Human Rights and Social Justice in a Global Perspective

Human Rights and Social Justice in a Global Perspective

An Introduction to International Social Work

Second Edition

Susan C. Mapp

OXFORD
UNIVERSITY PRESS

Oxford University Press is a department of the University of Oxford.
It furthers the University's objective of excellence in research, scholarship,
and education by publishing worldwide.

Oxford   New York
Auckland   Cape Town   Dar es Salaam   Hong Kong   Karachi
Kuala Lumpur   Madrid   Melbourne   Mexico City   Nairobi
New Delhi   Shanghai   Taipei   Toronto

With offices in
Argentina   Austria   Brazil   Chile   Czech Republic   France   Greece
Guatemala   Hungary   Italy   Japan   Poland   Portugal   Singapore
South Korea   Switzerland   Thailand   Turkey   Ukraine   Vietnam

Oxford is a registered trademark of Oxford University Press
in the UK and certain other countries.

Published in the United States of America by
Oxford University Press
198 Madison Avenue, New York, NY 10016

© Oxford University Press 2008, 2014

Library of Congress Cataloging-in-Publication Data
Mapp, Susan C.
Human rights and social justice in a global perspective : an introduction
to international social work / Susan C. Mapp. — Second Edition.
    pages cm
ISBN 978-0-19-998949-2 (pbk. : alk. paper)   1. Social service—International
cooperation.   2. Human rights.   I. Title.
HV41.M2796 2014
361.3—dc23
2013043627

Contents

Preface   vii

1. International Social Development   1

2. Human Rights   15

3. Human Trafficking   27

4. International Child Welfare   55

5. War and Conflict   87

6. AIDS   121

7. Issues Particularly Affecting Women   153

8. Social Work and the Physical Environment   187

9. Millennium Development Goals and Beyond   204

10. A Call to Action   216

   Appendix A: Universal Declaration of Human Rights   221

   Appendix B: Opportunities in International Social Work   231

   References   281

   Index   341

Preface

The social work profession promotes social change, problem solving in human relationships and the empowerment and liberation of people to enhance well-being. Utilising theories of human behaviour and social systems, social work intervenes at the points where people interact with their environments. Principles of human rights and social justice are fundamental to social work. (International Federation of Social Workers, 2000, ¶1)

As illustrated by this definition of social work, no matter where social workers are or who their clients may be, the fundamental concepts of social work remain grounded in social justice and human rights. We believe that all humans have the right to access the same basic essentials no matter what their status, and we work to help them achieve that right. Social workers work most often on local issues—issues pertaining to their clients who live by them, whether this work is on the micro, mezzo, or macro level. However, in this new millennium, the boundaries of social work are expanding as the boundaries of our world do. Issues that are confronted on a local level in countries in the Global North are the same issues faced by people struggling across the world, although they take a different form depending on the cultural context.

While it is easier to prioritize the needs of those who are close to us over those who are further away, this approach is damaging in the long run. First, social work's ethic of care requires that no distinction be drawn between "our" poor and "their" poor. Second, with the globalization of our world, social, economic, and political forces in one region of the world can affect other regions of the world, and injustices experienced in local communities can emanate from forces beyond national borders (Diaz,

Mama, & Lopez, 2006). Thus, the struggles of those who live half a world away can affect us locally. For example, in Afghanistan and Colombia, the stresses of poverty lure farmers to grow illegal drugs, while social workers in the Global North combat the effects of drug abuse.

The term "international social work" is becoming more common and encompasses several different concepts. This term can be used to refer to working with immigrants from other nations in one's home country, but in this book it will be primarily used to refer to conducting social work to help with social issues faced by citizens of other countries in their home nations. One group of nations at high risk in regard to the social issues to be considered are those nations formerly referred to as "Third World" or "developing" nations. These two terms have now been largely discarded. Although the term "Third World" was selected by these nations them-selves, over the decades it has come to be associated with such terms as "third class" and "third rate," denoting a lower status. Likewise, the term "developing" nation implied that the country was evolving to become like the "developed" nations, an ethnocentric notion that has become out of vogue. Therefore the term "Global South" will be used in this text, even though not all of these countries are located in the Southern Hemisphere, nor are all the countries in the Southern Hemisphere included in this term.

Issues pertaining to international social work have been gaining impor-tance, and schools of social work are increasingly adding this context to their classes to give their students the preparation they will need to be the most effective practitioners possible. Even social workers who never leave their country increasingly find themselves addressing these topics. For example, social workers in domestic violence shelters are working with clients who have immigration issues, and social workers in mental health settings encounter clients who are traumatized from war and conflict.

We are also seeing the globalization of social issues. The role of social workers is to help improve the human condition, regardless of the envi-ronment, but the environment can have a major impact on the develop-ment of an issue and thus on its resolution. As will be shown in this text, issues that are faced by people all over the world vary from culture to culture, depending on factors within that culture that inhibit or encour-age development of the issue. The issues that are faced by clients in the Global North are often the same issues faced by clients in the Global South, although the cultural context may affect their development. For instance, AIDS is a disease that knows no national boundaries, but who is affected, why, and the impact of the infection vary between cultures. Economic exploitation occurs across the globe, but who, why, and in what form can vary.

This textbook will help introduce those in the Global North to social problems as they occur in the Global South. There are both similarities and differences to how these issues have developed in different regions of the world due to issues of culture and access to resources. Each of these issues is a violation of the Universal Declaration of Human Rights. The human rights documents developed by the United Nations provide a lens through which these issues will be viewed. Woven throughout each chapter are descriptions and case studies from multiple countries in the Global South to help illustrate their impact. At the end of each chapter is a "Culture Box" which explores the issue in detail in one specific country so that the reader can understand the impact of culture on the development of a particular issue. The text is written from the orientation of a person located in the United States but is intended to be useful to those from other nations as well. It is aimed at all those who want to learn more about the world around them, both those who have the formal label of "student" and those who are simply seeking to educate themselves.

This edition is a thorough review of the first edition, updated where needed. I have attempted to include more material on effective solutions from around the world, because there is much progress to celebrate. The book still begins with an introduction to international social work and social development. To help illustrate how the way we think about the world affects how we view problems and solutions, the impact of map views and development theories is discussed. In Chapter 2, different human rights documents and the human rights approach are discussed. New material has been added on the role of the United Nations in promoting human rights. Chapters 3 through 8 discuss different issues, and readers of the first edition will notice the changes, and often improvements, in conditions discussed in the first edition. For example, Chapter 6 on AIDS has been completely revamped in order to reflect the remarkable progress made in fighting this epidemic. In Chapter 3, readers will note the change in terminology and understanding of the definitions of human trafficking and forced labor. Chapter 8 is brand new to this edition and represents the growing awareness in the profession of the linkage between the physical environment and issues with which social workers work. Chapter 9 discusses a potential path to developing solutions—the

Millennium Development Goals—but it is updated to discuss the pro-posed post-2015 Goals. In Chapter 10, how social workers and social work students can be a part of developing solutions is discussed. The size of the issues does not diminish the importance of attempting to reach solutions, and this book will help provide a path for those who want to be a part of this work.

No book is a product solely of its author. Many thanks go to many peo-ple, including my mother for her proofreading and encouragement, and to the rest of my family and friends for their support (especially trolls). A big thank-you to my student Eileen Kroszner, who updated Appendix B to help students with dreams of having an impact in other countries. There were many others who encouraged me who are too numerous to mention, but your support is valued.

International Social Development

As discussed in the Preface, the importance and spread of global social problems have been growing rapidly. While the need to see beyond our borders increases, the skills with which to do so may be lacking, particularly for those born in the United States. Currently the United States stands alone as the world's only superpower. Due to this dominant position, its citizens often put less emphasis on learning about other countries and cultures than these countries put on learning about the United States. English is considered the international language of business, and Americans traveling abroad typically encounter citizens of other countries who are fluent in English, reducing the perceived need to learn another language. In a recent poll, three-quarters of young Americans thought that English was the most common native language; in fact, Mandarin Chinese is the most common first language (National Geographic, 2006). The number of US elementary and middle schools that taught a foreign language decreased significantly between 1997 and 2008 from 31% to 25% for elementary schools and 75% to 58% for middle schools. The number of high schools stayed approximately the same at 91% (Center for Applied Linguistics, 2010). These statistics decline further as students enter college, where approximately 8% of students take foreign language classes (Modern Language Association, 2009). Study abroad numbers have risen and though fewer than 1% study abroad each year, 14% of graduates have studied abroad at some point in their undergraduate curriculum (Institute of International Education, 2012).

Those in the United States also have a notorious lack of geographical knowledge, both of the world and of the United States itself. The Nation's Report Card from the US Department of Education found that fewer than 30% of tested students were proficient in geography (US Department of Education, 2010). A 2002 study of nine major countries found that youth in the United States aged 18 to 24 years ranked next to last (after Mexico) in their knowledge of geography. Ten percent were unable to locate the United States on a world map, and almost 30% could not locate the Pacific Ocean (National Geographic, 2002). If 10% cannot locate their own country on a world map, it does not bode well for knowledge of other countries. Indeed, 85% were unable to locate current world hot spots Iraq, Afghanistan, or Israel on the map either (National Geographic, 2002).

If Americans are to become world citizens, they must know their place in the world, both figuratively and literally. When US aid is sent abroad, either as armed forces or as financial resources, its citizens should know where they are going. America has fought two wars in Iraq in recent years, but in the National Geographic survey only 13% could find Iraq on a map that depicted only the Middle East and Asia, not even the entire globe.

The Effect of Maps on Our Worldview

Even for those who are geographically knowledgeable, how people learn about geography can influence their perception of the world, even through something as simple as the map used to learn about other countries. When developing a two-dimensional depiction of a three-dimensional object, it cannot be exactly accurate; something must always be sacrificed to preserve another feature accurately. Such is the case with maps; when manufacturing a depiction of reality, only selected features are included. For example, if you draw a map of the route to your house for a friend, it will not include roads that will not be needed. The state map from your Department of Transportation will most likely not include the road on which you live. No one representation can include everything that exists in actuality; no map looks exactly like what it portrays. Thus, each map focuses on a particular feature or features that are considered important. As with any document, a map

represents the needs and perspective of the mapmaker. What is preserved and what is lost depend on what is important to the mapmaker.
This can be seen clearly in the map with which most Americans are
familiar, the Mercator projection.

Developed by a Flemish cartographer in 1569, the Mercator projection preserves longitude and latitude as straight lines. It also is literally
Eurocentric, placing Europe in the middle of the map. This map projection was a great benefit to seafaring ships, of particular importance
at that time in Europe. Mercator titled his map "A New and Enlarged
Description of the Earth With Corrections for Use in Navigation," a very
precise and accurate name (Kaiser & Wood, 2001). However, what is
lost is relative area, especially near the poles. The correction Mercator
described to keep latitude and longitude as straight lines resulted in dis-
tortions of relative size. Land masses located near the poles appear much
larger than they actually are, especially in comparison to other land
masses. This can be seen in the image on page 4 comparing the actual
land mass of Greenland and Africa and their depiction in the Mercator

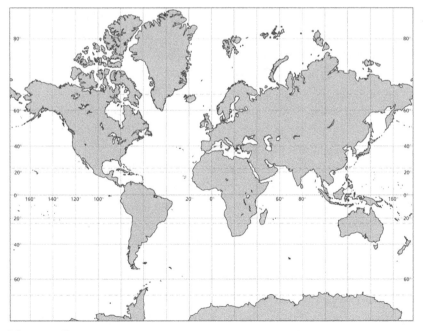

Mercator Projection

Land Mass Comparisons: Greenland has .8 million square miles and Africa has 11.6 million square miles, but on the Mercator projection they look as though they are the same size.

projection. Additional comparisons can be seen at http://www.peters-map.com/table.html.

To correct this limitation, subsequent map styles have been developed. One of the most popular (and controversial) of these is the Peters projection (see page 5). The map preserves relative land mass at the expense of distortion of shape. The Peters projection has been the subject of much debate, and its developer, Arno Peters, was one of the first to declare that mapmaking was inherently political.

His statement causes us to question how maps affect the way in which we view the world. Compare the Peters projection with the Mercator projection. The majority of Americans grew up with the Mercator projection on the wall of the schoolroom and accepted it as the way the world looked. To view such a radically different map can be jarring: Suddenly the United States and Europe do not appear so large in comparison with other areas of the world. Human nature tends to equate size with importance, so seeing these areas of the world that have larger roles on the global political stage suddenly shrink in size may cause a perception that they have shrunk in importance.

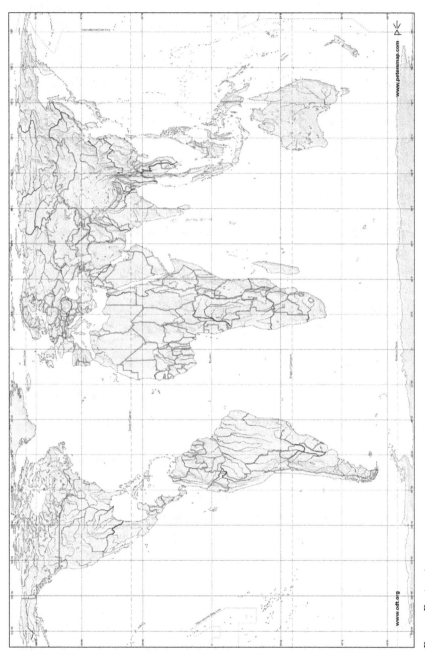

Peters Projection

Since all maps are a depiction of reality rather than the reality itself, they can appear different from the ones to which we are most accustomed in a number of ways. For example, some maps center the world on the Pacific Ocean to illustrate the Eurocentric approach of putting Europe in the middle. Still others, such as McArthur's Universal Corrective Map of the World, rotate the map so that south is on top. Since the Earth is a sphere floating in space, there truly is no such thing as "up"; putting north on top is only a convention. Take a moment to think about how this different perspective might change your viewpoint. How does the notion of choices of what to include on a map affect how people view that which it depicts? Why is it important to recognize conventions of mapmaking are just that—conventions?

Maps can depict whatever the cartographer wants to portray at the expense of other details. They do not need to focus on physical geography. Maps can depict national population, number of those infected with AIDS, votes for a candidate in an election, and a host of other concepts. They remain an accurate depiction of the world and the information portayed, but other information is sacrificed at the expense of this information, thus illustrating how two-dimensional maps are always a win-lose scenario.

When examining any map, the Department of Geography at the University of London (n.d.) suggests asking a few questions:

- What are the key features that are included and that are excluded?
- Why do you think the mapmaker made the decision to include and exclude those features?
- How do those decisions regarding the content of the map impact how those viewing the map see the world (e.g., what is considered important and what is considered unimportant)?

Your Geographical Knowledge

How is your geographical knowledge? Test yourself and work to improve your knowledge. An excellent Web site for this is www.sheppardsoftware.com/Geography.htm. Try these exercises (these are from a US perspective but can be adapted to citizens of other nations by focusing on knowledge of your own country first and then moving out to other regions with which your country has close ties).

- Label all 50 states on the US map.
- Name the capitals of the US states.
- Once you have mastered the geography of your own country, move on. Label the countries in Europe. Many Americans consider themselves familiar with Europe, but often that is only Western Europe. Can you label the Eastern European nations, especially those which have emerged, or re-emerged, since the fall of the Soviet Union? Europeans are typically familiar with nations on their own continent, but how about those on other continents?
- Now look at other continents around the world. How familiar are you with the location of countries? As globalization increases, the importance of being familiar with the world outside of our borders increases proportionally.

The Social Development Approach

Just as the map we use can affect how we view the world, the lens with which we view its problems will affect how we approach a solution. The values of social work tie closely together with the concept of social development, particularly in relation to the idea of empowerment. Social development can be defined as encompassing interventions and programs to improve social conditions. Social development works to build capacity within a client, often at the macro level, to avert the problem as opposed to helping to alleviate the effects of the problem after it occurs. It is focused on primary prevention—stopping the problem before it starts by address-ing it at its roots. Many times efforts of international nongovernmental organizations (NGOs) may focus on relief as opposed to prevention, and intervention will occur after a problem has become severe—tertiary pre-vention (Herscovitch, 2001). For instance, food assistance will be given after the famine has already occurred; medical assistance will be pro-vided after the epidemic is raging. However, by using a developmental approach, assistance is provided before the problem has metastasized, which is not only more cost-efficient but also more effective. At the world conference on social development held in Copenhagen in 1995, 117 heads of nations agreed that people should be at the center of development. Toward that end, they agreed to "make the conquest of poverty, the goal of full employment and the fostering of stable, safe and just societies their overriding objectives" (United Nations, 1999, ¶1). The Millennium Development Goals (discussed in Chapter 9) attempt to draw together a road map for the achievement of social development through designating core issues that block the achievement of full human development and setting clear-cut goals for their reduction.

Blocking the realization of this pledge is the fact that nations often argue that they must focus on economic development before they turn to social development. However, in order to achieve the greatest success, these two must occur together; social development and economic development are inextricably linked. When one occurs without the other, distorted development will occur. The most frequent type of distorted development is when economic development occurs without social development. This will result in a concentration of wealth and resources and difficulty in economic growth. If citizens are not educated, they will not be able to be as economically productive; if they do not receive adequate health care, they will be too unwell to work; and if they are hungry, they will not be as productive as they could otherwise. This was seen with the Structural Adjustment Policies of the World Bank. Designed to increase economic growth through reduced government intervention, they created "cost sharing" policies in which citizens of low-income countries were expected to share in the cost of services such as education and health care. This created widespread lower achievement in these areas as then only wealthy families were able to access these services; these policies have since been altered.

However, neither should social development be attempted without economic development. If social development occurs without economic development, there will be a lack of financial resources to pay for the programs. For human potential to be reached, economic and social development must occur together. This balance is one of the goals of social work in the international arena (Diaz et al., 2006).

Distorted development can occur in several ways: within a country or between countries. When global inequality between countries is examined, a number of theories have been developed to explain why these differences have occurred and some countries have remained "underdeveloped." We will examine two of the primary theories: modernization theory and dependency theory. These are only two from a multitude of possible theories and were selected to provide contrasting viewpoints.

Modernization Theory

A predominant theory when examining the underdevelopment of certain countries and regions in the world has been modernization theory, also known as the neoclassical approach. This theory states that the reasons for the origins of underdevelopment and poverty in a country are internal; they are located within that country itself and may include the lack of democratic institutions, capital, technology, or initiative on the part of its citizens. Modernists believe that underdevelopment is a state or condition that is synonymous with tradition. They state that the essence of the traditional society is that it is unchanging. Daily work is carried out just as it has always been, not to secure a profit, but to maintain one's place in society. It is not a negative view, but from an economic viewpoint it is a stagnant one, as there is no hope of gaining wealth. This equilibrium, while stable and predictable, will not generate economic wealth. Capitalism, on the other hand, can. Capitalism has created far higher overall levels of production, income, and wealth than ever before by decentralizing the wealth of nations. In its ideal form, through individuals trying to do the best for themselves, constant change and growth are created, spurring the society on to better things and producing economic changes to the benefit of all socioeconomic classes in the society (Isbister, 2003). In contrast, traditional societies maintain equilibrium. For example, as China has moved from a communist model economy toward allowing more capitalism, prosperity within the country has surged to levels previously unknown.

Modernization theory believes that global inequality exists due to technological and cultural differences between nations and that every country can achieve the level of development seen today in the Global North through a free market economy tailored to the culture of that country. This development can be a cooperative process with wealthier nations: rich countries can help poorer countries by serving as role models and by providing assistance. The wealthier nations can help these countries overcome the internal limitations that have stagnated economic growth, specifically through helping to limit population growth, increasing food production, increasing technology, and providing foreign aid (Macionis, 2006). As modernization theory operates from a cooperative model, there is no antagonism between nations in this model and all countries can work together to achieve the maximum good for all citizens.

However, all theories have their limitations. Modernization theory does not examine the role of wealthy countries in creating impoverishing conditions in poorer countries; it focuses almost exclusively on internal causes. Modernization theory tends to focus on economic growth as the goal; however, this can result in concentration of wealth in the hands of a few as opposed to economic redistribution. This theory is also inherently optimistic as it believes that any country can find the means from within to achieve the correct "mixture" of savings and investment, which together with foreign investment can achieve development. This optimism ignores limitations that may prohibit economic growth, such as poor agricultural conditions or a poorly educated workforce. By promoting the industrialized countries as the model of optimal development, it has an inherent ethnocentric bias (Macionis, 2006).

Dependency Theory

Dependency theorists believe that currently dominant nations developed to their current level of prosperity because they *depended* on the resources from the less developed nations: cheap raw materials and a captive market for the goods (Schultz & Lavenda, 2005). They believe that underdevelopment is a process, not a state of being; the underdeveloped nations are in their current state not because of their inherent nature or traditional society, but due to the process of impoverishment they experienced at the hands of the dominant nation-states, and they are now dependent on those dominant nations. Dependency theory does not focus on the conditions within individual nation-states but rather on global interactions between the nation-states by focusing attention on the international context of the Global South. Similar to systems theory, it examines nations in relation to their suprasystems (e.g., their regional context and relations with the Global North). Dependency theory asserts that as a result of economic growth in advanced capitalist countries, poverty increased in developing nations. It states that poor countries are not poor merely in comparison to countries of the Global North, but that the industrial system impoverished the developing countries to further their own growth (Isbister, 2003). This process occurred not only during colonization but also continues today as the high-income nations continue to block the growth of developing nations.

Dependency was first created through the colonization of countries, with the prime agricultural land and resources being allotted to a concentrated few—the colonists. These colonists used the natural resources of the land for their own benefits, such as the diamonds and gold of South Africa. Goods were produced for export to foreign markets as opposed to use by the country itself. For example, cotton was grown in Sudan and Uganda, but these countries imported cotton goods (Rodney, 2005). Some of the new "cash crops" were much harder on the soil than the sustenance crops, especially when the native Africans were relegated to the poorest soil. This led to further impoverishment, first of the soil and then of the people trying to eke a living from it (Rodney, 2005). Infrastructure was designed to benefit this export-oriented economy, with roads and railroads leading to ports as opposed to internal access (Thomas-Slayter, 2003).

Even though formal colonialism is gone, these orientations remain and poor countries continue to be dependent on wealthy countries. They export raw goods to them, they work for their companies, and they are required to learn their languages. This economic subservience leads to political subservience. For example, the United States provides aid to countries that help us economically by welcoming private enterprise and American businesses. As seen in the Cold War, large established nations played out their ideological battles on the grounds of smaller developing nations such as Panama, Vietnam, and Angola.

Dependency theory asserts that modernization theory is mistaken in stating that traditional societies are unchanged. They are not in an unchanged state; they have been changed through centuries of contact with, and exploitation by, the economically dominant nations. The existing poverty is not traditional or accidental; rather, it is necessary for the enrichment of the dominant nations. Over time, the price of poorer nations' exports has fallen and the price of imports has risen. Trade policies currently favor wealthier nations and their tariffs and subsidies make it difficult, if not impossible, for those in the Global South to compete

economically in the world market. For example, tariffs on goods manufactured by members of the Organisation for Economic Co-operation
and Development (OECD) (primarily countries in the Global North)
are one-quarter of those on goods manufactured by countries who are
not members (primarily countries in the Global South). This makes the
goods from countries in the Global South far more expensive and thus
less desirable. Agricultural subsidies in wealthy countries total more than
$300 billion each year, again making it more difficult for farmers in the
Global South, who do not have such aid, to price their goods at a competitive rate (UNDP, 2003).

Dependency theorists also argue that poor countries are not strangers
to capitalism; they have been subjects of it for centuries. They provide the
raw materials for the development that has occurred in the "developed"
nations. While modernization theorists state that there is a clear path
to development for all to follow, dependency theorists disagree, arguing
that the current economic powers rose to their current status by exploit-
ing the developing nations, a path not open to those nations today. An
obvious example of exploitation is slavery: Numerous African societies
were destroyed through the theft of their most able members, and it took
them centuries to recover. In addition, these nations in the Global South
currently face competition from well-established economic superpowers.

In assessing the limitations of dependency theory, it is clear that just as
modernization theory focused on internal causes to the exclusion of external ones, dependency theory does just the reverse: It focuses on external
causes to the exclusion of internal ones. Internal difficulties such as being
a landlocked nation or tolerating internal corruption are not considered.
It is a pessimistic theory in its belief that as long as wealthier countries
dominate the world, there is little opportunity for developing nations to
succeed. It also excludes from its premises the nations that were colonies
at one time but now have succeeded in the global marketplace, such as
the "Asian Tigers" (South Korea, Hong Kong, Taiwan, and Singapore).

Distorted Development Within Countries

Midgley (1997) notes that there are many examples of distorted development in the world. In some countries in the Global South, such as in Latin
America, extensive economic growth has occurred without corresponding

social development. This can also be seen in wealthier nations, such as the United States and the United Kingdom. These countries are among the wealthiest in the world, yet a high percentage of their population still lives in poverty with their basic needs unmet.

Certain populations within a country are more likely to be victims of distorted development. Those who are left out of social development frequently share common characteristics. According to the economist Goulet, development should offer three things: life sustenance, self-esteem, and freedom (Thomas-Slayter, 2003). Those who are left out typically lack access to these due to discrimination, poverty, and/or lack of access to education. These barriers make it difficult for these people to make such basic decisions as where to live, whom to marry, how to earn a living, and with whom to engage in sexual relations. The barriers can lead to social problems such as AIDS, refugees, and slavery. For example, women frequently receive less than their share of the benefits of development. Although women perform two-thirds of the work in the world, they receive only 10% of the income and own less than 1% of the property (United Nations, 2005). These three barriers are discussed in further detail in Chapter 2.

Goals of This Text

This text will provide not only an introduction to common issues in international social work and social development but also frameworks for analyzing these issues. In this chapter, lenses through which the world is viewed were examined. One is physical (how we actually see the world) and one is theoretical (why different parts of the world have achieved higher levels of development and how can the situation be rectified). Depending on which lens is used, different reasons will be perceived for why conditions exist, and this will affect how solutions are devised. An approach from modernization theory standpoint will focus on conditions within that country to overcome internal limitations. It may attempt to create a free market economy to generate greater wealth. A dependency theory standpoint will examine the role of wealthier nations in creating the problem and will be more externally focused in determining the source of the problem. It may focus on creating greater independence for that nation. As each issue in this text is discussed, think about how its existence might be explained from either the modernization or dependency standpoint. How has the issue developed as a result from forces within the nation or external to it?

This text has been thoroughly reviewed and updated from the first edition, and a new chapter on changes in the physical environment has been added. In many cases, hopeful progress has been made, but many challenges still remain. Chapter 2 will introduce common human rights documents, the framework that will undergird this work. International human rights documents provide a preliminary way to compare social development across cultures. Each chapter of this text will examine what human right is being violated through the existence of the issue. In the last chapter, a possible road map to achieving social development will be discussed, the Millennium Development Goals from the United Nations—their progress and what may lie beyond 2015. Throughout this text, the impact of culture on the development of an issue and how the three common barriers—poverty, discrimination, and lack of education—can foster their growth will be examined. This text will not only increase readers' knowledge of issues in international social work but will also deepen their understanding of how and why the issues vary from culture to culture.

2

Human Rights

*Sustainable human development means expanding all
people's choices and creating the conditions for equality
so that they may realize their full potential. This goal
is unrealizable if all human rights—economic, social,
cultural, civil and political—are not promoted, preserved
and defended.* (UNICEF, 1999, p. 1)

In the aftermath of World War II and its atrocities, the fledgling United
Nations decided to create a Universal Declaration of Human Rights
(UDHR). This document would elucidate the rights to which all humans
would be entitled, regardless of nationality, political system, religion, or any
other grouping, simply by the fact of their humanity. The United Nations
appointed a special commission to draft the document and appointed as
its head the US representative to the United Nations, Eleanor Roosevelt.
Eleanor Roosevelt was the widow of US President Franklin D. Roosevelt
and a formidable advocate for the poor and disenfranchised in her own
right. The final document was presented to the General Assembly of the
United Nations and adopted on December 10, 1948.

The full text of the UDHR is in Appendix A of this text (see Box
2.1 for a summary). The rights it defines were intended to be universal
and indivisible—that is, all humans have the right to them regardless of
culture, political system, ethnicity, or any other characteristic (universal), and a country cannot select which rights it should grant; all humans
should have all rights (indivisible).

BOX 2.1 Summary of the Rights Contained Within the Universal Declaration of Human Rights

Article 1: All humans are born free and equal in dignity and rights.
Article 2: Everyone is entitled to all of the rights in the UDHR regardless of any distinction.
Article 3: The right to life, liberty, and the security of the person
Article 4: Prohibition of slavery
Article 5: Prohibition of torture
Article 6: Right to recognition as a person before the law
Article 7: All must be treated equally under the law.
Article 8: Right to a remedy of any violation of these rights
Article 9: Prohibition of arbitrary arrest, detention, or exile
Article 10: Right to a fair trial
Article 11: People shall be presumed innocent until proven guilty.
Article 12: Right to freedom from arbitrary interference with private life
Article 13: Right to freedom of movement
Article 14: Right to seek asylum
Article 15: Right to a nationality
Article 16: Right to marry; marriage must be consented to by both parties; the family is entitled to protection from the state
Article 17: Right to property
Article 18: Right to freedom of thought, conscience, and religion
Article 19: Right to freedom of opinion and expression
Article 20: Right to freedom of assembly and association
Article 21: Right to participate in the government of one's country
Article 22: Right to economic, social, and cultural rights necessary for dignity and free development of personality
Article 23: Right to work and equitable compensation
Article 24: Right to rest and leisure from work
Article 25: Right to an adequate standard of living, including food, clothing, housing, and medical care
Article 26: Right to education
Article 27: Right to participate in cultural activities and to share in scientific achievements
Article 28: Right to a world order in which these rights can be realized
Article 29: Everyone has duties to the community; rights shall be limited only in regards to respecting the rights of others.
Article 30: None of the rights may be interpreted as allowing any action to destroy these rights.

Within the UDHR, there are three areas of rights: political and civil rights; social, economic, and cultural rights; and collective rights. Political and civil rights are often referred to as "negative freedoms" as they require a government to refrain from an overuse of its power against individuals. Included in this are rights such as freedom of speech and the right to a fair trial. The second grouping of rights—social, economic, and social rights—is referred to as "positive freedoms" as they require a government to take action for them to be realized for individuals. They include such rights as medical care, the right to an education, and the right to a fair wage. The last group, collective rights, includes rights for groups of people and includes the rights to religion, peace, and development.

A declaration does not impose on a ratifying government any obligation to fulfill the principles contained within the document; that is the purpose of a covenant, convention, or treaty. To codify the rights within the UDHR, there has been a succession of covenants and conventions that nations must ratify in order to be bound by its provisions. In this process the universality and indivisibility of human rights was immediately called into question. The two most powerful nations in the post–World War II era, the United States and the USSR, had substantially different ideas about the relative importance of the sets of rights and governmental responsibility for them. The United States argued that its Constitution was in concordance with civil and political rights, but the economic, social, and cultural rights went against its cultural preference for individual responsibility. The USSR had the opposite stance: They had a totalitarian government that granted few civil and political rights, yet its communist ideology supported the importance of economic, social, and cultural rights. This division led to these sets of rights being split into two different covenants (Amnesty International, 2005). The International Covenant on Civil and Political Rights (ICCPR) was ratified by the United States in 1992, but it has not yet ratified the International Covenant on Economic, Social and Cultural Rights (ICESCR). The USSR ratified both in 1973, one of the first countries to do so (UNHCR, 2006a, 2006b), but it tended to grant more of the economic, social, and cultural rights than the civil and political rights.

Universal and Indivisible?

There continue to be arguments over the universal and indivisible nature of the human rights in the UDHR. Governments argue that the human rights should not be regarded as indivisible. The United States has yet to ratify the ICESCR, illustrating its lack of support for economic and social rights, while groups of nations in Asia and Africa argue that civil and political rights should be secondary to the more urgent human needs recognized through economic, social, and cultural rights (Ghai, 2001). China states that while it is vilified for not granting civil and political rights, it does, however, meet economic, social, and cultural rights, which the United States does not. It argues that it is more important to meet the basic human needs for life than the more abstract political rights (Human Rights Watch, 1996).

Different countries have argued that the rights are not universal, and they should not be mandated to abide by that which is not appropriate in their culture. They state that human rights are not "one size fits all" but vary according to culture. This is known as *cultural relativism*. Some Asian countries argue that the document reflects a Western approach to rights, with a greater emphasis on the individual than on the society. They state that the community should be more important than the individual and prefer a strong government and deference to authority (Muntarbhorn, 2005). Freedom of speech may be viewed as a threat to a harmonious society, a key value in Asian culture (Reichert, 2003).

Social workers may find themselves in a bind trying to recognize both the right to one's culture as well as one's human rights. George (1999) argues that human rights cannot be both universal and culturally relevant and states that social workers have put themselves in a dilemma by arguing for both human rights and the right to one's own culture. For example, in some cultures women are treated as subordinate to men, yet the UDHR states that treating any person as less than another due to a characteristic is prohibited. How can the traditional order of a society and the UDHR both be respected?

The United Nations has stated that these two ideals are not in opposition. The human rights declared in its conventions, covenants, and declarations are a minimum standard, and each culture can choose the most appropriate manner in which to realize those rights. Ife and Fiske (2006, p. 302) state that "universality does not mean 'sameness,' rather it is a principle that emphasizes the essential worth of every human being without the need to reach a certain status or fit a certain model of desirable citizen." However, cultural variations may not be used in order to deny rights. While the right to one's culture is protected within human rights, that right is limited in that it may not infringe on another protected human right (Ayton-Shenker, 1995). Thus, each culture and the ordering of society within it must be respected, but only to the extent that the traditional order of a society does not impinge on the human rights of another.

Other Human Rights Documents

Even before the development of the UDHR, there were standards for the treatment of people during war and conflict. First developed in 1864, these standards have evolved over the years and are known as the Geneva Conventions. These conventions have established universal rules to protect victims of war and conflict. The Geneva Conventions state that people who cannot, or do not, take part in the conflict must be protected. This includes civilians as well as military personnel who have been wounded or have surrendered. All sides have an obligation to provide medical assistance to any wounded personnel, regardless of allegiance. Medical personnel are considered neutral and must not be attacked; they are marked by a standard emblem of a red symbol on a white background. In addition, prisoners of war are entitled to be treated with respect and must be allowed to exchange news with their families. An international monitoring body may visit prisoners of war to exchange this news and to ensure that they are being treated with respect.

The volunteers who assisted in the implementation of these new rules are known as the International Committee of the Red Cross. Today, the organization has evolved to include the International Conference of Red Cross and Red Crescent Societies and the Red Crystal from Israel. The symbols reflect the religious background of each: Predominantly Christian nations use a red cross on the white background, while primarily Muslim nations use a red crescent. Israel uses a red diamond to represent the Star of David. These are the neutral organizations that ensure that the Geneva Conventions are implemented during conflict (International Committee of the Red Cross, 2006; Red Cross of Latvia, n.d.).

In the years since the UDHR was developed, a host of other human rights documents have been written focusing on more specific areas and more vulnerable populations. Table 2.1 summarizes the documents, the year they were introduced, and the year they entered into force. To enter into force means that enough countries have ratified the document to consider it binding.

Table 2.1 Human Rights Documents

Document	Introduced	Entered into force
Convention on the Elimination of All Forms of Racial Discrimination (CERD)	1966	1969
Convention on the Elimination of All Forms of Discrimination Against Women (CEDAW)	1979	1981
Convention Against Torture and Other Cruel, Inhuman or Degrading Treatment or Punishment (CAT)	1984	1987
Convention on the Rights of the Child (CRC)	1989	1990
International Convention on the Protection of the Rights of All Migrant Workers and Members of Their Families (ICRMW)	1990	2003
Convention on the Rights of Persons with Disabilities	2006	2008
International Convention on the Protection of All Persons from Enforced Disappearance	2006	2010

CEDAW and CRC are particularly relevant to topics discussed in this book and will be discussed in detail in their respective chapters.

The Role of the United Nations

All of these Conventions have a specific committee within the United Nations that is responsible for overseeing and evaluating its implementation. Ratifying countries are responsible for submitting a report to this committee every 5 years that evaluates their progress in achieving the goals established by the Articles of that convention. Nongovernmental organizations are also able to submit a "shadow report," which offers their interpretation of the nation's achievement, or lack thereof. These shadow reports help the United Nations make sure that nations do not paint an overly positive picture of the state of human rights within their borders.

The committee then publishes a report summarizing where that nation has done well in achieving the convention and where further progress is still needed.

In addition, the United Nations itself works to further achievement of human rights through its various bodies. UNICEF works in all areas related to child development (www.unicef.org), while Womenwatch gathers information related to women's equality (www.un.org/womenwatch).

Monitoring Human Rights

Although these conventions and covenants have been ratified by a vast majority of countries, it is clear that not all countries abide by their provisions. Although the United Nations has the responsibility for monitoring human rights abuses, there is little it can do in terms of enforcement. While each convention has a monitoring body, as discussed earlier, the official body responsible for monitoring violations of the UDHR is the United Nations Human Rights Council. This Council was reorganized in 2006 due to dissatisfaction with the ineffectiveness of its predecessor, the Human Rights Commission, including that notorious human rights offenders sat on it. The new council consists of representatives from 47 countries who are elected by the General Assembly, and it meets almost twice as often as the commission did. Membership is based on population distribution as follows (United Nations, n.d.):

- African States: 13 seats
- Asian States: 13 seats
- Latin American and Caribbean States: 8 seats
- Western European and other States: 7 seats
- Eastern European States: 6 seats

The United States, under the Bush Administration, originally refused to join the new council. However, with the election of President Obama, this view was revised to one that stated change could more effectively occur from within, and the United States joined in 2009 (MacFarquhar, 2009).

The US State Department produces a report each year assessing the level of civil, political, and worker rights, as recognized in the UDHR, in 196 countries. The purpose of this assessment is to promote democracy.

Countries that are consistently assessed as faring poorly in these areas are typically non-democracies such as North Korea, Myanmar, and China. China, in response, has developed its own assessment of the United States that emphasizes more of the violations of social and economic rights but also what it sees as violations of civil and political rights, including the high level of violent crime and high rate of incarceration. The 2011 report is available at http://www.chinadaily.com.cn/cndy/2012-05/26/content_15392452.htm. Its purpose appears to be that the United States should be cautious about evaluating others' achievement of rights when it violates rights as well.

Nongovernmental organizations (NGOs) also take responsibility for monitoring human rights abuses; two of the more well known in the United States are Human Rights Watch and Amnesty International. Both of the organizations regularly investigate and assess violations of human rights abuses around the world. Their reports on many different topics are available on their Web sites. Amnesty International traditionally focused on violations of civil and political rights but broadened its mission to monitor economic, social, and cultural rights as well as civil and political ones as "there are many more prisoners of poverty than prisoners of conscience" (Amnesty International, 2005, p. 3).

The Human Rights Approach

These human rights documents and the rights contained within them will provide the undergirding of the discussion of issues in this text. Each issue in this book will be discussed together with the human right that is being violated through the existence of the problem. Jahan (2005, p. 2) states that "human development and human rights are closely linked as they have a common denominator—*human freedom* [emphasis original]. They both relate to choices or the lack thereof for all to live their life as they would." Looking back on the previous chapter about social development, it becomes clear how lack of social development creates situations in which violations of human rights can thrive.

Three main barriers exist that prevent full access to human rights and the fruits of social development. These barriers are poverty, discrimination, and lack of education. In each chapter, we will discuss how these barriers assist in creating the issue and help to perpetuate it. The existence of poverty violates economic human rights—the right to an income adequate to sustain oneself. Poverty inherently prohibits access to the realization of social human rights. The lack of adequate income typically prohibits adequate housing, nutrition, and other necessities. Money confers independence and autonomy. Those living in poverty find their options are limited due to their lack of financial resources. This can create dependence on others or on the state to help them meet the basics needed for life, the basic human rights guaranteed to all humans. They are placed at further risk of violation of other rights through economic exploitation and discrimination due to their lack of financial resources to meet their basic needs.

Discrimination involves grouping people into a category and denying them full access to human rights based on that category. This category may be sex, gender, ethnicity, race, caste, social class, or any other categorization. While discrimination itself is a violation of human rights, these categories are used to deny access to other rights as well, such as access to a job that pays a living wage, adequate medical care, a fair trial, and the right to vote. Lack of access to education is a larger problem than many of us realize: Without an education, the individual is not only locked into poverty but also placed at risk for the issues discussed in this text. This is due not only to their lack of education but also to the fact that school serves as a protective activity to help shield children from exposure to social risks. Also, parental education helps children to be healthier and more prosperous, particularly in the case of mothers.

These three barriers are often intertwined and difficult to separate. People are locked into poverty due to their lack of education, and they do not have access to education due to their poverty. They may be systematically denied education due to discrimination. As you read through the book, notice in each chapter how these issues affect people's lives and inhibit their access to human rights.

Applicability of the Human Rights Approach to Social Work

Contemporary human rights are based upon the ideal of social justice, a concept so central to social work that it is considered "fundamental" in the IFSW definition of the profession. All people should be equal under the law and should have equal opportunities to develop to their potential.

The UDHR can serve as a guide to putting into operation the often vague concept of social justice. Skegg (2005) suggests that an approach to social work based on human rights and empowerment tells oppressed people that they have rights to the basics for life, as opposed to regarding assistance as a charitable handout. In addition, self-determination, a concept for which social workers often advocate, is protected under the UDHR. Focusing on violations of human rights can help social workers focus on social justice as opposed to individual pathology (Healy, 2001).

The concepts and theories typically used in social work can aid in analyzing the issues to be discussed in this text. The systems perspective that is central to the social work perspective will continue to be valuable here. We regard the individual as the micro level, the family as the mezzo level, and communities or nations as the macro level. Try to assess in each chapter how the individual is affected by events occurring on higher levels and how the macro system is affected by events occurring on the mezzo and micro levels. For example, the family of an individual who lacks access to education will be more likely to live in poverty and struggle to meet their basic needs, and it impedes the development of the nation if its workforce is uneducated and struggling with social problems. The macro level will in turn affect the micro level because when the nation is struggling economically due to the lack of development, it will have difficulty affording adequate education. As you read each chapter, you will see the linking of these issues. An issue in one chapter will often make reference to issues described in detail in other chapters. Just as human rights are universal and indivisible, unfortunately so are the problems. But as discussed in the final chapter, fortunately, so are the solutions.

The following chapters will examine various violations of human rights. These are not the only violations occurring, nor are these the only countries in which they occur—they are simply an illustration of the violations that occur all too often. Using the human rights framework, this text will examine the social issues, how culture has affected their development, and what people are doing to try to solve the problems.

World Wide Web Resources on Human Rights

Access to all United Nations treaties: http://www2.ohchr.org/english/law/

Amnesty International (www.amnesty.org): One of the world's largest international voluntary organizations dealing with human rights and political repression.

Bayesky.com (www.bayefsky.com): Provides a range of data concerning the application of the UN human rights treaty system by its monitoring treaty bodies since their inauguration in the 1970s.

Global Rights (www.globalrights.org): Nonprofit human rights organization active in more than 20 countries, working directly with organizations and human rights advocates inside each country to help groups and individuals become more effective within existing infrastructures by helping local organizations build their internal capacities for challenging injustice.

Human Rights First (www.humanrightsfirst.org): "Works in the United States and abroad to create a secure and humane world by advancing justice, human dignity and respect for the rule of law," to guarantee observance of human rights and to strengthen independent human rights advocacy at the local level.

Human Rights Internet (www.hri.ca): An online resource, information, and documentation center for human rights actors, organizations, and interested individuals around the world.

Human Rights Watch (www.hrw.org): Dedicated to protecting the human rights of people around the world by investigating and exposing human rights violations and holding abusers accountable.

HURISEARCH (http://www.hurisearch.org/): An search engine that searches the content on the sites of over 5,000 human rights Web sites.

Interights (www.interights.org): Aims to enforce human rights through law, providing protection and redress, in particular regions and on issues of strategic focus; to strengthen human rights jurisprudence and mechanisms through the use of international and comparative law; and to empower legal partners and promote their effective use of law to protect human rights.

International Network for Economic, Social and Cultural Rights (www.escr-net.org/): A coalition of organizations and activists from around the world dedicated to advancing economic, social, and cultural rights.

Project Diana: An Online Human Rights Archive (avalon.law.yale.edu/subject_menus/diana.asp): The Yale Law School's segment of the International Human Rights Database project called DIANA (www.law-lib.utoronto.ca/Diana/about.htm), with many documents and links.

Social Watch (www.socialwatch.org): An international NGO watchdog network monitoring poverty eradication and gender equality.

United Nations High Commissioner for Human Rights (www.ohchr.org/english): Publications, documents, treaties, databases, special programs, conferences, links.

United Nations Human Rights Page (www.un.org/rights): Master page for all United Nations sites on human rights, with full documentation and activities.

United Nations Human Rights Treaty Information Portal (www.humanrightsinfo.com): A site with multiple links to other sites with information on human rights.

United States Department of State (www.state.gov/j/drl/rls/hrrpt): Country Reports on Human Rights Practices: Texts of yearly reports by the US Department of State, and related documents.

University of Minnesota Human Rights Library (www1.umn.edu/humanrts): Contains more than 25,000 documents relating to human rights. Included in this is the Human Rights resource Center at hrusa.org.

3

Human Trafficking

Article 4 of the Universal Declaration of Human Rights states, "No one shall be held in slavery or servitude; slavery and the slave trade shall be prohibited in all their forms." While many people in the United States believe that slavery ended after the American Civil War, the unfortunate truth is that slavery still continues around the world. The most recent estimate by the International Labour Organisation (ILO) (2012a) is that 21 million people around the world are currently in situations of forced labor. They state this is a "conservative estimate," and the Walk Free Foundation (2013) estimates 29 million. While ILO's estimate is substantially higher than the 12.3 million stated in their 2005 report, they note that this does not mean that the numbers themselves have grown, just that they were better able to estimate the number.

A relatively small percentage of those enslaved are kept under conditions similar to those with which we are familiar from the United States. Currently, most slaves are not bought and sold; there are no ownership papers. Today's slaves typically are not born into slavery and kept enslaved their whole lives, except for certain countries in Western Africa (as discussed later in this chapter). Most of those enslaved will be slaves for only a brief period; the average amount of time spent in a trafficking situation is 18 months (ILO, 2012a). Slavery now occurs more often as a result of desperation resulting from poverty rather than from one's freedom status at birth. Modern slavery is much more "cost effective" than old-fashioned slavery in that people are enslaved for only as long as they are productive and able to earn money for their "own-ers." After their ability to earn a profit has been exhausted, they are discarded, leading Kevin Bales, author of a book on this topic, to title his book *Disposable People* (2004).

Trafficking is prohibited in a wide variety of other human rights docu-ments as well. Article 6 of the Convention on the Elimination of All Forms of Discrimination Against Women (CEDAW) prohibits traffick-ing and the exploitation of prostitution. Within the Convention on the Rights of the Child (CRC), Article 34 provides the child with the right to be free from sexual exploitation, and Article 35 specifically references the right to be free from child trafficking. The CRC has two Optional Protocols: one on the Sale of Children, Child Prostitution, and Child Pornography and the other on the Involvement of Children in Armed Conflicts. As the use of child soldiers is considered to be a form of labor trafficking (US Department of State, 2011), both Protocols address traf-ficking. Although the United States has not ratified the Convention itself, it has ratified these Optional Protocols. The International Labour Organization's Convention Number 182, which defines the worst forms of child labor, also notes the use of children in armed conflicts as a type of labor trafficking:

> (a) *all forms of slavery or practices similar to slavery, such as the sale and trafficking of children, debt bondage and serfdom and forced or compulsory labour, including forced or compulsory recruitment of children for use in armed conflict*
> (b) *the use, procuring or offering of a child for prostitution, for the production of pornography or for pornographic performances*

Human trafficking was formally defined in international law for the first time in 2000 when the United Nations Convention against Transnational Organized Crime was opened for signature and entered into force. A standard definition was needed in order to help nations coordinate their anti-trafficking efforts, as well as coordinating services to those who had been trafficked (United Nations Office on Drugs and Crime, 2013). There were three Protocols that supplemented this Convention—the Protocol to Prevent, Suppress and Punish Trafficking in Persons, especially Women and Children being the relevant one. It is sometimes referred to the "Palermo Protocol," even though there are actually three Protocols.

This Protocol entered into force in 2003 and defines trafficking as follows (United Nations Office on Drugs and Crime, 2013):

_____

"Trafficking in persons" shall mean the recruitment, transportation, transfer, harbouring or receipt of persons, by means of the threat or use of force or other forms of coercion, of abduction, of fraud, of deception, of the abuse of power or of a position of vulnerability or of the giving or receiving of payments or benefits to achieve the consent of a person having control over another person, for the purpose of exploitation. Exploitation shall include, at a minimum, the exploitation of the prostitution of others or other forms of sexual exploitation, forced labour or services, slavery or practices similar to slavery, servitude or the removal of organs.

_____

According to this definition, trafficking has three central elements: act, means, and purpose. The act is what was done: recruitment, transportation, transfer, harboring or receipt of a person, while the means is how: threat, force, abduction, fraud, and so on. The purpose is for exploitation. Although this definition was established in 2000, what exactly constitutes human trafficking has continued to evolve. While the first edition of this text noted that trafficking was considered to be a form of forced labor, they are now considered to be largely equivalent terms (ILO, 2012a). Forced labor is defined as "all work or service which is exacted from any person under the menace of any penalty and for which said person has not offered himself [sic] voluntarily" in the Forced Labour Convention of 1930. The only form of trafficking that is specified in the Protocol that is not covered under the definition of forced labor is trafficking for the purposes of organ transplant. Trafficking for forced marriage and adoption are excluded from both (ILO, 2012a).

Part of the evolution of understanding what is defined as trafficking revolves around the term "transportation" within the act. Due at least in part to the fact that this definition was part of the "transnational" protocol, only those who moved across international borders were initially considered to be trafficked. However, opinion has now coalesced around the idea of the word "or" within the definition and that movement need not occur for trafficking to occur. The ILO (2012a) estimates that fewer than half of those in forced labor are moved (44%); 30% are moved across an international border, primarily those trafficked for the purpose of sexual exploitation. Women and girls represent a little more than half (55%) of those affected and three-quarters are adults.

The ILO (2009) notes a set of indicators that a situation may be considered as trafficking. These indicators fall into six categories: deceptive recruitment; coercive recruitment; recruitment by abuse of vulnerability; exploitative conditions of work; coercion at destination; and abuse of vulnerability at destination. They state that for trafficking to be determined as occurring, there should be two strong indicators; one strong and one medium or weak indicator; three medium indicators; or two medium and one weak indicator. These indicators include the following, among others, including additional indicators for children as well:

- Debt bondage
- Violence, or threats of violence, against the victim
- Confiscation of documents
- Excessive working days or hours
- Deception regarding the nature of the job or location
- Isolation or confinement

What makes people vulnerable to exploitation through slavery is some type of difference from others in their society (Bales, 2004). While in US history, that difference was based on skin color, in today's slavery these differences encompass a range of possibilities. As discussed earlier in this book, poverty, lack of education, and discrimination place people at higher risk of a number of social problems. When people have difficulty providing for themselves and their families, they may be more willing to take chances for a job for the money they require for basic needs. Discrimination within a society can limit their opportunities to obtain a wage through safer methods. This chapter will highlight limited opportunities due to discrimination based on caste, sex, socioeconomic status, ethnicity, and citizenship status, which make people vulnerable to being trafficked, whether it is for labor or sexual exploitation.

Types of Human Trafficking

The ILO (2012a) breaks down the types of forced labor into two basic types: that imposed by the state or other armed forces, and that imposed by private citizens. The exploitation committed by private citizens can be further broken down into exploitation for the primary purpose of labor or sexual exploitation. While sex trafficking receives the bulk of media attention, it makes up only about a quarter of trafficking situations. As noted later, trafficking is defined not by the type of labor performed but by the type of relationship between the worker and the employer (ILO, 2012a). The work may be perfectly legal, but it is the exploitation of it that causes it to become trafficking.

All immigration is due to what are termed "push and pull" factors: factors that push people to leave their current situation and factors that pull them to a new place. In economic migration, pull factors are typically promises of better paying jobs, while push factors are typically the poverty and oppression found in their place of origin. For example, since the disintegration of the Soviet Union, poverty has increased in the nations that constituted it, especially among women. Job segregation is common and women have had difficulty accessing employment that pays sufficient wages. This has made women from countries such as Russia, Ukraine, and Moldova vulnerable to sex trafficking (Tavcer, 2006; Tverdova, 2011; Vijeyarasa, 2012). These countries also have comparatively high levels of governmental corruption (Transparency International, 2012). Governmental corruption has also been found to be a strong predictor of why trafficking occurs in a source country; it is also a predictor of a country being a destination country (Bales, 2007).

Exploitation by the State

Approximately 10% of forced labor victims are exploited by the state or armed forces—approximately 2.2 million people (ILO, 2012a). According to the ILO, states do have some authority to mandate service, but only under certain specific conditions, such as compulsory military services; normal civic obligations (e.g., jury service); and emergencies (ILO, 2012b). In some cases, it is not the state that requires the labor, but those fighting against it in rebel or militia groups. As noted earlier, the use of child soldiers is considered to be a form of human trafficking (discussed further in Chapter 4).

Myanmar, a major offender in this category at the time of the first edition of this text, has been working to make reforms and in 2012 signed a joint plan with the United States to address trafficking of its citizens (US Department of State, 2012a). Myanmar had been noted for its governmental use of child soldiers and for forcing its citizens to provide free labor for the government. Villagers were required to travel from their homes to build roads, dams, and temples as well as act as porters for the military. Not only were villagers not paid for this compulsory labor, they were forced to provide their own food and face physical consequences, including beatings and death, if they did not fulfill their duties (Human Rights Watch, 2001; ILO, 2005). The situation in Myanmar is not yet free of forced labor, but it continues to show signs of improvement (US Department of State, 2013a).

In contrast, Uzbekistan has gained increasing notice for its use of state-sponsored forced labor. During the cotton harvest each year, people are forced to work in the fields to bring in the crop. The government sets such a low price for cotton, it is impossible for farmers to recruit and pay a voluntary workforce. While the number of children under 15 years old who have been trafficked has been decreasing, older children and adults are still subjected to this forced labor (US Department of State, 2013b).

China and North Korea have been cited for their use of forced labor camps. The ILO Convention number 105, adopted in 1957, prohibited nations from using forced labor as a form of political coercion or as punishment for expressing political views (ILO, 2012b). North Korea uses these camps to punish political prisoners, who are forced to labor in such work as logging, mining, and farming (US Department of State, 2013b). It is estimated that 80,000 people are held in these camps, a reduction from the previous estimate of 120,000. This is due in small part to the release of prisoners, but it is primarily because of the high mortality rate of those sent there (Harlan, 2013). While China originally used the camps for the detention of government critics, they have expanded to include "re-education" of those addicted to drugs, sex workers, and followers of Falun Gong (Bodeen, 2013). At the beginning of 2013, China stated they would be closing them (Bodeen, 2013). While progress has yet to be observed, later that year a woman won a court case against the state after being sentenced to a labor camp for protesting the sentences given to men who raped and trafficked her daughter (Jacobs, 2013).

Economic Exploitation by Private Citizens

The largest proportion of forced labor victims (90%) are used by private citizens for economic exploitation—for either primarily labor (68%) or sexual (22%) exploitation (ILO, 2012a). While trafficking for purposes of sexual exploitation has received the lion's share of media coverage, it is actually debt bondage that entraps the largest number of people.

Debt Bondage   The most common type of forced labor worldwide is debt bondage. Debt bondage occurs when a worker is lent a sum of money by an employer and is unable to leave this employment until the debt is paid. However, through a series of mechanisms, the debt can be impossible to pay. For example, the employer may charge enormous interest rates, ensuring the debt continues to grow. The employer may also charge large sums for (substandard) food, shelter, and clothing while paying the worker below-market wages. Many workers trapped in debt bondage are illiterate and thus unable to track their debt. International law defines debt bondage as:

The status or condition arising from a pledge by a debtor of his/her personal services or those of a person under his/her control as security for a debt, if the value of those services as reasonably assessed is not applied towards the liquidation of the debt or the length or nature of those services are not respectively limited or defined. ("Supplementary Convention," 1957)

Debt bondage is most prevalent in South Asia, including the countries of India, Pakistan, Bangladesh, and Nepal. Debt bondage illustrates very clearly how certain segments of society are most at risk. India has the highest number of people enslaved in the world (Bales, 2004), although bonded labor is illegal in India. Those of the lower castes are much more likely to be in debt bondage. The caste system in India, although outlawed, still permeates the thinking of many Indian citizens. The majority of those in debt bondage (80% to 98%) are from the "Scheduled Castes or Tribes," or Dalit people (Srivastava, 2005), thus illustrating how discrimination can lead to poverty, which can lead to desperation. People from this lower caste group are traditionally assigned "dirty" jobs such as sweeping, removal of animal and human waste, and snake catching. Historically, higher caste people would not allow themselves to become unclean through performing these tasks, and thus the Dalits were mandated to do so without any payment. Debt bondage originated in this tradition of giving a service to upper caste people without payment (Anti-Slavery International, 2001). Many bonded laborers are in agriculture, but there is a growing number in other areas, including quarries, mines, and brick kilns (Srivastava, 2005). Women tend to suffer disproportionately to men, through sexual and physical abuse, indirect bondage through their husbands, and heavier workloads (ILO, 2005).

The Indian government has set up programs to assist workers who are freed from bonded labor. When the laborers are identified and registered, they are eligible for a grant in money, land, or livestock. They can receive cash immediately to help them get home or get started. However, corruption can prevent this system from working as well as it could. In some cases, corrupt officials help the landlord claim the money in the name of the laborer, leaving the laborer still in bondage and no better off (Bales, 2004). A nongovernmental organization (NGO), Volunteers for Social Justice (www.vsj-ddva.org), has been working in India to arrange the release of people kept in debt bondage and to punish those who commit crimes against people of the Dalit caste.

Nepal has names for bonded labor, referred to as *Kamaiya*, *Haliya*, and *Haruwa/Charuwa* in different parts of the country (United Nations—Nepal Information Platform, 2012). These workers primarily labor in agriculture but also in domestic labor, brick kilns, and embroidery workshops (Anti-Slavery International, 2009). In 2002, the *kamaiya* system was legally abolished and there was a program to identify these workers and provide rehabilitation services, including land and access to vocational training. While successful in some instances, in others, the land provided was infertile or the vocational training unrealistic (e.g., providing electrical training in an area without electricity), causing some to be rebonded (Anti-Slavery International, 2009). In 2008, the Nepalese government announced the abolishment of the *haliya* system, but a law has not yet been passed and rehabilitation services are lacking (United Nations, 2011).

In Qatar, large numbers of Nepalese men were trapped in forced labor while working in construction for preparation for the World Cup; 44 died in a 2-month time span in the summer of 2013. Their passports had been confiscated, they had not been paid, they were denied drinking water while working in the desert, and they were forced to sleep 12 to a room.

Most felt trapped by the debt they owed for transportation from Nepal (Pattisson, 2013).

Debt bondage also occurs in Brazil. Forced labor situations exist on cattle ranches and plantations, with some in the charcoal industry (Seelke, 2012; Shahinian, 2010a). The economic boom in the 1960s and 1970s in Brazil caused a large-scale migration from rural to urban areas. This mass migration increased poverty in the urban areas and resulted in the creation of slums known as *favelas*. The economic boom passed and the poverty in the *favelas* worsened, increasing the desperation of workers eager to support their families.

Workers, primarily men, are lured to rural areas by promises of good pay. Recruiters (known as *gatos*) will go into the slums and announce they are looking for workers. They may use loudspeakers or go door to door to spread the word of these employment opportunities. They promise transportation to the work site, food and salary, and free trips home for family visits. The *gatos* will even give some men money to give to their families before they leave. They transport them to the work site and buy as much food as the men like on the trip. However, when they arrive at the work site, they are informed they must repay the cost of the food and transport, as well as any money they have already been given (Bales, 2004; Shahinian, 2010a).

Several factors change this activity from simple economic exploitation to forced labor. The work sites are typically located far from home, which acts to imprison the workers since they have no way to leave. They are also often watched by armed guards (Shahinian, 2010a). The *gatos* will also collect the worker's state ID card and labor card. As people are unable to gain employment without these documents, the workers are unable to leave because they will not be able to get another job without them. Third, as with debt bondage in India, there is no honest accounting of what the debt owed is and how the worker's labor counts to reduce the debt (Bales, 2004).

A fourth factor also acts to keep these men in their enslaved conditions: their cultural beliefs about debt. In Brazilian culture, it is extremely important to repay your debts, and a person who does not do so is looked upon very poorly. Thus, the men are reluctant to leave the work site while they still believe they owe a debt to their employers for the transportation and food. Although the men are not informed as to how great a debt they owe or how their wages are used to help pay it off, their cultural sense of honor binds them until the debt is repaid (Bales, 2004).

The situation in Brazil has improved since the first edition of this text. In the 2012 update to his book, Bales credits two government officials for this achievement: government official Luis Antonio Carmago de Melo and the then-president of Brazil, Luiz da Silva (known as Lula). Lula established the National Commission for the Eradication of Slave Labor within 4 months of taking office and freed over 40,000 people. The UN Special Rapporteur on Contemporary Forms of Slavery, Gulnara Shahinian (2010a), also praised the Brazilian government for its excellent policies but also noted that there have been few consequences for traffickers, including *gatos*, landowners, and the corporations who benefit from the labor.

Shahinian (2010a) also noted the recruitment of workers from Bolivia into Brazil to cities such as São Paulo for work in the garment industry. Once in Brazil, they are easier to exploit than Brazilians due to the strong Brazilian unions. They are held in debt bondage, with their papers taken and their movements restricted to the factory. Due to their low wages, as well as the fact that they must pay for the use of tools and machines, they will never be able to earn enough to pay the debt.

Domestic Workers   Due to the isolated nature of the work, those employed as domestic workers are vulnerable to exploitation. To address the issue of exploitation of domestic workers, in 2011 the ILO adopted the Convention on Decent Work for Domestic Workers. This convention established global minimum standards such as minimum wages, number of working hours, and the right to time off as well as requiring governments to protect workers from abuse (Human Rights Watch, 2011b). However, many remain exploited.

This inherent vulnerability caused by isolation in the home is heightened when workers are removed from their support system. In certain countries, such as Sri Lanka and the Philippines, women are trained to enter the household service of employers in other countries (Waldman, 2005). They will leave their own families for years at a time so they can travel abroad and earn money they cannot earn in their own country. Their destination countries are often in Asia or the Middle East, although Western European countries and the United States are not uncommon. These workers are typically traveling voluntarily and may even have signed a contract stipulating their work conditions and salary. However, even with these seeming protections, their travel can turn to trafficking all too easily. They may or may not be in the host country through legal channels. Even if they have entered legally, employers often take their passports and work papers, thus rendering them unable to flee. If they have signed a contract, it may be torn up or replaced with a new one with different conditions. The workers are told they cannot go to the authorities of that country about the abuse because they will not be believed. Once they are isolated, the workers work long hours every day and are paid minimal amounts of money, or even nothing at all. They are given poor places to sleep, such as the floor, and are forbidden from leaving the house (Vlieger, 2012). A number of domestic workers have been subjected to physical and sexual abuse (Waldman, 2005).

Due to the *kafala* (sponsorship) system in Saudi Arabia and the United Arab Emirates, foreign workers are unable to change employers without permission of their original employer, thus trapping them in exploitive situations (Vlieger, 2012). This system places the legal responsibility for the employee on the employer, giving the employer justification for taking the passport and confining the person to the house (ILO, 2013). A form of debt bondage can also exist as the worker may be expected to repay the cost of her plane ticket, recruitment fee, or other costs (Shahinian, 2010b).

Many women and girls emigrate from Indonesia to Malaysia for employment as domestic workers. Due to the vast numbers being exploited, Malaysia placed a ban on women migrating to Indonesia to work as domestic aides between 2009 and 2011 (Gooch, 2012). When the ban was revoked, a system was put in place to provide women with 200 hours of training before they departed ("Indonesia revokes ban," 2011). However, none of this addressed the true problem, the exploitation. During the ban, the void was filled by workers from Cambodia who were also exploited (Human Rights Watch, 2011a). After the ban was lifted, Malaysian women were again exploited (Gooch, 2012).

The following is a typical story:

"Sujatmi told me that I would take care of her children and would be paid 300,000 rupiah [$33] a month. I worked at Sujatmi's house for 3 months. Sometimes I did not get any food. I woke up at 4 a.m.

and slept at 10 p.m. I would sweep the floor, wash the clothes, and take care of the children. Sujatmi shouted at me, 'You are a poor person. You have to know your position, you are here to work.' I was not allowed to go out of the house. I had not seen my family since I left home. I was not paid any salary. Sujatmi would say to me, 'I have your 300,000 rupiah with me and I will take you back…to see your family.' She was lying. She never took me home. She hit me when she was angry. Three times she hit. Once she slapped my face and then kicked me above my right hip. It hurt and swelled up. I did not go to the doctor. She laughed when I asked that I want to see the doctor."—Asma, 15, Medan (summarized from Human Rights Watch, 2005)

In some cases, diplomats bring workers from their home country to their posting. If the workers do manage to complain of exploitation, the employer will claim diplomatic immunity. In some cases in the United States, judges have ruled that since the situation was outside of their diplomatic duties, they are not immune to prosecution (Fitzpatrick, 2009). However, this remains more the exception than the rule (Neubauer, 2012).

A large number of children also work as domestic servants, the vast majority of whom are girls. They are regarded as cheaper and more compliant than adults (Shahinian, 2010b). In many cases, this derived from a positive tradition in which children were fostered by a wealthier relative and sent to school in exchange for assistance with chores. However, this tradition has now been perverted in many cases. In Haiti, the term *restavèk* (meaning to stay with) has become a pejorative term for these trafficked children (Shahinian, 2010b). It is estimated that there are approximately 225,000 *restavèks* in Haiti (Seelke, 2012). The following story summarizes the situation faced by one child:

Ten-year-old Larissa lived in rural Haiti with her family when one of her sisters convinced her to come to Port-au-Prince to work for a family. In exchange, they would send her to school and take care of her. Instead she was forced to rise at 4 a.m. each day to clean, fetch water, and prepare lunch. She was whipped if there was no water in the house. She was also in charge of watching the family's 4-year-old. After the family went to bed, she was then able to go to

*bed herself—a cloth on the floor. After 3 years, she built the courage
to escape. She jumped in a taxi, but had no idea where to go; the
passengers took her to the police.* (Summarized from UNICEF, 2012)

Descent-Based Slavery   In certain countries in Western Africa, such as
Mauritania and Niger, situations resembling slavery from centuries ago
persist. In these areas, slavery is something into which people are born,
and it lasts a lifetime. While slavery has been outlawed by the laws or con-
stitutions of these countries, it continues to exist because the ruling class
is not interested in enforcing these bans. It is in these nations that slavery
based on racism and skin color continues. Slave owners are of Moorish
descent, while slaves are of African descent (Bales, 2004). Slaves may
be responsible for herding cattle, performing agricultural labor, or doing
domestic work. Slaves are the property of their owners and can be sold or
given to a new owner. They are not paid for their labor and are given no
choice about their work and lack freedom of movement.

The family of the slave has often served the family of the master for
generations. Religious authorities often support the notion that slaves
deserve their bondage. Those enslaved are taught that God has placed
them in bondage and that to leave would be to disobey God's will (Special
Rapporteur on Contemporary Forms of Slavery, 2010). These slaves
remain tied to their masters through economic, cultural, and psychological bonds. Due to continuing discrimination against their caste, they typically have few options for survival and those that do leave usually live
segregated in an *adwaba*, a camp outside the city (Special Rapporteur on
Contemporary Forms of Slavery, 2010).

National movements have worked to try to stop slavery in these countries. In 2013, Mauritania announced its first governmental agency to provide support for those who have been enslaved ("Mauritania pledges,"
2013). In Mali, those formerly enslaved were given a reprieve in 2013
when the Arab Moors fled Timbuktu after the brief rebellion in Mali's
north (Raghavan, 2013). In Niger, a group called Timidria was founded
in 1991 to eliminate slavery and all forms of discrimination in Niger
through nonviolent means. Although the organization has faced resistance from the slave-owning classes, it has grown into a strong movement with thousands of members. Timidria operates through multiple

methods to accomplish its goals. It holds meetings and uses poetry and drama to spread the messages that slavery is illegal and that members of the population do not have to be enslaved. Members also lobby the government and use the media to spread their message. They provide assistance to former slaves, including microcredit and schooling (Anti-Slavery International, n.d.). A case in which they supported a woman through the legal system is described next:

_____

Hadijatou Mani was born to an enslaved woman in Niger and inherited her enslaved status. When she was 12, she was sold to a friend of her master's as a Wahiya, *a slave to both do chores and be a concubine. From this age, she was forced to have sex with her master, to clean, and to work the land. This provided her only a few hours of sleep a night. She was violently beaten at any hint of disobedience. In 2005, her master granted her a 'liberation certificate' due to the then new law criminalizing slavery as well as negative publicity, but he refused to let her go, insisting she was his wife based on customary law. The first court ruled against him, but the higher court overturned this ruling. Hadijatou Mani, with the help of Timidria, took the case to the Community Court of Justice of the Economic Community of West Africa States and sued Niger for failing to protect her. The court ruled in favor of Ms. Mani and ordered the State to pay her compensation of 10 million West African Francs, which will help her build a new life.* (Summarized from ILO, 2009)

_____

Other Industries   The situations described earlier by no means cover the totality of labor exploitation. While forced labor can occur in any field, there are some in which people are more vulnerable for several reasons, including a migrant workforce, temporary/seasonal work, not speaking the dominant language of that nation, not holding the necessary documentation to be legally within a nation, and having one's residency being dependent upon a marriage or family reunification, as in the case of female migrant workers (ILO, 2013; Smit, 2011). These fields include agriculture outside of debt bondage, construction, factories, and seafaring.

Brick kilns are places where trafficking occurs in Asia, including such nations as China, Nepal, and India (Anti-Slavery International, 2009; Shen, Antonopoulos, & Papanicolaou, 2013). Restaurants have also been found to be sites where labor trafficking exists, while children or those with a disability may be forced to beg ("Disabled," 2011; Smit, 2011).

Sexual Exploitation by Private Citizens

Approximately 22% of those who have been trafficked experience primarily sexual exploitation—currently approximately 4.5 million people. Ninety-eight percent of these sexually exploited individuals are women and girls; 21% are children (ILO, 2012a). While some victims of economic exploitation, such as those in domestic labor, are sexually exploited as well, many others find that sex work is their main "employment." Sexual trafficking is often an outcome of dual oppression: poverty and gender discrimination. Poor girls often have no other means of economic survival or perceived skills other than the sexual use of their bodies. Gender discrimination and poverty have often barred them from an education or other skills, while cultural expectations in many parts of the world require females to support their families.

The money that girls are able to send back to their villages encourages families to send their daughters to work in the sex trade. For example, families in Yunnan province in China would send girls to work in the sex trade in Thailand as the money they earned paid for large new houses with air conditioning for their families (French, 2005). While not all women in the sex trade are forced into it, virtually all suffer from a lack of other economic options.

Thus, poverty plays an important role. As the vast majority of those who experience sex trafficking migrate, either internationally (74%) or internally (19%; ILO, 2012a), it is not the extremely poor who experience this, as they do not have the funds to travel (Danailova-Trainor & Laczko, 2010).

Sexual exploitation provides a clear example of how voluntary migration may become trafficking. Many are tricked with false job offers or offers of marriage. While some of the women realize that they will be working as prostitutes, many do not until it is too late. Even those who do know this do not know the conditions under which they will be working—they are often forced to service 10 men a day without protection while suffering additional physical and sexual violence (Tverdova, 2011). When village girls in Thailand were asked what a prostitute was, the most common answer was "wearing Western clothes and eating in restaurants" (Caye, 1996, as cited in Bales, 2004). Globalization has increased knowledge of other nations, but only to the extent portrayed in the media. Therefore, to those living in impoverished nations without job opportunities, the Global North appears to be a place where it is easy to make money. In some nations, "employment agencies" are set up as fronts for recruitment into sex trafficking. Girls are told they will be working in Western nations as models, nannies, or waitresses (Hodge & Lietz, 2007). Girls have idealized notions of these countries. Believing they will get wealthy there, the girls eagerly sign up. These situations have been found in such diverse countries as Malawi, Mozambique, the Philippines, Thailand, and Colombia (International Organization for Migration, 2003; Lee, 2005) as well as countries in Southeast Europe (Dottridge, 2006).

India is a source, destination, and transit country for trafficking. In both India and its neighbor Nepal, females have few opportunities for education or employment. Girls are regarded as an economic burden because not only are they typically unable to access well-paying employment but their family must provide a dowry upon marriage. These factors all contribute to trafficking (Deane, 2010; Patel, 2013). If a girl's parents are unwilling or unable to pay a dowry, she may be sent to the city to find work. Typically, the work she is able to find will be in the sex trade. In other cases, parents trade their child for a sum of money, either knowing or not knowing the type of work into which their daughter will be forced. Thus, one is able to see how the double burdens of poverty and discrimination against women can lead to sex slavery in these highly patriarchal cultures. Females from Nepal or rural India may also be lured with false job or marriage offers (Deane, 2010; Patel, 2013). The border between Nepal and India is open, making migration across it extremely easy. In response, NGO workers monitor the border where possible to try to spot those who are being crossed to be trafficked ("Keeping watch," 2010).

Turkey provides another example of this phenomenon. It has become a destination country for women from Eastern Europe seeking better employment because it is relatively easy for them to enter Turkey due to its visa policy and because it is close to their home nation (Demir & Finckenauer, 2010). While prostitution is legal in Turkey, many of the immigrating women either do not realize they will be working in this trade or do not realize the conditions under which they will be forced to work. After they enter the country, their passports are taken away and they are beaten into submission and forced into prostitution. They are kept locked up unless they are being sold to a customer (Demir & Finckenauer, 2010; Smith, 2005).

Thailand has become both a destination and a sending country. Women from China, Myanmar, and Cambodia are trafficked into Thailand, while Thai women are trafficked abroad to places such as Japan and Taiwan. Thai women have entered Japan legally under "entertainment visas," believing that they will be working in dance clubs, only to find themselves forced into prostitution (Bales & Trodd, 2008; ILO, 2005). Other Thai women who emigrate to Japan are aware that they will be working in the sex trade, but they are unaware they will accumulate large debts to the traffickers, which will place them in servitude. They may have their passports confiscated by the traffickers or be sold to Japanese gangsters after their arrival in Japan (Onishi, 2005). The Culture Box at the end of this Chapter provides a more in-depth look at trafficking in Thailand.

While sex tourism has received a lot of media attention, most of the women working in the sex trade who serve foreigners are not working under conditions of forced labor. They face conditions of economic oppression, often due to limited opportunities for females, but they are not enslaved (Blackburn, Taylor, & Davis, 2010). Most of the trafficked women in the sex trade serve men of their own country or low-income migrant workers from neighboring countries (Bales, 2004; Pearson, 2001). Thus, when we focus on eliminating sex trafficking, sex tourism should be only a piece of that focus. The exception to this, of course, is children who are sexually exploited and the tourists who seek them. A number of countries in the Global North, including the United States and Canada, have enacted laws criminalizing such acts and have sent their citizens to prison for violating them.

Other cultural factors such as religious customs can also lead to conditions of institutionalized sex slavery. Known as *trokosi* in Ghana or *devadasi* or *devaki* in India and Nepal, young virgin girls are given to the priest at a shrine if a calamity strikes the family. The girl is then bonded to the priest and expected to perform domestic and sexual services for him for no payment for the rest of her life. There is no limit as to the number of girls that can be bonded to each priest, so a "harem" may be developed. The girls can be beaten or denied food for infractions such as refusing sex, running away, or lateness (Pearson, 2001).

Forced Marriage   North Korea is among the poorest countries in the world, and the situation for its citizens is even direr due to the repressive nature of its government. Citizens from North Korea will emigrate to China with the hope of finding jobs that will pay enough to allow them to send money back to their families in North Korea. Despite the repressive government, their primary reasons for leaving tend to be economic (Muico, 2007). However, illegal border crossings have become more difficult in recent years with reports of border guards being told to shoot to kill (US Department of State, 2013a). However, those who successfully cross are at risk for being trafficked in China (US State Department, 2013b). Women are most at risk as their work tends to leave them isolated within a household. They may become domestic workers or sold into prostitution. Many North Korean women in China, however, are sold into forced marriage (Kim, Yun, Park, & Williams, 2009; Muico, 2005). China has an imbalance of men to women, and some men have difficulty finding a wife. This imbalance is due in large part to China's "one child" policy, discussed further in the Culture Box in Chapter 4. These women often face physical and sexual abuse in their marriage. Women of other nations such as Myanmar and Cambodia are at risk of forced marriages to Chinese men as well, a situation not calculated in the ILO's estimate.

Trafficking victims are reluctant to approach Chinese authorities for fear of repatriation. Leaving North Korea without permission is a crime that can result in the death penalty, and the Chinese government is known to forcibly return them there (US Department of State, 2013b). Typically, returned immigrants will be sentenced to a labor camp (US Department of State, 2013a). In the camp, they receive little food and are forced to work at hard physical labor. The following case study summarized from Muico (2005) illustrates the plight of these people:

My eldest daughter went to China to sell a porcelain bowl at a market but didn't return. To look for her, I took my youngest daughter and crossed the icy Tumen River into China in the middle of the night.

Once there, I worked as a nanny for a Korean-Chinese family. After a week, I was sent out to the market on an errand and when I returned, my younger daughter was gone. The family said they didn't know anything about it. I ran out of the house in despair searching for her. To get her back, I had to pay 4,000 yuan ($500).

After two years in China, four men came to our house at night and kidnapped us. They were planning to sell us as "brides" to men in a mining town for 10,000 yuan ($1,200) each. The neighbors suspected foul play and called the police. My daughter and I spent 40 days in a Chinese detention centre before being deported to North Korea. In North Korea, we were stripped naked, checked for hidden money, and sent to a labour training camp. My daughter was beaten and interrogated on whether we met any South Koreans or missionaries in China. All we had for food was porridge made from black, rotten flour and watery soup. We worked in the cabbage patches and carried heavy logs from the mountains. The guards threw stones at us if we didn't run fast enough. I escaped after four days, but my daughter remained in prison for two and a half months.

What Can Be Done

As noted in the US Trafficking Victims Protection Act, fighting human trafficking is often conceptualized as "three P's": prosecution, protection, and prevention. Prosecution of traffickers has been the major focus for countries, and the number of countries adopting laws to criminalize human trafficking continues to grow. As of 2013, 83% of nations had human trafficking legislation ("UN member states," 2013). However, protection of those who have been trafficked has not kept pace. Oftentimes, assistance to the person trafficked is tied to the person's assistance in prosecution of the offender (Nikolic-Ristanovic, 2010). This type of legislation is thus operating from a criminal justice standpoint, not a rights-based approach.

When focusing on protection, the diverse impacts of the different forms of trafficking should be noted. The majority of studies in the peer-reviewed literature have focused on women who were trafficking for exploitation, especially in South Asia (Oram, Stöckl, Busza,

Howard, & Zimmerman, 2012). These women were found to have experienced both physical and sexual violence and as a result suffered from a myriad of issues. Physical complaints included back and stomach pain as well as memory issues, while mental health issues included depression, Post-Traumatic Stress Disorder, and anxiety. Some studies also found high levels of HIV infection (Oram et al., 2012). The one research study on working with those formally in descent-based slavery notes that important clinical issues can include "survivor's disempowerment, disconnection, co-dependency, self-blaming, and PTSD symptoms" (Blumhofer, Shah, Grodin, & Crosby, 2011, p. 328). Blumhofer et al. also note that supporting these survivors in learning to chart the course of their own days is an important skill because they did not have that luxury while enslaved.

Due to the focus on trafficking for the purposes of sexual exploitation, almost all services are designed to serve this population. Survivors of labor trafficking, especially males, typically have few available services (Smit, 2011). Also too often lacking are trained providers of mental health services. For example, in Cambodia, many services are provided by foreign faith-based NGO workers without clinical training. While their intentions are good, they lack the skills needed to effectively address the complex trauma that trafficking survivors have suffered (Blackburn et al., 2010).

In terms of prosecution, laws have a major impact and, as noted, more and more countries have been passing laws to criminalize human trafficking. However, not all of these laws cover the full range of trafficking outlined in the Palermo Protocol. For example, China's law excludes adult males and children between 14 and 18 years old who have been labor trafficked (Shen et al., 2013). Additionally, countries tend to focus more on the prevention aspect of laws as opposed to prosecution or protection (Cho & Vadlamannati, 2012).

Opinions have been divided on the best legal approach to reduce trafficking. In terms of sex trafficking, some countries believe it is best to legalize the buying and selling of sex in order to eliminate the criminal element, while others have criminalized only the buying of sex in order to focus on the demand side. Research has found that legalizing prostitution tends to increase sex trafficking (Cho, Dreher, & Neumayer, 2013). In contrast, in 1999, Sweden outlawed the buying, but not the selling, of sexual services. This was done in order to address the demand factor for these services, a factor noted as important by the UN High Commission on Human Rights (2002) but often left unaddressed.

A 2010 evaluation of the law in Sweden found that street prostitution had been reduced by half, while in contrast it grew dramatically in Norway and Denmark—neighboring countries without such a law. Internet prostitution did grow in Sweden, but not as extensively as in Norway and Denmark. Thus, there was not support for the concern that the law would merely move prostitution. It appears to have led to a decrease in demand (Swedish Institute, 2010). Swedish police and social workers report that criminal groups involved in prostitution regard Sweden as a "poor market" and avoid it due to this law. Norway and Iceland have now adopted their own version of the law (Ask, 2011).

In terms of prevention, more needs to be done on the demand side of this issue. Much attention has been paid to warning those deemed at risk about trafficking, but when people are in economic desperation, they will act to meet that need. In contrast, those on the demand end have more control over their choices. This correlates well with Sweden's approach. In contrast, in the United States, Dr. Melissa Farley conducted a study on men who purchase sex—such as through prostitution, pornography, or stripping—but she had difficulty finding 100 men who did *not* purchase sex in some form (Bennetts, 2011). The widespread buying of people for sexual use (and cultural acceptance of it) needs to change if trafficking is to be stopped. After the passage of the law in Sweden, a person who purchases sex is now referred to as "a cod," another term for a loser (Shubert, 2011).

Businesses can play an important part in prevention. The Global Business Coalition Against Human Trafficking (gBCAT) consists of major corporations including Coca-Cola, Ford, and Microsoft, as well as a number of businesses associated with travel and hospitality, who have pledged to focus on eliminating/preventing trafficking in their businesses, including monitoring their supply chains and training employees to monitor for those who have been trafficked (Balch, 2013). In 2012, a law came into effect in California that requires businesses with USD$100 million or more in sales that do business in California to state what they are doing to prevent human trafficking in their supply chain. This information must be displayed on a prominent place on their Web site ("New California law," 2012).

The Professional Role of Social Workers

Social workers can wear many of their hats in responding to conditions of human trafficking in the world. We are able to work nationally and internationally, on the micro level and on the macro level. Within the United States, social workers can push for effective legislation to assist survivors of trafficking in our country. These efforts can include both increasing awareness of the issue among citizens as well as providing effective services to victims, such as legal assistance, financial assistance, and help with food and housing. Social workers can also work for policies that punish those who exploit others into forced labor. In addition, these efforts can be focused on those who commit their crimes within our borders, as well as extraditing citizens who commit crimes in other countries.

In countries and areas from which people are emigrating or experiencing forced labor, social workers can use their education regarding community building and development to work to eradicate the conditions that support forced labor, including poverty and gender discrimination. By working with indigenous leaders to support the community, social workers will be better able to work in a culturally sensitive fashion that will meet the needs of the community. Social workers can also seek employment at agencies in other countries that assist victims of forced labor.

Pearson (2001) identifies the following conditions as ones that can contribute to situations of trafficking. Many of these fall under the purview of social work:

- Poverty and unemployment
- Globalization of the economy
- Feminization of poverty and migration
- Development strategies such as tourism
- Situations of armed conflict
- Gender-based discrimination
- Laws and policies on prostitution
- Corruption of authorities
- High profits; involvement of organized crime
- Cultural and religious practices

Pearson (2001) also states that when working against trafficking, it is more effective to work on strengthening the rights of those oppressed than to work on oppressive responses such as more restrictive immigration policies or more severe penalties. The first will help eliminate the conditions that drive forced labor, while the second relies on "catching" the person who is committing the crime. The second may also work against those who are victims of forced labor by restricting their freedom of movement and perpetuating the violation of their human rights. For example, the Philippines and Bangladesh barred female citizens of their nations from emigrating for work as domestic workers due to the abuse that former workers had suffered. However, this only served to limit the official freedom of movement and did nothing to eliminate the root causes of why women were emigrating for employment. Therefore, it did not stop the practice but only drove it underground. Once women were forced to resort to illegal means to gain employment, it increased their vulnerability rather than reducing it (Pearson, 2001).

An example of empowering oppressed people, thus reducing their vulnerability to forced labor, can be found in the case of the Self-Employed Women's Association (SEWA) of India (discussed further in Chapter 7). Its goal is to assist self-employed women in South and Southeast Asia who face personal barriers such as high rates of illiteracy, having to care for multiple children, and living in slum conditions, as well as macro barriers such as exploitation by moneylenders and harassment by employers and officials. Today, SEWA is the largest single union in India and has founded a bank in order to provide micro-finance loans to its members. The bank also provides insurance for its members, while the union assists with child care and legal aid. Through methods such as these, the women are able to provide for themselves and their families without resorting to forced labor.

Conclusion

This chapter has illustrated how the three vulnerabilities—poverty, discrimination, and lack of access to education—can lead to human slavery, a horror many thought long dead. Although it is experienced differently in different cultures and the specific vulnerabilities will vary from place to place, the phenomenon of enslavement remains. Social workers can play a unique role in stopping this violation of human rights. We are equipped to work on the micro level with the victim and also on the macro level to stop the conditions that create the atmosphere where this can occur.

Culture Box
HUMAN TRAFFICKING AND THAILAND

Thailand has received a lot of international attention for the existence of sex trafficking within its borders; however, labor trafficking is also a major issue in this country. Whether the purpose of the exploitation is for labor or sex, those affected tend to be citizens of neighboring countries, often irregular migrants. They often migrate to Thailand of their own accord and then find themselves in trafficking situations after their arrival (US Department of State, 2013b). However, there are a number who are trafficked from the outset, especially those who will be sexually exploited.

While prostitution has existed in Thailand for hundreds of years, as it has in many countries, the sex trade expanded greatly during the Vietnam War when American soldiers would visit Thailand on "R&R" (rest and relaxation). Thai culture has had a large impact on the development of the sex trade in Thailand. Traditionally, there has been no stigma placed on men using prostitutes. Thailand was a polygamous society for many years and remnants of that remained in the acceptability of male use of prostitutes.

The economic boom in the 1990s added to this. While wealthy men had always been able to afford prostitutes, it was not until the economic boom that men of average and low wages were able to do so as well. This fueled the demand for low-cost prostitutes and resulted in a greater number of girls being brought from the north of Thailand, since that area did not experience the economic boom until many years after central Thailand did. Consequently, these girls were still living in dire poverty and seeking a means to support their family. Theravada Buddhism favors boys over girls, and this can result in a society that regards women as objects to be used (Bales, 2004). Boys are favored because if a boy serves as a monk for a period of time, it is believed this service adds a great deal of good karma toward his parents' reincarnation. There is no such benefit to having a daughter.

While sex tourism in Thailand has received a great deal of press, the vast majority of prostitutes are not enslaved. Those who are serve the "lower" end of the market, Thai laborers (Bales, 2004). In Thailand, most of those in the sex industry are aged 16–25 years old, while young children are much more difficult to locate, although they are forced to work in this industry as well (Blackburn et al., 2010). One study found that 10% of its sex worker sample were trafficked—of these, 15% had been tricked or forced, and 89% had been under 18 years old when they began. However, the vast majority (95%) was Thai, and this should be taken into account (Decker, McCauley, Phuengsamran, Janyam, & Silverman, 2011).

In the past, those who were trafficked for sexual exploitation were poor Thai women primarily from the northern and more rural areas of Thailand. However, in recent years, they are increasingly from other countries such as Laos, Cambodia, and Myanmar. Whether they are from Thailand or other countries, they are typically members of ethnic minorities, such as the Hill Tribes (Jayagupta, 2009; US Department of State, 2013b). The girls and women often come to Bangkok of their own accord in search of better opportunities. They may be escaping poverty, searching for a job, or simply looking for more excitement than is found in their village. In some cases, they are aware that they will be working as prostitutes, but they have little idea as to what that will actually entail, such as the conditions of the brothel and the number of customers they will be expected to serve each night. In other instances, they have no idea; they believe they will be working in a restaurant or other business. There is an informal network that will arrange for the girls' transport. Often these brokers are known in the villages and are trusted.

In some cases, those trafficked are refugees, such as from Myanmar. As noted in Chapter 5, these refugees have been restricted to camps and unable to earn a living legally, causing them to resort to working illegally to earn money, which creates vulnerability for trafficking. In other cases, they are from countries that lack the economic opportunities of Thailand, such as Laos or Cambodia.

A review of research regarding children who migrated from Laos to Thailand for work found that in the vast majority of cases, the children voluntarily migrated of their own accord. One-third of them wound

(continued)

up in the sex industry, but the majority were in other fields, including domestic labor, construction, factory work, and agriculture (Huijsmans, 2008; US Department of State, 2013b). Children have been trafficked to sell flowers or to beg for money on the streets of Bangkok. In most cases, these children are not Thai ("Children trafficked," 2012; US Department of State, 2012b). For many years, children born to Burmese refugees in Thailand were not granted citizenship, rendering them stateless and excluding them from the benefits of citizenship and making them vulnerable to trafficking.

Men from Cambodia or Myanmar are frequently found to have been trafficked in the fishing industry. One study found that 57% of workers on these fishing boats experienced forced labor (US Department of State, 2013b). They endure 20-hour working days, lack of food, and physical abuse while at sea for several years at a time ("Men trafficked," 2011; Nadi, 2013; US Department of State, 2013b). If a person is too ill or weak to work, it is common for him to be killed (US Department of State, 2013b).

Thailand has been trying to combat trafficking through a multipronged approach. First, it passed legislation in 1996 that provided stiffer penalties for customers of prostitution, brothel owners, and parents who sell their daughters into prostitution. These penalties were even stiffer if the girl is underage. In 2008, the Anti-Trafficking in Persons Act took effect, which further increased jail time and financial penalties for traffickers (Blackburn et al., 2010). However, awareness of this law remains low, even among law enforcement (US Department of State, 2012b).

In 2013, Thailand approved a new "Master Plan" to improve its response to trafficking. This plan would improve monitoring for labor trafficking, addressing sex tourism, addressing law enforcement interventions, and providing sufficient resources to accomplish its goals ("Cabinet approves," 2013). This plan prevented Thailand's ranking from being downgraded in the US Trafficking in Persons report of 2013 (US Department of State, 2013b). However, Thailand is not yet a party to Palermo Protocol, although it signed it in 2001 (United Nations, 2013).

Thailand has been criticized by the United States for the extraordinarily long time that it takes to process trafficking cases through its judicial system ("US concerned," 2013; US Department of State, 2012b). Additionally, the Trafficking in Persons Report states that the number of those convicted of trafficking is "disproportionately small" compared to the scope of the problem (US Department of State, 2012b). As noted in other nations, corruption of police is part of the problem, with brothels paying protection to them or even police outright owning the brothel (Blackburn et al., 2010; US Department of State, 2013b).

More attention needs to be given to the reintegration phase. As noted, the legal process is exceedingly slow, causing some to give up in frustration. Thailand provides several protection centers and a number of temporary shelters for those who have been trafficked. In them, survivors are offered psychological services, medical treatment, and vocational training. However, some survivors view it more as a detention center, causing them to avoid it (Jayagupta, 2009). Foreign survivors of trafficking, especially women who were sexually exploited, are required to stay there and may not leave without an escort (US Department of State, 2013b). Additionally, the main center—Kredtrakarn Centre, located outside Bangkok—receives a number of official visitors, resulting in a lack of privacy for those living there (Jayagupta, 2009). Services are lacking for children who have been trafficked, and if they are unwilling to testify against their trafficker, they are required to return to their home country, often resulting in their retrafficking (US Department of State, 2013b).

In some cases, survivors learn a trade that they are unable to apply when back in their home village. They are typically returning to the same lack of economic opportunity that they left initially, which can compel them to migrate again and possibly be retrafficked. In addition, they may face stigma due to their experiences while trafficked ("Family pressures," 2011; Jayagupta, 2009). As many of those who were found to be trafficked in Thailand have migrated of their own accord due to economic opportunities, it cannot be assumed that simply informing people of trafficking will prevent it from occurring (Huijsmans, 2008). People will act to meet their needs, even if it bears a risk. Therefore, economic development in their home regions should be an important focus.

What Can I Do Now?

- Use your consumer power. Buy products that are made as "Fair Trade." This can include coffee marked as Fair Trade or rugs marked with the "Rugmark" label to show they were not produced with child labor. Boycotts are often not encouraged as that only directly hurts the slaves since the market for the product dries up. You can check companies' records of human rights at www.responsibleshopper.org. Learn more at www.sweatshopwatch.org.
- Take the quiz at slaveryfootprint.org to see how many slaves work for you based on your buying habits, including clothing, food, and electronics. Educate others about the problem. Break the ignorance. MTV has excellent resources located at http://thebackstory.mtv.com and http://www.againstourwill.org
- Convince those you know to stand against the buying of people for the sexual use of others—whether in prostitution, pornography, or strip clubs.
- Support groups that are working to solve the problem. See the section on Web sites to learn more about these organizations.
- Ask your state representatives to pass strong antitrafficking legislation. Monitor your state at the Polaris Project Web site.
- Report suspected cases of trafficking. Call the hotline at 1–888–3737-888 to report cases of suspected trafficking.
- Know that although this chapter focuses on citizens of the Global South who have been trafficked, it happens frequently to those in the Global North as well.

What Can I Do as a Professional Social Worker?

- Work to assist victims of human trafficking within the United States. Various NGOs in cities such as San Diego (Project Safe Haven), New York City (ECPAT-USA), and Washington, DC (Polaris Project) are working in this arena.
- Work for an international humanitarian organization such as Save the Children, World Vision, or Catholic Relief Services.

- Work with a community development organization such as Oxfam to help prevent the conditions that make people vulnerable to trafficking.

World Wide Web Resources on Forced Labor

Anti-Slavery International (www.antislavery.org): This organization has been working since 1839 to end slavery around the world. It offers a host of reports compiled by its staff.

Coalition to Abolish Slavery and Trafficking (www.castla.org): This organization focuses on the issue of trafficking within the United States. It offers training on trafficking issues as well as providing services to victims of trafficking.

ECPAT (End Child Prostitution, Child Pornography and Trafficking of Children for Sexual Purposes) (www.ecpat.net): One of the best-known international organizations, this is a coalition of agencies working to end commercial sexual exploitation of children.

Forced Migration Online (www.forcedmigration.org): The site offers a variety of electronic resources on topics relating to forced migration.

Free The Slaves (www.freetheslaves.net): An agency in Washington, DC working to end global slavery.

Global Alliance Against Trafficking in Women (www.gaatw.org): An international coalition working to end trafficking in women. Their Web site offers a variety of high-quality resources.

International Labour Office (www.ilo.org): The agency of the United Nations that works to address issues involving workers' rights. An excellent site for resource material.

Polaris Project (www.polarisproject.org): This organization focuses on the issue of trafficking within the United States. It advocates on issues related to trafficking as well as providing services to victims of trafficking.

Save The Children (www.savethechildren.net): The International Alliance of Save the Children offers many high-quality reports and resources on any issue relating to children.

Transfair USA (www.transfairusa.org): This site offers information about fair trade products and ethical shopping.

Volunteers for Social Justice (www.vsj-ddva.org/index.html): This agency in India is working to end bonded labor.

4

International Child Welfare

When people from the United States think of "child welfare," they commonly associate the term simply with child abuse and neglect. But globally, children face many other, even more severe, threats to their well-being than abuse and neglect. Children who do not receive the basics of what they need for optimal adult development, as outlined in the Convention on the Rights of the Child, will struggle more throughout their lives. Children need proper physical, emotional, and educational care to reach their adult potential. Far too many children do not have these needs met. Children lack safe drinking water, adequate sanitation, food, shelter, education, health care, and family support and care, just to name a few.

As a result, 6.6 million children under the age of 5 years die each year, mostly from preventable causes ("Global child mortality rates," 2013). In addition to these mortal threats, almost half of the world's 35 million refugees are children; 153 million children are orphans; 25% of all children live in extreme poverty; and 215 million are child laborers (International Labour Organization [ILO], 2010; UNHCR, 2011; UNICEF, 2012b). The majority of threats to children discussed in this chapter will fall into the categories of child labor and child abuse and the conditions that can make children more vulnerable to violations of their human rights. As awful as these numbers are, it is important to remember that in almost all areas, they represent substantial progress. While more work needs to be done, children have made substantial progress, even since the first edition of this text (UNICEF, 2012b).

Convention on the Rights of the Child

The Convention on the Rights of the Child (CRC) was written by the United Nations in recognition of the fact that those under 18 years of age are especially vulnerable to violations of human rights. Children are entitled to the same rights as all people under the UDHR, but they have the additional protection of the CRC to recognize the special barriers and threats they may face. This document was based on the Declaration of the Rights of the Child, which was proclaimed by the General Assembly of the United Nations in 1959. The declaration was updated in 1989 and was renamed the Convention on the Rights of the Child. The convention operates from the point of view that children are neither the property of their parents nor are they "helpless objects of charity" (UNICEF, 2005, ¶2). UNICEF (2005, ¶2) states that "the Convention offers a vision of the child as an individual *and* as a member of a family and community, with rights and responsibilities appropriate to his or her age and stage of development. By recognizing children's rights in this way, the Convention firmly sets the focus on the whole child."

Currently, all but three nations in the world have ratified the Convention: Somalia, the United States, and the new nation of South Sudan. The United States signed the document in 1995 but has not submitted it to Congress for ratification. Previously, the biggest stumbling block was the Convention's prohibition against capital punishment (the death penalty) for juveniles, which the United States allowed until the Supreme Court declared it unconstitutional in 2005. Currently, the largest barrier is that those opposing ratification fear that the convention would undermine parental authority. This was cited as a fear in the 2012 US Senate vote not to ratify the Convention on the Rights of Persons with Disabilities (CRPD)—that ratification would give the United Nations the right to determine how US parents raise their children. Despite the fact that prominent Republicans, including former President Bush, sought to achieve ratification of the CRPD, it was defeated (Helderman, 2012). In addition, the CRC provides for economic, social, and cultural rights of children. As previously discussed, the US government does not protect this group of rights.

Child Labor

Many of the threats to child well-being fall under the umbrella of child labor. According to Article 32 of the CRC, children have the right to be protected from economic exploitation. It states that children should not perform "any work that is likely to be hazardous or to interfere with the child's education, or to be harmful to the child's health or physical, mental, spiritual, moral or social development." This definition separates out work that assists in the child's development—such as after-school jobs, assisting on the family farm, or apprenticeships for a child of age in that society—from work that is harmful to the child. Approximately 168 million children worldwide were engaged in some form of child labor (ILO, 2013), 120 million of whom were ages 5–14 years (UNICEF, 2011b). Of these, about 85 million were engaged in hazardous work (ILO, 2013), which is included as what are defined as "the worst forms of child labor," which also includes commercial sexual exploitation, participation in armed conflict, and slavery (including trafficking and debt bondage). The vast majority of child laborers (59%) work in agriculture (ILO, 2010).

These numbers have been shrinking markedly, with the largest progress in the 2008–2012 period (ILO, 2013). The number of children ages 5–14 years who work has decreased by 10%, as has the number of children in hazardous work by 31%. Girls have seen their labor rates drop 40%, while boys' rates decreased 25%. All world regions have seen their numbers and percentages of child laborers decrease. The least progress has been made in Sub-Saharan Africa, which currently has the highest proportion of child laborers of any region. The number of child laborers there has decreased, but 21% of children are still engaged in child labor (ILO, 2013).

As noted, the majority of child laborers work in agriculture. Agriculture can be hazardous for children due to the chemicals and heavy machinery often used. The most common source of accidents for children involved in this form of labor is from operating motor vehicles, including farm machinery. These vehicles were not designed for use by children and require specialized training that children typically do not receive. Cutting tools are another source of frequent injury for the same reasons. Other threats can include the chemicals used for fertilizer because they are often more harmful for children's developing bodies than adult systems (International Labour Organization, n.d.).

Children also work as factory workers, making such items as bricks, fireworks, clothing, and rugs. For example, over 2,000 children in eastern Afghanistan work in brick factories alongside their parents to help their families pay off debt to the factory owners. These children work 8 to 12 hours a day, and 90% of them do not attend school ("Children work," 2008). Children also work for brick manufacturers in India, again typically alongside their parents (Bales, 2004).

Children who work by making fireworks in India often work in a dark and dingy shed where they roll and pack the fireworks. The gunpowder mix that is used is corrosive, and over time it eats away at the children's fingers. They breathe in the chemicals constantly, such as zinc oxides and powdered potassium chlorate, leading to long-term breathing problems and blood poisoning (Bales, 2004). Among child factory workers in India in such industries as garments or carpets, it has been found that they are forced to work in small spaces and maintain the same repetitive work for hours on end, resulting in chronic pain and growth deformities. Children working with looms often develop lung or skin diseases resulting from prolonged exposure to the wool (Child Workers in Asia, 2007). Following is the story of Yeramma, one of the children working in the silk industry (Human Rights Watch, 2003, ¶1):

At 4:00 a.m. I got up and did silk winding....I only went home once a week. I slept in the factory with two or three other children. We prepared the food there and slept in the space between the machines. The owner provided the rice and cut it from our wages. He would deduct the price. We cooked the rice ourselves. We worked twelve hours a day with one hour for rest. If I made a mistake—if I cut the thread— he would beat me. Sometimes [the owner] used vulgar language. Then he would give me more work. —Yeramma S., 11 years old, bonded at around age 7

Other children in countries in Central America, such as Honduras, are employed in the *maquilas,* or textile factories. They often produce clothes for major US companies. There have been cases in these factories of girls forced to take birth control pills or undergo abortions in order to keep the workers productive (Zelaya & Larson, 2004).

Approximately 1 million children work in mines in Africa, Asia, and South America (Save the Children UK, 2007). This may be gold mining, salt mining, or rock quarry mining. Confined underground, they breathe toxic fumes from such elements as mercury used to crushed ore. They do not have protective equipment while using these toxins and use tools designed for adults, which can lead to the same types of hazards facing children in agricultural labor. Children involved in salt mining experience adverse effects from the corrosive nature of salt, including cracking of the skin on their hands and discoloration of their irises (ILO, 2006c).

The main reason that children around the world work is due to poverty. For example, in Nigeria, the most common reason children gave for working was to provide their parents with money (Omokhodion, Omokhodion, & Odusote, 2006); and in India, 23% of family income is earned by children working in part due to adult unemployment or wage cuts (Cunningham & Stromquist, 2005). There is a circular relationship between poverty and child labor. While poverty leads to an increase in child labor, child labor leads to an increase in poverty. Children who work during their childhood are not able to receive a solid education, which inhibits their ability to obtain well-paying jobs as adults. Additionally, they will most likely suffer long-term health consequences from their labor, which will impede their ability to work as adults. If child labor is banned but no attention is given to wages earned by adults or social supports, the situation may worsen through increases in malnutrition and other calamities. It is also important to differentiate child labor that is harmful from child labor that is culturally appropriate and designed to assist children in their long-term goals, such as assistance with household chores or apprenticeships (Ajayi & Torimiro, 2004).

Therefore, alternative means of familial income are needed. The International Labour Organization (2003) proposes income transfers to families to offset the income lost in the short term when children attend school rather than work. The Bolsa Familia program in Brazil gives very poor families a stipend if their children attend school and get regular health check-ups. This is known as a Conditional Cash Transfer because it is dependent on a condition being met: the child's attendance at school.

Conditional Cash Transfers (CCTs) can now be found in a number of countries; they are very common in Central and South America but also can be found in Asia and Africa. CCTs have been found to have a broad variety of positive outcomes. In Brazil, Bolsa Familia families are more likely to have their children attend school and to successfully complete a grade. Additionally, pregnant women have more prenatal visits and infants are more likely to receive their vaccines (International Food Policy Research Institute, 2010). In Chile, children were also found to have increased school participation as well as enrollment with public health services. The CCT was found to help lift families out of extreme poverty (Martorano & Sanfilippo, 2012). One fear was that these cash payments might encourage workers to drop out of the labor force; that has not been found to be the case (Fiszbein & Schady, 2009; Martorano & Sanfilippo, 2012). However, one concern is that the improved attendance at school and health visits does not always mean that there are improved educational and health outcomes (Fiszbein & Schady, 2009).

International pressure can help reduce child labor as well. In Bangladesh, the number of female child laborers has been reduced substantially due to the pressure from international garment makers (Global March, 2006b). A number of manufacturers have created codes of conduct that outline the expectations for the production of goods for their company and their refusal to purchase products that do not meet those standards, including child labor. However, due to the multinational locations of production and subcontracts, production is not always monitored and violations can flourish (ILO, 2004). This was made vivid after over 900 workers died in Bangladesh when their garment factory building collapsed in 2013.

Some countries have passed laws to try to reduce the number of child laborers. For example, India, a major country where child labor occurs, has been reforming its laws. Adding to the existing ban on hiring children in occupations considered hazardous, India passed a new child labor law in 2006 that forbade the hiring of children under 14 years of age to perform domestic labor or work in hotels and restaurants (Gentleman, 2007). The government had been reluctant to implement a full ban in recognition of the high poverty that many families faced and the desperate need for the children's income. However, it was decided that permitting employment of children under 14 clashed with the government's guarantee of education to all under 14, and in 2012, a complete ban for those under 14 was approved, together with a strengthening of protections for those aged 14–18 years (Kazmin, 2012).

Street Children

Children working on the streets, for example as peddlers, shoeshine boys, or selling sex, are among the most visible of child laborers. While their exact numbers are difficult to quantify, UNICEF (2006a) estimates it to be in the tens of millions, possibly ranging as high as 100 million. Article 27 states that children have the right to a standard of living adequate for their development. However, for some children, their family cannot or does not provide this. While the term "street children" is used as a generic label, there are several subcategories. "Working children" work in the streets, typically to earn money for their families, but live at home with these families. "Homeless children" both work and live in the streets, either on their own or with other children. "Displaced children" live and work in the streets with their families (Pinzón-Rondón, Hofferth, & Briceño, 2008). These are general definitions because, of course, there are always children who do not fit neatly into these categories.

Boys are the majority of street children worldwide for a number of reasons, part of which is definition. For example, girls on the street are often defined as prostitutes, not street children. Further, female child laborers who are not working in the sex trade are often working in jobs located off the streets (such as maids), while male child laborers are more visible on the streets working as shoeshine boys or peddlers (Lalor, 1999). Finally, girls still living with their families are less likely than boys to work on the street as they are more vulnerable to violence on the streets and are more often needed at home for chores (ILO, 2003a).

Worldwide, most children come to the streets due to poverty, being orphaned, or familial conflict. Other reasons may be more regional. For example, in certain African nations such as Angola, Democratic Republic of the Congo, Nigeria, and Ghana, there has been an increase in accusations of sorcery against children, which has led to their maltreatment, including murder, or being forced out of their homes (Adinkrah, 2011; Cimpric, 2010). The accusation may result from a death in the family or a job loss, but it often stems from a family member not having the financial resources to care for a child. The accusations have been growing due to issues resulting from increased urbanization and the weakening of family structures in which families care for each other, as well as the impact of conflict in affected regions. These families need a culturally acceptable reason to push the child onto the street—thus the accusation of sorcery. These children who are thus accused are rarely being cared for by both biological parents, but more often by stepparents or extended family members, who are less likely to want the responsibility and burden (Cimpric, 2010). In the past, elderly women were more likely to be accused of witchcraft and these accusations of children are new. Most of these children are boys aged 8–14 years, and they often have something that distinguishes them such as being a twin, having a disability, or being more aggressive or solitary than the norm (Cimpric, 2010). This phenomenon has been more likely to occur in Christian, rather than Muslim, nations and appears to be influenced by Pentecostal or charismatic churches (Cimpric, 2010). In order to help fight this, child protection officials have been working with allies in the churches, as well as striving to increase basic services available to children and families (Cimpric, 2010).

Other reasons why children are in the streets vary by whether the child is a working child, a homeless child, or a displaced child. Working children are more likely to be there because of poverty. The children typically need to work to support their families and return home in the evenings (Kombarakaran, 2004; Pinzón-Rondón et al., 2008). This work will prevent them from attending school. In Mumbai, India, it was found that only 40% of the street children had ever been to school, and only 10% had ever progressed past primary school (Kombarakaran, 2004). Displaced children have typically fled with their families from conflict and are often younger (Pinzón-Rondón et al., 2008). Homeless children are more likely to have experienced familial problems such as parental death, abuse, or other conflict; they live on the street because they have nowhere else to go (Pinzón-Rondón et al., 2008; Plummer, Kudrati, & Yousif, 2007; Ward & Seager, 2010). The following case study, summarized from Lalor (1999), illustrates the often complex path to the streets:

At age 2 Eshete's mother gave her into the care of relatives because she could not afford to care for her (gudifecha, an Ethiopian custom whereby children are accepted by those willing to raise them if parents are unable to do so). At age 9 Eshete's adopting father died and she went to live with his brother for 2 years. At age 11 she went to Addis Ababa to search for her birth parents, whom she found were separated. She decided to live with her birth father, but he struggled with alcoholism and often beat her. She ran away and went to stay with her birth mother, but her mother had two other children and could not afford to look after Eshete. So Eshete left and found work in a rural hotel as a maid but the work was so hard that she soon left. A rural family adopted her and she minded their cattle for 7 months. Eventually Eshete came back to Addis Ababa at age 16 and began living by begging. For a short time she lived as the "wife" of a taxi-boy but he eventually left her and she returned to living on the streets with friends.

Street children typically receive attention for being perpetrators of crime, including theft, assault, and drug use (Lalor, 1999). However, children of the streets are typically very vulnerable to being crime victims. For example, Kudrati, Plummer, and Yousif (2008) found that the majority of both boys and girls on the street in their study in Sudan had been victims of sexual assault. They stated that the gang rape of girls was so common, there was a special term for it—*fatah*. In India, Mathur, Rathore, and Mathur (2009) found that 99% of their sample had experienced moderate to very severe levels of abuse, with over one-third experiencing severe or very severe levels. While the perpetrators of these crimes are commonly other children, children are also at risk from those assigned to protect society—the police. Kudrati et al. (2008) found that the majority of interactions between their participants in Sudan and the police were negative and could involve beatings, robberies, and rape. Street children are also vulnerable to forcible recruitment into armed forces, both governmental and rebel forces (Singer, 2005; UNICEF, 2001).

There are a number of health risks to street children. They typically do not get sufficient food, do not have access to clean water or toilet facilities, and lack access to medical care (Kombarakaran, 2004). In malaria-prone areas, they are more likely to contract the disease because they are not sleeping under mosquito nets (Orme & Seipel, 2007). They are also likely to have psychological and emotional problems; one study in Kyiv, Ukraine, found that 70% of children in their study had some form of behavioral and emotional difficulty, while three-quarters were depressed

(Kerfoot et al., 2007). Harmful habits are common among street children, including use of drugs and alcohol as well as risky sexual practices.

Street children's work typically reinforces their dependence on others. Therefore, when working with them, an empowerment approach is especially important as it can help offset this. While it may be necessary to meet short-term immediate needs such as food, provision of goods should be part of a long-term developmental approach to help children become self-sustaining adults as well as to create a durable approach that will not disappear when the outside funding does (Ennew, 2000).

Programs must be perceived as inviting to the children, and the programs must help children meet their needs as they see them. In Sudan, if street children are caught and arrested, they are whipped and sentenced to government camps, where they experience frequent beatings and sexual assault (Kudrati et al., 2008). Lam and Cheng (2008) note that the shelter for street children in Shanghai is desperately avoided by children because they are not free to leave once they enter, and even within the compound, their movements are controlled. They must wear a uniform and are required to be picked up by their parents, whose abuse many of them have fled. Also, they are not offered classes or services to meet their needs. In short, the design of the shelter does not regard children as active agents in deciding their future.

In contrast, Karabanow (2003) notes that programs that incorporate street education, where the cause of children on the street is viewed as a societal structural deficit, and concurrent prevention strategies have higher levels of success than programs that view street children as delinquents or in need of rehabilitation. He notes that organizations should meet basic needs and avoid cumbersome regulations. Providing a place where the children feel comfortable and welcomed is key to helping to rebuild linkages between them and mainstream society. Respecting the children is vital to recognizing their strengths and independence, as well as acknowledging implicitly the disrespect they typically receive from society (Dybicz, 2005).

In the Philippines, one program uses "street educators" in an attempt to perform outreach with street children. These street educators are young people, some of whom are former street children themselves. They provide the street children with education about sexually transmitted diseases, sexual abuse, drug abuse, HIV, as well as intangible things such as attention and concern. The street educators will also escort the children to temporary shelters, if they desire. Children often need help to reconnect with their families. Program social workers help them to reconcile with their families and work toward getting off the street (Silva, 2002). Schwinger (2007) notes that reconciliation is an underutilized option in Brazil, where foster care tends to dominate and many children desire to return home but need assistance in doing so.

Children in the Sex Trade

Another of the worst forms of child labor is the use of children in sexually related activities, discussed in greater depth in Chapter 3. Article 34 of the CRC explicitly forbids the use of children in prostitution. Due to the increase in child trafficking, an Optional Protocol to the CRC was ratified by the United Nations in 2000; it addresses the sale of children, child prostitution, and child pornography. As of this writing, 158 countries are parties to this protocol, including the United States. The number of children experiencing commercial sexual exploitation is difficult to estimate but estimated to be almost 1 million children, the majority of whom are girls (ILO, 2012). As discussed in Chapter 3 on human trafficking, various factors can push children into sex work, including poverty, discrimination, and lack of access to education. The effects of sexually related labor on children can be traumatic and can include anxiety, depression, posttraumatic stress disorder, substance abuse, and suicide (Clawson, Salomon, & Grace, 2008; Willis & Levy, 2002).

Children in Armed Conflict

The last of the worst forms of child labor to be discussed is the involvement of children in armed conflict. Article 38 of the CRC requires that those taking a direct part in combat must be at least 15 years old, and children younger than 15 may not be recruited into the armed forces. An Optional Protocol to the CRC in 2000 raised these ages to 18. It states that there will be no compulsory recruitment of children under 18 and voluntary recruitment must be truthful, genuinely voluntary, and only with the consent of parents or guardians. As of this writing, 147 countries have ratified this protocol, including the United States.

Myanmar was the country whose government was most likely to recruit and use child soldiers. However, in 2012, in conjunction with the United

Nations, they created an 18-month plan to release and reintegrate the children currently in their armed forces. Additionally, the plan included methods to prevent future recruitment. While this is an ambitious goal, there is a set timetable for actions to occur and methods to determine whether the goals are being reached ("No more child soldiers," 2012).

Child soldiers not only take part in combat but may also serve as spies, messengers, porters, and forced sexual partners. In some cases, children voluntarily join the forces, while in others, they are forcibly recruited. However, the United Nations Special Representative of the Secretary-General for Children and Armed Conflict successfully argued before the International Criminal Court that there should be no distinction made between these two recruitment methods. She stated that this "choice" was made in the context of poverty, familial loss, and lack of protection; therefore, it could not truly be regarded as voluntary. The Court agreed stating that "children could not give 'informed' consent because they possessed limited understanding of the short-term and long-term consequences of their choice and actions and did not control or fully comprehend the structures and forces with which they were faced" (United Nations, 2012, p. 4).

Children often "voluntarily" join armed forces in a search for stability in the upheaval generated by armed conflict. It may be the only manner by which to get daily food and some semblance of protection from harm. Some child soldiers have said that they joined the fighting to escape the poverty in their families (UNICEF, 2001). They may believe the propaganda disseminated about the conflict (Shakya, 2011). Other children join to get revenge upon the killers of their families; not to do so would be a great shame in their culture (Singer, 2005). However, in most situations, the children are forcibly recruited in some manner (Singer, 2005).

This was seen most vividly through the work of one of the most infamous users of child soldiers, the Lord's Resistance Army (LRA). The LRA, a rebel group in Uganda, has been fighting against the government since 1986 (Briggs, 2005). The LRA kidnapped as many as 25,000 children during the height of the conflict, 7,500 of them girls (Amnesty International, 2005). The boys were trained to be soldiers and the girls were given to an officer as a "wife" and forced to become sex slaves. Typically the children were coerced into the army by being forced to kill those they know, such as family and friends. They then felt such guilt that they thought they could not return to society after such shame. The following quote from a child kidnapped by the LRA illustrates this method (Human Rights Watch, 1997):

One boy tried to escape [from the rebels], but he was caught....His hands were tied, and then they made us, the other new captives, kill him with a stick. I felt sick. I knew this boy from before. We were from the same village. I refused to kill him and they told me they would shoot me. They pointed a gun at me, so I had to do it. The boy was asking me, "Why are you doing this?" I said I had no choice. After we killed him, they made us smear his blood on our arms....They said we had to do this so we would not fear death and so we would not try to escape....I still dream about the boy from my village who I killed. I see him in my dreams, and he is talking to me and saying I killed him for nothing, and I am crying.

In order to avoid being captured by the LRA, approximately 30,000 children slept en masse at their schools, churches, hospitals, and other central locations every night, watched over by the adults in their communities (Amnesty International, 2005). These children were known as the "night commuters" for their nightly journey. The conflict has subsided substantially—the LRA is estimated to only have approximately 500 members (United Nations Security Council, 2012), but as of this writing, Joseph Kony remains free and continues to terrorize civilians. As of 2012, they had left Uganda and were operating within South Sudan, the Democratic Republic of the Congo (DRC), and the Central African Republic. In the DRC, they were repeating their tactics of forcible recruitment and continuing to force children to kill their family or other children. In the Central African Republic, they had developed the new tactic of kidnapping people for ransom in the form of food, clothing, or other goods (United Nations Security Council, 2012).

While countries in Africa often receive the bulk of attention for this issue, countries in other regions are not immune. The use of children by rebel groups and militias is widespread in Colombia. The government has used children for intelligence gathering, but the vast majority fight for the guerrilla groups— the Revolutionary Armed Forces of Colombia (FARC) and the National Liberation Army (ELN) (United

Nations Security Council, 2012). Children as young as 8 years old are recruited by FARC and face severe punishment if they attempt to return home. Children are used to spy, run messages, and place bombs, as well as participate in direct combat (Briggs, 2005). (See Chapter 5, War and Conflict, for a more detailed explanation of this conflict.) Another country that had a large number of child soldiers was Sri Lanka. The rebel group known as the Tamil Tigers received international condemnation during the conflict there. Approximately 40% to 60% of their forces were under the age of 18, most of them recruited when they were between 10 and 16. The Tamil Tigers were particularly known for their use of girls in direct fighting; about half of the soldiers were female (Singer, 2005).

Once child soldiers have been released from the armed force with which they were fighting, it can be difficult for them to reintegrate into society. The biopsychosocial approach common to examining human behavior in the social environment can be a useful tool for examining the barriers to reintegration. Biologically, they may have suffered wounds from combat in addition to having been undernourished. Thus, physically they may encounter difficulties. As discussed, they may have been forced to kill family or community members by the group that captured them. This, as well as the other deaths they caused or witnessed, can create psychological difficulties. Socially, the former child soldiers may encounter resistance in the community to which they are returning due to anger at their actions while in combat. In addition, they will encounter difficulties in education as they are typically substantially older than other schoolchildren at their level due to their lack of educational opportunities while involved with armed forces.

Reintegration can be particularly difficult for girls. One reason is that they are often not viewed as soldiers since they typically do not participate in combat. As a result, they often do not receive the reintegration services that boys do, leaving their psychological trauma unresolved. Additionally, due to the nature of the services they were forced to perform, they may be rejected by their family and community, especially if they return with children born of the rape.

Child Maltreatment

While child abuse and neglect by caretakers is not the only threat to children's well-being, it certainly cannot be excluded from this discussion.

Unfortunately, far too many children worldwide experience child maltreatment. An estimated 86% of children between the ages of 2 and 14 years experiences physical or psychological aggression from their family; two-thirds experience physical aggression (UNICEF, 2009). Article 19 of the CRC provides that the state will ensure that all children are protected from child maltreatment. However, even within a culture, there are different definitions of what is "maltreatment." For example, within the United States, there is no single clear-cut definition of child physical abuse; some would include corporal punishment, while others would not. It has been a concern of many of those working in the area of culture and child maltreatment that a balance be found between respecting a person's culture and not allowing maltreatment to occur. This is similar to the discussion on human rights and cultural relativism in Chapter 2. In an attempt to create a cross-cultural definition of child maltreatment, Finkelhor and Korbin (1988, p. 4) define it as "the portion of harm to children that results from human action that is proscribed, proximate, and preventable."

This definition allows for cultural variation in childrearing but is inclusive of child maltreatment as well. Some behaviors might meet a cultural norm but be considered maltreatment by other cultures. For example, some cultures are appalled that Americans have infants sleep in separate rooms from their parents, considering this practice to be detrimental to the child's development (Small, 1998). Other cultures may accept a behavior that is considered abusive by most other cultures, such as Female Genital Cutting (see Chapter 7). It is important to differentiate between what are cultural differences and what is maltreatment. Despite some differences in definition about what constitutes maltreatment, there is general agreement that certain acts are definitely maltreatment. Globally, sexual abuse is the type of abuse most commonly considered to be maltreatment, followed by abandonment and physical abuse by a parent (Bross, Miyoshi, Miyoshi, & Krugman, 2000).

Maltreatment has long-lasting consequences. In the short term, death and injury may be the immediate most visible results. In the long term, it can result in an increased likelihood of mental health diagnoses, especially depression, substance abuse, and low self-esteem. It has also been linked to physical health conditions, including cancer, chronic lung disease, and liver disease (Pinheiro, 2006). Women who have experienced child sexual abuse are more likely to be victims of intimate partner violence in their adulthood (Speizer, Goodwin, Whittle, Clyde, & Rogers, 2008). Child maltreatment can also permanently alter the developing brain structure in a child, causing the child to be hypervigilant to threats and be less able to react positively to others and engage in complex thought (Pinheiro, 2006; US Department of Health and Human Services, 2009).

Programs to prevent child maltreatment have been concentrated in countries in the Global North, and there have been relatively few in the Global South and these have tended to focus on sexual abuse. As this is the most universally recognized form of abuse, this is logical. Educating children about sexual abuse can be an effective primary prevention tool. In Thailand, a child abuse prevention project teaches the children the mantra "Why, no, go, tell" to help children protect themselves from sexual abuse by teaching them they have the right to refuse a person seeking to abuse them and to tell another person about what happened ("Mantra may help," 2005).

However, many parents consider it to be inappropriate to discuss topics of a sexual nature with their children. For example, in Afghanistan, many parents consider any discussion of sex with their children to be indecent, even though 40% of child sexual abuse occurs within the home. Rates of child sexual abuse have been rising in that nation in the post-Taliban era, but few children will speak of it due to the associated disgrace and stigma ("War, poverty and ignorance," 2007). A survey of parents in China found that although almost half of respondents were concerned that education about child sexual abuse might cause their children to know too much about sex, 95% thought such programs should be offered in elementary school and were willing to have their children attend (Chen, Dunne, & Han, 2007).

International Adoption

While in the United States being available for adoption is often associated with having experienced parental maltreatment, this is typically not the case of children worldwide. Children in other countries are often available for adoption due to disabilities, parental poverty, or governmental policies limiting the number of children per family. In recent years, the number of children being adopted into the United States has been declining. After peaking at 22,991 in 2004, the number has shrunk to 8,668 in 2012, a decline of 62% (Swarns, 2013). The top sending countries are China, Ethiopia, and Russia. Ethiopia is the only nation to continue to increase its numbers in recent years (US State Department, 2011). The numbers of international adoptions from China, Russia, and South Korea have been declining primarily due to a greater emphasis on domestic adoption in those nations (Swarns, 2013). However, the relationship between Russia and the United States has been tense, and adoptions have received some of the backlash. There have been a few high-profile deaths after adoptions from Russia, as well as deteriorating discussions over human rights resulting in a ban on American adoptions passed at the end of 2012.

International adoption first began in force after World War II with the adoptions of orphaned children from Germany and Greece by US families. A second wave began after the Korean War with children from Korea (who were often fathered by US soldiers). From these beginnings as a child-focused phenomenon, international adoption has evolved to one that is more focused on meeting the needs of adoptive parents. As fertility has declined in Western nations, as well as the number of healthy White infants available for adoption, interest in international adoption has risen. However, international adoption is of concern not only due to illegal practices such as trafficking (discussed later) but also because of overall social justice issues. Hollingsworth (2003) questions whether social justice is served by international adoption by families in the United States. On the one hand, children are being brought from conditions that are at the best impoverished and at the worst harmful. On the other hand, the question remains whether it is the best method to remove a few select children from these circumstances and leave the circumstances unchanged.

In order to attempt to minimize unethical practices, international adoption is regulated by the Hague Convention on Intercountry Adoption. Developed in 1993, its goal is to regulate procedure and set minimum standards for international adoptions in order to protect all parties—birthparents, adoptive parents, and the children being adopted. The Hague Convention requires governments to make it the first priority that children are able to remain with their birthparents and that international adoption is an option only after attempts at familial reunification, as well as domestic placement, have failed. There are currently 89 contracting states to this convention, including the United States.

In order to assure that the principles of the Hague Convention are being upheld, Family Group Conferencing has been promoted as a method for inclusion of the child's extended family. As described by Rotabi et al. (2012), the family's information is gathered from the birthparent(s) and they are invited to the meeting. If they cannot attend, they are welcome to information via a letter or another format. The situation is explained to the family by the birthparents and the social worker adds additional information as needed. The family then meets in private to determine the best course. In the Marshall Islands, this method has enabled the child to find a home within the country in 70%–80% of cases and is being promoted as a method in other countries (Rotabi, Pennell, Roby, & Bunkers, 2012). However, in some countries, international adoptions are perceived as favored over domestic adoptions due to the greater revenue they provide. For example, in China, each international adoption brings $5,000 to the orphanage; this is not true for domestic adoptions and creates concerns of trafficking (Custer, 2013; Johnson, 2012). Cases have been documented where children were kidnapped, brought to orphanages, and then adopted by US parents, but there is no information on how widespread this form of trafficking is (Custer, 2013).

Adoption trafficking has been a growing concern. In 2001, the United States halted the processing of adoptions from Cambodia due to reports of widespread corruption and trafficking. They were joined by France, the Netherlands, Switzerland, Belgium, and Britain in 2004 and Canada in 2005 (Blair, 2005; Ministry of Children and Family Development, n.d.). In some cases, children in Cambodia were being purchased, or even stolen, from birth mothers for international adoption (Corbett, 2002; Mydans, 2001). In other cases, poor women, especially those who were widowed or divorced, were convinced to place their newborn in a "children's center." They were told that the placement would be temporary and they would be able to visit the child; they were also given a "donation." However, when the mothers would try to visit the child, they were refused, and if they asked for the child back, they were told they would have to pay an amount of money several times the amount of the "donation" they had received. Fraudulent paperwork was then created stating that the child had been abandoned and the parents were unknown. Government officials appear to have been receiving large bribes for their assistance in the process (Cambodian League for the Promotion and Defense of Human Rights, 2002).

In Guatemala, an estimated 1,000 to 1,500 infants were being trafficked to the United States and Europe each year (UNICEF, 2009).

Guatemala had been sending such huge numbers of children to the United States that 1 of every 100 children born every year was growing up in the United States ("Adoptions," 2008); overall, more than 30,000 Guatemalan children were adopted by foreign families between 2000 and 2007 (Rotabi et al., 2012). In September 2008, Guatemala announced that it was suspending international adoption in order to allow itself time to establish guidelines for accrediting adoption agencies as well as process transition cases. At the same time, the United States announced that although Guatemala had ratified the Hague Convention, it was not meeting its Convention requirements and therefore no new adoptions from there would be processed (US State Department, 2008). This was despite a new law in Guatemala passed at the end of 2007 that was designed to tighten the adoption system to reduce the widespread corruption ("New Guatemala adoption law," 2007). Canada has suspended adoptions from Guatemala since 2001 (Adoption Council of Canada, 2006). Additionally, the United Kingdom, Germany, Canada, Spain, and the Netherlands all filed objections regarding Guatemala's adherence to the Hague Convention (Huntenburg, 2008).

A growing ethical issue tied to the decline in intercountry adoption is the use of intercountry surrogacy. In this scenario, people from the Global North who wish to be parents contract with a person in the Global South to bear a child for them using In Vitro Fertilization. This may be due to the fact that commercial surrogacy is banned in their home country or the drastically reduced cost by going to another nation (Rotabi & Bromfield, 2012). For example, in the United States, surrogacy is a complex legal procedure that can cost over $70,000, while in India, the cost is approximately $12,000 (Rotabi & Bromfield, 2012). Ethical issues arise, as in India, these surrogates are often recruited using fraudulent means, must sign documents they do not have the ability to read (due to illiteracy or because they are in another language), and then are kept guarded during their pregnancy. These means highly resemble the methods used by human traffickers (Rotabi & Bromfield, 2012). Legislation to regulate the procedure has been drafted, but it has not been introduced in Parliament for consideration (Lakshmi, 2013). In Guatemala, the agents who used to work in intercountry adoption have now shifted to surrogacy and are marketing their services as one might market a vacation (http://www.advocatesforsurrogacy.com/) (Rotabi & Bromfield, 2012).

Other concerns related to intercountry adoption are the conditions in which children live prior to adoption. In many cases, children available in sending nations live in orphanages prior to adoption as this is the most cost-efficient means of caring for them; however, the use of orphanages has been a controversial topic. Many children who live in orphanages are not truly orphans but have parents who are too poor to care for them, so they relinquish them to an orphanage. While some research has found outcomes for children raised in orphanages are equivalent as compared to children raised in the community (Whetten et al., 2009), most research has found worse outcomes for children who were raised in institutions (e.g., Norman & Bathori-Tartsi, 2010; Wilson, Weaver, Cradock, & Kuebli, 2008). Many of the former Soviet countries are working to close down their orphanages, due to these outcomes as well as the fact that conditions in orphanages in some countries have been found to be abusive. Extraordinary neglect and abuse have been documented in orphanages in countries such as Romania and China (the situation in China is discussed in this chapter's Culture Box).

In Romania at the end of the Cold War, it was found that hundreds of thousands of children had been abandoned due to their parents' inability to care for them. There had been a prohibition on birth control and abortion, causing parents to have more children than they could afford to raise. The conditions in these orphanages were squalid and the children were typically severely neglected (Hunt, 1990). As a condition of being able to join the European Union, Romania promised to move the children from orphanages without resorting to international adoption for them (Laffan, 2005). However, thousands of children were simply moved from orphanages to psychiatric institutions and other state-run facilities where horrific conditions persisted (Mental Disability Rights International, 2006). In an effort to reduce poor adoption practices in international adoptions and increase domestic adoption, Romania stopped all international adoptions, Currently, they are extremely limited and children may only be adopted by a relative, a step-parent, or a Romanian citizen living abroad (US State Department, 2012).

Stateless Children

UNICEF (2011b) estimated that in 2007 approximately half of all births in the Global South were unregistered. This equals 51 million births in

2007 alone (UNICEF, 2009). South Asia and sub-Saharan Africa are the most severely affected regions; approximately two-thirds of all births there are estimated to go unregistered (UNICEF, 2012a). In recognition of this problem, the United Nations Human Rights Council passed a resolution in 2012 urging all countries to provide free universal birth registration. Article 7 of the CRC states that all children should be registered at birth and that they have the right to a nationality.

Birth registration is important because it provides access to the other rights that can come with citizenship, such as access to education, health care, employment, and the right to vote. It can also help protect children from trafficking, underage military conscription, child marriage, and child labor. Therefore, it helps children achieve the other rights ascribed to them in the CRC. Birth registration is also important on the macro level as it helps a government plan accurately for the needs of its population (Mouravieff-Apostol, 2006).

There are a number of reasons why a child's birth may not be registered. While the international community believes that birth registration should be free, a number of countries charge a fee, shutting out those too impoverished to pay it. In all regions, birth registration is higher among the wealthiest 20% of households (UNICEF, 2012b). Those living in rural areas are also less likely to have births registered. There may also be a lack of funds for a national birth registration program, limiting offices and services to major cities. In some countries there are registration centers only in major cities. This can impose transportation difficulties for those in rural areas. Additionally, rural dwellers may not understand why birth registration is important because they traditionally do not use government services, therefore necessitating education for parents on its importance (Mouravieff-Apostol, 2006; "No ID," 2012). If armed conflict is occurring in the country, this can also limit opportunities to register a child's birth due to displacement or disruption of government services. It may also result in the loss of documents from a birth that was registered (UNICEF, 2007).

Migration can also affect birth registration. In certain countries, such as Malaysia, a child is not automatically given citizenship upon birth within its borders. If the mother has migrated there without the appropriate documents, the child will be left in limbo, as the country in which it was born will not grant citizenship and the mother's home country is often reluctant to grant citizenship to a child born outside its borders. Without citizenship, children are unable to attend the public schools and their parents cannot afford to send them to private school. Therefore, they tend to start working at an early age (Refugees International, 2007). In some cases, the problem has gone on so long that some children, now grown to adults, have turned to crime to earn a living since they cannot do so in the legal labor market (Hamid, 2006). For many years, children of refugees from Myanmar who are born in Thailand were denied a nationality. As discussed in Chapter 3, it is illegal to leave Myanmar without governmental permission; therefore, the Burmese government will not grant citizenship to these children. However, since few have official refugee status from Thailand, they were also denied Thai citizenship (Refugees International, 2009).

Another barrier to birth registration for ethnic groups is that information may not be available in their native language (UNICEF, 2006b). Governments may refuse to register children whose names do not conform to expectations (Mouravieff-Apostol, 2006). For example in China, the move to digital identity cards has limited the number of available characters and the approximately 60 million people with characters in their name that are considered obscure are not able to get identity cards until they change their name (LaFraniere, 2009).

In some cases, lack of birth registration can be political. Certain ethnic groups who do not have equal standing in societies may be denied the right to register their child's birth, such as non-Muslims in Kuwait (Refugees International & Open Society Justice Initiative, 2011). The Dominican Republic changed its laws in 2010 to allow citizenship only to those born to two legal Dominican Republic residents. Therefore, children born to those who have migrated from Haiti without documentation are being denied citizenship, even retroactively. This prohibits them from attending school, getting married, and even buying a cell phone (Casey, 2012; "Stateless," 2011).

Sex discrimination can be a barrier to registering a child's birth. In Kuwait, women do not have the right to confer their citizenship upon their child, thus rendering the child stateless if she marries a stateless man (Refugees International & Open Society Justice Initiative, 2011). According to a report from Plan International (2012a), laws in a number of countries inhibit a woman from registering the birth of her child. In countries such as India, Laos, and Nepal, it is the head of the household who is legally responsible for registering a birth. This is considered to be the husband or, in his absence, the child's grandfather or another male relative, thus inhibiting the mother from registering the birth herself. If the birth occurs out of wedlock, that can create an additional barrier. Not only can stigma and shame inhibit the mother but also fear. In Sudan, a woman who bears a child out of wedlock must be able to prove the child is a result of rape or she risks being arrested. In Cameroon, two witnesses must support her assertion of the child's paternity in order to have a birth certificate issued. Even in countries such as Egypt and Burkina Faso, where women are legally permitted to register their child, cultural norms still exist and officials may not allow her to do so (Plan International, 2012a).

Although much work needs to be done, a concentrated effort can be very effective. Countries have been developing different campaigns to increase registration. In a region of Nepal, registration has been linked to food grants. Families can receive a small grant up to twice a month to purchase nutritious food for their children whose births have been registered. In addition, Hindu priests have been brought into the campaign to help promote the importance of birth registration ("Cash grants," 2011).

In Bolivia, it was estimated that only 56% of children under 18 were registered due to the previously discussed barriers of money and distance. Following a policy change in which registration became free for children under 12, as well as a transition period of 3 years where it was free for all under 18, that percentage rose to 87% in 2008. In order to reach remote areas, a "mobile brigade" was developed. The brigade's arrival and requirements for registration would be announced ahead of time by the media so people were prepared and included equipment such as a photocopier, computer, and a generator so that everything could be handled on site (Plan International, n.d.).

In India, a massive campaign was launched to increase birth registration. Media spots were developed for TV and movies, as well as booklets and posters, to raise awareness of its importance. Special campaigns were developed for what were termed "Children in Difficult Circumstances," children who were hard to reach, such as those living on the street, those from the scheduled castes, or those who were nomadic. To reach these children, "birth registration camps" were implemented, as well as street plays, wall writing, and rallies (Plan India, 2010). The rate rose from just over half of all births in 1996 to three-quarters of births by 2007 (Sinha, 2012).

Technology has been helping create new methods of birth registration to overcome barriers. In Senegal, birth registration from rural areas was traditionally low due to the time and expense to travel to a center to register a child's birth. Families were unable to afford the trip as well as the time away from their fields; however, this then barred their children from entering school. Village elders have now been given mobile phones preloaded with an app to text a child's birth information. As a result, the number of births being registered has soared ("Texting for birth certificates," 2012).

Access to Education

Article 28 requires primary education to be offered free of cost to all children, that secondary education appropriate to the child's interests and abilities (i.e., vocational or college preparatory) be made available and accessible, and that higher education be made accessible. Much progress has been made in this area. Since 2000, the number of children enrolled in school has increased markedly, as has spending on education. However, approximately 57 million primary school-aged children are not enrolled in school (UNESCO, 2013); thus, more work remains. As discussed in Chapter 5, war and conflict pose a large barrier to school enrollment and attendance; half of all children who are out of school are in conflicted areas (UNESCO, 2013). Barriers to school enrollment include safety concerns, poverty, and traditions that do not emphasize schooling.

The majority of children who are not enrolled in school are girls (UNICEF, 2012c). Girls who live in poverty, in rural areas, or who are members of ethnic groups likely to experience discrimination are at particular risk to be out of school (Plan International, 2012b). Some do not attend due to safety concerns such as danger walking to school and harassment at school. Many schools in rural Africa do not have private toilet facilities, and after girls experience their first menstrual cycle, there is no private place for them to tend to these needs and they will drop out of school rather than be shamed (LaFraniere, 2005).

Some cultures believe it is not useful to educate girls as they will "only" grow up to marry and have children. Other girls may start school but may not be able to finish due to early marriage or a need to help with the housework at home. However, research has found that education of girls has an impact far beyond the immediate learning. Children of mothers who have been educated have lower child mortality rates due to improved nutrition and immunization rates and are more likely themselves to be educated (UNICEF, 2012c). As explained in Chapter 6, education serves as a protective factor for girls, not only by educating them about potential risks such as HIV but also by serving as a productive activity that reduces high-risk activities.

Three-quarters of the children not in primary school in the Global South are from the poorest 60% of households (UNICEF, 2006a). Poverty inhibits schooling in two fashions. First, the family may need the children to stay home and help earn a living. Second, many countries charge fees for school attendance. Even if the country does not charge fees, there are still often costs for supplies and uniforms. In the 1990s the World Bank encouraged its debtor nations to charge fees for textbooks and other school expenses to reduce the amount of federal money spent on social and educational services in these countries. However, this substantially reduced the number of children able to attend school, and in 2002, the World Bank reversed its policy (Dugger, 2004). A number of countries, such as Kenya, Malawi, and Ghana, have now eliminated school fees under the banner of the drive for Universal Primary Education (UPE). Kenya's "cost-sharing" program under the World Bank plan, where families were expected to "share" in the costs of education, resulted in higher rates of dropouts and students repeating a grade while simultaneously lowering graduation rates (Nafula, 2001). In contrast, there was rapid enrollment growth under UPE (World Bank, 2009).

In Uganda, enrollment rose 240% over 6 years (Avenstrup, 2006). However, not only have enrollments increased greatly, but delayed enrollments have decreased and more children are completing grades. Girls in poor households in particular have experienced these positive benefits. Only about 10% of children not in primary school state that the money is the main barrier to attendance (even though tuition is no longer charged, there are still costs for supplies and uniforms). However, the percentage of children out of school due to cost rises sharply for secondary school, which is not free. In addition, more girls drop out during secondary school due to marriage/pregnancy or sexual harassment, including from teachers (Nishimura et al., 2008; Plan International, 2012b). Additionally, the risk associated with eliminating fees is that the rapid increase in students can overwhelm the system. The rapidly rising enrollments associated with

UPE led to overcrowded classrooms; running classes in shifts; acute short-ages of teachers, textbooks, and other materials; as well as the problem of overage students in the classrooms (Avenstrup, 2006).

In 2012, the United Nations launched a new campaign focused on achieving universal primary education. Named "Education First," its goals are to put every child in school, have them receive a quality edu-cation, and to foster global citizenship (United Nations, n.d.). It imme-diately gathered USD$1.5 billion in pledges to achieve its goals, both from governments as well as businesses (Niles, 2012). These pledges will help improve education in a number of nations around the globe. This is needed because aid for primary education has been declining as interna-tional donors have slashed their budgets (Provost, 2013).

The Professional Role of Social Workers

When social workers in the Global North are employed in child welfare, they are almost always working with issues of child abuse and neglect. However, the brief sections in this chapter are designed to give an over-view of the additional issues that may affect a child's well-being. As has been demonstrated, the topic of child welfare encompasses more issues than maltreatment. Many things that children in the Global North may take for granted, such as freedom from military service, education, and citizenship, may be concerns that threaten the welfare of millions of chil-dren around the globe. By the same token, other issues, such as maltreat-ment, threaten children worldwide. Social workers can work on reducing these threats to child well-being by working on the micro level to help individual clients or their families to attain child well-being. Social work-ers in the Global North may also often work with international adoption, performing home studies and helping parents and children to adjust to each other and overcoming cultural differences. Social workers can also work on the macro level to make education and birth registration more accessible. They can work to help families be able to provide for their children so that the children do not need to be given up for adoption or be sent to work at an early age. Working with multiple system levels enables social workers to help those who are currently experiencing the problem while helping to prevent others from suffering the same prob-lem in the future (see Box 4.1).

BOX 4.1 Social Worker Profile—Mai-Lynn Sahd, MSW

Mai-Lynn Sahd's mother was born in northern Vietnam. Due to a mental illness, her mother was stigmatized and shunned by her fellow villagers and family. She moved to Hanoi to find work, but then lost her job as a result of Mai-Lynn's birth. Both Mai-Lynn and her mother were forced to live in the streets and scavenge for food. At times, her mother would go off on her own and leave Mai-Lynn to fend for herself. When Mai-Lynn was about 6 years old, a worker convinced her mother to place Mai-Lynn in an orphanage so she could receive constant care; Mai-Lynn lived there for about 3 years.

Conditions there were overcrowded and undersourced. Corruption permeated the orphanage administration; most of the monies received were used to supplement salaries rather than care for the children. There were about 80 children, with five caregivers. Twenty children lived in a room, with five children per bed. There was no education provided, no structure, and the food was poor—both in quality and quantity. In order to survive, the children would sneak out and steal food from the local villagers. If visitors came, the children were cleaned up and given nice clothes in order to present well. But once they left, those clothes as well as the toys that they had been gifted were taken away. Mai-Lynn felt very abandoned and cried frequently for her mother.

She saw parents come to adopt children and witnessed the love they had for their adopted child. She yearned to have that special connection for herself. She was supposed to be adopted by one couple, but they later backed out after Mai-Lynn had already been given their picture and told they were her new parents. By this time, she was getting older, approximately 9, and was placed on a special needs adoption list. Her picture was seen by an American couple who were in the process of adopting another Vietnamese child, and they decided to adopt Mai-Lynn as well.

Her mother was a social worker who had founded an agency, Brittany's Hope, in the memory of their first adopted daughter, Brittany, who died in a car accident during her senior year of college. Brittany's Hope was developed to facilitate international adoption of special needs children who were otherwise unlikely to find a permanent family. Her mother and father personally lived this mission and adopted children from around the world who had been designated as "special needs" for a variety of reasons, including Mai-Lynn's "advanced age."

Mai-Lynn came to the United States and acclimated very well. She went on to earn her BSW and MSW. In the interim, Brittany's Hope expanded their mission to promote sustainable development projects for orphans and other at-risk children around the world and create hope for those children who will not be adopted. Mai-Lynn now serves as the Executive Director at Brittany's Hope. Her own adoption story led her to strive to create change for children in orphanages worldwide. She remembers that craving for love and a human touch and uses that memory to motivate her on a daily basis. Through this, she states that she creates healing for herself.

(continued)

Brittany's Hope connects with the local government and community to determine what needs and desires they have before ever beginning a project. Many of the Brittany's Hope projects have occurred in the nation of Vietnam, including Emily's Canes to provide canes to community members with vision impairment and teach them to use them, as well as Brittany's Cribs to provide safe cribs in orphanages. They also sponsor the House of Love orphanage, where they have funded a number of building projects such as shower and kitchen facilities, underwritten sustainable development including potable water and farm animals, and also facilitated sponsorship of individual children at the orphanage. Many children living at the House of Love are not eligible for adoption as they have a living parent, but in many cases their parents are not able to adequately care for them due to poverty or illness. The money provided through sponsorship helps assure an adequate diet, schooling, and a safe place to eat and sleep for all children living at this facility. The HOPE project (Helping Orphans by Providing Education) provides funding for orphans to receive education, either higher education or vocational skills.

They have now expanded operations to Injibara, Ethiopia, where, in consultation with the local community, they have built an orphan care facility. This model facility is not an institution but has a number of small homes in which the children live with a housemother, who is hired from the local village. Brittany's Hope also runs a number of other projects that work to help children in need around the world. You can learn more about their work at www.brittanyshope.org.

INTERNATIONAL ADOPTION AND CHINA

China is one of the largest nations in the world and has the largest population of any country, with 1.3 billion citizens (CIA, 2012). It became a communist country in 1949 and has maintained strict controls over its people. In recent years, there has been loosening in the economic sector, with capitalist-like ventures such as a stock market being introduced. However, in terms of personal control, the government still regulates citizens' lives. One way in which the government does this is by working to control the size of the population. In 1979, a policy was introduced that is commonly referred to in the West as the "one-child policy." This name is misleading as the policy is not strictly "one child." Urban families have been restricted to one child, but rural families may have two if the first child is a girl, and ethnic minorities are typically exempt altogether from the policy. Families may also pay large penalties for having additional children past their limit if they want additional children. Wealthy families are easily able to pay the fines and therefore the fine was raised for these elites. In 2012, a family paid a record fine of 1.3 million yen (over $200,000) (Moore, 2012).

In the Confucian culture that still predominates in China, sons are needed for the family. When a couple marries, they live with the husband's parents and take care of them in their old age. Therefore, a daughter grows up to take care of someone else's parents, not her own. If given a choice, Chinese families prefer children of both sexes, but due to the impact of the policy restricting the number of children, combined with the lack of an old age social security plan, families require sons to care for them (Johnson, 2012).

The consequence of this policy was a sharp rise in the number of abortions, infanticides, and infant abandonments. In the 1980s and 1990s, when the government began enforcing the policy more strictly, the number of abandonments increased sharply (Johnson, Banghan, & Liyao, 1998). Children who were abandoned were most often girls or disabled boys. The vast majority of these children were not abandoned to die but were typically placed where they would be found by someone else whom the parent believed would be able to care for the child, such as an orphanage or potential adoptive family (Johnson, 2004). At that time, the orphanages in China became overwhelmed and were unable to adequately care for all of the children. Human Rights Watch (1996) found that the mortality rate in the orphanages was frighteningly high, with over 50% of admissions dying in the first year from the lack of proper care; in some institutions, the mortality rate was closer to 90%. The orphanages were also unable to pay high-quality staff to care for the children, and thus high rates of abuse were documented as well. Since that time, conditions have improved, and children report that living conditions are better than with their previous foster families, and they receive better education and medical care. However, there are still problems associated with institutional living, such as stigma and insufficient emotional support (Zhao et al., 2009).

International adoption has both helped and hurt China. The large number of adoptions from China, particularly Chinese girls, has helped to raise money for the orphanages and therefore raise the quality of the care. Each adoption contributes a substantial sum of money for the orphanage (Johnson, 2002). However, these adoptions also removed a large number of its citizens from its borders. According to the Hague Convention, the first priority should be to help the children find a home within their own culture. Until recently, Chinese law has inhibited this. Prior to 1999, if a Chinese couple wished to adopt a child, they had to be at least 35 years old and childless. This was to reduce the number of "illegal" children who violated the one-child policy; the government did not want couples to "hide" the birth of a daughter as an adoption so that they could try again for a son. However, it is a great shame in Chinese society to remain childless so late in life, and this policy greatly reduced the number of potential adoptions. In 1999, the law was changed to allow couples 30 years and older to adopt, and if the child was abandoned and living in an orphanage, the couple is permitted to already have one other child as well. These changes have helped substantially increase the number of domestic adoptions; however, intercountry adoptions are still often favored (Johnson, 2002).

It appears that in recent years, the sex of the child is becoming less important to parents. While some believe that the Chinese are reluctant to adopt nonrelated children, many Chinese families have been found to be willing to adopt, including daughters, if they could. The "ideal" family in China is often seen to have one child of each sex (Johnson, 2002). While families believe they need a son in order to care for them, they believe that a daughter is more loving, loyal, and obedient (Johnson, 2002; Johnson et al., 1998). The tradition of honoring the elderly and one's parents has been lessening in recent years, and as a result, the city government of Nanjing has even taken to publicly shaming people who do not visit their elderly parents often ("Penalties for neglecting," 2006). Daughters are seen as more willing to care for their parents and have a closer emotional bond, thus reducing the concern that elderly parents will have no one to care for them (Johnson, 2002). With the improvement in living standards in China, fewer healthy infants are being abandoned, including infant girls (Crary, 2010).

This does not mean, however, that the desire for a son has faded. In some cases, traffickers kidnap male children and sell them to local families desperate for a son (Jacobs, 2009). Trafficking has also occurred by government officials who seize children from parents unable to pay the fine for a second child or produce needed paperwork. These children may be brought to an orphanage, where they are made available for international adoption (Custer, 2013; LaFraniere, 2011).

Another impact of the one-child policy and its resulting gender preferences has been to create a severe gender imbalance in China. While worldwide there are 105 boys to 100 girls, in China this has become 117 boys to 100 girls for those under 15 years old. This is improving, and at birth, it is 1.13 (CIA, 2012). However, this imbalance results in there not being enough women for the men to marry when they age and can result in the marriages to trafficked women described in Chapter 3. In an effort to stem this imbalance, China has outlawed sex-selective abortions and has piloted programs to pay the school tuition for poor families with a girl or from a family with two girls (Zijuan, Shuzhuo, & Feldman, 2012).

The number of children being adopted out of China has shrunk in recent years and the eligibility criteria have been tightened. Currently, married, heterosexual couples are highly preferred. They must be between 30 and 50, unless they are adopting a child with special needs. Single women can only adopt a child with special needs. Applicants must be in good physical and mental health, and they cannot be morbidly obese (BMI of more than 40). The current waiting time for a child without special needs from date of submission of their application to reception of the referral is almost 5 years (US State Department, 2012).

In sum, the fertility control policy, in combination with the traditional need for a son, resulted in substantial increases in the number of girls and children with disabilities being abandoned to orphanages due to their parents' inability to raise them. China is now increasing its efforts to have these children adopted by families in their own country as opposed to parents from other countries, and the abandonment of healthy infants is decreasing, but the impact of the sex ratio imbalance will continue to have severe consequences for China. The control in population growth has resulted in a situation where there are now many more elderly persons who need to be supported than there are workers supporting them. There are concerns that this will inhibit China's economic growth. Due to this, there are signs that China may be expanding the exceptions to its one-child limit. In 2013, China announced that it would further relax the policy, allowing a second child if a husband or wife is an only child (Buckley, 2013).

It appears that the economic costs of having a child are holding down birthrates to only one child, even in areas that are allowed two. Importantly, in these areas, the sex ratios are less skewed than in other regions ("China's one child," 2013). Therefore, it appears that even if the policy is reversed, it will not affect the birthrate and, therefore, this economic impact will be difficult for China to avoid (LaFraniere, 2011; Wong, 2012).

What You Can Do Now

- Work with an organization such as the Coalition to Stop the Use of Child Soldiers that is trying to prevent the use of children in combat.
- Monitor where and how your clothes and other purchases are made to make sure you do not fund child labor.
- Raise money to help UNICEF or Save the Children in their work to help children.
- Volunteer to tutor children in your own area to help their education.
- Participate in a service trip to help children.

What You Can Do as a Professional Social Worker

- Work to promote ethical international adoption.
- Conduct psychosocial counseling for children caught up in combat, either as soldiers or as victims.
- Work for an international NGO such as UNICEF or Save the Children.
- Raise awareness of the problems surrounding birth registration within your agency, particularly if you are employed in a development agency.
- Create programs to help children stay in their homes or create welcoming ones for children who are living on the street.

World Wide Web Resources on International Child Welfare

ChildInfo (http://www.childinfo.org): UNICEF's site for statistical information related to children on a multitude of topics.

Children's Rights Information Network (www.crin.org): This is a global network whose purpose is to disseminate information concerning the rights of children. They have information on a broad variety of topics relating to children and their rights.

Childwatch International Research Network (www.childwatch. uio.no): A network of institutions that conduct research relating to children. The research is aimed at improving children's lives and well-being. They provide links to information from sites worldwide.

Coalition to Stop the Use of Child Soldiers (www.child-soldiers. org): An international coalition that works to stop the use of child soldiers. They have a number of resources on the issue.

Human Rights Watch (hrw.org/children): Human Rights Watch children's section. Provides reports on a number of different issues.

International Labour Organization: International Programme on the Elimination of Child Labour: IPEC (www.ilo.org/public/english/ standards/ipec/index.htm): Provides information and statistics relating to child labor and the organization's work to eliminate it.

PLAN International (www.plan-international.org): An international NGO that works from a developmental approach to improve the lives in children in poor nations.

Save the Children (www.savethechildren.net; www.savethechildren. org [US Branch]): An international NGO with branches in a number of countries. It works to improve the lives of children worldwide, including in the Global North. Its Web site offers a number of reports on issues that affect the lives of children.

Street Kids International (www.streetkids.org): A Canadian-based NGO that works around the world to help street children.

UN Education First (www.globaleducationfirst.org): The UN official Web site for its Education First campaign.

UNICEF (www.unicef.org): The United Nations agency that focuses on children; its Web site offers a wealth of information concerning their different projects and reports.

5

War and Conflict

It was after World War I, then known as the "Great War," that social workers became aware of "shell shock," the trauma that many soldiers experienced after battle. Shell shock has now received the formal diagnostic name of Post-Traumatic Stress Disorder (PTSD). As our knowledge regarding the impact of violence and conflict on the human psyche has expanded, so have the categories of people experiencing it. Those affected by war are no longer primarily soldiers. No longer are there clearly defined battle lines in wars between nations; the impact of conflict spreads far beyond the battlefields. Wars today are often fought within nations between governments and rebel groups, rather than between nations.

As discussed in Chapter 2, the Geneva Conventions are the central documents for the humane treatment of people involved in conflict, whether they are combatants or civilians. The American Red Cross (2011, p. 2) states that "The Geneva Conventions apply in all cases of declared war, or in any other armed conflict between nations. They also apply in cases where a nation is partially or totally occupied by soldiers of another nation, even when there is no armed resistance to that occupation." All nations in the world are parties to the conventions. These treaties are categorized under a branch of law known as international humanitarian law; this section of law is founded on the principles of humanity, impartiality, and neutrality (American Red Cross, 2011).

The central tenets of the conventions require that warring parties make distinctions between combatants and civilians and provide protection for those civilians. Soldiers "placed out of combat" by sickness, wounds, or detention must be given medical care and treated humanely, regardless of on which side they fought. The taking of hostages and the torture of prisoners of war is expressly forbidden. Additionally, a representative from a neutral "protecting power" must have access to any person detained; this power is most commonly the International Committee of the Red Cross. The Universal Declaration of Human Rights supports these principles found in the Geneva Conventions. Article 5 states that "No one shall be subjected to torture or to cruel, inhuman or degrading treatment or punishment." The impact of conflict on civilians is also addressed in the Universal Declaration of Human Rights; Article 14 provides rights to refugees and asylum seekers: "Everyone has the right to seek and to enjoy in other countries asylum from persecution." The primary document in establishing who is a refugee, together with their rights and responsibilities, is the 1951 Convention relating to the Status of Refugees, together with its 1967 Protocol (UNHCR, 2011).

Impact of War and Conflict

The impact of violence and conflict today goes far beyond the battlefield. Long-term impact is felt through the damage to infrastructure, including roads, businesses, and school buildings, as well as the economic impact, making recovery from conflict extremely difficult. The impact on civilians has also markedly increased. It is no longer primarily soldiers who experience the physical impact of conflict. Wars have moved from isolated battlefields to cities and towns. Civilians are often caught in the fighting or must flee their homes to avoid it. In some cases, civilians are direct targets of violence, as seen in Iraq and South Sudan (Burnham, Lafta, Doocy, & Roberts, 2006; Médecins Sans Frontières, 2012).

However, typically the majority of deaths that occur as a result of armed conflict are not from violence, but rather result primarily from the conditions created by wartime, such as malnutrition and an increase in communicable disease. The lack of access to health care, sufficient food and water, or adequate shelter creates mass casualties. For example, in the Darfur region of Sudan, while the majority of deaths were initially from violence, this changed as people fled; disease then became the biggest killer (DeGomme & Guha-Sapir, 2010). Young children are particularly vulnerable. Children under 5 years of age have the highest mortality rates in areas affected by conflict (Zwi et al., 2006) and the infant mortality rate has been found to increase 10% in countries with conflict (Gates, Hegre, Nygård, & Strand, 2012). In Afghanistan, 41 people froze to death in camps for internally displaced people in the winter of 2011–12; the vast majority of them were children ("Dozens of children," 2012).

Physical and Mental Health Impacts

Numerous physical health impacts have been noted as a result of armed conflict. Death and dismemberment as a direct result of combat are obvious ones, especially as civilians have been increasingly targeted in recent conflicts, such as through roadside bombs or suicide bombers in public places. However, other physical health impacts occur, including a greater number of chronic medical conditions. An increase in high-risk behaviors has also been found, such as substance use, including tobacco, alcohol, and other drugs (Médecins Sans Frontières, 2011).

However, the mental health impacts of conflict can last long past the physical impacts if intervention is not provided. Common psychological difficulties include depression, anxiety disorders, and PTSD (Attanayake et al., 2009; Médecins Sans Frontières, 2011; Murthy & Lakshminarayana, 2006). These impacts are even more pronounced among those who have been displaced from their homes (Husain et al., 2011). Prolonged conflicts typically erode traditional community coping mechanisms and supports, leaving them even less able to cope. While many people are able to recover from psychological distress once the trauma ends, others will need assistance in doing so. For others, they lack the ability to leave the traumatic situation.

While Doctors Without Borders/Médecins Sans Frontières (MSF) is better known for its physical health interventions, they also offer psychosocial services. As one staff member stated, "What do you do if there is enough food, but no one wants to eat?" (Doctors Without Borders, 2005a, ¶2). Social workers are among the mental health professionals who volunteer to work with Doctors Without Borders. These volunteers are experienced in working with trauma issues and PTSD (Doctors Without Borders, 2013).

The core of their psychosocial approach is for their mental health workers to work with local residents to build the community's capacity to resolve the trauma in a culturally appropriate manner. The staff adapts cognitive-behavioral therapy and brief therapy techniques to the cultural context in which they are working. Recognizing the context of a crisis situation, the goal is not to cure people but to "support and improve the coping mechanisms of beneficiaries" (De Jong & Kleber, 2007, p. 490). MSF also coordinates with local staff and traditional healers to work together with the person's cultural context, particularly to address spiritual concerns. Readers are referred to the handbook developed by Médecins Sans Frontières (2011) for further detail.

Local social workers also offer services to help people recover from conflict. These services may look different from those offered by the international community. Doucet and Denov (2012) found that Sierra Leonean social workers were likely to offer direct advice and incorporate their personal stories to help their clients. While this would run counter to social work practice in a number of Western nations, their clients reported it was helpful.

Traditional healers may also be sought out to help individuals who are having a difficult time returning to community life. In countries such as Mozambique and Angola, those who have engaged in conflict must be cleansed before they are accepted back into society. They are carriers of the spirits of the dead; if the former soldiers are not cleansed, they will carry the anger of the spirits back into the community. These vengeful spirits cause the psychosocial issues from which the person is suffering (Green & Honwana, 1999; Honwana, 2006). Rituals and healings will be conducted to help the individual, the nature of which will depend on the primary religious identification of the individual and how rural his or her village is (Honwana, 2006).

Sexual Violence During Conflict

During conflict, the risk of sexual violence increases, both for civilians and those involved with armed groups. Sexual violence can include rape, genital mutilation, forced incest, sexual torture, sexual humiliation, and sexual slavery (Médecins Sans Frontières, 2009; Onyango & Hampanda, 2011). In recent decades, more attention has been given to this trauma and in 1993, after the conflict in the Balkans, it was recognized as a crime against humanity. While both males and females are at risk of this crime, the majority of reported cases have been by females.

During most of the world's recent conflicts, such as in Central African Republic, Democratic Republic of the Congo, Sierra Leone, and Sudan, reports of sexual assault and sexual violence have spiked (Doctors Without Borders, 2005b; U. N. Special Representative on Sexual Violence in Conflict, 2012a; UNICEF, 2005). Sexual violence has been recognized as a war crime for its tactical use to inspire fear and humiliation in a population. It can be used a psychological tactic to terrify or intimidate the population or as a reward mechanism for soldiers. It can also be used as a form of "ethnic cleansing" by impregnating women from the opposing side (Machel, 1996). In the Democratic Republic of the Congo, it has been used for economic or political control (United Nations Security Council, 2012a).

The United Nations' top relief official, in referring to conflicts in sub-Saharan Africa, stated that "organized, premeditated sexual attack had become a preferred weapon of war..., with rapists going unpunished and victims of rape shunned by their communities" (Hoge, 2005, ¶1). Even in camps for those who have fled the violence, the risk of sexual assault remains high. This is due in part to the fact that these criminals are aware that there are a high percentage of women living there unprotected, not even by a front door (Ali, 2013; "Sexual violence continues," 2008). The perpetrators may also be government troops assigned to protect the camp or nongovernmental organization (NGO) workers who are supposed to aid them ("Camps offer little refuge," 2008; "Rape on the rise," 2011). Even UN peacekeepers have been found to sexually exploit the population, such as exchanging food for sexual intercourse (Martin, 2005).

Although awareness of sexual violence during times of war and conflict has risen and it is now recognized as a war crime, for the most part perpetrators continue to act with impunity. Regardless of gender of the person assaulted, there is often a lack of faith in the justice system, especially if the perpetrator was a member of the state forces ("Sexual abuse survivors," 2007). In some cases, national law may be insufficient for prosecution. For example, the rape of a man may not even be recognized as a crime under the laws of that nation (Médecins Sans Frontières, 2009). Prior to 2006, the law in the Democratic Republic of the Congo lacked a definition of rape and was not gender-neutral. These shortcomings have now been addressed, but prosecutions remain extremely low, while sexual violence remains extremely high (Zongwe, 2012). Male victims may fear reporting could lead to a prosecution against them if homosexual acts are outlawed in their country (Onyango & Hampanda, 2011; Sivakumaran, 2007).

In the Democratic Republic of the Congo, sexual assault has become extremely widespread. While it is committed by all sides in the conflict, the vast majority recently has been by government forces, apparently to punish community members for suspected collaboration (United Nations Security Council, 2012a). In addition, the situation in this nation exemplifies how conflict can help tear down societal norms and the rule of law as sexual violence perpetrated by civilians has also increased markedly (Bartels et al., 2012; Nelson et al., 2011). However, this may be due in part to the demobilization; those who were soldiers are now in civilian clothes rather than a uniform (United Nations Security Council, 2012c).

The genocide in the Darfur region of Sudan caused a high level of chaos and sexual violence. A report compiled by Doctors Without Borders (2005b) stated that as a result of the violence, almost 2 million people in the region fled their homes. However, even when they reached a camp for displaced persons, the violence continued. Women had to leave the relative safety of the camp to collect firewood and water, and they were attacked while pursuing these daily activities. In a 6-month period, Doctors Without Borders treated almost 500 rape victims and believed that number was only a portion of the actual victims. In more than half of the cases, physical assault accompanied the sexual assault, and almost one-third were raped more than once. Eighty-one percent of the women were assaulted by military or militia forces that were armed. Women are typically discouraged from reporting by police and can face great shame in their community if the attack is known. Doctors Without Borders included the following case study in its report to illustrate the repercussions of sexual assault:

A 16-year-old girl was collecting firewood for her family when three armed men on camels surrounded her, held her down and raped her, one after the other. When she arrived home, she told her family what had occurred. They threw her out of the house and she had to build her own hut away from them. Her fiancé broke their engagement, stating that she was now disgraced and spoiled. When she was eight months pregnant as a result of the rape, the police came to her home and they asked about the pregnancy; she told them she had been

raped. They told her that since she was not married, this was an
illegal pregnancy. They beat her with a whip and placed her in jail
for 10 days in a cell with 23 other women in the same position. These
women were forced to clean, cook and fetch water for the police officers.
The only food and water she had was that which she could scrounge
in the course of her duties. (Summarized from Doctors Without
Borders, 2005b)

While women have received the bulk of the attention for being victimized through sexual assault, this is not to say that men do not experience
this trauma or that women cannot be perpetrators. For example, a survey
conducted in the Democratic Republic of the Congo in 2010 found that
40% of the women and 24% of the men experienced a form of sexual
violence; these numbers may actually be low as the interviewers could
not enter areas with active combat. Women were perpetrators in 40% of
the violations against women and in 10% of those against men (Johnson
et al., 2010).

As men rarely report sexual violence due to cultural stigma, it goes
untreated (Christian, Safari, Ramazani, Burnham, & Glass, 2011). Men
may discuss "torture" they have experienced but are reluctant to name it
as sexual assault. This shame is why it is an effective tool against men. It
is meant to be shaming, to state that they are not truly men, as a "man"
should not only be able to have prevented the assault but also be able to
deal with its consequences (Sivakumaran, 2007). Some male survivors
report that their wives left them after learning of the assault and that
other villagers refer to them as "bush wives" (Gettleman, 2009). In other
cases, the men left their families due to their shame. They felt that two
wives could not live in the same family and the assault had made them
a wife of the armed force, rather than a husband (Christian et al., 2011).
However, due to the lack of attention, there is little funding for services
for men and policy manuals do not include them.

Men may also be violated in other ways than being assaulted themselves. A man may be forced to witness the rape of his wife or daughter,
or be forced to commit the act himself, in order to degrade and humiliate
him (Ward & Marsh, 2006). It is meant to show that he cannot fulfill his
gender role of protector. Enforced sterilization, nudity, and masturbation
are also other ways that men may be victimized (Sivakumaran, 2007).

Readers are referred to Sivakumaran (2007) for an excellent exploration of this topic.

Sexual violence can have many long-term impacts. Physical impacts can include vaginal or anal tearing, fistulas, pregnancy, and HIV, among others. The psychological scars can be even more devastating. One study in Liberia found that of the 40% of female combatants and 32% of male combatants who experienced sexual violence during the war, 74% and 81% percent, respectively, had symptoms of PTSD, significantly higher than those who had not (Médecins Sans Frontières, 2009). As noted earlier, the shame and stigma experienced by male survivors can break families apart and isolate them from their communities. Men may feel unable to work due to the trauma they have experienced, increasing poverty for the household (Christian et al., 2011). The stress placed upon men, including the shame of the rape of their wives, can lead to domestic violence, causing further problems within the household (Suárez-Orozco, 2001). The mental health impact of these sexual assaults can be long standing and require targeted interventions to heal.

UNICEF has established programs in affected countries to provide counseling and to help decrease the stigma associated with their assault (UNICEF, 2005). Medica Mondiale (www.medicamondiale.org) is a German organization dedicated to helping women and girls heal from the trauma of rape during times of war and conflict. Founded in 1993 in reaction to the mass rapes occurring at that time in Bosnia, it currently operates in a number of countries, including Afghanistan and Democratic Republic of the Congo. Through networking of women and advocacy, they are helping to create change to heal those affected by wartime sexual violence.

Médecins Sans Frontières (2009) has established programs in a wide variety of countries where conflict-related sexual violence occurs. Social workers and psychologists help survivors through the initial physical exam as well as considering the long-term impact. In Democratic Republic of the Congo, sexual violence had become so common that survivors did not consider it as something special that would require attention. Therefore, Médecins Sans Frontières worked with each village to have them select a *maman conseillère* (mama counselor) who would be a point person within the village for anyone who was a victim. This person would support the victim and encourage him or her to seek prompt medical care.

Impact on Men, Women, and Children

The impact of violence and conflict differs by population: Men, women, and children are affected differently by the same phenomenon.

Men   Men are more likely to experience direct acts of violence. Coghlan et al. (2006), in their survey of the impact of the conflict in Democratic Republic of the Congo, found that 71% of those who died as a result of violence were men. As noted earlier, a man may be forced to witness the rape of his wife or daughter, or be forced to commit the act himself, in order to degrade and humiliate him (Ward & Marsh, 2006). Not only may they be unable to fulfill their role of protector but also their role of provider. Economic impacts are common and widespread during wartime and unemployment is rife. Access to sufficient food and water can be very difficult. In Democratic Republic of the Congo, 75% of men in one survey reported that they were ashamed because they were unable to provide for basic needs and 78% were depressed due to unemployment (Sonke Gender Justice Network, 2012). This stress can contribute to the occurrence of domestic violence, causing further problems within the household (Giacaman, Rabaia, & Nguyen-Gillham, 2010; Suárez-Orozco, 2001).

For young men, who have traditionally had more freedom than young women, the restraints imposed by conflict can be oppressive. Tavernise (2006) reports that in Iraq, the ongoing conflict resulted in young adults being kept inside their houses. Their parents did not allow them out even for school or work for fear they would be killed. The nature of the sectarian violence caused the loss of friends, due to death as well as increased sectarian allegiances. Tavernise states that due to the lack of jobs and little faith in governmental justice, more young men joined armed gangs and militias, further increasing their risk of death as well as the death of others.

Women   Women face many risks during times of conflict; as noted earlier, one of the largest is the risk of sexual assault. Another threat is the increased risk of domestic violence during times of conflict due to the higher levels of stress of their husbands, as noted earlier. Women may also experience restrictions on their movement for a variety of reasons. They may fear attack, they may not be able to go out without a male escort (who might be missing due to combat), or they might not have the proper documents for free movement (Governance and Social Development Resource Centre, 2009).

The end of conflict does not necessarily mean the end of difficulties for women. Women may face additional burdens due to the death of their husbands. In countries where women do not have equivalent legal standing, they may be prohibited from inheriting their husband's possessions, lowering them into further poverty. In Iraq, a man's body is necessary to prove his death, but due to the high rate of disappearance and conflict deaths, this is often not possible and therefore women are unable to receive a widow's pension (Oxfam International, 2009).

Women who have moved into positions of leadership or employment during the conflict due to the lack of men may lose those positions at the end of the conflict. Women who were involved in the conflict, serving as combatants or sex slaves for example, can have difficulty reintegrating into the community after the conflict. There may be a backlash against them in the community for their actions during the conflict, regardless of whether their participation was voluntary (UNICEF, 2005).

Afghanistan has one of the highest rates of widowhood due to the length of conflict within that country ("Bleak prospects," 2008). Due to social norms, these women typically lack education and literacy skills. Two widows of the attacks in the United States on September 11, 2001, have founded an organization called "Beyond the 11th" that works to raise money to help the widows of Afghanistan (www.beyondthe11th. org). These women felt that they received a great deal of public support after their husbands' deaths and that the widows in Afghanistan received none of that. Their organization raises money and partners with other NGOs to help these women support themselves.

Children   According to the United Nations (n.d.), there are six "Grave Violations" that occur in armed conflict that negatively affect children: killing or maiming of children; recruitment or use of children as soldiers; sexual violence against children; attacks against schools or hospitals; denial of humanitarian access for children; and abduction of children. As noted earlier, many of these affect adults as well.

Landmines and cluster munitions have been identified as a special risk to the killing and maiming of children. These ordnance often remains in place long after battle due to the time, expertise, and money it takes to clear it. Children are at special risk for being landmine victims because they are less able to read warning signs and less likely to be aware of the dangers of landmines. Children in poor families are at particular risk because these children are more likely to be in mined areas when scavenging for firewood, fetching water, cultivating their crops, or herding animals (Machel, 2001). Additionally, some of the landmines are brightly colored and can appear as toys to a child. The "butterfly" mine, once common in Afghanistan, came in several colors and had a "wing," creating an attraction to young children (Machel, 2001).

The Convention on the Prohibition of the Use, Stockpiling, Production and Transfer of Anti-Personnel Mines, and on their Destruction has been adopted by 161 countries. All NATO countries with the exception of the United States have signed it (International Campaign to Ban Landmines [ICBL], n.d.). Since this Convention, the global production of landmines has greatly decreased and there has been no intercountry trade of landmines since the 1990s. While the death rate remains unacceptably high, it is approximately one-third of what it was a decade ago (ICBL, 2012). An international treaty to ban cluster munitions entered into force in 2010 and currently has 111 state parties. Unfortunately, a number of the largest users, including Israel, the United States, China, and Russia, have not joined. However, the United States has put in place a moratorium on export of cluster munitions (Cluster Munition Coalition, 2012).

War and armed conflict disrupt children's education. While the overall number of children who are out of school has decreased, the proportion of them who live in conflicted areas has increased from 42% to 50% (UNESCO, 2013). While children who are involved with armed groups or who are displaced from their homes by the violence are especially likely to be out of school, children who are not combatants or displaced due to the conflict also have their educations affected. During times of violence, parents are more apt to keep children home in order to protect them. Children can be at risk of becoming targets of violence during their journey to school. They also fear being accused of giving aid to the "other" side during their travels or being forced to help one side or the other (IBON Foundation, 2006). While schools should be a safe place for children, isolated from the conflict, this is too often not the case. The trauma the children have witnessed and the state of fear can inhibit them from concentrating and learning, and malnutrition can impact their cognitive development and thus their ability to learn (Kohli & Mather, 2003; Machel, 2001).

School buildings themselves can also be targets for attack, either for physical destruction or recruitment of child soldiers (Kilpatrick & Leitch, 2004; Machel, 1996; Risser, 2007; Shakya, 2011). Schools are often attacked both by rebel groups as well as official state forces. In countries such as Afghanistan, Colombia, Iraq, and Somalia, schools and teachers have been a repeated target of rebel groups. Schools have been bombed, burned, and forced to closed, while teachers were intimated, kidnapped, or killed (United Nations Security Council, 2012a). Teachers can be a target for armed forces, due to their high status in the community or their strong political views. Teachers in Sri Lanka who tried to protect the children from forced recruitment by armed forces were targeted by guerrillas, while in Colombia, schools are regularly attacked and/or occupied by armed factions and schoolteachers are threatened or killed (Coalition to Stop the Use of Child Soldiers, 2007; Machel, 2001; United Nations Security Council, 2012a). Readers are referred to Mapp (2013) for further discussion on the impact on conflict on children.

Refugees and Asylum Seekers

The UN High Commissioner for Refugees (UNHCR) monitors the condition of people it identifies as members of "populations of concern." In addition to refugees, this definition includes asylum seekers, stateless persons, and returned refugees as well as internally displaced persons (IDPs) and people fleeing a broad threat such as war or a natural disaster. A refugee is legally defined as a person who has fled his or her country because of a well-founded fear of persecution based on race, religion, nationality, political opinion, or membership in a particular social group (UNHCR, 2004). US law also specifically states that a person fleeing, or who has suffered, a forced abortion may be considered a refugee. The condition of being a refugee is determined by the UNHCR. An asylum seeker is a person who states he or she is a refugee but whose claim has not yet been established (UNHCR, n.d.). Those who flee their home, but remain within the borders of their nation, are known as IDPs. Chapter 2 discussed how the Universal Declaration of Human Rights focuses on the rights of the individual rather than on community-level rights. The same is true of the definition of refugee: It focuses on the persecution of the individual and neglects community-wide persecution.

In 2012, the size of the "population of concern" to the UNHCR was 42.5 million, of whom 25.9 million were under UNHCR protection (UNHCR, 2012). Children are estimated to make up almost half of this population. Representing the change in current warfare, the proportion of refugees within that population has been decreasing over the past decade, while the number of IDPs has been increasing. Those from the Occupied Palestinian Territories are the largest actual population of concern (4.8 million), but they are not served by the UNHCR, but another agency. Countries in the Global South by far host the greatest number of refugees—four-fifths of the total. The top five countries hosting populations of concern to the UNHCR are (in order) Colombia, Sudan, Pakistan, Democratic Republic of the Congo, and Iraq (UNHCR, 2012).

The countries with the largest populations of IDPs (in order) are Colombia, Sudan, and Democratic Republic of the Congo (UNHCR, 2012). While many people are not aware of the situation in Colombia, the violence that has been occurring for decades has resulted in it being the country with the highest number of displaced people (3.9 million), the vast majority of whom are IDPs, a situation addressed in this chapter's Culture Box. Afghanistan is the source country for the second largest number of "populations of concern" to the UNHCR, with 2.7 million affected people; these people are spread throughout 79 countries, but 95% are in Pakistan and Iran. Pakistan hosts the greatest number of these refugees, followed by Iran and then Syria (UNHCR, 2012).

As noted, the status of being an asylum seeker is different from that of being a refugee, although the same criteria of the five areas of persecution are applied. A person who has a fear of persecution in his or her home country may apply to another country for asylum in that nation. According to the 1951 Refugee Convention, the principle of *nonrefoulement* forbids any nation from returning a person to a country where he or she would face persecution because of any of the five areas of persecution. However, this persecution must be proved in court, and the evidence required for asylum is much greater than that of refugee status and therefore has a much higher rate of denial. For example, those seeking asylum due to gender-based persecution claims have traditionally had great difficulty in proving their case in many Global North countries, where it can be difficult to prove that the discriminatory treatment of women in such areas as domestic violence and female genital cutting can rise to the level to be considered persecution (Human Rights Watch, 2004). Those who face persecution due to being a member of a sexual minority have also faced high hurdles for being granted refuge or asylum ("The plight," 2013). Due to the skepticism with which most refugees and asylum seekers are viewed, their treatment in host countries has often been questionable in terms of violations of human rights. A "culture of disbelief" tends to exist, and in some countries, such as South Africa, asylum officers fail to apply applicable law or seek to be bribed for a favorable recommendation ("Culture of disbelief," 2013; "South Africa's flawed," 2013). There is a need to identify asylum seekers and provide them with the services to which they are entitled, while differentiating them from economic migrants as well as those who would pose a security threat to the nation. This balance is very difficult, as will be illustrated in the following section. This text will examine conditions in three Global North countries (Australia, Israel, and the United States) and two Global South countries (Thailand and Pakistan).

Thailand

While Thailand is not a signatory to the 1951 Refugee Convention, due to its location and relative stability, it has hosted approximately 1.3 million refugees since it began working with UNHCR in 1975 (UNHCR, n.d.). Currently, Thailand is host to refugees from Myanmar fleeing the repressive government there as well as fighting between that government and rebel groups. There are approximately 140,000 Burmese individuals living in refugee camps and 2 to 3 million living outside of them in Thailand (Human Rights Watch, 2012a). In 2005, the Thai government stopped registering new arrivals ("Aid workers," 2011), and it is estimated that only about 60% of the refugees in the camps are registered (Human Rights Watch, 2012a).

As Thailand has not ratified the Refugee Convention, it has no refugee law or asylum procedures. The Thai government considers most of the Burmese to be economic migrants, but research by the International Rescue Committee has found that many of them would likely qualify for refugee status (Green-Rauerhorst, Jacobsen, & Pyne 2008). Under Thai law, all foreign nationals without proper documents are considered illegal immigrants, and those who are not officially registered as refugees are considered in violation of Thai law (Human Rights Watch, 2012a). Those who are registered must remain in the refugee camps set up on the Thailand/Myanmar border and are not allowed to leave. If they do leave, they are considered to be in violation of the law and may be arrested and deported. As a result, these refugees are unable to seek employment or go to school outside of the camps, limiting their prospects for improving their lives and becoming self-sufficient.

Progress is being made in several areas. In 2008, changes to Thai law permitted the citizenship of all children born in the country, regardless of the status of their parents, thus reducing the number of children born stateless (UNHCR, 2013a). In 2005, resettlement to third countries began for a large number of the refugees, largely to Australia, Canada, and the United States (Human Rights Watch, 2012a). However, those who have been resettled were the more educated, for example, teachers and health workers, meaning those who remain are more likely to need assistance (Human Rights Watch, 2012b).

In 2011 and 2012, vast progress was made in peace talks between the Burmese government and rebel groups. The government also loosened its draconian hold on the country. This raises hope that refugees may be able to return home in the near future. Fortunately, Thailand is not pushing the refugees to hurry back but is allowing them to wait and see if this stability continues. Aid groups are beginning to change their assistance from survival needs such as food and shelter, to providing those in camps with skills to allow them to survive outside of the camp (Human Rights Watch, 2012a).

Pakistan

Pakistan is host to approximately 1.6 million refugees from Afghanistan, making it the country hosting the largest number of refugees (UNHCR, 2013b). This number includes only registered refugees, making the actual number of refugees in Pakistan much higher. Pakistan also has almost three-quarters of a million of its own citizens displaced (IDPs). While approximately 3.8 million Afghans who had fled their country have returned home since 2002, large numbers remain in the countries of refuge (UNHCR, 2013b). Despite the fall of the Taliban in 2001, many Afghans have been reluctant to return home due to continuing security concerns, as well as drought and extreme poverty, and therefore remain in their host countries (IRIN, 2012).

Pakistan and Iran (the other country to which Afghans have fled in large numbers) have resisted integrating Afghan refugees into their populations, due in part to the large number of people involved. Pakistan and Iran, even before the fall of the Taliban, stated these people were economic migrants, not refugees, in order to avoid providing services guaranteed to refugees. Instead, they were contained within refugee camps or struggled in the community fearing identification. It was not until 2006 that Pakistan agreed to register and provide identification for Afghan refugees in their country (UNHCR, 2006a, 2006b). However, Pakistan stated that at the end of 2012, this registration would no longer be renewed (UNHCR, 2013b). Even at the beginning of 2012, Afghani refugees in Pakistan reported increasing harassment, including arbitrary arrests and detentions, home invasions, disappearances, and beatings (IRIN, 2012). There was high concern about Afghanistan's ability to receive back all its citizens due to the still fragile nature of the country. It was feared that those who are not able to integrate due to lack of adequate employment, housing, and food will be easy recruitment targets for the Taliban (IRIN, 2012). At the end of 2012, this was extended for 6 months and then extended again in June 2013 (United Nations, 2013).

United States

In countries in the Global North, the process of obtaining asylum is a long and difficult one. In the United States, when persons are found to have entered the country without the proper documents, they are supposed to be asked if they fear being sent home. Those who say yes are to be given a hearing before a judge to assess if this is a credible fear that would qualify that person for asylum. However, "expedited removal" is typical, where those who do not evidence fear are immediately returned and those who do are housed in detention facilities. Additionally, the UNHCR (2013c) states that who is determined to be a "member of a particular social group" is inconsistent throughout the country and the government has not issued any guidelines to correct this.

A 2005 federal study found extreme variation in the treatment of asylum seekers between US airports and concluded that a person's chance of obtaining asylum may depend on where he or she entered the country. Kennedy Airport was the most difficult; personal interviews assessing fear of return were typically conducted at public counters (inhibiting disclosure) and shackles were routinely used on asylum seekers. The study found that in general the question-and-answer forms used during these preliminary interviews were "unreliable and incomplete" and were later used by immigration judges to impeach the testimony of the asylum seeker. In some cases, although the person stated he or she had a fear of returning to his or her country, the immigration officer recorded on the interview form that the person stated no fear. In approximately half of all cases, the officers did not inform the person of the protections afforded them by US law, although it is mandatory to do so. The study found that asylum seekers were typically treated in the same manner as criminals: being strip-searched, shackled, and put in detention centers while their claims were evaluated was common (United States Commission on International Religious Freedom, 2005).

The commission made five recommendations to improve the process, but while improvements have been made, they have yet to be fully implemented. Even when an asylum seeker is granted a hearing before a judge, there is no guarantee of a fair hearing. Federal appeals judges, who review the asylum decisions upon appeal, state there is a pattern of biased and incoherent decisions in asylum cases (Liptak, 2005). The courts are regarded as swamped, with each judge having up to 70 cases scheduled at a time without law clerks, stenographers, or sufficient competent lawyers (Bernstein, 2006; Wasem, 2011).

Approval rates of asylum claims have been found to vary markedly between asylum officers, between judges, and between regions. For example, in Atlanta, only 7% of asylum seekers from China received asylum, but in Orlando, the rate was 76% (Wasem, 2011). The US Government Accountability Office stated that applicants in San Francisco were 12 times more likely to be granted asylum than in Atlanta Wasem, 2011). A 2008 study found that the majority of judges appointed under the Bush administration's illegal political litmus test were much more likely to reject asylum claims than their peers. This litmus test, conducted from 2004 to 2007, was designed to assure that judges were sufficiently conservative and screened out Democrats and those deemed too liberal. Of the 31 immigration judges appointed, 16 had a sufficient record for analysis. Nine were significantly more likely to reject claims, three were more likely to accept them, and four were in line with their peers (Savage, 2008). Thus, there are significant legal barriers to being granted asylum within the United States as demonstrated by the following case study:

Joseph is an Egyptian man, but does not follow the religion of the majority in Egypt; rather, he is Christian. Muslim fundamentalists, with the full cooperation of Egypt's secret police, tried to forcefully convert him and members of his family, including trying to force him to marry a Muslim woman. Due to his refusal to convert and accept the forced marriage, he was detained and tortured. Due to the injuries sustained during the torture, they had to seek treatment for him at a hospital. At this time, Joseph was able to escape from them and flee the country. However, upon landing in the United States, he found that Egyptian authorities had declared him wanted for murder and he was detained upon arrival. During his detention, he came to the attention of Kathleen Lucas, founder of CIRCLE, an agency to assist refugees and asylum seekers. Kathleen helped lead an effort to prevent him from being deported and to obtain his release from prison, including research missions which found the woman Joseph was accused of murdering to be alive. Yet despite this evidence, Joseph remained detained. They secretly flew Joseph's mother to the United States so that she could testify as to the persecution they had faced in Egypt due to their religion at a hearing under the Convention Against Torture. Joseph was granted relief under the Convention Against Torture and his mother was granted asylum due to her testimony, yet still Joseph remained in prison. Finally, after over 8 years of detention, Joseph was allowed to move into the community. However, he remains ineligible for permanent residency due to the false murder accusation, even after his marriage to a US citizen.

The conditions under which most asylum seekers are held continue to be jail-like, although some improvements have been made. The controversial Hutto Family Detention Center in Texas has been closed. This was a former state prison run by a for-profit correctional company to house families of asylum seekers. Children were housed there with their families in a cell with an open toilet. They received only an hour of schooling each day and were threatened by guards with separation from their families. Only judicial intervention permitted them such freedoms as changing into pajamas at night and taking crayons into their cell (Bernstein, 2009).

Those held in detention had great difficulty accessing legal representation because even if they located a person to defend them, they could be transferred to a facility across the country with no warning and were unable to be tracked. To reduce this issue, in 2010, the Immigration and Customs Enforcement agency (ICE) established a locater system on the Internet to allow detainees to be located and, in 2012, issued a new policy establishing criteria for transfers in order to reduce arbitrary decisions (ICE, 2012).

However, conditions for those held in immigration detention remain controversial. The number of those held in immigration detention has exploded to 400,000 in 2012; the majority of them are undocumented immigrants but include asylum seekers as well. More than half of them are held in private, for-profit facilities, increased from 10% only a decade previously. These for-profit facilities are not bound to follow the ICE standards and do not have the same transparency of reporting as is required in the governmental facilities ("Private prisons," 2012). These private companies, also located in Britain and Australia, have been found to commit abuse, as well as lethal neglect, but do not lose their contracts, worth billions of dollars (Bernstein, 2011).

Israel

Israel has been facing an asylum-seeker crisis in recent years. Between 2006 and 2012, the number of people seeking asylum in Israel climbed sharply and reached approximately 60,000 people in this time frame, most of whom were from Eritrea and Sudan. In Eritrea, a repressive dictatorship compels lengthy forced service to the government and persecutes religious minorities and political dissenters. Sudan has been dealing with ongoing conflict, both in the Darfur region and more recently with the newly independent South Sudan. People had not traditionally sought refuge in Israel due to the enormous difficulty in reaching it. They must cross the Sinai Peninsula, where many fall victim to starvation or to Bedouin smugglers who enslave travelers (Paz, 2011). However, this changed after refugees experienced brutality in Egypt by officials (Schwartz & Hetfield, 2013).

Israel is a signatory to the 1951 Refugee Convention, but it has granted refugee status to fewer than 200 people ever (Greenberg, 2012). Between 2009 and 2012, it granted asylum to only 16 people out of 7,000 applications (Kershner, 2012, June 18). It is more likely to grant group protection to people from countries such as Eritrea and Sudan; however, while this allows them to legally remain, they are not allowed to work or receive assistance from the state and therefore struggle to survive (Greenberg, 2012).

Due to the growing influx, there has been a backlash in Israel as some felt that these migrants were not truly asylum seekers but economic migrants. Prime Minister Netanyahu stated that they threatened "the Jewish character of Israel" (Kershner, 2012, June 18, ¶9). In 2009, asylum seekers were forbidden to live and work in cities such as Tel Aviv and Eilat, where many had settled ("African asylum-seekers," 2009; "Asylum-seekers detained," 2009). The growing resentment of Israelis resulted in violent demonstrations, physical attacks, firebombs, and arson, as well as attempts by parents to keep the "infiltrator children" out of school (Greenberg, 2012; "Israel's migration policy," 2012; Kershner, 2012, June 4). In 2012, Israel updated its "Anti-infiltration Law" to state that any attempting to cross the border without proper paperwork would be labeled "infiltrators" and could be detained for up to 3 years. They also built a fence along their border with the Sinai and prohibited entry, even to those seeking asylum, and enforced it with use of tear gas and stun grenades (Greenberg, 2012; Human Rights Watch, 2012b). Eritreans were detained in prisons along the border and were not informed of their right to claim asylum or given the documents to be able to do so. Rather, multiple reports stated that they were being coerced to return to Eritrea or to Uganda ("Imprisoned Eritreans," 2013). This violates Israel's obligations as a signer of the refugee convention as petitioners must have their claims examined and cannot be summarily rejected as this violates the principle of *non-refoulement* (Human Rights Watch, 2012b).

Australia

The treatment of asylum seekers in Australia has been controversial for a number of years. Since 1992, the government has automatically detained all persons attempting to enter the country without proper documents despite the fact that the 1951 Refugee Convention specifically states that people fleeing persecution often cannot follow regular procedures for entering a country and should not receive adverse treatment for arriving in a country without proper paperwork or approval. They were typically detained in remote camps or on the island of Manus (part of Papua New Guinea) and the island state of Nauru. This policy disproportionately affected those arriving by boat (Refugee Council of Australia, 2012a). Those arriving by boat were subjected to open-ended detention, whereas those arriving by airplane were permitted to live in the community while their claim as processed (Siegel, 2011). This was despite the fact that 90% of those arriving by boat were eventually determined to be refugees (Refugee Council of Australia, 2012b). In 2011, the end to the disparity in treatment between those arriving by boat rather than by airplane was announced. Known as the "no advantage" policy, asylum applications are to be processed in the same time period regardless of from where the person applies ("Australia's offshore asylum," 2012).

After 2010, immigration detention swelled again (Pazzano, 2012). In 2012, the government raised the number of refugees it will accept from 13,750 to 20,000 ("New Australian refugee," 2012). However, at the same time, they also reverted to allowing offshore detention in Nauru and Manus for those arriving by boat. Community detention was available only for unaccompanied children and "vulnerable" families (Pazzano, 2012). Australia had hoped to have Malaysia process asylum seekers; however, they are not party to the 1951 Refugee Convention ("Australia asylum bill," 2012). In 2013, the Prime Minister of Australia, Kevin Rudd stated that absolutely no one arriving by boat without a visa would be settled in Australia, even if they were determined to be a genuine refugee. Instead, they would be sent to Papua New Guinea, including the facility on Manus Island ("Australia to send," 2013).

The conditions in the centers in Manus Island and Nauru have drawn condemnation from UNHCR and Amnesty International (UNHCR, 2013d). On Manus Island, detainees are assigned to tin huts with no doors or windows ("Activists rap," 2013). On Nauru, the asylum seekers are housed in army tents with a fan. On both islands, temperatures reach 40 degrees Celsius (104 Fahrenheit) with high humidity, and inside the shelter, it can get even hotter (Amnesty International, 2012a). On Nauru, there is no process to apply for asylum (although the government is working to establish one), nor are there lawyers to assist in the process.

These conditions exacerbate the deterioration of mental health, and suicide attempts have occurred (Amnesty International, 2012a).

Unaccompanied Child Asylum Seekers   The issue of unaccompanied children seeking refuge in new countries has concerned human rights activists for some time. Article 22 of the Convention on the Rights of the Child requires nations to provide protection and assistance to child refugees. Children may have been sent without their parents or other caregivers for a number of reasons: in a bid to keep them safe, because they were separated from their family during the conflict, or because their caregivers may have died in the conflict (Mitchell, 2003). Children of impoverished families are more likely to be caught in the conflict as child soldiers or refugees, while wealthier families are able to send their children abroad to escape the conflict.

A common problem that arises is that of documentation of minor status. Minors must supply documents to prove their age if their appearance does not substantiate their claimed age. Due to their often-sudden departure and the conflict they are fleeing, many lack documentation and may be erroneously referred to adult services, where they will not receive services appropriate to their age (Cemlyn & Briskman, 2003; Mitchell, 2003). They may also have been given an adult's documents to enable them to travel.

Once they arrive in the country where they claim asylum, they typically face additional barriers, including being held in a detention facility. In Australia, some unaccompanied minors were placed in detention facilities, while those in the community lack access to postsecondary education and counseling services (Cemlyn & Briskman, 2003). In contrast, the United Kingdom and the United States have been working to change their detention policies for unaccompanied children.

In 2010, the British government pledged to end the detention of children, including unaccompanied minors. However, subsequent reports found that the practice continued, although the time periods appear to have been considerably shortened to less than 24 hours (Gower, 2013). A study in the United Kingdom found that children are typically detained and subjected to a lengthy interview immediately upon arrival even if they are sick or exhausted. They typically do not have an adult representing them in these procedures, and the information can be used against them in denying their asylum claim (Children's Commissioner, 2012).

In the United States, policies were changed after studies in the early part of this century that found asylum-seeking children were routinely shackled and kept in detention facilities with juvenile offenders or adults. As part of the 2008 Trafficking Victims Protection Act reauthorization, new standards were developed and children now are primarily placed in appropriate residential facilities with access to education and recreation unless they have been documented with criminal or dangerous behavior (Levinson, 2011). However, the legal system is still very difficult to navigate. While 40% of unaccompanied children who enter custody are identified as potentially eligible for legal relief to remain, such as through asylum, ultimately, only 1% of these children are granted such status (Byrne & Miller, 2012).

Services for Affected Populations

Refugee camps, while affording some protection from the upheaval caused by conflict, offer little else. The camps often do not have adequate sanitation, food, or medical care. While groups such as the United Nations and the International Rescue Committee attempt to meet people's needs, there are always more people than money or ability to help them, causing supplies to be inadequate. The close quarters and aforementioned lack of access to adequate health care, food, or water cause disease to be rampant. Diseases such as malaria, diarrhea, and typhoid become common in refugee camps, raising mortality rates, especially in children (Meleigy, 2010; Zwi et al., 2006). Support for the deleterious mental health consequences is extremely limited, if available at all.

The limited supplies may also not reach the people who need them due to denial of humanitarian access by combatants. In some areas, combatants will refuse to allow resources such as food or medicine to reach civilians affected by the conflict, exacerbating the situation. For example, in a region of Somalia, a blockage of humanitarian access by rebels affected 3.5 million people who were also dealing with famine. In Syria, hospitals were attacked by government forces; medical workers were threatened for suspicion of having provided medical care to the opposition (United Nations Security Council, 2012a).

In some cases, refugees are unable to return to their home country and are assisted with resettlement in a new country. The United

States accepted the highest number of refugees for resettlement in 2011: 51,500 (UNHCR, 2012). However, the new laws created as a result of the attack in the United States on September 11, 2001, have reduced the number of refugees eligible to resettle in the United States. The Patriot Act and the Real ID Act both ban entry to the United States to anyone who belongs to, or has provided material support to, armed rebel groups. This requirement does not vary if the rebel groups fought alongside US troops or opposed governments to which the United States government was opposed, or if the group is not considered to be a terrorist organization. This has created great difficulty for Iraqis and Afghanis who have worked for the US government while US troops were in the country. Once the troops leave the country, those who assisted them are typically targets for the opposition. However, they are frequently prohibited from being granted refugee status within the United States for having fought against the previous government. As of late 2012, visas for only 50 of the 6,000 Afghan interpreters had been approved (Sieff, 2013).

While all immigrants to a new country face challenges in adapting to a new culture, refugees and asylum seekers face special barriers (Suárez-Orozco, 2001). They have not chosen to leave their home country but were forced to migrate. All that was familiar and comfortable has been lost. There is often an economic impact, as professionals in their home country are often not granted equivalent status in their new country and may be forced to work multiple low-wage jobs for economic survival, resulting in financial stress as well as emotional stress from the loss of status. For example, Italy grants asylum to a fairly high number of applicants (40%–50%); however, there is a lengthy waiting list to receive support in resettlement. This leaves refugees to figure out the school systems, health care, and how to find employment on their own or with volunteers (Povoledo, 2012).

Asylum-granting countries within the Global North often have very different cultures than those from which the refugee is fleeing. These cultural differences, including differences in the treatment of women and expectations of children, can create strife within the family as some family members become more acculturated than others. Refugees who look different from the majority in the host country may experience discrimination (Suárez-Orozco, 2001).

Because they have been granted the status of refugee, it can typically be assumed that they have suffered trauma. The trauma may have been inflicted upon them or upon those dear to them and often results in long-term psychological impacts. Basic trust in humankind has often been lost, and survivors will be mistrustful, especially of those in positions of authority. This group may also have suffered torture, and this should be assessed. Engstrom and Okamura (2004) note that the experience of torture often goes undocumented, and the unaddressed trauma can cause problems for the individual and family.

Women can experience unique impacts. If resettled in a Western nation, they are often expected to become economically independent, including being able to get around by themselves. Due to their experiences in their home country, they may not have had the opportunity to get an education, learn to drive, or develop employment skills, which can inhibit their ability to become self-sufficient in their new country. They may not feel comfortable going out by themselves or understand the day care system (Deacon & Sullivan, 2009).

Youth who migrate with their families may have a difficult time adjusting. Although they have the support of their families, there may be tensions with their parents as they try to adapt to the new culture. These children may wish to fit in with their peers, yet their parents may desire that they maintain their native culture and values. Furthermore, there will often be financial difficulties in the new country because working parents are typically not able to obtain employment at their previous level from their home country. Parents can also be coping with their own trauma and adjustment issues and may not be available as a support for their children. Xenophobia in the new country may also be a barrier to successful adjustment. Children's education can also be affected if they do not speak the language of the new country or if schooling is at a different grade level than it would be in their home country. Refugee children may also be bullied by other children ("No school today," 2012).

Children who arrive as unaccompanied minors have additional issues, including the impact of trauma-related mental health issues. Living in a state of fear can create permanent trauma for children if it is not addressed. The separation from parents can exacerbate this trauma. Children who arrive unaccompanied are more likely to have higher levels of trauma and stress than those who arrive with family (Barrie & Mendes, 2011). Children can overcome this trauma, but it requires culturally sensitive care, including supportive caregivers and a secure community (Machel, 2001). They may also be dealing with uncertainty about their legal status within the country. In the United Kingdom, about half of this population is permitted to remain only until their 18th birthday (Barrie & Mendes, 2011).

Even if these children are granted refugee status, the difficulties for these children are not yet over because they then face the stress of acclimating to a new country, a new culture, and often a new language. In some cases, symptoms of PTSD do not start developing until 8–10 months after resettlement as they become comfortable in their new surroundings and begin to process the trauma to which they have been subjected (Schmidt, 2005). In addition, they frequently have the stress of concern for those who have remained behind and are still in danger (Cambridge & Williams, 2004). They must also cope with concerns around basic needs. It was found that in Scotland that unaccompanied children were sometimes placed in homeless shelters. In other cases, they were housed for extended periods of time in hotels, which left them isolated and unable to cook for themselves. This is an important need for children who miss the food of their native culture or have dietary needs, such as Muslim children who require halal meat (Hopkins & Hill, 2010).

Conflict Diamonds and Conflict Minerals

Conflict diamonds are defined by the United Nations as "rough diamonds used by rebel movement to fight legitimate governments" (Thomas, 2012, ¶1). They received notoriety as a result of the 2006 film *Blood Diamond*. Most commonly associated with the conflict in Sierra Leone, the purchases of these diamonds by consumers in the Western world helped to fuel the conflict there. To help regulate the trade, and to assure that these purchases were not financing the type of atrocities described in this chapter, the Kimberley Process was developed. This agreement between the United Nations, the European Union, 74 national governments, the World Diamond Council, and a number of NGOs created a

certification to consumers that their purchases did not meet the definition of a conflict diamond (Armstrong, 2011).

However, it has not been as successful as hoped. It has largely been
self-policing and has not evolved to address the use of diamonds to fund
other human rights abuses, including those by sitting governments. While
the war in Sierra Leone has now ended, there continue to be concerns
around the world about continuing human rights abuses funded by
these sales.

In 2011, Global Witness, a leading NGO involved in the Kimberley
Process, pulled out after purchases of diamonds were authorized from an
area in Zimbabwe where numerous human rights violations were committed by the Zimbabwean army, including the murder of 200 miners
(Global Witness, 2011). In 2012, there was an attempt to expand the
definition to "rough diamond used to finance armed conflict or 'other
situations' relating to violence affecting diamond-mining areas"; however,
this was not successful (Thomas, 2012, ¶1).

More recently, the role of "conflict minerals" coming out of
Democratic Republic of the Congo has been highlighted. The minerals tungsten, tin, and coltan are needed for the manufacture of such
items as laptops and cell phones. However, it has been found that the
profits from these purchases were funding armed groups, thus fueling
the conflict in Democratic Republic of the Congo as was seen in Sierra
Leone (Global Witness, n.d.). Both the rebel groups and the militias
have carried out mass atrocities against civilians for control of areas
with minerals (Zongwe, 2012). To attempt to address this, laws have
been passed by the European Union Parliament, Australia, and the
United States, requiring disclosure of the supply chain of these minerals
(KPMG, 2012).

The Professional Role of Social Workers

Social workers can work with refugees and asylum seekers in countries
in the Global North, as well as in countries from which people are
fleeing and their neighboring countries. The issues will vary depending
upon where one engages them. In countries of refuge in the Global
North, the immediate fears of danger have ebbed and cultural difficulties

will dominate, as well as dealing with the physical and psychological aftermath.

The ability of social workers to work on the macro level to develop effective policy or coordinate culturally appropriate services combines well with our abilities on the mezzo and micro levels to work with people who have experienced trauma to help them resolve it. Social workers can work with many different types of organizations in this field. The United Nations, international NGOs such as Médecins Sans Frontières/Doctors Without Borders, and advocacy organizations and local service providers are all potential employers. Due to our broad training, social workers are able to work directly with victims of war and conflict, advocate for better policies affecting this population, and conduct research on issues of concern; these are only a few options. As with most areas of international social work, starting as an intern or volunteer is an excellent way to get experience in this competitive area. Another strong skill is the ability to speak a language other than English.

Conclusion

The impact of a regional conflict is felt worldwide in our globalized world. Social workers in the United States work with refugees and asylum seekers and must be knowledgeable about the impact that conflict has had on their lives and the trauma they may have suffered. The impact will vary by where they are from and whether they are male or female, adult or child. We must be prepared to help them resolve their trauma so they can begin to reconstruct their lives.

Culture Box
COLOMBIA

Although Colombia's ongoing conflict does not receive much attention in the world press, Colombia has the world's largest population of IDPs—approximately 3.9 million. This is almost double the number reported in the first edition of this book. Additionally, approximately 400,000 have fled to other nations (UNHCR, 2013e). However, these are only the number of people who are officially registered and the actual number is likely much higher. The NGO *Consultoría para los Derechos Humanos y el Desplazamiento* has recorded over 5 million displaced (Internal Displacement Monitoring Centre [IDMC], 2011). These figures had been shrinking, but then reversed course sharply in 2011 (International Committee of the Red Cross [ICRC], 2012). Médecins Sans Frontières (2006) notes that Colombians, when referring to displacement, do not use the phrase *estar desplazado*, which would indicate a temporary displacement. Instead, they use *ser desplazado*, which indicates a permanent state of being, for even those who are able to return home are permanently affected by the displacement.

The roots of the violence in Colombia are difficult to untangle and stem from a variety of sources, but the social and political exclusion of the poor is a driving force (Refugees International, 2005a). During colonialism, land was unequally divided, with the wealthy colonists having the largest proportion of the best land. The upper class consisted of predominately White, locally born landowners, while those in the lower class were primarily *mestizo* (mixed-race) laborers and farmers (Loughna, 2002). This inequality continued after independence from Spain in 1810. Colombian society continued to be highly stratified, with divisions based on types of employment, wealth, and Spanish heritage. It is one of the countries with the worst inequality levels in the world (World Bank, 2011). This social stratification has helped drive the violence. What follows is a basic explanation of a complex problem.

After independence, two political parties were formed: the Liberals and the Conservatives. The Liberals supported free trade, a federal government, and secularism; in contrast, the Conservatives wanted a central-ized authoritarian government and strong Roman Catholicism and tended to favor the landed elite (Loughna, 2002). In the late 1940s, the assassination of the leading Liberal party presidential candidate resulted in a mass uprising. This helped trigger a period known as *La Violencia* (The Violence) from 1948 to 1958. In 1958, the Liberal and Conservative parties developed a power-sharing system known as the National Front, which ended *La Violencia*, but due to its elite nature, it shut out the disenfranchised (the peasants). The peasants had survived *La Violencia* by moving to uninhabited areas of the country. They cleared their land for farming only to have it taken by the government. These rural dwellers decided that their only chance to achieve social justice was to wage a guerrilla war. The basic goal was agrarian reform, but they also were fighting for improved services, social equality, and improved distribution of income. The organization was formalized in 1964 as FARC (*Fuerzas Armadas Revolucionarias de Colombia*—Colombian Revolutionary Armed Forces). In that same year, another rebel group, ELN (*Ejército de Liberación Nacional*—National Liberation Army), was formed by university students on the principles of guerrilla warfare. During the 1960s these rebel groups remained in the rural areas of the nation and focused on achieving their goals of social justice.

However, they controlled these areas through terror and intimidation of local peasants, including such acts as kidnapping, murder of civilians, torture, and forced recruitment (IDMC, 2006). In 1974, the National Front power-sharing scheme was dissolved, but fundamental issues affecting the poor remained unresolved and the rebel groups fought on. In the 1970s and 1980s, the coca trade boomed, fueled by Americans' and Europeans' desire for cocaine as well as the drop in coffee prices (IDMC, 2006). Many of the rural peas-ants migrated to FARC-controlled areas to grow coca and to make money. This source of wealth provided

(continued)

the income they had long sought. However, the drug trade soon brought increased problems: Drug-related violence increased, drug barons bought up large farms to grow coca, and the production of food decreased as fields were used to grow coca instead of crops. FARC and ELN have now largely abandoned their original social justice goals and are focused on the wealth and power to be obtained through the drug trade.

While the rebels and the drug lords were originally in sympathy with each other, this ended as the drug lords became rich, bought land, and became the wealthy land owners against whom the rebels were fighting. The guerrillas began kidnapping family members of the drug lords as a good source of income, and the drug lords and other large landowners formed their own paramilitary armies to fight the guerrillas. However, the paramilitary did not restrict itself to only fighting the guerrillas: They also used this as an excuse to displace whole villages on the premise of fighting rebels, but in actuality to clear the land for the drug lords. These paramilitary forces were also aligned with the government, but the government forces were unable to control them. In 1989, membership in paramilitary groups was made illegal, but this did little to diminish their numbers or influence. The paramilitary forces were also known for human rights violations, including massacres, torture, and mass displacement. They engaged in "social cleansing," killing those of whom they disapproved, including homosexuals, the homeless, prostitutes, and drug addicts (IDMC, 2006).

There was a major demobilization of the paramilitary groups in the mid-2000s; however, since that time, new groups have emerged and are now causing displacements as well (IDMC, 2011). The government refers to these groups as "criminal gangs" (bandas criminales, commonly referred to as Bacrim) and does not recognize them as part of the ongoing conflict (Amnesty International, 2011). Many of the leaders of these new groups were mid-level commanders in the previous groups, but either did not demobilize or demobilized fraudulently (Human Rights Watch, 2010). These groups are much more disparate and less unified than the previous paramilitaries, but they operate in many of the same manners, including such human rights violations as violence, sexual violence, and "social cleansing" (Amnesty International. 2011).

While in many countries, fighting would be the primary cause of displacement, in Colombia, it is threats by the armed forces (IDMC, 2011). Threats have been increasing as the reason for displacement in recent years as compared to murders of loved ones, which have been decreasing (IDMC, 2011). Other reasons include fighting, sexual violence, and potential recruitment of children to fight (ICRC, 2012). Recruitment and use of children in armed groups is "widespread and systematic" according to the United Nations Special Representative of the Secretary-General for Children and Armed Conflict (2012, ¶2). All three of the factions fighting in Colombia use child soldiers, but the vast majority are fighting for FARC (United Nations Security Council, 2012a). Children as young as 8 years old are recruited by FARC, typically by force, and face severe punishment if they attempt to return home. The guerrilla groups have a relatively high use of females, with one-quarter to one-half of their soldiers being females (Human Rights Watch, 2003). FARC has refused to even engage in talks on their use of child soldiers.

Sexual violence has been widespread in the conflict. The United Nations Special Representative of the Secretary-General on Sexual Violence in Conflict (2012b, p. 1) noted that the Constitutional Court in Colombia stated that sexual violence was "a habitual, extensive, systematic and invisible practice in the context of the Colombian armed conflict, perpetrated by all of the illegal armed groups and in isolated cases, by individual agents of the national armed forces." Sexual violence is often used to force displacement of people from areas desired for their mining or agricultural wealth or for movement of drugs. She stated that that women and children are systematically targeted, particularly by FARC and the Bacrim. However, reporting is very low due not only to the shame and stigma, but fear of retribution. Confidence in the government to pursue justice is very low as in the cases that have been reported there is typically little investigation and even fewer prosecutions (Amnesty International, 2011).

(continued)

Colombia's laws governing services to those who have been internally displaced are among the most advanced in the world, but they have not been fully implemented and Colombia's Constitutional Court has decreed the governmental response to be inadequate and unconstitutional (IDMG, 2011; UNHCR, 2006b). Seventy percent of IDPs have two or more unmet basic needs, including housing, basic sanitation, and school enrollment, compared to only 10% of urban dwellers (IDMC, 2006). Almost all (99%) of those displaced live below the poverty line as compared to 29% of nondisplaced persons; 83% live in extreme poverty compared to 8.7% of nondisplaced (Albuja & Ceballos, 2010). Due to difficulties with registration and bureaucracy, it can take up to 2 years for IDPs to begin receiving the assistance to which they are entitled (Albuja & Ceballos, 2010).

Those who have fled to the cities have difficulty re-establishing themselves. Those who do register receive only 3 months of assistance, such as emergency food and supplies. The displaced typically experience stigmatization in the urban areas to which they have fled; residents believe that these displaced persons are trying to "take advantage of the situation and try to get some free assistance." They wonder what the displaced "have done to feel so threatened. Maybe they are guerrillas themselves" (Médecins Sans Frontières, 2006, p. 30). This stigma makes it even more difficult for them to re-establish themselves after displacement.

Therefore, these people have great difficulty meeting their survival needs. They typically reside in illegal urban settlements where exploitation is common and threats to safety remain. Women and girls are vulnerable to sexual violence and youth face recruitment from the armed groups (Refugees International, 2012). Women may also have to engage in transactional sex in order to obtain goods for their families' survival (Refugees International, 2009). Many children are among the displaced, and they have great difficulty accessing the national educational system, often due to associated costs such as uniforms, books, or transportation (IDMC, 2006).

The impact on family structure has been noticeable. Approximately three-quarters of IDPs are from rural areas where the traditional patriarchal family structure predominates. However, displacement frequently negatively impacts it. The male head of household may have been murdered or forced to flee separately from his family. Even for families that remain intact, the change in life in the urban environment can have a negative impact. Many of these men were small-scale farmers, with skills unsuited to an urban environment. Therefore, the woman will frequently have to become employed in order to bring money into the family. The loss of the provider role negatively impacts the man, while the increase in responsibilities negatively impacts the woman (Vélez & Bello, 2010).

Those most disproportionately affected by displacement are the traditionally most vulnerable and stigmatized groups: the indigenous people and Afro-Colombians. They constitute almost one-third of IDPs, despite their relatively small share of the population (IDMC, 2011). This disproportionate impact is due largely to the fact that these peoples were the most likely to be living in the affected rural areas, where there is commercial interest or the potential for drug production. Additionally, their skills are ill-suited for the urban environments to which they fled for safety, and they struggle to survive. The indigenous and Afro-Colombians have lower rates of employment and are less likely to be earning the minimum salary when they do find work. This is even more pronounced for women than for men. These groups also have lower rates of adequate housing and education than other IDPs (IDMC, 2011).

The displacement and persecution threaten the loss of their traditional culture. Many of these people traditionally have not had government identification, but they may be considered by paramilitary groups to be rebel sympathizers and face persecution if they cannot show identification (Spindler, 2003). One group noted that in the city to which they had fled, they lived in substandard conditions, families broke up, girls began working in the sex trade, and employment was difficult to find. They desperately wanted to return to their land, stating, "A *campesino* without land is like a fish without water. We need land to

(continued)

survive and maintain ourselves" (Refugees International, 2005b, ¶8). Therefore, some decided to return even though it was not yet safe.

The aim of the government of Colombia is to return to their homes those who have been displaced, but this is difficult due to the continuing violence. Many do not want to return, and those who do have too little support to ensure their safety. Many returned civilians have been forced to flee again due to continuing instability in their home regions or because their land has become occupied by someone else in their absence (Refugees International, 2006). The vast majority of those displaced do not want to return if security concerns remain (IDMC, 2011; Lidchi, Tombs, Magalheas, & Lopez, 2004).

The governmental response to the situation of the IDPs has improved under the presidency of Juan Manuel Santos. In 2011, the Victims and Land Restitution Act was passed to provide compensation to those who had been displaced. If implemented correctly, it could return millions of acres of land to its rightful owners and provide justice to survivors of sexual violence. However, there are a number of limitations in the law. As the government does not recognize the *Bacrim* as paramilitaries in the conflict, those who experience violations at their hands are not eligible for restitution (Amnesty International, 2012c). Additionally, only those who lost their lands after 1991 will be eligible to gain them back (Amnesty International, 2012c). Advocates for land restitution and against sexual violence working against these and other barriers have been targets for murder (Amnesty International, 2012b; IDMC, 2011).

The physical and mental health of Colombians has obviously been affected. For many years, violence was the leading cause of death for both men and women in Colombia (Médecins Sans Frontières, 2006). While it is no longer the number one cause, it remains one of the primary causes (International Association of National Public Health Institutes, 2013). Due to the conflict, it is difficult for health providers to reach rural residents, increasing their health needs. Those who have fled their homes will settle in urban slums, with the health risks associated with such living conditions. Médecins Sans Frontières (2006) has noted the high level of physical symptoms associated with stress during medical examinations; patients frequently state that they have headaches, neck pain, back pain, and difficulty sleeping, among other symptoms. Rural villagers live in a high state of fear due to the frequent acts of violence that occur in their area. The children often have behavioral issues, such as being highly aggressive or withdrawn, and have difficulty concentrating in school.

The mental health implications of this trauma are far-reaching. Patients of Médecins Sans Frontières frequently state that they need to tell their story, indicating the high need for mental health services to assist in resolving the trauma. Médecins Sans Frontières psychologists have found that half of their consultations in the urban areas are triggered by experiences of violence; 37% of patients had experienced the murder of a close family member and 10% had a family member "disappear." One study found that 52% of displaced women had suffered physical violence and 36% had suffered sexual violence (IDMC, 2006).

Mental health providers have worked to provide services in a manner that is accessible and effective for the population. As those in rural areas have limited access to mental health services, Médecins Sans Frontières has developed a mobile clinic. However, due to the instability and geography, they are unable to provide regular ongoing visits and therefore have developed a single-session model for intervention. The vast majority reported improvement at the end of the session (Urrego, Abaakouk, Roman, & Contreras, 2009).

The family biogram has been found to be useful in working with those who have been internally displaced (Lidchi et al., 2004). This tool maps medical, socioeconomic, employment, and housing data over a longitudinal period. Themes have included changes in family structure, living conditions, trauma and loss, and available resources. This tool is useful to the family as it helps them examine how they have coped.

The needs in Colombia are great. The violence has been going on so long that most citizens cannot remember a time when it did not occur. As of 2013, talks for peace were occurring between the government and FARC, focused on land reform; however, progress has been described only as "modest" ("Columbia peace talks," 2013).

What You Can Do Now

- Volunteer to teach English as a Second Language.
- Intern at an agency serving refugees and asylum seekers.
- Visit asylum seekers detained in prisons.
- Lobby for humane laws for asylum seekers.
- Write letters to media outlets asking them to cover stories relevant to refugees and asylum seekers to help others become aware of their plight.
- Volunteer or intern at an agency serving survivors of sexual assault.
- Support organizations such as Beyond the 11th by fundraising, screening a showing of their documentary, or other ways noted on their Web site
- Make sure diamond sales and purchases adhere to the Kimberley Process. Tell those you know if they must buy diamonds, to buy only from stores that certify they are conflict-free.
- Look at the company from where you buy your electronics. Do they certify they are not using conflict minerals?

What You Can Do as a Professional Social Worker

- Work for an organization helping to resettle refugees and asylum seekers in the United States.
- Work to create policies for more humane treatment of asylum seekers.
- Work for an international organization such as UNHCR or ICRC.
- Work in refugee areas to provide services in or near their home countries.
- Provide mental health services through an organization such as International Rescue Committee or Doctors Without Borders/ Médecins Sans Frontières.

World Wide Web Resources

Bridging Refugee Youth and Children's Services (www.brycs. org): Provides information for social service practitioners working with refugees, especially children.

Doctors Without Borders/Médecins Sans Frontières (www.dwb. org; www.msf.org): Their Web site provides information about the countries in which they work and the services they provide.

Forced Migration Online (www.forcedmigration.org): Provides access to a variety of online resources relating to forced migration. Offers a variety of resources, including a focus on international law.

Internal Displacement Monitoring Centre (www. internal-displacement.org): The leading international body monitoring conflict-induced internal displacement worldwide. They provide information regarding people who have been internally displaced.

International Rescue Committee (www.theirc.org): Works around the world to provide assistance to refugees, both in emergency situations and assisting in resettlement programs.

Refugee Council USA (http://www.rcusa.org/): A coalition group of US agencies concerned with refugees and asylum seekers. The Web site has numerous links to information for advocates of this population.

Refugees International (www.refugeesinternational.org): An agency that works as an advocate for refugees both within their home countries and in receiving countries, such as the United States. Provides information about their projects and the situations of refugees around the globe.

United Nations High Commissioner for Refugees (www.unhcr. org): The UN agency in charge of refugee issues. Its main purpose is to lead and coordinate international action to aid refugees to help ensure their rights.

6

AIDS

Article 25 of the Universal Declaration of Human Rights states the right of all people to medical care adequate for their health and well-being. Without this right, people's access to their other rights, including the right to life, is limited. In many nations, including the United States, people's access to medical care is based on their personal financial resources. Examining AIDS in a global context sharply highlights this social injustice.

AIDS, first identified in 1981, has become a worldwide epidemic, growing far beyond initially affected populations. UNAIDS (2012a) states that almost 34 million people are currently living with HIV/AIDS, almost 70% of whom live in sub-Saharan Africa; South/Southeast Asia is the next most affected region. In terms of percentage of population, 5% of those in sub-Saharan Africa are affected, followed by the Caribbean, Eastern Europe, and Central Asia. And yet, even as we look at these numbers, the vast progress that has been made must be acknowledged. The number of AIDS-related deaths has been declining globally due both to the reduced number of new infections and increased access to antiretroviral drugs (UNAIDS, 2012a). The rate of new infections was 20% lower in 2011 than it was in 2001, including a 25% decrease in sub-Saharan Africa. More people are able to access life-saving antiretroviral (ARV) treatment, causing a 25% decrease in mortality from 2005 to 2011 (32% in sub-Saharan Africa) (UNAIDS, 2012a).

However, these numbers mean that the battle can be won, not that it is over. Infection rates in regions such as North Africa/Southwest Asia are rising. Mortality rates are rising in this region as well as Eastern Europe/

Central Asia (UNAIDS, 2012a). Reflecting the shift from initially affected populations, UNAIDS has stated that women and girls "bear the brunt" of AIDS (UNAIDS, 2005a). The proportion of women has risen in every region worldwide and is approximately 50% of those infected globally; in sub-Saharan Africa, it is almost 60% (UNAIDS, 2012a, 2012b). As will be discussed, women are at high risk of this disease for both biological and social reasons. Overall, young people aged 15 to 24 make up 39% of all new infections worldwide (UNICEF, 2012a), while young women are the population determined to be at highest risk. Globally, young women have infection rates twice those of men their age; in sub-Saharan Africa it is almost 2.5 times higher (UNAIDS, 2012b).

AIDS exists in a broad socioeconomic situation that must be considered when developing responses to the disease. UNAIDS (2005b) stated that if AIDS is viewed in isolation as only a medical illness, the epidemic will only worsen. They state that what must be done to eradicate the epidemic is to reduce poverty and increase development and to address the roles of men and women in society, in addition to other macro-level interventions. These issues, seemingly unrelated to a medical disease, are vital to stopping the epidemic.

The Intertwining of AIDS and Poverty

In many parts of the world, high infection rates are caused by factors related to living in poverty. AIDS can also cause a vicious cycle in which it creates further poverty, leading to increased vulnerability. On the micro level, in nations around the world, people in rural areas struggle with poverty and dream of moving to urban areas where they believe they will be able to earn more money. Unfortunately, this economic migration has also led to an increase in HIV infection in countries as diverse as China, Thailand, Haiti, Kazakhstan, and Lesotho.

Often it is the men of the family who will migrate for labor. While they are away from their families, they may engage in activities that put them at high risk for contracting HIV, such as using intravenous drugs and visiting sex workers. When they return to their villages, they bring the disease back with them. The common belief is that AIDS first became widespread in this fashion. A main highway in southern Africa served as a primary trucking route; infected sex workers worked at the main rest areas and subsequently many truck drivers became infected with HIV. Upon returning home, these husbands gave the disease to their wives, posing a risk to subsequent children (Sunmola, 2005). Workers would also migrate to South African mines and bring the disease home in the same fashion; 90% of surveyed HIV-positive men in rural Lesotho had worked in the mines at one point (Furin, 2007, as cited in Furin et al., 2008).

Similarly, during the economic boom of the 1990s, many Thai workers left the rural countryside for the urban areas to find higher paying work. While in the cities, a number of them were infected with AIDS. When these workers returned to the countryside, they also transported the infection (Lim & Cameron, 2004). This economic migration pattern was also seen in India. Truck drivers traveled long distances on the highways and employed sex workers while away from home. They then returned home to their wives and spread the HIV infection (Waldman, 2005). The HIV epidemic has been growing in Central Asia, including Kazakhstan. Among migrant market vendors (both men and women), longer trips to sell one's goods and more frequent travel were significantly associated with multiple sexual partners as well as unprotected sex. Additionally, the workers had low levels of HIV knowledge, especially the women (El-Bassel et al., 2011).

When women migrate for economic reasons, they are also vulnerable to HIV infection. Many of these women end up in the sex trade, since it is typically the highest paid work available to them. Once employed as a sex worker, they earn more money, often to two to three times as much, if they engage in intercourse without using a condom, raising the risk of infection. As a result, female sex workers are 13 times more likely to be infected with HIV than other women (UNAIDS, 2012b).

Poverty affects non-migrating people as well. In China, what is considered to be "the third wave" of AIDS in that country (from about 1994 to 2001) particularly affected the rural poor. Due to the poverty in China's rural areas, these citizens earned extra money by donating blood and plasma to illegal traveling blood banks. These blood banks not only reused needles from donor to donor but would also mix all the blood together before giving it to the recipient. Therefore, if there was any infected blood, both donors and recipients were certain to receive it, causing high rates of infection in these areas (Kanabus, 2005).

On the mezzo level, increased familial poverty is due not only to the money that must be spent on health care and medicine but to lost income as well. AIDS is a particularly devastating disease in that it is centered not in children and the elderly, typically the most vulnerable, but in young and middle-aged adults. As discussed, it is often the men in the family who are infected first. With no access to treatment, the family's income is sharply reduced as the man is typically the primary breadwinner. He may be too ill to work or may be fired due to stigma and discrimination. Even if he is not the first to become ill, he often loses income when taking time off from work to care for the person who is ill (Rajaraman, Russell, & Heymann, 2006). Mothers are often the next in the family to fall ill. With parents too ill to work, the family is in a desperate situation.

The loss of a father often results in lowered income and decreased access to resources such as land; the loss of a mother typically results in increased malnourishment and less care for the children (Commission on HIV/AIDS and Governance in Africa, n.d.). In agrarian societies in southern Africa, fields go untended due to the dire illness of the work-force. This pattern increases malnutrition and poverty, feeding back into the epidemic as medications must be purchased and then taken on a full stomach for optimal effectiveness (Panos, n.d.).

The death of middle-aged parents causes a rise in the number of orphans, straining the traditional kinship care systems. Children are dou-bly affected by AIDS: They are at risk of contracting it from their mothers, and when their parents die from the disease, they are left even closer to poverty. While access to medication to prevent transmission during child-birth has risen and almost 60% of women in low- and middle-income countries receive it, only 30% of them are able to access medication for their own treatment (UNAIDS, 2012a). Illustrating this impact, 3.3 mil-lion children worldwide are estimated to be infected with HIV or AIDS, but an additional 17.3 million (as of 2011) have lost one or both parents to the disease. More than 90% of these children are living in sub-Saharan Africa, putting a huge strain on traditional support systems within the family (UNICEF, 2012a).

Caregivers of these children have reported concerns about the abil-ity to afford food, clothing, health care, and school fees; in addition, the health of the caregivers can deteriorate due to the added stress and bur-den of their caretaking duties. In response, "Granny clubs" have been started in Andhra Pradesh, India, to help grandparents who were car-ing for their grandchildren due to the death of their child from AIDS. Support is offered in a variety of ways: material support, including food and clothing; psychosocial support for grieving and the burdens of raising grandchildren; and childrearing training specific to children affected by HIV. Groups are formed so that members are geographically close to each other so they can attend monthly meetings (Vasavya Mahila Mandali, 2009).

School acts to provide a productive activity for children, keeping them away from high-risk activities, in addition to educating them about the risks of sexual activity. However, the increased poverty in the families of children who have been orphaned often forces the children to leave school for two reasons. First, they often must work to help replace family income; second, they can no longer afford the cost of school. Although some countries have eliminated school fees, these fees remain in other countries or they have been eliminated only for primary school. Even if there is no tuition, there may still be fees for uniforms, texts, and supplies. Some orphans receive financial support for education, but others do not. There are also often unmet needs for adequate food and medical care (Mhaka-Mutepfa, 2010). Some children own only one threadbare outfit and are too embarrassed to attend school due to their lack of adequate clothing.

Examining the impacts from the macro level, in Africa, the structural adjustment policies dictated by the World Bank in order to increase exports and imports for participation in the world economy were financed through large cuts in social services, including education and health care (Commission on HIV/AIDS and Governance in Africa, n.d.). In general, this lack of social services caused by the shift in funding results in less knowledge about HIV/AIDS, fewer protective factors (as will be discussed), and less ability to assist people who have been infected (Tlilane, 2004). The imbalance in global trade resulted in spreading, not reducing, poverty levels, increasing again the risk factors for AIDS (McCoy et al., 2005).

Continuing the cycle of AIDS and poverty, AIDS spreads poverty, which further increases vulnerability on all systems levels. On a macro level, a high HIV infection rate can threaten the development of a nation. As AIDS attacks the working-age population, the impact of the disease can result in loss of economic productivity due to illness and death. There are also fewer consumers to participate in the economy. Children orphaned by AIDS are forced to leave school, reducing the number of potential educated workers and thus the country's economic output.

Some countries have what is known as a hyperepidemic, in which a high percentage, for example, over 15%, is infected with the disease (United Nations Development Programme, n.d.). With such high rates, it raises concerns that countries will be able to continue to function—economically, politically, and socially—if such a high percentage of their population is ill.

The following story, adapted from Paul Farmer (2005) (see Box 6.1), illustrates how personal poverty and structural factors in the culture led one young Haitian woman to die from AIDS:

Acephie was born in the small village of Kayin. The Riviere Arti-bonite, Haiti's largest river, ran through this village. Her family was initially relatively well off. However, her village was flooded to make a dam to provide electricity for the urban Haitians and the villagers were forced up into the stony hills on the sides of the new lake. This new land was not nearly as fertile as their old land and they struggled to survive. Acephie would carry the family's meager agricultural produce to the local market to earn money. The road to the market led past a military barracks and the soldiers often flirted with the girls as they passed. This flirtation was rarely openly rejected, as the soldiers were among the few men with an income in this now poor region. When a captain, Jacques, began to pursue Acephie, she eventually agreed, even though she knew that Jacques was married and had several other partners. The sexual relationship lasted less than a month, as Jacques fell ill and died a few months later of unexplained fevers.

Acephie eventually moved to Port-au-Prince and found a servant's job. She also began seeing a boy, Blanco, with whom she once attended school. He was doing comparatively well chauffeuring a small bus, and they planned to marry. However, when Acephie became pregnant, Blanco was not happy and eventually disappeared from her life. Due to her pregnancy, Acephie lost her job. She returned to her hometown to give birth to her daughter. Shortly thereafter, she soon fell ill and eventually died of AIDS.

BOX 6.1 Paul Farmer

Thanks to the work of Dr. Paul Farmer, a Harvard-trained physician, ideas about treating patients in poor countries have changed. Prior to his work, the common belief in the global health arena was that offering treatment to impoverished people in poor countries would not only be ineffective, as they would not be compliant in taking medications, but it would worsen the epidemic by increasing medication-resistant illnesses. In the early 1980s in rural Haiti, Farmer and his organization, Partners in Health (PIH), established a medical clinic where fees were nominal or nonexistent. Haiti has one of the highest adult HIV infection rate in the Western Hemisphere: 1.8%, equaling about 100,000 people (UNAIDS, 2012a).

Farmer developed a model known as the directly observed treatment model (DOT). In this model, local community members are trained to assist and support HIV/AIDS patients. The DOT model has a third person (who is a local resident) responsible for observing the patient swallowing his or her medication. This local liaison helps the patient with particularly complicated prescriptions or medications with adverse side effects in order to help maintain medication compliance. In Farmer's model, since the third person is also a fellow village member, it decreases the power structure and helps increase trust and community support (D'Adesky, 2004). This person is known as an *accompagnateur* (one who accompanies) to emphasize the equal relationship. This model had great success and demonstrated that if a program was properly structured, individuals in impoverished countries could have higher treatment compliance rates than those in industrialized nations. Partners in Health is the nongovernmental organization providing health care in Haiti and in 2013 opened a 300-bed facility (Partners in Health, n.d.).

Partners in Health now works in 10 countries across five continents and in the Caribbean, fighting not only AIDS, but tuberculosis, cholera, and cancer. They also focus on mental health and how vulnerable populations such as women and children are affected (Partners in Health, 2013a). PIH has a "four pillars" approach to health. The first pillar is to integrate HIV care and treatment with primary health care. For example, PIH has helped to build houses, develop potable water projects, and help people gain access to education (PIH, 2005). The second is a focus on maternal and child health, and the third is to establish tuberculosis control. The fourth is the detection and treatment of sexually transmitted infections. They now provide antiretroviral treatment to more than 20,000 people in Haiti, Rwanda, Lesotho, and Malawi. Additionally, they have also provided survival needs such as housing, water, food, and psychosocial support. In this way, they are able to address the intertwining of poverty and AIDS (Partners in Health, 2013b).

The story of this one Haitian woman illustrates a number of the concepts discussed. Events on the macro level, in this case the building of the dam and the flooding of her family's farm, sharply increased the poverty within the family. This increased poverty, in turn, increased her vulnerability to a relationship with the captain. This brief liaison eventually led to her death from his "mysterious illness." Her story also illustrates how the female gender role increased her risk of becoming infected. It was the man who had greater social power, while she relied on either her family's attempts at farming in the poor soil to which they have been relegated or to a servant's job, which she lost when she became pregnant. Acephie's story demonstrates how factors on the micro, mezzo, and macro levels all contributed to her eventual death.

Fighting Back

Progress is being made in the worldwide battle against the AIDS epidemic, and these victories give hope for the future that this war can be won. A comprehensive plan must be developed in order to effectively target and eliminate this epidemic. UNAIDS states that in order to reduce the sexual transmission of HIV, the following aspects must be targeted: "behaviour change, condom provision, male circumcision, focused programmes for sex workers and men who have sex with men and access to antiretroviral therapy" (2012a, p. 16).

Behavior Change

Behavior change encompasses a broad range of concepts and vulnerable populations that should be addressed. A major factor that shapes the progress of AIDS within a nation is the country's specific culture. Cultural traditions and beliefs can affect the transmission of HIV/AIDS within an ethnic group. Cultural practices that developed to meet traditional needs can become harmful in a rapidly changing society. These traditional beliefs can deter prevention and treatment efforts due to cultural clashes if the intervention efforts are not conducted with knowledge and respect of these traditions. If the information is not presented in a manner that enables the intended recipient to accept it, it will inhibit behavior change.

Addressing the roles of men and women in society is a necessary step in fighting the epidemic (UNAIDS, 2005b). Gender norms can impact transmission, testing, and mortality. Those affecting women are discussed in the next section, but men are also affected. Gender norms can increase the risk of infection for men through glamorizing high-risk practices such as multiple partners or lack of a condom (UNAIDS, 2012a). In many cultures, men are unwilling to admit illness and seek treatment. Thus, they have lower rates of testing and are typically sicker than women when they are formally diagnosed. Once diagnosed, they are less likely to take their medications as they should and therefore have higher mortality rates in a number of nations (UNAIDS, 2012a). One study in Malawi found that men were significantly more likely to be in Stage 4 of the illness when they started treatment, and their mortality rate was twice that of women (Taylor-Smith, Tweya, Harries, Schoutene, & Jahn, 2010).

Unlike in the early days of the disease, women and young adults (especially girls) are now the fastest growing population of those infected. Young people are seen to be at high risk due to ignorance about how HIV is transmitted as well as ways to reduce risk; only 32% of males and 20% of females aged 15–24 years have correct knowledge on these topics. Educational programs have been implemented in numerous countries, and the 15 countries with the highest prevalence rates have seen their rate of young people infected fall by 25% (UNICEF, 2012b).

The risk is particularly high for young women; globally, approximately two-thirds of infections among young people are female. In sub-Saharan Africa, young women are more than twice as likely to be infected as young men (UNICEF, 2012b). Women of all ages are at greater biological and social risk for contracting HIV than men. Biologically, women are two to four times more likely than men to become infected during heterosexual intercourse due to the larger surface area exposed to contact (National AIDS Commission, 2003). This is especially true for young women, who are more apt to become infected than older girls due to their immature physical development (UNAIDS, n.d.a).

Girls are also more likely to be removed from school due to societal expectations for caretaking and household duties, poverty, or marriage than boys, raising their risk of contracting HIV. Orphaned girls are at even higher risk, as girls who have been orphaned are more likely to be withdrawn from school than girls whose parents are alive, and they are also more likely to have had sex (Birdthistle et al., 2009; Kang, Dunbar, Laver, & Padian, 2008). Girls who have lost their father are significantly more likely to have had sex for the first time because they need goods such as food or clothing, while those who have lost their mother are more likely to be HIV-positive (Kang et al., 2008). Orphans, both boys and girls, are also more likely to have sex earlier than nonorphans (Mkandawire, Tenkorang, & Luginaah, 2013).

Girls who are not in school typically have to find a way to meet their basic needs in some manner. This may include marriage to an older man who will pay a good bride price for a young wife, or it may include "survival sex." Survival sex is when a female begins a relationship to help acquire goods she needs or desires. This relationship will often be with an older man. The formal term is "cross-generational relationship," if he is 5 or more years older than her, while the informal term is "sugar daddy." "Sugar mommies" also exist, but they are not as common (Bajaj, 2009). Female orphans are at particular risk for engaging in transactional sex in order to acquire food and clothing (Mmari, Michaelis, & Kiro, 2009). Not all young people will engage in these relationships for simple survival; some also do so in order to gain material goods. This is more common in urban areas, while rural girls are more likely to use them for subsistence purposes (Cockcroft et al., 2010). This is not prostitution, in that she does not engage in intercourse with a variety of men for money, but she will have intercourse with one man who will help provide for her financially.

However, all too often the girl begins a relationship only to find that those promises go unfulfilled and she has been placed at risk for contracting HIV, as the man is rarely faithful to her and she will not have the power in the relationship to insist that he use a condom. Older men are more likely to be infected with AIDS than boys of the same age of the girl. They are also likely to be engaging in multiple sexual relationships at the same time (Wood, 2010). However, Wyrod et al.'s research (2011) in Zimbabwe found sugar daddies to be much less common than supposed and the assumption should not be made that this phenomenon is ubiquitous.

The girl may also be married at a young age. For men who are knowledgeable about methods of transmission of AIDS, young girls and virgins are seen as a safe recourse. Men will marry as young a girl as possible in order to have a wife with the highest likelihood of being disease-free. This has the effect of pulling girls out of school at a young age, reducing not only their educational opportunities but also the aforementioned protective factors that school provides. In some cultures, grooms will pay the bride's family a bride price; typically, the younger the bride, the higher the bride price. Again, the link between poverty and increased vulnerability to HIV infection becomes evident, as impoverished families are more likely to need the funds and agree to the early marriage. Early marriage often places girls at higher risk for contracting HIV rather than offering them protection from it. In addition to these young girls being at higher risk biologically for contracting HIV after exposure to it, their older husbands are more likely to be infected with HIV and less willing to use a condom (Hageman et al., 2010; Hindin & Fatusi, 2009).

In order to help combat this and create the needed behavior change, interventions have been designed to affect the root cause: poverty. Unconditional cash transfers have been found to be an effective means of reducing risky behaviors and increasing protective ones for young people. These cash transfers have been found to reduce sexual activity and pregnancy, delay first intercourse among girls, decrease the number who had more than one sexual partner in the previous year, significantly lower HIV rates, lower dropout rates, and reduce absenteeism ("Cash payments," 2012; Department of Social Development, South African Social Security Agency, & UNICEF, 2012; Pettifor, MacPhail, Nguyen, & Rosenberg, 2012).

Based on the right of social protection in the Universal Declaration of Human Rights, Kenya offers its most vulnerable citizens cash assistance each month. Young adults whose families received assistance were more likely to delay initiation of intercourse, and when they did have sex, they were more likely to use protection and to have fewer partners. They were also more likely to stay in school (Shaban, 2012). A program in Zimbabwe provided participants with school fees, supplies, and uniforms, as well as helpers at each school to monitor attendance and assist with overcoming barriers to attendance. The school dropout rate was significantly lower among participants than the randomized control group, as was early marriage (Hallfors et al., 2011; Miller, Hallfors, Cho, Luseno, & Waehrer, 2013). However, when this intervention was attempted in Kenya, it was not as successful, possibly due to students being overage for their grade (Hallfors, Cho, Mbai, Milimo, & Itindi, 2012).

Some children and youth are at higher risk than others. Street children are one such population. They are more likely to use drugs and engage in sexual activity, including risky sexual behaviors, than other children. These risky behaviors vary some by gender, although children of both sexes engage in both behaviors. Girls tend to be at higher risk for sexual transmission of AIDS as they are likely to engage in high-risk sexual activity: involuntarily, for money, or willingly. Male street children tend to be at higher risk for HIV infection through intravenous drug use, although they also engage in risky sexual activity. Research in countries as diverse as Egypt, Ukraine, Nepal, and the Democratic Republic of the Congo have noted these trends (Busza et al., 2011; Karmacharya et al., 2012; Nada & Suliman, 2010; "Reducing the HIV risk," 2012).

The following two stories help illustrate the risks faced by street children and how they can result in HIV infection. Pham Huy Hoang, a 17-year-old boy in Vietnam, left his home to live in Hanoi, the capital city, so that he could work to financially assist his family. Some of his new friends in the city convinced him to try injecting drugs. Due to his lack of education, he did not know that this activity could give him HIV. In time, he discovered he had become HIV-positive (Van & Dung, 2006).

In the Democratic Republic of the Congo, Sarah is 16 years old but has been living on the street since she was about 8, soon after her mother died. She found out that sexual assault was commonplace and that if she screamed, she would just be beaten. Selling sex is necessary for survival and she says that while men offer USD$1, with negotiation, that can be raised to USD$10. She bears the scars from where she was attacked by a group of girls with a razor. Services are difficult to offer to girls like Sarah because typically reintegration with their families is not an option due to abuse in the family or rejection of what the girl has done to survive ("Reducing the HIV risk," 2012). Aide à l'Enfance Défavorisée, together with its international partner Médecins du Monde, provides a mobile health clinic as well as a drop-in center. At the drop-in center, girls can learn vocational skills, such as tailoring. Music is also used as a therapeutic tool. Girls are typically raped about twice a week; music and dance help them reconnect to their bodies in a positive way ("Reducing the HIV risk," 2012).

Women   As noted earlier, women are at higher risk of being infected with HIV in many nations due to cultural impacts. This is seen most vividly in sub-Saharan Africa, where 60% of those infected are female. Girls and young women were discussed earlier, but increasing age does not decrease the risk. Women of all ages are at higher risk of HIV infection than their male counterparts. Socially, women are all too often not in a position to control what happens to their bodies due to cultural traditions and financial difficulties. Practices throughout the life span such as female genital cutting, early marriage, and traditions relating to widowhood expose females to the risk of HIV infection. Women are often in a position of cultural social inferiority, which limits their ability to protect themselves against infection, including following HIV-prevention strategies such as the ABC model.

The public health motto that has been used to help promote the prevention of HIV infection is the ABC model: A, abstinence; B, be faithful; C, use condoms. This model is effective if both partners abide by its tenets. However, women often do not have the cultural standing to insist on abstinence, faithfulness, or condom use. Due to epidemic violence against women, including intimate partner violence, women often find themselves impotent when it comes to HIV prevention (Rosenberg, 2006). Women who experience coerced or forced sexual initiation, as well as sexual intimate partner violence, are at a significantly higher risk to contract HIV (Stockman, Lucea, & Campbell, 2013).

Since women are often not in a position of power to negotiate safer sexual practices, marriage therefore can actually become a risk factor for HIV infection. UNAIDS (2005c) reports that many women who develop new HIV infections are in a relationship, typically marriage, in which they are faithful to that partner. However, that partner is often not faithful to them and the woman is unable to insist on the use of condoms.

Women's empowerment has been found to correlate with reduced dependence on male partners and improved decision-making power (UNAIDS, 2012b). This was supported by a study in Ghana that found an association between women's sexual empowerment and use of contraceptives. Women with higher levels of education, with greater wealth, and who were unmarried were all more likely to report the use of contraceptives (Crissman, Adanu, & Harlow, 2012). Education has been found to be particularly important as women with higher levels of education delay sexual initiation, have fewer partners once they do have sex, and are more likely to use condoms both before and after marriage (Adamczyk & Greif, 2011; Tenkorang, 2012; Zuilkowski & Jukes, 2011).

Microfinance, discussed in Chapter 7, has been found to help empower women in a variety of contexts. Therefore, it would stand to reason that it could be used to help combat these conditions that can further spread AIDS. This is supported by a study in South Africa, which found that HIV education paired with microfinance created both economic improvements as well as higher levels of empowerment and lower levels of intimate partner violence and HIV risk behaviors (Kim et al., 2009).

New prevention strategies are also being developed that women can control, rather than relying on male cooperation. A microbicide, typically a gel or cream, is being tested that women can insert in their vagina to help prevent HIV infection. Women who tried it in South Africa liked the fact that it could be hidden from their boyfriends and it was under their control (Rosenberg, 2006). This method would rely only on the woman to protect herself and she would be able to do so unobtrusively. There are currently several in clinical trials that show promise in preventing HIV transmission. Results to date have been mixed, due at least in part to lack of regular use (Cairns, 2013).

Traditions relating to widowhood can also increase HIV risk in the current social context. In some African societies when a man dies, his property reverts not to his wife but to his family of origin. This custom developed from the concept that the man is the breadwinner of the family and the property of a married couple represents the fruits of his labor and thus should return to his family, as his wife did not contribute to it. Fights between wives in a polygamous household are also eliminated through this custom. However, this loss of material goods pushes a family further into poverty and has now been outlawed in multiple African countries.

Swaziland and Zimbabwe both passed laws in 2005 that provide more rights to women. In Swaziland, the new constitution makes women the legal equivalents of men, while Zimbabwe's law allows them to inherit property from their husbands and fathers (LaFraniere, 2005). Botswana's high court overturned a customary law that prohibited women from inheriting the family home ("Botswana women," 2012). However, even if the widow is aware of her rights, she is typically unable to secure legal representation to assert those rights due to lack of availability or poverty. Organizations such as the Zimbabwe Widows and Orphans Trust, the Federation of Women Lawyers Kenya, and the Rwanda Women's Network have been formed to help women in these matters ("Protecting widows," 2007; UNAIDS, n.d.b).

In some parts of sub-Saharan Africa, when a husband dies, his wife must have intercourse with a designated "widow cleanser" to ensure that his spirit does not return to the village and haunt them. However, if the husband died of AIDS, his wife will typically be infected as well. She can pass the infection to the widow cleanser, who can infect subsequent widows. Culturally, women feel they must have this procedure; thus, they are not a good target for intervention, due to their lack of societal power. Therefore, interventions with widow cleansers have been developed. Progress is being made, and some have left the profession as a result (Curnow & Watts, 2013).

Some areas of sub-Saharan Africa practice the tradition of "widow inheritance" in which the widow is taken as a wife by a relative of her deceased husband, typically a brother or cousin. The inheritor also performs certain required sexual rituals with the widow. If these rituals are not performed, she may lose her property. While this is intended to act as a social and financial safety net for the widow and her children (Phiri, 2002), it can act to spread HIV to new partners. In recent years, fewer relatives are willing to inherit a widow due to the growing stigma of the practice as a result of AIDS campaigns, the economic burden, and exposure to Western culture. As a result, professional inheritors, known as *jokowiny*, have emerged so women can complete the required rituals (Agot et al., 2010). However, this increases the risk further. Widows who are inherited by nonrelatives for sexual ritual purposes have more than twice the risk of being HIV-positive than widows who were not inherited; widows inherited by a relative for sexual ritual purposes were 1.34 times more likely to be positive. However, widows inherited by relatives for companionship purposes were *less* likely to be HIV-positive than uninherited women (Agot et al., 2010).

As noted, cultural traditions that place women at biological risk of HIV infection, such as widow cleansing and widow inheritance, or social risk, such as loss of property upon their husband's death, have been targets for intervention. However, Gausset (2001, p. 511) notes that Westerners are often quick to point fingers at African cultural traditions and practices that can increase the risk of HIV/AIDS while being less willing to look at their own practices. He states, "Today in the West, AIDS prevention campaigns do not suggest that homosexuals or drug addicts have to stop being homosexuals or drug addicts; rather they advise them to make their practices safer—to use condoms and clean needles." He states that similarly, the problem is not about whether people practice monogamy or polygamy; the problem is unfaithfulness outside of the marital arrangement.

Preventing the transmission of HIV from pregnant and breast-feeding women to their children (Preventing Mother-to-Child Transmission—PMTCT) has been a major global focus in recent years and has resulted in marked drops in infection rates. In 2011, 57% of pregnant women globally received this treatment (UNAIDS, 2012b). Barriers such as lack of access to medical care due to poverty or distance, lack of access to clean water for formula, and stigma experienced from health workers can reduce women's ability to access the needed care ("Eliminate bottlenecks," 2010; UNAIDS, 2012b). Including men in PMTCT programs such as antenatal attendance has been found to significantly decrease the rate of HIV infection among infants (Aluisio et al., 2011). South Africa has seen marked success in this area, reducing infection rates of newly born infants to 2.7% from 8% between 2008 and 2012 ("Mother-to-child," 2012). However, caution must be taken as disclosure of HIV-positive status can increase a woman's risk of experiencing partner violence ("The downside," 2012). Additionally, marketing campaigns can lead to the idea that women who give birth in health care facilities rather than at home must be HIV-positive, resulting in women avoiding them for fear of stigma ("Study shows," 2012).

Stigma   Behavior change is necessary not only among those who have HIV or are at risk of infection but also the broader society. Stigma against those with HIV or AIDS has been documented around the world with varying impacts such as loss of employment, being gossiped about, experiencing verbal or physical violence, and denial of health services, as well as internalization of the stigma resulting in thoughts of suicide or being ashamed of oneself (U.N. AIDS, 2012a). As of 2012, only about 60% of nations had laws prohibiting discrimination against those with HIV/AIDS, and a number of those countries that have laws do not implement them (UNAIDS, 2012a).

For example, extensive stigma against those with HIV/AIDS in India has been documented. A literature review assessing studies from the early 1990s through the first decade of the new century found that stigma and discrimination had not lessened much over the years. Negative attitudes, victim blaming, and avoidance of people with AIDS, as well as fear of infection from casual contact, remained common (Bharat, 2011). Married women are often blamed for bringing the disease into the family; they are told they should have been able to keep their husband from straying if he were infected first. People with HIV reported discrimination within the family (such as being forced to use different utensils), within the health care system (including the denial of treatment), and community settings (such as having their children be expelled from school). However, interventions in health care settings show promising results in changes in attitudes, although they lack long-term follow-up to assess changes in practices (Bharat, 2011).

In China, stigma against those with AIDS and those who work with them is still common, even among health workers. One doctor stated, "Other doctors are afraid they'll catch HIV from my lab coat" (Levin, 2013, ¶19). While China has passed a law banning discrimination against people with HIV, in 2010, a man lost his suit against an employer who denied him a teaching job due to his HIV-positive status (Jacobs, 2010).

The stigma associated with HIV/AIDS in many cultures has also led to its spread. As has been seen in the United States, some cultures stigmatize homosexuals, believing them to be immoral or sinful. In 40% of nations, same-sex relations are criminalized and in some of them, a conviction can result in death (UNAIDS, 2012a). This, in conjunction with the early link between gay men and AIDS, causes a rise in infections for a number of reasons. First, the stigma against homosexuality causes many homosexuals to lead a double life in which they are married but engage in homosexual acts outside the marriage. As in heterosexual relationships, nonmonogamy can lead to an increase in infections.

Second, the link between stigmatized homosexual behavior and the disease has caused people to stigmatize those with HIV/AIDS. Thus, people did not want to go to clinics for testing, to pick up medication, or participate in HIV research for fear that they would be stigmatized ("HIV stigma," 2012; "Stigma hinders," 2011). Some of this stigma and discrimination is coming from the health care workers themselves; they may insult the person or refuse to treat him or her ("HIV-positive people," 2011; "Insensitive health workers," 2009). This social exclusion also causes these populations to be excluded from AIDS intervention plans, as will be discussed in the next section.

Campaigns to counter stigma have been found to be successful in a variety of nations, including Haiti and Lesotho, resulting in increased willingness to be tested and an easing of attitudes such as willingness to care for a person with HIV or to have that person working in such occupations as teacher or fruit vendor (UNAIDS, 2012a).

Focused Programs

Two groups who are designated by UNAIDS as being at particularly high risk are sex workers and men who have sex with men. The lack of power and control previously discussed for women is even truer for women who are sex workers. Women commonly work in this field due to poverty and lack of access to other means to earn sufficient money for survival (Oyefara, 2007). As noted earlier, they can earn much greater sums for not using a condom. These women are often left out of prevention schemes, due to the illegality of their work and/or their presence in that nation ("Criminalization of sex work," 2011; "Migrant sex workers," 2012). Even when sex workers are included in HIV/AIDS intervention plans, often only female sex workers are targeted, leaving out male sex workers—who are also shunned by men who have sex with men ("New light," 2011). The World Health Organization has urged the decriminalization of sex work in order to lower stigma and discrimination, and thus hopefully, lower rates of HIV ("New WHO guidelines," 2012). Having access to jobs that pay a living wage will reduce the need to engage in sex work.

The term "men who have sex with men" (abbreviated MSM) is favored by activists over "gay" or "homosexual" as many men do not see themselves as gay, even if they engage in intercourse with other men. Therefore, a more inclusive term was needed in order to include these men in prevention work (Lacey, 2008). Although the groups of people considered at high risk for infection has broadened, this initially affected group also remains at high risk. Due to the high level of stigma, and in some countries illegality, of homosexual acts, MSM are often excluded from HIV outreach and prevention. According to the World Health Organization (2011), the criminalization of same-sex relations increases vulnerability to infection as it inhibits the free discussion of these issues between doctors and their patients.

It was not until after the millennium that Saudi Arabia began to face the AIDS epidemic within its borders, as the association of the disease with homosexual behavior made it anathema in this Muslim nation (Fattah, 2006). The Kingdom has now been working to help certain affected populations, such as intravenous drug users or pregnant women, but states that focusing on sex workers or MSM is not relevant in their country (Ministry of Health, Kingdom of Saudi Arabia, 2012).

In research examining the inclusion of MSM in AIDS National Strategic Plans of 46 African countries, only 34 even mentioned MSM. Few of these discussed the impact of the stigma against MSM or the criminalization of homosexuality. Some plans conflated experiences of MSM together with other high-risk groups, including commercial sex workers, and did not address the unique experiences of the groups (Makofane, Gueboguo, Lyons, & Sandfort, 2013). Even when MSM are included, outreach can be insufficient. For example, one survey found that while 44% of respondents could access free condoms, only 29% could obtain lubricant ("Survey reveals," 2011).

Condom Provision

The use of condoms is another central piece of the fight against HIV transmission. For those using them as a method of family planning, it can be even more important as injectable hormonal birth control has been found to increase the risk of HIV infection (Heffron et al., 2012). Unfortunately, the public health message to be faithful or to use a condom can equate the concept of condom use with unfaithfulness or promiscuity, thus increasing the stigma associated with condom use. Additionally, an understanding of the risk and how condoms can reduce it is often insufficient; self-efficacy in their use is an important piece (Rimal, Böse, Brown, Mkandawire, & Folda, 2009).

Many countries have had to face issues about the use of condoms to spread the prevention message. Worldwide, problems remain with access to, and willingness to use, condoms and water-based lubricants. For example, there has been difficulty in countries such as Kenya and Uganda with condom availability and promotion ("Condoms continue," 2013; UNAIDS, 2012a). Uganda has been accused of "bowing to U.S. pressure to emphasize abstinence over condom use" ("Condoms continue," ¶2, 2013). Much of the money coming to Uganda from the United States is through pro-abstinence organizations, which can also be anti-condom. Some Ugandan teachers reported that they were instructed by US contractors not to discuss condoms (Human Rights Watch, 2005).

Religious leaders, including Catholics and Pentecostals in Uganda, and Christians and Muslims in Kenya, have campaigned against the use and promotion of condoms, fearing that they will promote immorality ("Condoms continue," 2013; "Muslim clerics," 2008). In Kenya and Uganda, campaigns to promote condom use in the case of infidelity were very controversial, despite high rates of infidelity and infections in this manner. These campaigns were viewed as promoting cheating and contrary to the "Be Faithful" message ("Kenya condom advert," 2013;

"Ugandan HIV campaign," 2013). Stores in certain areas of Kenya refused to carry condoms, stating they promote infidelity ("Muslim clerics," 2008). Use of condoms has declined sharply in Uganda since 2005, and it is believed that this, combined with the high level of stigma against MSM and sex workers, is driving the rising HIV prevalence rate ("Condoms continue," 2013).

In some cultures, the value of a woman depends on how many children she can bear, greatly limiting the incentive to use a condom, as it would inhibit conception (Plusnews, 2003). In India, it has been found that the association of condoms with family planning reduced the likelihood that married women would use them, even though married women are considered a risk group due to the extramarital sexual activity of their husbands (Bhattacharya, 2004). In Malawi, AIDS was originally said to stand for "American Invention Depriving Sex" and was viewed as a US family planning plot, family planning being contrary to indigenous cultural values (Lwanda, 2005).

In India, the social stigma associated with condom use acts as a barrier to their purchase. Therefore, one intervention set up "condom depots" in offices, banks, and marketplaces where people could simply pick up condoms. Therefore, they were easily accessible and no one could be identified as using them. They were found to be 30 times more effective at distributing condoms than condom vending machines (Tamboli, 2010).

In China, there was a stigma against condom use: Those who use condoms must be promiscuous. However, this is being overcome and the sale of condoms in China has boosted the profits of the makers of Durex condoms; sales in China grew 46% in a year (Ford, 2010). Mechai Viravaidhya, an internationally known Thai AIDS activist and politician, worked in Thailand to de-stigmatize condoms by sponsoring contests to blow up condoms and having police officers pass them out in traffic in his "Cops and Rubbers" program (D'Agnes, 2001).

Male Circumcision

Male circumcision has been found to reduce the likelihood that a man can contract the virus from a woman. It is estimated that widespread male circumcision prevents infection in 20% of those who otherwise would have contracted the disease (UNAIDS, 2012a). Additionally, men who are themselves circumcised are more likely to agree to having their infant son circumcised (Young et al., 2012). Countries have been utilizing different strategies to promote this to their citizens. In Kenya, men are given vouchers that can be redeemed for cash (100 Kenya shillings) when they return for a follow-up visit. This helps reduce the impact of loss of income men experience by missing work for the procedure ("Push to meet," 2012). In Uganda, response to circumcision campaigns has been high and the main limiting factor has been the number of health workers able to complete the procedure ("Supply," 2012). However, concerns exist among women whether this might mean that men will then be less willing to wear a condom or more willing to cheat ("Mass male circumcision," 2007).

Access to Antiretroviral Treatment

Antiretroviral treatment (ARV) treatment has proven very effective in helping those infected with the disease to maintain their health. In the earlier days of treatment, patients had to take numerous pills (sometimes as many as 20 a day) to try to maintain their health. The expense and burden of this was a barrier for many people. With ARV treatment, the drugs are often combined within one pill, thus greatly reducing the number of pills the patient needs to take on a daily basis. In 2013, French researchers announced 10% of those treated very early in the stages of infection (within 10 weeks) could be "functionally cured" after ARV treatment (Sáez-Cirión et al., 2013). However, this was based on a sample of 14 people, so it should be viewed with extreme caution at this point.

Even South Africa is now aggressively promoting ARV medication. Initially these medications did not find favor with top South African officials. Instead, their minister of health promoted good nutrition as equivalent to ARV medication in fighting HIV (Nullis, 2005). But South Africa has now reversed course and has seen substantial progress. ARV medications are now promoted, and new HIV infection rates have been drastically reduced, including mother-to-child transmission (UNAIDS, 2012a). The South African government was able to negotiate a USD$250 million reduction in medication costs for ARV, a savings of almost 50%, which will allow them to treat many more people ("New ARV," 2012).

Children require a special focus, as diagnosis and treatment present special barriers in young children. It is difficult to detect HIV early in children, especially in the Global South, because the mother's antibodies are still in the child's bloodstream, which may render blood test results incorrect in children. Thus, antibody tests are typically not used in infants, but rather another test (Avert, 2013a). However, diagnosis does not mean treatment. If untreated, the disease kills one-third of infected children before their first birthday and one-half before their second birthday (UNICEF, 2012c). Children's access to ARV medication has been increasing markedly in recent years, although it still remains too low. In 2005, approximately 6% of children who need ARV medication were receiving it; by 2010, that figure had risen to 23%. Coverage varies markedly by region with access highest in the CEE/CIE countries and lowest in North Africa and Southwest Asia (UNICEF, 2012c).

Improvements have been made in children's medications. Early pediatric medications had to be refrigerated, mixed with clean drinking water, or split from adult dosage pills (difficult to do accurately) (Doctors Without Borders, 2005). The cost of pediatric medications has dropped sharply; in 2009 it was about $50 a year for first-line medications compared to about $20,000 only a few years before (Avert, 2013a). Syrups are now available and granular sprinkles are being developed. The sprinkles are easier for babies to swallow and are easier to transport and store ("Better paediatric," 2012). However, as noted, even with the recent rapid increase in access to medications, children do not have the same access to medications that adults do.

ARV medications were traditionally very expensive, but generic alternatives have been developed that are much cheaper. Brazil, India, Cuba, and Thailand have all developed generic medications for their own populations; India supplies 80% of the donor-funded medications to low- and middle-income countries (Avert, 2013b). Indian pharmaceutical companies helped lower the price for AIDS treatment from $15,000 per patient in the mid-1990s to about $200 in 2005, while also simplifying treatment by combining three medications into one pill, known as "triple therapy" (Avert, 2013b).

However, pharmaceutical companies argued that generic medications were reducing their profit and thus inhibiting them from recouping the money they spent on developing the drugs. In response, the Agreement on Trade Related Aspects of Intellectual Property Rights, known as TRIPS, was developed. After 2005, developing countries such as India and Thailand were not able to continue to develop generic drugs. They could continue to manufacture the older drugs, but not the newer medications, including second-line medications. Therefore, the most effective medications continue to be out of reach for poorer nations (Avert, 2013).

Almost all patients need to switch medications after a few years (due to reduced effectiveness) from more common "first-line" medications to stronger "second-line" medications, and eventually third-line medications. Generics have brought the cost of first-line treatment down to about USD$60 a year, but second-line treatment costs about USD$400 for the most affordable option—over three times as much (Médecins Sans Frontières, 2011). In low-income countries, if people have to pay for their medication, many cannot afford it and will die. Even if funding is available through their government or international donors, the more expensive the medications, the fewer people who can be treated, again increasing the number of people who will die.

Several ways to deal with TRIPS have been developed. The patent holder can grant a "voluntary license" for manufacture, which has occurred in a number of instances. Second, a country can issue a "compulsory license" for drugs needed to fight a public health emergency without paying royalties to the patent holder. Several countries such as Brazil, Thailand, and Indonesia have chosen to do this; however, Thailand has received backlash in the world trade market as a result (Avert, 2013b; "Indonesia to override," 2013). A "patent pool" has also been developed which holds the license to certain medications, thus easing and speeding the negotiations for generic equivalents (Avert, 2013b). The Least Developed Countries have been granted extensions to comply with TRIPS, most recently extended to 2021 (McClanahan, 2013).

The cost of the medications is not the only barrier. The medicines can have severe side effects due to their potency, especially for people who cannot afford food to help digest the medicine. Dr. Paul Farmer has pioneered an approach in Haiti called directly observed treatment (DOT). He employs village members to serve as *accompagnateurs*, who observe the patient taking the medicine at least once a day. This helps improve compliance with medication and offers the patient a local liaison if he or she is having difficulty with the side effects of the medication (Kidder, 2003) (see Box 6.1 for further information on Dr. Farmer and his work).

The use of local residents as health workers can be especially helpful in Africa as the medical infrastructure is lacking—another major barrier to treatment. Not only is there a lack of physical buildings and roads to transport medications, but trained medical personnel have been leaving their home countries for better working conditions and pay in the Global North, especially Britain. There is a shortage of almost a million health professionals on the continent. The ratio of health care workers per 1,000 population is 2.3 as compared to 24.8 in the Americas with the shortage particularly acute in the countries of sub-Saharan Africa (Naicker, Plange-Rhule, Tutt, & Eastwood, 2009).

Working with the local community to help devise solutions is extremely effective. For example, in Uganda, transportation costs and the distance to the health clinic to get medication every month was a large barrier to local residents being able to maintain their medication. Therefore, they determined each person would go every 3 months for his or her own check-up, and each month someone is nominated to collect medication for the other residents and bring it back to the village ("Basic health care," 2009).

Additionally, providing widespread basic health care is vital for the population, including those with HIV. In Rwanda, universal health coverage has been developed; subscribers pay premiums together with a 10% co-pay, but preventative measures as well as treatment for HIV and others are completely covered. Based on a system of rewards for good health of its patients, Rwanda has seen a huge payoff in health outcomes, including an almost 80% decrease in AIDS-related mortality, the largest in the world (Farmer at al., 2013).

Country-Wide Interventions

Countries around the world have been developing campaigns to stem new HIV infections. Many governments tried to ignore AIDS when it first began developing in their country. However, they soon learned it could not be ignored and a variety of culturally-specific interventions have been developed.

Thailand

Thailand has been recognized worldwide for its battle against HIV/AIDS. Initially, AIDS was seen in foreigners and then some injecting drug users;

therefore, it was not seen as a "Thai problem." Thailand initially did not want to mount a large anti-AIDS campaign because a large portion of its revenue is derived from tourism, and it believed that attention to the AIDS problem would deter tourism (D'Agnes, 2001).

The most prominent figure in Thailand's effort has been Mechai Viravaidhya. Known internationally for his anti-AIDS crusade, he was initially unsuccessful in getting his government to start a public health campaign against AIDS, as they insisted there was no "Thai to Thai" transmission. He refocused his target and was successful in getting the military to support him in fighting AIDS due to the rising infection rates among new recruits. The military leaders supported broadcasting AIDS awareness messages and stopped the stigmatizing of HIV-infected soldiers.

He then broadened his focus and convinced businesses to support his efforts by reminding them that "sick people cannot work and dead people cannot buy" (D'Agnes, 2001). When a new government came to power, he was given the support, including a large budget, to develop a broad campaign. He developed a widespread public awareness campaign, including radio and TV ads, subsidized songs and movies about AIDS, and educational programs in both schools and businesses. He also made certain to include the Buddhist monks, a very important sector of Thai society. He launched the "100% condom program" in an attempt to get Thailand's sex workers to use a condom 100% of the time (D'Agnes, 2001).

Thailand achieved remarkable success in the battle against AIDS and saw its rate of new infections fall from 140,000 in 1991 to 21,000 in 2003 to 9,700 in 2011 (Kanabus & Fredriksson, 2005; UNAIDS, 2012c). However, he and other activists warn of complacency, stating that with decreased government spending and awareness, infection rates are again rising. Funding for free condoms was cut back in 1998 after the Asian financial crisis. With the availability of accessible treatment, it appears that some have come to view HIV as a treatable disease. Few young people are using condoms during intercourse. Free condoms have been brought back and a new advertising scheme has been developed (World Health Organization, 2010).

China

China has developed a policy entitled "Four Frees and One Care" under which people are provided with free antiretroviral drugs, free prevention of mother-to-child transmission, free testing and counseling, free schools for AIDS orphans, and care for people infected with HIV or AIDS at sites across the country (UNICEF, n.d.a). Orphanages have been developed for children who have lost parents to the disease and do not have any relatives able to look after them. Children feel that these orphanages offer the advantages of providing basics, such as shelter, food, and clothing, as well as education, health care, and psychosocial support. However, children felt restricted by the regulations on movement, as well as experiencing stigma for living in an orphanage designated for those affected by AIDS (Zhao et al., 2009).

Botswana

To combat the reluctance to be tested for HIV due to the stigma associated with the disease, Botswana has implemented routine testing of everyone who seeks medical care. Pretesting counseling as practiced in Western nations, with its full disclosure about the impact of the disease if the person were positive, did not work well in Botswana, as no one wanted to be tested by the end of the session. With routine testing, people are identified earlier in the progression of the disease, making it more likely that medication can assist them. It is part of a standard exam, and it has an "opt out" clause. Wives who suspect their husbands may have infected them no longer have to be tested surreptitiously; they are tested as a routine procedure, freeing them from potentially violent repercussions at home. This has all helped to reduce the stigma associated with testing and with the disease, leading to increased ability to fight it (LaFraniere, 2004). Specific services have been developed for couples, children, and adolescents and people with disabilities, but these services are still underutilized (Ministry of Health-Botswana, 2012).

Professional Role of Social Workers

While many challenges remain in the global battle against HIV/AIDS, there are also signs of hope. Many more people await diagnosis or treatment, but effective, affordable medications can be made available. The rapid increase in funds dedicated to the fight after 2001 led to a slowing in the epidemic, offering hope for the future. However, funds have been reduced in recent years due to the global recession, raising fears of a reversal of this progress.

Social workers can help fight this battle. Social workers can work on the macro level to help develop culturally appropriate interventions to help stem transmission, assist those who are already infected, and help to reduce stigma against the disease. Social workers can assist in the case management of those who are battling the disease, as well as helping to create a system of social supports to assist those who are indirectly affected by the disease, such as orphaned children. Traditional methods such as kinship care are being overwhelmed by the epidemic, and social workers can assist in the creation of formal services to help care for those left behind, as well as supporting these caregivers. By focusing on social development, as opposed to a strictly medical approach, social workers can help turn the tide against HIV/AIDS.

Culture Box
THE FIGHT AGAINST HIV/AIDS IN MALAWI

Malawi is a small country in Southern Africa. Its official languages are English and Chichewa, with other dialects of Bantu spoken as well (Rankin, Lindgren, Rankin, & Ng'ona, 2005). According to the Central Intelligence Agency's *World Factbook* (CIA, 2013), Malawi was established as a British colony in 1891 and achieved independence in 1964, with the first democratic elections held in 1994. It has a total area of 118,480 square kilometers, making it slightly smaller than Pennsylvania. Women bear an average of five children and have a lower literacy rate than men (69% vs. 81%); however, it should be noted that this literacy rate is substantially higher than in the first edition of this text, then 50% to 76%. Eighty-three percent of the population is Christian and 13% is Muslim, with the rest declaring other (1.9%) or none (2.5%).

It is one of the world's least developed nations, ranking 170 out of 187 countries on the Human Development Index and 124th out of 148 in gender equality (UNDP, 2013). Approximately half of the population lives below the international poverty line of USD$1.25/day, an improvement from 65% in 1998 (World Bank, 2013). Malawi has been heavily affected by AIDS, but it has made good progress in turning around the epidemic. The current life expectancy in Malawi is 52 years, a substantial increase from the 41 years expected at the time of the first edition of this text (CIA, 2013). The rate of infection was 14.1% in 2005; in 2011, the adult prevalence rate was 10% (UNAIDS, 2006, 2011b). The rate of new infections decreased more than 50% between 2001 and 2011 (UNAIDS, 2012a). Prevalence among young people and pregnant women has also decreased (Malawi Government, 2012).

The primary method of HIV transmission in Malawi is heterosexual sex (Malawi Government, 2012). Mother-to-child transmission had been quite high, but it has been substantially reduced. The number of sites providing PMTCT services increased to 544 in 2011 from 152 in 2006. In 2011, 82% of pregnant women who tested positive for HIV received ARV drugs; all women who are pregnant now receive them regardless of how far the illness has progressed (Malawi Government, 2012). About 20% of men are circumcised, but it varies widely by region and ethnic group (Malawi Government, 2012).

The previously discussed risk factors, such as orphanhood, condom use, circumcision, MSM, and low levels of knowledge, are all evident in Malawi. While awareness of HIV/AIDS is universal, comprehensive knowledge remains low—under 50% (Malawi Government, 2012). Orphans are more likely to have sex earlier than non-orphans (Mkandawire, Tenkorang, & Luginaah, 2013). Homosexuality is illegal in Malawi with a punishment of 14 years of hard labor ("Queer Malawi," 2011). Interestingly, HIV continues to be correlated with *higher* wealth in Malawi; it is also more common in urban areas as opposed to rural ones. High-risk groups have included truck drivers (14.7% 2006 prevalence rate), police (28.3%), schoolteachers (23.4% primary, 17.2% secondary), sex workers (70.7%), and MSM (21.4%) (Malawi Government, 2012).

Stigma against those with HIV/AIDS has been decreasing, although it does still exist. Half of those living with HIV reported being gossiped about and 35% stated they had been verbally insulted, harassed, or threatened; one-third had been excluded from a social gathering (Malawi Government, 2012). Condom distribution remains below target. While traditionally faith-based organizations have denounced the use of condoms, recently some are now privately advising their members to use them (Malawi Government, 2012).

Economic migration assisted in the spread of AIDS in Malawi as it did in other nations. Between 1985 and 1993, the Malawian Army fought in Mozambique to defend a railway line. This army, consisting primarily of single men, took its "rest and relaxation" with sex workers in Malawi and Mozambique. Similarly, Malawian men emigrated to work in the South African gold mines and visited sex workers while there. Upon their return to Malawi, these gold miners were favored as husbands due to their comparatively high income. When both groups of these men returned to Malawian society, they transmitted the disease they had obtained while working outside of the country (Lwanda, 2004).

(continued)

The government was reluctant to acknowledge the AIDS crisis at first. Even in 1994, when 20% to 30% of those hospitalized had HIV-related illnesses, the government continued to deny the crisis (Lwanda, 2005). There is a strong taboo in Malawian culture against speaking about sexual subjects not only in public but also within the family, even between husband and wife (Rankin, Lindgren, Rankin, & Ng'oma, 2005). In 2012, Joyce Banda became the president of Malawi after the sudden death of the previous president, Bingu wa Mutharika. Malawi had a series of proposals rejected by the Global Fund due to lack of faith in the fiscal management of the Mutharika administration, and Banda set out to increase international confidence in Malawi again. She also pledged to decriminalize homosexuality, but as of this writing, that has not yet occurred ("Where is HIV/AIDS," 2012).

The cycle of AIDS increasing poverty can be seen easily in Malawi. The nation is dependent on its agriculture. As adults of working age are disabled or killed by the disease, familial poverty increases. Children are pulled from school for caretaking or farming duties. On a macro level, the decreasing agricultural output due to the disabled workforce increases food insecurity. In addition, the structural adjustment policies of the World Bank mandated that Malawi switch its agriculture to more exportable goods, as opposed to those that would feed its nation, again resulting in greater food insecurity. These policies also mandated the elimination of the subsidy for fertilizer (Bryceson & Fonseca, 2005), reducing its accessibility and thus lowering agricultural output. Food insecurity is an ongoing problem due to overuse of fields, natural occurrences such as floods and droughts, and rising inflation (World Food Programme, n.d.). This lack of food further weakens those infected with HIV and AIDS, pushing the cycle to start again.

Under colonial rule by the British, health care was highly segregated. "European-only" hospitals were in existence until 1972 (despite independence in 1964), and many of the qualified medical personnel focused on the care of the small European population. Therefore, people living in rural areas continued to rely on traditional medicine for their health care. In the early days of the AIDS epidemic, Malawians believed that talk of an epidemic was a family planning plot of the Americans, family planning being contrary to the values of their culture. Early public health interventions, with their reliance on condoms, violated both these values and the economic realities of the nation (Lwanda, 2004).

John Lwanda (2003, 2005), a physician from Malawi, notes the following cultural practices among ethnic groups in Malawi that can lead to HIV infection: *nthena*, when a widower is given his deceased wife's younger sister; *m'bvade*, a practice in which the abstinence after childbirth of an unmarried woman is ceremoniously ended by surrogate sex with a designated man; *chokolo*, widow inheritance; and the use of *fisi* (surrogates) in infertility rites and in initiation ceremonies. There is also a strong faith in traditional medicine to protect against and heal HIV. However, he states that the strongest cultural contributor to the spread of HIV is the weak position of women in Malawian society. Rankin et al. (2005) noted that the Chichewa term for sexually transmitted infections translates as "women's disease." If a man discovers he has an infection, he will tell his wife he has a "women's disease," thus blaming her for the infection.

In Malawian society, women are expected to be subordinate to men. A woman is socialized never to refuse having sex with her husband, even if she suspects him of being unfaithful or of being infected with HIV (National AIDS Commission, 2003). It is seen as unnatural for men to go without sex: "manhood without sex is considered incomplete" (Lwanda, 2005, p. 134). This social inequality translates to increased infection rates for women. Among younger people, females have a much higher infection rate than males. Among those aged 15 to 24 years, approximately 1.9% of males are reported to have AIDS compared to 5.2% of females. This disproportion is true for every age group except those 40–44 years (Malawi Government, 2012).

Women living with HIV in Malawi have also reported marriage to be a risk factor. Women who never married have a much lower infection rate (4.2%) than those who are currently married (11.7%), divorced/separated (24.8%), or widowed (50.1%) (Malawi Government, 2012). They report often getting married in a search for companionship but also due to poverty. Many were orphaned and lacked basic necessities

(continued)

such as food, which led them to accept marriage proposals. However, once married, they reported high levels of infidelity and forced sex, as well as other forms of abuse and abandonment. Once abandoned, they were once again faced with the choice of poverty or a new marriage (Mkandawire-Valhmu et al., 2013).

Despite its struggles, Malawi has been a leader among African nations in many areas, including the care of the children left orphaned by AIDS. In 1992, it became the first nation in the region to develop guidelines for the care of these children, recommending that orphans be kept within their home communities (Mutume, 2001). Malawi has eliminated school fees and other educational costs to enable more students to attend schools (UNICEF, n.d.b). Education still remains problematic, however, due to familial poverty. Children are often needed to help bring money into the family rather than attending school, and Malawi has had difficulty retaining teachers due to the high number of deaths among working-age adults.

Malawi has developed child care institutions for children whose families are unable to care for them, community-based child care centers, and a cash transfer program. Similar to other nations, the cash transfer program has had very promising results to date. Health outcomes include increased food security and reduced malnutrition, as well as increased school enrollment and retention. Program recipients also have lowered dropout rates, reduced early marriage, and reduced sexual activity (Malawi Government, 2012). Another initiative has provided vocation skills training to orphans and other vulnerable children, such as carpentry or tailoring, skills in high demand (Rowan & Kabwira, 2009).

Malawi was the first nation in the region to develop and implement a national system for monitoring and evaluating the responses to HIV/AIDS within its borders (UNAIDS, 2004). ARV treatment is free and this access has greatly increased the life span for those living with HIV. However, drug shortages have become an ongoing problem ("Malawi's never-ending," 2013). There is also a severe shortage of health workers, facilities, and equipment to care for the affected population.

Therefore, organizations from around the world have been assisting the government of Malawi. Doctors Without Borders has been working with the government on "task shifting," in which routine duties are shifted from doctors to other health workers. These duties include HIV tests and dispensing ARV medications (Doctors Without Borders, 2011; "Solving health worker," 2008). Patients who are medically stable also need to see a medical worker only every 6 months rather than every 3 months, a 50% increase in available time for health workers (Doctors Without Borders, 2011).

The US Centers for Disease Control (2012) has also been assisting in training of health care workers, as well as supporting the improvement of laboratory services. Partners in Health, Dr. Farmer's organization, has adapted its *accompagnateur* model. Its worker has a dirt bike, due to the poor roads and expense of fuel, and makes home visits to those who have stopped taking their medication. He is able to help determine why they have stopped (e.g., food insecurity or depression) and to talk with them about the consequences. This approach helps increase medication adherence (Partners in Health, 2013c).

The Coalition of Women Living with HIV/AIDS (COWLHA) in Malawi has been a major force in fighting against some of the factors that have particularly affected women (http://www.cowlhamw.com). They work on issues relating to women's rights and sustainable livelihoods in order to address social and economic empowerment, as well as issues directly related to HIV/AIDS, such as gender roles in Malawian society. Their "Stepping Stones" program separates participants by sex and then helps them explore issues relating to relationships such as love, intimacy, violence, and decision-making, in order to help them move to a model where they make decisions as a couple rather than having the man make the decisions (UNAIDS & The Athena Network, 2011).

Malawi offers a microcosm of the global epidemic of AIDS. The disease is furthered by poverty, discrimination, and certain cultural traditions, but targeted, culturally relevant interventions have stemmed the tide and offer hope for the future.

What Can I Do Now?

- Advocate to reduce the impact of HIV and AIDS on women and girls:
  - Remove financial barriers that keep girls out of school.
  - Reduce violence against women.
  - Secure women's rights to own and inherit property.
  - Provide equal access to treatment, care, and prevention.
  - Develop an effective microbicide (a gel, cream, sponge, or suppository that women can use to protect themselves from HIV).
- Call on leaders—politicians, religious leaders, corporate managers, community leaders—to get engaged in the fight against AIDS. Make a call, write a letter, or go to a meeting. Ask them to advocate for support to the Global Fund to Fight AIDS, Tuberculosis, and Malaria.
- Advocate for low-cost access to life-saving medicines.
- Give your time to an organization or program that helps people affected by HIV and AIDS.
- Donate money to an organization that is working to reduce the impact of HIV and AIDS.
- Become knowledgeable about how the disease spreads, and then spread the word. Ignorance is the enemy.

What Can I Do as a Professional Social Worker?

- Work for an organization within the United States such as PSI (www.psi.org) that works to promote health in the Global South. They use social marketing techniques to address a broad range of health issues, including HIV/AIDS, malaria, and safe water.
- Work for an international organization in the countries that are directly affected. Doctors Without Borders (Médecins Sans Frontières) (www.doctorswithoutborders.org) seeks mental health workers, including social workers, to assist in its work. Save The Children operates a number of projects in affected countries. Partners in Health is another option.

• Work against stigmatizing those with HIV/AIDS, as this creates a barrier both to testing and to treatment.

World Wide Web Resources on AIDS

Avert (www.avert.org): An international AIDS charity that provides basic information on AIDS around the world.

Doctors Without Borders/Médecins Sans Frontières (www.doctors withoutborders.org; www.msf.org): An international humanitarian organization that sends doctors and other professionals, including social workers, to provide emergency aid where it is needed. Their Web site also provides reports related to their work.

Kaiser Family Foundation, Global Health Facts (www.kff.org/ hivaids/index.cfm): GlobalHealthFacts.org provides the latest country- and region-specific data on HIV/AIDS; demographic and economic indicators; program funding and financing.

Partners in Health (www.pih.org/): The organization of Dr. Paul Farmer and his colleagues. It provides information on their work and a few related reports.

UNAIDS (www.unaids.org): The United Nations agency that is responsible for coordinating the UN response to the AIDS epidemic. They have an abundance of information on their Web site.

UNICEF (http://www.unicef.org/aids/index.html): The UNICEF Web site that has information on their campaign for children affected by AIDS.

7

Issues Particularly Affecting Women

A major theme of this text is that while the issues discussed are experienced by members of all groups, certain forces can act to place some people at higher risk. These forces include discrimination, poverty, and lack of access to education. Due to widespread discrimination, women are more likely to live in poverty and more likely to lack an education than men. Although women perform two-thirds of the work in the world, they receive only 10% of the income and own less than 1% of the property (United Nations, 2005). In addition, there are issues that are unique to women due to their lower societal position. There are many areas in which women experience harmful or unequal treatment, and this chapter will not attempt to discuss them all. What will be covered in this chapter are some specific types of violence experienced by women throughout their lives, unique concerns relating to women's health, and a discussion of how gender can play a role in social development.

Due to these unique burdens borne by women and their vulnerable position in many societies, a human rights document focusing specifically on the rights of women was adopted by the United Nations in 1979—the Convention on the Elimination of All Forms of Discrimination Against Women (CEDAW). CEDAW defines what constitutes discrimination against women and what nations must do to eliminate discrimination. Discrimination includes both intentional discrimination as well as acts that have a discriminatory effect. Countries are required to work to eradicate harmful practices based on discriminatory attitudes toward women, such as female genital cutting and lack of access to education. As of 2013,

CEDAW had been ratified by 187 countries, over 90% of the membership of the United Nations (United Nations, 2013).

Despite ratification, a country is allowed to post reservations to certain parts of the document. CEDAW has had many substantive reservations posted, with countries claiming that pieces of it violate their cultural norms. A number of countries have expressed reservations to Articles 2 and 16 concerning the equality of men and women under the law and in marriage. As these are considered to be core principles of CEDAW, the United Nations considers these "impermissible reservations" (United Nations, 2009). Many times, these reservations have been posted due to perceived conflict with religious values. However, upon review, many countries have withdrawn some or all of their reservations, including Egypt, Malaysia, Morocco, and Turkey (Freeman, 2009).

The United States signed CEDAW in 1980 but has not ratified it, the only country in the Global North that has not. This is not the only international document for the equality of women from which United States has withheld support. In 1994, an international meeting in Cairo developed a plan of action to address reproductive health concerns in order to increase sustainable development and decrease poverty. This document was based on the concepts of gender equality and human rights (United Nations Population Fund [UNFPA], 2004). The United States was a signatory to this 1994 action program. In 2004, on the 10-year anniversary of the Cairo meeting, a statement was developed that was designed to show support for the UN plan to ensure women's rights to an education, health care, and family planning. However, the United States refused to sign the 2004 statement, claiming that the statement indicated support for "sexual rights." The US government expressed reservations about the statement as they saw it as endorsing abortion, the rights of gays and lesbians, and the use of condoms by unmarried couples to prevent the spread of AIDS (Lederer, 2004). However, with the election of President Obama, this course of action was reversed and the US again began financially supporting the goal of reproductive health as an important part of development (Dennis & Anderson, 2009).

Equity Versus Efficiency

When examining the quest for equal treatment of women, Van Soest and Crosby (1997) note that arguments tend to fall in one of two areas: equity and efficiency. Arguments for equity state that women should have equal rights because it is the morally correct position that women should be considered the equal of men and should have the same rights and opportunities as they do. Proponents in favor of efficiency argue that empowering women and increasing their rights is the correct thing to do because it benefits society as a whole. As will be discussed in this chapter, social development that focuses on women tends to have large payoffs beyond the individual female. Research has found that focusing on the social development of women leads to lower child mortality, increased education, and lower rates of HIV/AIDS (Coleman, 2005). The United Nations has stated that poverty cannot be eliminated until discrimination against women (social, economic, and physical) is eradicated (UNFPA, 2005).

Violence Against Women

One example of the discrimination that is experienced uniquely by women is the pervasive violence that threatens them throughout their life solely as a result of their gender. Women are much more likely to experience violence based on their gender than are men. The violence can take a variety of forms throughout their lives. It begins even before birth, as female fetuses are more likely to be aborted than male ones in some regions of the world, such as South and East Asia, as well as Southeast Europe and the South Caucasus (UNFPA, 2012). Male children are preferred over female children in these areas to the extent that if the parents can afford an ultrasound, they may choose to abort the fetus if the scan shows the fetus is female. The preference for a boy is demonstrated in the fact that this occurs more often in families with only daughters, as well as families with more children (UNFPA, 2012). Sons are considered necessary as it is their cultural responsibility to take care of their parents when they are elderly and they will be able to earn more as workers to do so. They also continue the family line (Hesketh, Lu, & Xing, 2011).

This preference has resulted in widespread sex imbalances and "missing" girls—girls who should be alive but due to sex-selective abortion, female infanticide, or poor quality care in their early years are not alive. In early childhood, sons are shown preferential treatment and are given more and better food and are more likely to receive medical care than daughters. As a result, boys are more likely to live to their fifth birthday than girls. Worldwide estimates of this number range as high as 160 million missing females (Hvistendahl, 2011).

In India, one study concluded that 10 million girls were "missing" over the previous 20 years due to sex-selective abortion (Jha et al., 2006), although this procedure has been officially illegal since 1994 (Sheth, 2006). Wealthy couples in India will even fly to the United States, which is one of the few countries where it is legal to test for sex in embryos prior to implantation, so that they can be sure to have a son (Kaur, 2006). While China, India, and South Korea all have laws banning sex-selective abortion, only South Korea enforces them (Hesketh et al., 2011).

This phenomenon has been driven further by lowering fertility rates. Most countries around the world have seen their fertility rates decline over the past decades. In most cases, this has been voluntary, but in the case of China, it is driven by the government's fertility control policy (described in the Culture Box in Chapter 4). In China, there is a high ratio of boys to girls, primarily due to a widely distorted ratio for second births, especially in areas where families are allowed a second child if the first one was a girl (Zhu, Lu, & Hesketh, 2009). This discrepancy among latter-born children has also been found in the United States among families from India, China, and Korea. The sex ratio for first children is equal, but if there is no son in the family, the ratio for second children increases to 1.17 and to 1.5 for the third child. The authors of the study believe this is due to prenatal sex selection and note that the practice continues despite the lack of in-country cultural factors, demonstrating the power of these cultural beliefs (Almond & Edlund, 2008).

Once the child is born, some poorer families resort to infanticide rather than bear the expense of raising a female child. Sex-selective abortion and female infanticide occur primarily among families living in deep poverty who cannot afford the expense of this child. In a number of cultures, the female moves to her husband's family upon marriage. Thus, she does not contribute any money to her parents' household but only costs money. Impoverished families cannot afford to raise a girl, particularly if they already have a daughter.

As will be discussed later in this chapter, in South Asia, the tradition of paying a dowry upon the marriage of a female has grown to the extent that paying the expected dowry can impoverish a family. If a family already has several daughters, the anticipated expense of raising another girl and then paying for her wedding and dowry can lead parents to the hard decision that they cannot afford to raise her. Girls are also seen as a burden to the family as they are perceived as needing constant protection. A son is needed in a family as only a male successor can light the funeral pyre of his father, an important cultural tradition (Devraj, 2003).

In China, neonatal mortality for girls in rural areas is double that of boys, and it is correlated with the number of children that a family already has. If the girl's birth is the family's authorized second pregnancy (allowed if their first child was a girl), the risk of neonatal mortality increases (Wu, Viisainen, Wang, & Hemminki, 2003). As discussed in the Culture Box in Chapter 4, the number of children born to each family in China is limited. While wealthy families are able to pay the fine for having "excess" children, this is not true for poorer families.

However, there is hope that these trends are shifting. Substantial change has already been documented in South Korea. The gender ratio reached its peak in the early 90s and has been decreasing ever since. This is attributed to a number of factors. While revealing the sex of a fetus was banned in 1987, enforcement was lax (Sang-Hun, 2007). Beginning in the early 1990s, the law against sex-selective abortion was strictly enforced and doctors could lose their license for determining the sex of a fetus; an immediate fall in the imbalance of the ratio was seen (Hesketh et al., 2011).

Part of the decrease is attributed to the improving economy in South Korea in recent decades that increased employment opportunities for women, as well as improving the ability of parents to save for their retirement (Chung & Gupta, 2007; Sang-Hun, 2007). Additionally, the government created a public policy campaign to change attitudes about having a girl baby. To address the perceived need for a son to care for parents in their old age, South Korea provided pensions for rural parents of daughters (Hesketh et al., 2011). Urbanization also assisted in the decrease as urban families were less likely to support traditional ideas about the need for sons. Urban families were better able to change inheritance structures as it was seen as easier to leave daughters monetary wealth rather than land, which historically only went to sons (Chung & Gupta, 2007). Changes were also made to the law that abolished the legal basis for the male headship of families (Chun & Gupta, 2009).

China has been working to follow suit. Laws have been strengthened and now include requirements that two doctors are present at each ultrasound and increasing punishments (Branigan, 2011). They have also created a public policy campaign, "Care for Girls," originally targeted to areas with very high imbalances in sex ratios. It focused on multiple system levels by both increasing enforcement of the law, while simultaneously addressing the economic factors that were driving the imbalance. Examples include providing free care for the elderly and reduced medical care cost for girls. They also conducted advocacy campaigns to raise the perceived value of girls. This campaign has been found to be successful in the targeted areas and has been expanded (Zijuan, Shuzhuo, & Feldman, 2012).

In India, poor families in states with the most severe imbalances will receive cash payments of about US$385 every year if they have a girl and raise her. They will also receive a lump sum of about US$2500 when she turns 18 if she completes her education and is not married ("Cash incentives," 2008). Recent data from India indicate that, while still markedly off-ratio, the sex ratio at birth is improving (Kotla, 2011).

Female Genital Cutting

The next type of violence that girls may experience is female genital cutting (FGC), a procedure that involves partial or total removal of a girl's external genitalia for cultural or nonmedical reasons (UNICEF, n.d.). This was previously known as female circumcision, but it is not equivalent at all to male circumcision; thus, currently it is more commonly referred to as female genital cutting or female genital mutilation. However, the term "mutilation" is considered pejorative by many cultures, and thus this text uses the more neutral term "cutting." Approximately 125 million women living today have undergone the procedure; about 30 million girls are at risk for the procedure (UNICEF, 2013). The majority of girls undergo FGC between 4 and 14 years of age, but it is sometimes performed as early as birth or as late as at marriage (Population Reference Bureau, 2010). It is practiced in about two dozen countries in Africa, as well as some countries in Asia. It is most common in northeast Africa: Prevalence rates range from 80% to 97% in countries such as Egypt, Somalia, and Eritrea. However, prevalence may vary widely within a country (Population Reference Bureau, 2010).

The procedure may be conducted for several reasons. A primary one is to increase chastity among women. The procedure is seen as an important rite of passage in some cultures. The external female genitalia are seen as unhygienic and unsightly in certain societies, and thus their removal is seen as beautifying and hygienic (UNICEF, n.d.). While rates are higher among Muslim families in countries where it is performed, FGC is not based in that religion and in fact predates the religion.

There are three basic types of FGC, differentiated by the extent of the cutting: clitoridectomy (type I), excision (type II), and infibulation (type III). Type I involves the removal of the clitoral hood and may include the removal of part or all of the clitoris. Type II is the removal of the clitoral hood, the clitoris, and part or all of the labia minora. The most severe form, type III, is the removal of part or all of the external genitalia (clitoris, labia minora, and labia majora) with a stitching or narrowing of the vaginal opening. Only a very narrow opening is left (about the diameter of a matchstick) for the passage of urine and menstrual blood.

The reason that FGC is not equivalent to male circumcision, nor considered a cultural tradition that should be protected as such, is the extensive damage that can result from the procedure. The procedure is traditionally performed by traditional practitioners using non-sterile instruments rather than in a medical facility by medical personnel (UNICEF, 2005). Extensive damage can result from the procedure, including painful sexual intercourse and menstruation, increased susceptibility to sexually transmitted diseases, infertility, increased risk during childbirth, hemorrhaging, and death. Psychological impacts, including Post-Traumatic Stress Disorder, anxiety, and depression, are higher in girls who have experienced FGC than similar girls who have not (Kizilhan, 2011). One study found that women who have experienced FGC are more than 50% more likely to die, or have their infants die, during childbirth than women who have not experienced the procedure. Women who had undergone more severe forms of FGC were more at risk than women who had experienced less severe types. The authors of the study believe that the results actually underestimate the risk to women, as only births in hospitals were included in their study; women giving birth at home are more at risk than women giving birth in the hospital due to lower levels of medical care and higher levels of poverty (World

Health Organization, 2006). This has prompted some girls to flee their countries and seek asylum in other nations.

———————

Fauziya Kassindja was a 16-year-old girl in Togo when her father died. A progressive man, he had not forced her to be circumcised. He sent all his daughters to school and allowed them to marry the man of their choice. However, after his death, her aunt took over the family; according to custom, a man's property reverts to his birth family upon his death. Her aunt tried to force her to marry an older man who already had three wives and to undergo FGC. Fauziya fled the country rather than submit, eventually seeking asylum in the United States. No one had ever been granted refuge on this basis before. Asylum laws were established originally to protect political and civil rights and were based on a male model of dissent. She was placed in prison during the evaluation of her appeal. After spending 16 months in prison, she was eventually granted asylum with the help of an American law student and a women's advocacy group. It was determined that having one's clitoris cut off against her will is an act of persecution. She tells her story in the book Do They Hear You When You Cry *(Kassindja, 1998).*

———————

While in some places efforts have been made to reduce these potentially negative outcomes by performing the procedure in a medical facility, many of the risks remain. Additionally, this is taken by some to be an endorsement of the procedure ("FGM/C regulations," 2011). Thus, most countries are looking to eradicate the procedure. In 2012, the United Nations passed a resolution calling for the worldwide ban of the procedure. It was sponsored by two-thirds of the member states, including the Group of African States ("Ban welcomes," 2012).

In order to eradicate the procedure, public opinion must turn against it. One of the major targets for revising public opinions has been men. Men must be willing to marry a woman who has not undergone the procedure, and fathers must believe it is not necessary in order to maintain family honor. Involving religious leaders to counter the belief that FGC is necessary for religious purposes is also important. In 2007, Egypt started a nationwide campaign against the practice and top religious leaders declared it *haram*, or prohibited by Islam (Meleigy, 2007). In Senegal, a grassroots movement (TOSTAN) that was developed in the native language of the Senegalese at the wishes of the local women and in conjunction with local religious leaders was successful in lowering FGC rates. Culturally sensitive terms were used for FGC, and all villages in the intermarrying community agreed to abandon the practice (Easton, Monkman, & Miles, 2003). At follow-up, awareness of FGC increased significantly and the women who believed it was a social necessity decreased significantly. FGC rates decreased significantly among girls 10 years and under (Diop & Askew, 2009).

Recent data demonstrate rates are lowering among younger women as compared to middle-aged women, giving hope that the procedure is being abandoned. For example, in Egypt, rates are 96% for women aged 35–39 years, but 81% among girls aged 15–19 years. In Ethiopia this is also seen with rates of 81% for older women and 62% among adolescents (Population Reference Bureau, 2010; UNICEF, 2013). Most studies have found that women with higher levels of education are less likely to have the procedure performed on their daughters, again demonstrating the power of education for women (Hayford, 2005; Sipsma et al., 2012).

One of the countries that has been hailed as a success story is Burkina Faso. They outlawed the procedure in 1996 and instituted and enforced stiff penalties, including fines and jail time, for those who violate it. They have trained religious leaders, police, and the media about the risks of the procedure and have set up a toll-free number that people can call to report if they suspect a girl is at risk of being cut ("Girl's death," 2007). While FGC is more common in girls whose mothers had the procedure, recent research in Burkina Faso has seen the intergenerational transmission drop markedly. One study found that 75% of the adult women had undergone the procedure, but only 25% of their daughters; this was the only country out of 10 in the study to show such a drop, showing the power of the change (Sipsma et al., 2012). This finding was echoed by another that found prevalence rate of 77% among adult women, but only 30% of their daughters (Karmaker, Kandala, Chung, & Clarke, 2011). However, these studies may have included girls who were too young for the procedure and other research has shown rates lowering from 80% for women in their thirties to 60% for adolescent girls (Population Reference Bureau, 2010). It has not been a complete success; some now perform the procedure on younger girls or cross into other countries to escape detection, but the reduction in rates is marked and shows that eradication is possible.

Early Marriage

Girls in the Global South are susceptible to being married at early ages. Although many countries have laws against child marriage, they are often weak or ineffectively enforced. More than 67 million women aged 20 to 24 years worldwide were married before the age of 18. Rates vary among countries, but South Asia accounts for more than half of these girls. Sub-Saharan Africa follows as the region with the next highest level—15% of the total (UNICEF, 2011a). Progress is being made, and prevalence rates are declining, but only slowly (UNICEF, 2011a).

A number of factors increase the likelihood of child marriage, but poverty is a primary one. Worldwide, women in the lowest quintile of income were three times more likely to be married as children as compared to women in the highest quintile (UNICEF, 2011a). If the girl can be married at an early age, her parents no longer have to bear the expense of raising her, and if a bride price is offered, she can be a source of income for the family. Conversely, in countries where a dowry is expected, a younger girl requires a smaller dowry ("Online birth data," 2012; "The hidden costs," 2012). Additionally, the family no longer needs to worry about premarital sex. Becoming pregnant outside of wedlock is the worst shame a girl can bring to her family, and early marriage is used to prevent this from occurring.

Girls who are married early face a host of potential negative outcomes. They face a higher risk of domestic violence than those who marry at later ages. They typically have to leave school once they are married or become pregnant, which usually soon follows. Additionally, an early pregnancy has a higher risk of maternal death or injury during childbirth. Girls aged 10 to 14 years are five times more likely to die as a result of childbirth or pregnancy than those aged 20 to 24 years, and girls aged 15 to 19 years are more than twice as likely to die (United Nations Population Fund [UNFPA], n.d.).

The International Center for Research on Women (2007) suggests several strategies to end child marriage. At the macro level, cultural norms needs to be changed and grassroots community-led programs should be supported. Girls need greater access to education as well as future job opportunities. With more education and greater earning potential, the risk of child marriage decreases due to the decrease in benefits. Within each country, there is a "tipping point" in age, after which a girl's risk decreases—typically 13 to 14 years old. Therefore, interventions must be focused on children younger than this age in order to reach them and their families prior to marriage.

The first International Day of the Girl Child, celebrated in 2012, focused on the theme of "Ending Early Marriage" (Vojvoda, 2012). Individual countries are also taking actions to work to reduce the number of child marriages. Bangladesh has been working to enter a child's birth registration data online in order to allow authorities to easily access a girl's birth date ("Online birth data," 2012). In India, peer educators visit schools to tell them of the risks of early marriage (Singh, 2011). Also in India, clubs for teenage girls have been formed to provide girls support, both for their development in general and as a strategy to delay marriage and continue their education (UNICEF, 2011b).

Intimate Partner Violence

While home is often perceived as safe shelter from the troubles of the world, for women it can be a dangerous place. Approximately one in every three women worldwide (about 1 billion women) has been beaten, coerced into sex, or otherwise abused by an intimate partner (United Nations Secretary General, 2006). Such violence would be considered illegal if it were perpetrated against someone who was not an intimate partner, but in such a relationship, it is often condoned. A global study of partner violence conducted in 15 sites in 10 countries throughout the world found that the prevalence of partner violence varied widely, but it was widespread. Between 15% and 71% of women in the study had experienced physical and/or sexual violence at the hands of an intimate partner, with most sites reporting between 30% and 60% (World Health Organization, 2005).

The violence takes different forms in different cultures, including honor killing, dowry deaths (discussed in a later section), and acid throwing. In countries such as Pakistan, acid throwing is a form of violence against women. If a man is angry with a woman, he will pour acid on her, resulting in disfigurement and blindness in many cases. As a result, the woman is confined to the home, leading to social isolation and depression. This occurs not only between spouses but has been used by the Taliban against Pakistani schoolgirls (Khan, 2012). This form of violence was finally specifically outlawed in 2011 (Azhar, 2012).

A common denominator throughout the world has been linked to partner violence: traditional gender roles and the inequality of women in society (McCloskey, Williams, & Larsen, 2005; United Nations Secretary General, 2006; Wipatayotin, 2005; Xu et al., 2005). Studies have also found that a low level of education for women is linked with a higher likelihood of experiencing partner violence (McCloskey et al., 2005; Rani, Bonu, & Diop-Sidibé, 2004). Violence against women is often seen as acceptable due to their lower societal status (Surtees, 2003). Leaving the relationship is not an option for women in many cultures. In Afghanistan, females who have left an abusive marriage have been imprisoned themselves for running away (United Nations Assistance Mission in Afghanistan, 2012). In other cases, she may be returned to her abusive husband by government courts or community leaders ("Afghan women," 2013). Divorce may not be legal or acceptable, and even if the woman did leave the relationship, she is likely to have difficulty surviving financially due to her lower status and education, making it difficult for her to obtain good-paying work. In many cultures, a woman's status is tied to her role as wife and mother, and if she leaves that, she loses the little status she did have (Surtees, 2003).

Progress is being made in that the number of countries outlawing intimate partner violence has been increasing. In 2009, there were only 21 countries of the 121 tracked by the Social Institutions and Gender Index (primarily countries in the Global South) that had laws specifically outlawing it and in 2012, there were 53 countries, or 2.5 times more (Social Institutions and Gender Index, 2012). However, these laws need to be well-enforced. For example, Turkey has a strong anti-family violence law; however, it has gaps, such as excluding unmarried women. It is inconsistently applied and police and judges have not always fulfilled their responsibilities (Human Rights Watch, 2011). In addition, while the law requires all cities with more than 50,000 residents to have a shelter, this requirement is far from being met (Human Rights Watch, 2011).

Dowry Deaths

A particular form of fatal partner violence that occurs in South Asia has been termed "dowry deaths." However, this is not a strictly accurate term. While many of the deaths may be precipitated by a desire for increased dowry, as with all domestic violence cases, the stated reason for the violence is often simply an excuse (Kishwar, 2005): Men may offer as an excuse for the violence that dinner was late or poorly cooked, but they are not called "lousy cooking murders."

Under the law in India, any death of a wife within the first 7 years of marriage is classified as a "dowry death"; it is up to her husband to prove it was not murder (Hackett, 2011). Thus, when news reports state that over 8,000 cases of dowry death were reported in India in 2010 (Bedi, 2012), it is unknown how many of these were truly such cases.

In India, regions with lower rates of gender equality and human development had higher rates of dowry deaths (Hackett, 2011). The link between dowries and the lower status of women is not a direct link, as even groups that did not practice the tradition of dowry were found to have committed female infanticide, demonstrating the low status of women in the culture regardless of the dowry burden (Oldenburg, 2002). As further evidence of the weaker link between dowry and "dowry death" and the stronger link with women's lower status, in Pakistan women are victims of deliberate burnings blamed on stoves; these deaths are not linked with dowries in that country but represent general violence within the family (Human Rights Watch, 2006). In Afghanistan, some women even set themselves on fire so that they can escape from the violence experienced at the hands of their husbands and in-laws (Rubin, 2010).

Conversely, in Uganda, it is the norm for the groom to give money or gifts to the bride's family, named "bride price." Research has found that women believe that this tradition contributes to domestic violence as the husbands feel they have "bought" their wives, and as their possessions, they may treat them as they like. Activists in Uganda want to change the name to "bride gift," as they do not believe they can eradicate the tradition, but hope the name change will reflect the intent of the tradition and not that women may be bought as possessions ("Ban term," 2013).

However, this should not obscure the fact that this does occur. The importance and amount of a bride's dowry has been growing in South Asia in countries such as India and Bangladesh, even though the giving and receiving of a dowry is illegal. To give an "appropriate" amount, many families are now driven into debt. However, some grooms and their families are not satisfied with the dowry and ask for more. If they do not receive it, they may kill the bride so that the groom is free to marry again and get another dowry.

A dowry was originally intended as an inheritance for the woman so that she would have her own wealth separate from her husband's. Women traditionally married out of their birth villages and moved away from the protection of their families. The dowry was developed to give her money and goods for her pleasure and possibly for times of need. It was intended to show the appreciation for, and the status of, the bride in her home village (Oldenburg, 2002). However, with the advent of the British colonialism and laws, inheritance for women waned. The British concept of inheritance was that land was passed down to first-born sons; thus, land was no longer passed down to women and they lost their traditional inheritances. This led to the concentration of land in the hands of a few wealthy landowners rather than many smaller farmers, increasing poverty. This increase in familial poverty led to difficulties in giving daughters a dowry and they began to be seen as liabilities (Kishwar, 2005). To combat this, a campaign in India has started urging couples to pledge to abstain from giving or receiving a dowry: (www.indiatogether. org/women/dowry/pledge).

Honor Killings

Another example of violence that women and girls face from their families, either at birth or by marriage, is honor killings. It is estimated that approximately 5,000 women are murdered each year in honor killings (United Nations Secretary General, 2006). In some cultures, if a female is seen to have besmirched the family honor by acting in a dishonorable way, the only way for the family to regain its honor is to kill her. The offense is typically due to violating cultural norms such as having an extramarital affair, wanting to choose her own husband, being seen in the company of a man who is not her husband, or even being raped. These violations may not even be proven but may be only a suspicion of her family. In some cases of rape, women have not been killed but have been forced to marry their rapist to preserve honor (Zaman, 2005). These situations have been documented in Turkey, Pakistan, and Egypt, as well as in countries in Europe where people from these countries have immigrated. While these are all predominately Muslim nations, the crime is not sanctioned by Islam and predates the development of Islam as a religion (Homolo, 2006; Sev'er & Yurdakul, 2005). Imams in Canada have declared a fatwa (a ruling based on religious law) against these murders (Csillag, 2012).

Research has found that there are distinct populations who are victims of this crime. Younger girls (average age 17 years) are more likely to be killed by their family of origin while older women (average age 36 years) are more likely to be killed by an intimate partner. Women living in North America and Europe were more likely to be killed for acting "too Western," while women in the Muslim world were more likely to be killed for allegations of sexual impropriety. Acting "too Western" included refusal to wear the hijab, refusal to marry the chosen husband, or a desire to have non-Muslim friends or boyfriends (Chesler, 2010). This is supported by research from Pakistan, which states that women over 18 years are more than three-quarters of the victims and are killed for suspected sexual impropriety in 92% of documented cases (Nasrullah, Haqqi, & Cummings, 2009).

Although honor killings are outlawed, they are frequently not punished severely. The family will also commonly have the youngest male in the family take the blame for the murder, even if he did not commit it, so that the courts will be more lenient with him due to his age (Kulczycki & Windle, 2011). Families may also pressure women perceived to have tarnished the family honor to commit suicide, or they will kill her in a manner that looks like suicide in order to avoid prosecution (Bilefsky, 2006).

The limited role of women in affected cultures often leads to men being seen as the absolute ruler of the household. In this scenario, it is his role and responsibility to discipline a female who violates cultural prescriptions for appropriate dress and action. Thus, discrimination is a clear factor in this violence, but poverty has also been found to play a role. Families in which honor killings occur are often very poor with low levels of formal education (Broom, Sibbritt, Nayar, Dorn, & Nilan, 2012; Kulczycki & Windle, 2011). Honor is seen as a valuable possession, and in the case of impoverished families, it may be the only thing of value they have. Therefore, when it is seen as damaged, it is extremely important to reclaim this only possession of value (Sev'er & Yurdakul, 2005). As one father who killed his daughters due to an adulterous affair of one stated,

"We are poor people and we have nothing else to protect but our honor" (Tanveer, 2005, p. A9).

In a famous case in Pakistan, Mukhtar Mai (also known as Mukhtaran Bibi) fought back against this system of honor. Her 12-year-old brother had allegedly committed transgressions, and a village council decreed that she should be gang-raped as punishment for her brother's actions. She was taken outside and raped by four men while others watched. It is typically expected that after she had been shamed in such a manner, she should commit suicide to reclaim honor. Instead, she pressed charges against the rapists. The men were found guilty in court and she was awarded monetary compensation from the government. She used this money to open schools in her village. She received pressure from the Pakistani government to remain silent, but with the help of Nicholas Kristof, a *New York Times* columnist, her story has become known worldwide. She now has a book telling her story: *In the Name of Honor* (Mai, 2006).

Unequal Under the Law

In a number of countries around the world, women have fewer rights under the law than men. Some countries place limitations on women's movements (including the right to go out without a male family escort), the right to work (including in mixed-gender environments), the right to a passport without permission of a male relative, and the right to drive. In Algeria, the 1984 Algerian Family Code treats adult women as minors under the law, stating that women are legally obliged to obey their husbands and that a man may have up to four wives (Salhi, 2003). In Saudi Arabia, women are not permitted to appear in public without a male relative or to drive. The male relative designated as their guardian is sent a text message if they leave the country (Harding, 2012). Israel has seen a public debate between the ultra-Orthodox, known as the Haredim, and other sectors of society over the role of women, resulting in women speakers being barred from a conference and protests over mixed-sex buses (Bronner & Kershener, 2012). As noted in Chapter 4, some countries also have limits on mothers being able to register the birth of a child or pass their citizenship to their child.

A number of nations have limitations on property ownership, inheritance rights, and credit access for women, therefore restricting their ability to earn income (UNFPA, 2005). According to the Social Institutions and Gender Index, 86 of the 121 countries tracked had discriminatory inheritance laws or practices (Social Institutions and Gender Index, 2012a). Inheritance laws discriminate against women in some countries, with some cultures passing all property to the husband's birth family due to the desire to retain property within that family as well as the difficulty of dividing property in polygamous societies. However, this leaves widows impoverished and at the mercy of others. Custody of children can also be an issue. For example, in the Democratic Republic of the Congo, a widow does not have sole guardianship of her children; rather, it is held jointly with members of her husband's family (Banda, 2008).

In some countries, women have differential access to divorce, including reasons why a divorce can be granted and how the divorce can be granted. For example, in Israel, a woman may not initiate a divorce without the consent of her husband because divorce is considered a religious rather than civil matter (Amnesty International, 2004). In Thailand, a man may be granted a divorce on grounds of adultery, but a woman cannot (Social Institutions and Gender Index, 2012b). In Afghanistan, a man can simply declare himself divorced; however, a woman faces very high barriers to obtaining one (Human Rights Watch, 2012).

Even when laws are changed, it can still be difficult for women to access the rights granted to them due to the lack of cultural agreement with the new law. In a number of countries in Africa, laws have been changed to allow women to inherit and own property, but they have encountered difficulties in trying to realize these rights ("Botswana women," 2012; "Fighting for," 2012; "Women's equality," 2009). However, this is not to say that progress cannot be realized under the law. Saudi Arabia has made a number of recent changes, allowing women the right to vote as of 2015, increased access to employment, and seats in Parliament ("Breakthrough," 2013; MacFarquhar, 2011; Watson, 2012). In contrast, Iraqi women used to have many more rights than other women in the region; however, they have now lost this status as these rights have been eroded as a result of the troubles experienced by their nation ("Women yet," 2013).

The most infamous cases of discriminatory treatment have occurred in Afghanistan. Under the rule of the Taliban, women were not allowed to leave the house without the escort of a close male relative, and when they did leave, they had to be completely covered. They could not seek medical care, even in an emergency, without the escort of a close male relative.

They were not permitted to be educated and could not work. This drove many women into desperate poverty and even death because their husbands and other male relatives had been killed during the decades of war. Readers are referred to Benard (2002) for more information on this topic.

Afghanistan remains a country where women experience extensive discrimination. While in 2009, laws were passed that criminalized child marriage, forced marriage, forced self-immolation, rape, and other acts of violence, these laws have not been fully implemented (United Nations Assistance Mission in Afghanistan, 2012). While reports to police of such violence have increased, investigations and prosecutions have been lacking. The law is considered to be quite weak; however, proponents fear that attempts to strengthen it could lead to a backlash that eliminates it entirely (Rubin, 2013).

According to Human Rights Watch (2012), almost all imprisoned girls and about half of imprisoned women in Afghanistan were incarcerated on charges of "moral crimes." These crimes include running away from a forced marriage or intimate partner violence, or for having sex outside marriage, after experiencing sexual assault or forced prostitution. In some cases, women had gone to the police to report crimes committed against them, only to be arrested themselves. Running away is not a crime under either Afghan law or *Sharia* law, yet this problem persists (United Nations Assistance Mission in Afghanistan, 2012). The UN report also noted that authorities would often refer cases to local *jirgas*, councils of powerful men, where decisions were made based on a mix of formal law, religious law, and personal relationships—typically resulting in a lack of justice for the woman.

The concept of cultural relativity comes into question in this discussion. A common argument is that these laws are in keeping with the tenets of Islam and should be respected. However, the merits of this argument do not hold up to close examination. Afkhami (2001) notes that these restrictions rely on a particular interpretation of the tenets of Islam—a strain of fundamentalism that exists in all religions, including Christianity, Judaism, and Buddhism. When women are kept silent, as occurs in many fundamentalist religions, their differing opinions cannot be heard. However, many of the women under these systems state that this inequality is not what they want, an opinion echoed by a number of the men (Benard, 2002). The term "gender apartheid" is sometimes used in these discussions to draw parallels to the differing systems that existed in South Africa for people for different races. This differential treatment was not considered to be a natural part of their culture and deserving of respect, but a system imposed specifically to benefit one group of people over another. As stated in Chapter 2, human rights protect the right to one's culture, but that right is limited in that it may not infringe on another protected human right (Ayton-Shenker, 1995).

Brodsky (2003, p. ix) notes that "the oppression of Afghanistan and particularly Afghan women did not start with the Taliban nor has it ended with their defeat." Women in Afghanistan have been fighting for equal treatment for decades and still have not achieved it, even after the fall of the Taliban. The Taliban continue to try to reassert their radical form of Islam and have attacked a number of women working to oppose it, including female ministers in the government.

Women's Health

Due to their reproductive abilities, women are at risk for health issues that do not affect men. Since women are seen as being of lower class than men and their reproductive capacity is often seen as "different," these medical issues typically do not receive the attention that they should, on the micro, mezzo, or macro level. This is also true in terms of defining human rights: Many documents do not include reproductive health, an issue that can be a matter of life and death (Agosín, 2001). Many women do not have access to contraceptives, which thus increases the likelihood of an unintended pregnancy. Approximately one in five women in the Global South is estimated to have an "unmet need" for family planning: She would prefer not to become pregnant but is not using any form of contraception (Social Institutions and Gender Index, 2012a). As discussed in Chapter 6, in a number of cultures it is considered inappropriate for a woman to refuse to have intercourse with her husband for any reason; thus, even if she would prefer not to become pregnant, she cannot refuse him.

When women experience an unintended pregnancy, some will opt to have an abortion, whether it is legal or not in their country; such illegal abortions can be fatal. The World Health Organization [WHO] (2012a) found that abortions occur across the world, regardless of abortion laws; however, unsafe abortions are correlated with stricter abortion laws, resulting in higher rates of death and injury. Unsafe abortion is defined by WHO (2012a, p. 1) as "a procedure for terminating an unwanted pregnancy either by persons lacking the necessary skills or in an environment lacking the minimal medical standards, or both." Approximately 47,000 women die every year from unsafe abortions, 13% of all pregnancy-related deaths (WHO, 2012a). The incidence varies greatly by region, with the highest rates in South America, as well as Eastern and Middle Africa (WHO, 2012b).

Reducing the maternal mortality rate is one of the Millennium Development Goals (discussed in Chapter 9), and significant progress has been made. Maternal mortality was cut almost in half between 1990 and 2010, with the number of deaths each year decreasing from 543,000 to 287,000; the greatest declines were seen in eastern Asia and northern Africa (UNFPA, UNICEF, WHO, & World Bank, 2012). Substantial progress also has been noted in Egypt, China, Ecuador, and Bolivia (Hogan et al., 2010).

However, this still means that each day, 800 women die due to pregnancy-related reasons (UNFPA, n.d.). The highest rates of mortality are in sub-Saharan Africa and southern Asia (UNFPA, UNICEF, WHO, World Bank, 2012). Half the deaths were concentrated in six countries in 2008: Afghanistan, Democratic Republic of the Congo, Ethiopia, India, Nigeria, and Pakistan (Hogan et al., 2010). Even within countries, disparities can be seen. Overall, Nigeria halved its maternal mortality rate between 1990 and 2010, but much of that progress has been in seen in the wealthier southern region of the country, rather than the more rural, poorer northern half ("Bridging the north-south divide," 2012).

Several factors are noted as important to reducing maternal mortality: reducing the number of births per woman, increased income, increased maternal education, and increased skilled birth attendance (Hogan et al., 2010). Trained midwives are seen as essential in the battle to reduce the number of these deaths. The World Health Organization has called the shortage of trained midwives "deadly" and estimates that their numbers need to more than double to meet the reduction goal set by the Millennium Development Goal ("Shortage of midwives," 2009). For example, Nepal has cut its maternal mortality rate almost in half, but this reduction is predicted to be unsustainable if the number of midwives does not sharply increase ("Nepal's maternal mortality," 2013).

Some countries have used Conditional Cash Transfers to increase mothers' use of medical facilities, while others work to increase access in other ways. In Bolivia, pregnant women who lack health coverage can register to receive four small stipends through their pregnancy if they receive prenatal check-ups and give birth in a hospital. In addition, they can receive 12 additional payments in the child's first 2 years if they bring the child in for scheduled check-ups and postnatal care (Moloney, 2009). In Bangladesh, women can receive vouchers for free prenatal care, subsidies for transportation, and cash for utilizing a trained attendant while giving birth ("Demand-side financing," 2012). In Sierra Leone, Médecins Sans Frontières provides free emergency obstetric care together with an ambulance service ("Slashing the maternal mortality rate," 2012), and in Mali, doctors go to rural villages rather than requiring the women to travel to them (Medical house visits," 2009).

While progress is being made in reducing the mortality rate, even more common, though, are long-lasting infections, injuries, and disabilities resulting from childbirth; 20 times more women suffer from these complications than from maternal death (UNFPA, n.d.). One example of an injury resulting from childbirth that has become extremely rare in the Global North, but is still common in other areas, is a fistula. Typically experienced by young mothers, especially those who are small (as is typical in females who are poor and undernourished throughout their lives), it occurs during extended labor. During contractions, the tissues between the uterus and the bowel, as well as between the uterus and bladder, rub against each other. When labor is protracted, this friction can result in tissue tearing, creating an opening between the two organs. In smaller women, the baby may be too large compared to her body for the birth to proceed easily. Due to the lack of access to medical facilities, the tear is not repaired, and the woman becomes incontinent. The leakage of urine and/or excrement causes a severe rash and a foul odor. As a result, the woman is typically cast off from her husband and her village. If she does not receive surgery to repair the tear, she can die as a result of this societal neglect.

It is estimated that approximately 2 million women are currently living with a fistula and 50,000 to 100,000 new cases occur every year. These numbers are based on women seeking treatment, and thus the actual numbers are likely much higher (UNFPA, n.d.). The problem is concentrated in sub-Saharan Africa due to a combination of reasons: poverty, lack of access to modern health care, the tradition of home birth, and early pregnancy. However, it also occurs in other nations where these factors cluster, such as Afghanistan and Pakistan (UNFPA, 2009).

Maternal mortality and morbidity helps illustrate how discrimination against women in other arenas can lead to permanent injury and death. As mentioned, women who are small are more at risk. Since girls are more likely to be malnourished than their brothers, this creates a risk factor. The stereotype that girls should not be educated but should be married as soon as possible to reduce the cost to their birth family again creates a risk factor, as younger women are more at risk for fistulas. Onolemhemhen (2005) states that to prevent fistulas, long-term solutions must include the education of girls and delaying their marriages until they reach maturity.

The following story helps illustrate the common scenario (adapted from Kristof & WuDunn, 2009):

Mahabouba was 14 when she gave birth. She had escaped from a marriage in which she was abused by her husband and his first wife. Her birth was unassisted by even a midwife, and after 7 days of labor, she lost consciousness and assistance was called. Mahabouba suffered a fistula to both her urethra and rectum and therefore leaked urine and feces. Additionally, she had suffered nerve damage to her pelvis and was unable to stand or walk. She was placed in a hut at the edge of the village, where she fought off hyenas with a stick before crawling for a day to a missionary for assistance. He took her to the Addis Ababa Fistula Hospital, where she was treated.

The surgery to repair fistulas is relatively easy and is typically successful. However, it is typically difficult to obtain because few doctors perform it and the cost, about US$100, is usually beyond the means of the woman. Therefore, UNFPA has launched the Global Campaign to End Fistula and has been working in a number of countries around the world to work on both prevention and treatment of fistulas in several ways. They have been working to help expand the number of people qualified to perform the surgery, as well as reducing the stigma around it. In addition, they have been working to help prevent it by promoting family planning, skilled birth attendance, and emergency obstetric care for those who need it (UNFPA, n.d.). The UNFPA works around the world to try to reduce these numbers of maternal deaths and injuries. However, in 2002, the Bush administration refused to pay the US share of dues, stating that UNFPA supported the one-child policy and forced abortion in China. Data supporting this claim were never found; in fact, the US State Department stated they had investigated and found no evidence to support it. Upon his inauguration in 2009, President Obama resumed the funding.

Access to Education

As discussed in Chapter 4, it is more common for girls to be denied access to an education than boys. Thus, the majority of children out of school are girls, leading to the fact that almost two-thirds of illiterate adults in the world are female (UNESCO, 2011).

There are a number of barriers to girls' education, including structural barriers, cultural beliefs, and safety concerns. Structural barriers to education can include a lack of female teachers or schools for girls in cultures that do not believe it is appropriate for male teachers to be teaching female students or for female students to be educated with male students. Additionally, many schools in rural Africa do not have private toilet facilities. For example, in Sudan, there is nowhere for girls to relieve themselves, and they will drop out of school rather than embarrass themselves in front of their male classmates by leaving the premises. This only gets worse after girls experience their first menstrual cycle; there is no private place for them to tend to these needs and they will drop out of school rather than be shamed (Abdelmoneium, 2005).

Cultural beliefs can also limit girls' education. Some cultures believe it is not useful to educate girls because they will only grow up to marry and have children. Other girls may start school but not be able to finish due to early marriage or a need to help with the housework and caretaking of younger children at home. This can be influenced by familial poverty— because girls are valuable at home, where they can assist with household chores, it can be perceived as more expensive to send a girl to school than a boy in terms of lost labor.

Concerns for safety can also act as a barrier to girls' education. Attacks by the Taliban in Afghanistan have made going to school dangerous, and many families are keeping girls home to ensure their safety. In Ethiopia, girls are at risk of being abducted and raped; they are then often married to the rapist because their honor has been ruined. This type of attack (known as *telefa*) is committed primarily while girls are walking back and forth to school, raising fears about this journey (Save the Children Denmark, Ministry of Education, & Ministry of Women's Affairs, 2008). In India, sexual harassment of girls on their way to school has caused parents to pull their daughters out of school (Williams, 2013).

Girls may not even be safe once they reach school. Teachers also sometimes sexually assault girls, promising them good grades in exchange (Save the Children Denmark et al., 2008). In some areas that lack qualified teachers, young, low-qualified men are hired, which has led to an increase in sexual harassment of female students (Valerio, Bardasi, Chambal, & Lobo, 2006). For example, in both South Africa and Ecuador, approximately one-third of sexual violence against girls is perpetrated by teachers (Plan International, 2008).

However, the importance of education of girls can be argued under both the equity and efficiency arguments. The United Nations has stated that not only does education for girls have the greatest payoffs for the empowerment of women, but it also pays off throughout their lives in ways that benefit society as a whole (UNFPA, 2005). Research has concluded that the education of women has a greater positive impact on social and economic development of a country than the education of men (e.g., Balatchandirane, 2003; UNFPA, 2005). As noted throughout the book, education of girls serves as a protective factor against a number of harmful issues. Educated women have increased economic capabilities and are more able to play a role in society and have a voice in their life. Education of girls has been found to reduce deaths due to childbirth, to lower child mortality and fertility rates, and to delay marriage; educated women are also more likely to send their children to school (UNICEF, 2012). It is estimated that there have been 4.2 million fewer child deaths due to the increase in women's education (Gakidou, Cowling, Lozano, & Murray, 2010).

Strategies to increase enrollment of girls in school include eliminating school fees, working to increase sanitation facilities, and working with male students to help them understand the burdens female students face and to be supportive of them. The United Nations has established a special initiative to increase the enrollment of girls—the United Nations Girls' Education Initiative (UNGEI). Additionally, the elimination of gender disparity in all levels of education is a target in the Millennium Development Goals.

Women and Development

Previously, the unique impacts of development on women were not considered and actually increased their hardships rather than relieving them. This is due in part to the fact that women's traditional contributions to society are unpaid and thus are unmeasured in terms of economic growth. What is unmeasured is cast as unimportant (see the work of Marilyn Waring for more information on this topic). For example, structural adjustment policies discussed in Chapter 6 had a disproportionate impact on women. As women's gender role casts them as caregivers, they were typically the ones who shouldered the additional burden when governmental services such as medical care or child care are cut. Van Soest and Crosby (1997) give the example of how an agricultural intervention enabled men to double the acreage of planting, which then doubled the workload of women who were responsible for weeding the fields by hand. Due to examples such as these, the World Bank and United Nations, as well as other institutions, have now implemented a policy of "gender mainstreaming" in which the impact of policies on each gender is examined prior to implementation. According to the United Nations, gender mainstreaming involves ensuring that "gender perspectives and attention to the goal of gender equality are central to all activities" (n.d., ¶1).

However, even when aid is given to support gender equality, it rarely goes to local women's rights organizations; in 2010, these groups received only 1.3% of such funding from countries in the Organization for Economic Cooperation and Development (OECD). The money typically goes to international nongovernmental organizations (NGOs), who then subcontract to local groups. This approach does not recognize the expert knowledge and leadership potential in such organizations but treats them as mere workers. It also inhibits their ability to earn funds to strengthen their own organization (Jackson, 2013).

Some of the most successful examples of empowerment and increased equity in development (both social and economic) have originated within nations rather than as a result of international development. The Self-Employed Women's Association (SEWA), mentioned in Chapter 3, is a labor union in India founded in 1972 by Ela Bhatt (see their Web site at www.sewa.org). SEWA's goals are full employment and self-reliance for its members. It is an unusual labor union in that its members consist of poor, self-employed female workers. These women are employed in such labor as selling vegetables, picking out recyclable materials from trash heaps, and weaving. They were excluded from India's labor laws as these were not recognized professions by the government (Bhatt, 2006). Bhatt, an experienced labor organizer, helped them organize and advocate for their rights. By organizing and working together, the women are able to advocate for higher wages and less harassment. They are no longer as afraid to stand up for their rights because they know that there are many others who will help them (Bhatt, 2006).

To achieve these goals, SEWA has organized a number of support services, including a microfinance bank and child care, health care, and legal services. These services also help SEWA members because those who provide the service charge for it, thus earning income at the same time they are helping others in their quest for employment (SEWA, n.d.). SEWA developed a bank in which these women, who previously could not access traditional financial institutions, can save money as well as borrow it. Traditional institutions would not lend to them because they were illiterate and without formal collateral. The only place they had been able to borrow money was from moneylenders, who charged usurious rates, keeping the women in poverty. At the SEWA Bank they can borrow money at reasonable rates once they have established themselves, helping them on the path out of poverty. This system is similar to that of microcredit.

Microcredit, in which small loans are made to those living in poverty, has been successful in helping to alleviate poverty and empower women. Originating with the Grameen Bank in Bangladesh (discussed in more detail in the Culture Box), it has spread to other countries. In recognition of the far-reaching impact of microfinance, the founder of the Grameen Bank, Muhammad Yunus, was awarded the Nobel Peace Prize in 2006.

However, together with its successes, there have been problems as well. Vonderlack-Navarro (2010) points out that microfinance only seeks to operate within the current societal structure that makes it difficult for the poor, especially women, to become financially stable, rather than seeking to change that system. By focusing on women, because they are more likely to repay the loan and spend the money on their families, it implicitly gives the men permission to not contribute to the household and to spend the money on what they choose.

In countries such as Mexico and Nigeria, interest rates have remained extremely high due to lack of competition, and one lender in Mexico has even become a publically traded company with huge profits (MacFarquhar, 2010; Malkin, 2008). This focus on investor outcomes can lead to a lack of interest in alleviating poverty. In India, borrowers in one state protested against companies by stopping their payments. They stated that the focus on profit spurred companies to aggressively seek to issue loans regardless of the person's ability to repay it. As Ela Bhatt pointed out, people need more than loans to become successful entrepreneurs; they also need support in the form of sound financial and business advice (Polgreen & Bajaj, 2010).

A review of the impact of microfinance in sub-Saharan countries found mixed results, both between countries and between variables. Generally, positive impacts were seen on health, health behaviors, food security, housing, and women's empowerment, while negative results were more common for children's education and no impact on child labor. Results varied on the impact on income (Van Rooyen, Stewart, & De Wet, 2012).

These mixed results may be the result of subpopulations. In the Philippines, it was found that increases for wives in household decision-making participation and household expenditures on goods for female use increased significantly for women who were lower than average in these measures at pretest, but not for women above average. Thus, the impact was greatest on those who benefitted most (Ashraf, Karlan, & Yin, 2010). Another study in India found that results improved with the number of years a woman was in the program (Basargekar, 2010). Of course, it should also be considered that a woman may only stay if it is beneficial for her.

The cultural context is also important to consider. Haile, Bock, and Folmer (2012) conducted a study assessing the impact of two different microfinance programs in Ethiopia with markedly different cultures, including expectations about the role of women. While positive results were generally seen across both sites in how money was spent, who owned assets, and domestic conflict, Haile et al. stated that where traditionally the sexes have separate incomes and make decisions separately about spending money, such programs are more likely to increase female empowerment. It should also be noted that they found that microfinance tended to increase women's workloads as they maintained responsibility for their traditional roles, including domestic chores and child care, while adding the responsibilities created by the economic activity generated by the loan, such as caring for livestock.

Professional Role of Social Workers

Throughout this chapter, different issues that affect women solely because of their gender have been discussed, but the impact of poverty and lack of education has been clear. The research findings of multiple international organizations support the fact that for global social and economic development to occur, women must become empowered. Due to our ethical grounding in empowerment, social workers are an ideal group to help empower disenfranchised groups. We are able to work both with international NGOs and local movements to help women achieve a culturally relevant model of equality.

Due to varied means by which women experience discrimination, there are a variety of methods that social workers can use to help alleviate the situation. Social workers can work on the macro level to help change laws to allow women equal rights under the law; they can also work on the mezzo and micro levels to increase acceptance of the new laws and open up opportunities for women. The vision of equality for women should not be based on a Western model but should evolve from within the society and should take into account what those citizens want to achieve. Recognizing the client as the expert is another method in which social workers can help achieve a culturally relevant, more equitable world.

Culture Box
MICROFINANCE IN BANGLADESH

Bangladesh is located in south Asia to the east of India. After India received its independence from Britain, Pakistan (located to the west of India) and Bangladesh (then known as East Pakistan) separated from India due to religious differences and were one nation. Due to its wide geographical separation from Pakistan, however, Bangladesh declared independence in 1971. The majority of the country is Muslim (90%), with a minority Hindu population (10%). Thirty-two percent of the population lives below the poverty line (CIA, 2013). This is a noticeable decrease from the 45% poverty rate in the first edition of this text; the economy has grown 5%–6% each year (CIA, 2013).

As is true all over the world, Bangladeshi women are more likely than men to be poor and have fewer opportunities for moving out of poverty. Some of the reasons for this are that inheritance rights favor men and that cultural norms emphasize *purdah* for women (female seclusion) and strict adherence to the appropriate gender role: caregiver in the home. Any monetary contributions to the household by women tend to be devalued (Bernasek, 2003). Poor women were often engaged in small-scale economic activities to help feed their families but lacked access to credit to expand these businesses. As was true for most Bangladeshis living in poverty, they did not have access to traditional banks due to lack of collateral and could not get financing for self-employment enterprises. Women faced additional barriers in obtaining financing as they were not considered credit-worthy and needed a male relative to cosign the loan (Bernasek, 2003). Their only options were moneylenders and loan sharks who charged exorbitant interest rates.

In 1976, Muhammad Yunus of the University of Chittagong in Bangladesh started an enterprise to help impoverished people gain access to loans at market rates to help them pull themselves out of poverty. This is known as microfinance (Grameen Bank, 2002). Microfinance is defined as "offering very small loans to poor people, usually women, to help grow their small-scale businesses or start new ones" (UNFPA, 2006c, p. 6). Although loans were initially made to men and women equally, women now represent 96% of the more than 6 million borrowers (Grameen Bank, 2011). Women are preferred as borrowers as research has found that they are more likely to invest income in their families, resulting in increases in child survival rates and child growth. They are also more likely to repay their loans (Coleman, 2005). Loans are used for a variety of commercial activities, including agriculture, the selling of agricultural products, opening a shop, or selling a service, in attempts to move out of poverty (Jahiruddin, Short, Dressler, & Khan, 2011). Grameen Bank assesses reductions in poverty through a combination of factors, not only income but also housing quality, access to clean water and sanitation, and food security (Grameen Bank, 2013).

The Grameen Bank has been joined by other organizations in Bangladesh, the largest of which is the Bangladesh Rural Advancement Committee (BRAC), and they operate in a similar manner. The difference is that Grameen Bank utilizes what is termed a "credit-only" approach, where it focuses on the provision of loans, while BRAC is "credit-plus," as it also provides training, raw materials, and consultations (Jahiruddin et al., 2011). There are also other nongovernmental and governmental organizations operating within the country, but these are the two largest.

To take advantage of the cultural importance of social networks, villagers interested in participating are gathered into groups of five. One loan at a time is given to one member of the group and the entire group is held responsible for repayment. This helps create peer pressure and solidarity for increasing the rate of repayment, as well as creating social support for the women who are breaking gender norms by engaging in economic activity. As repayment rates have been above 90% and social stigma has decreased, this appears to be a highly successful method (Basher, 2007; Develtere & Huybrechts, 2005). However, this method has been criticized for using cultural norms of shaming women to regulate behavior (Karim, 2008).

(continued)

Demonstrating the broad definition of poverty and how its reduction is assessed, the Grameen Bank has created social development goals known as the Sixteen Decisions by which participants must agree to abide. These decisions are designed to help influence all aspects of their lives, not just the financial part (Grameen Bank, 2006b).

The Sixteen Decisions of the Grameen Bank

We shall follow and advance the four principles of Grameen Bank—Discipline, Unity, Courage, and Hard Work—in all walks of our lives.

Prosperity we shall bring to our families.

We shall not live in dilapidated houses. We shall repair our houses and work towards constructing new houses at the earliest.

We shall grow vegetables all the year round. We shall eat plenty of them and sell the surplus.

During the plantation seasons, we shall plant as many seedlings as possible.

We shall plan to keep our families small. We shall minimize our expenditures. We shall look after our health.

We shall educate our children and ensure that they can earn to pay for their education.

We shall always keep our children and the environment clean.

We shall build and use pit-latrines.

We shall drink water from tubewells. If it is not available, we shall boil water or use alum.

We shall not take any dowry at our sons' weddings; neither shall we give any dowry at our daughters' wedding. We shall keep our centre free from the curse of dowry. We shall not practice child marriage.

We shall not inflict any injustice on anyone; neither shall we allow anyone to do so.

We shall collectively undertake bigger investments for higher incomes.

We shall always be ready to help each other. If anyone is in difficulty, we shall all help him or her.

If we come to know of any breach of discipline in any centre, we shall all go there and help restore discipline.

We shall take part in all social activities collectively.

While microcredit has been given credit for everything from reducing poverty to empowering women to increasing education, in reality the research findings have been more mixed. Overall, microcredit has been found to improve the living conditions in a variety of ways for its users, including increases in income, food security, children's school enrollment, and access to health care (Chemin, 2008; Mahjabeen, 2008; Nawaz, 2010). However, some research has found that microcredit can increase child labor due to the requirements of the business (Islam & Choe, 2013).

Women who participate in microcredit were found to be "empowered" in a variety of ways, including non-economic ones such as participation in national elections and decreasing preference for sons (Basher, 2007). Women participating in microcredit were more likely than similar women to contribute to the household income, participate in family decision-making, and be aware of gender issues. However, they were less likely to have access to resources such as education. Among women participating in microcredit, these benefits were more likely to be observed among borrowers from the Grameen Bank as opposed to other institutions (Hoque & Itohara, 2009).

However, microfinance has not always reached the poorest of the poor (Chemin, 2008; Nawaz, 2010). It has also been criticized for making loans to those who lack the ability to repay them ("Microfinance institutions," 2011). In interviewing the small subset in their study who stated their financial situation was worse as a result of microfinance, Jahiruddin et al. (2011) found there were four interrelated barriers that helped create this situation: a business that took a while to provide financial returns (such as agriculture);

(continued)

suffering a loss at the beginning of the business; using the money for a household emergency (such as illness); and using the money for household expenditures. These poorer households have no financial reserves to help see them through these financial bumps and thus are at higher risk to default on the loan.

To address this, an approach that provides greater supports has been suggested. Ahmed (2009) tested a capacity development approach among the ultra-poor in Bangladesh that included skill training, initial monthly stipends, and technical assistance. Health support, including sanitation and financial assistance for health care, as well as social development knowledge on topics such as women's rights, early marriage, and dowry, were also provided. Participating families demonstrated an improvement in income, assets, food security, and access to health care. The health care and nutrition was seen was as a vital factor as people will be unable to work if they are ill or malnourished.

In 2011, Mohammed Yunus left his position at the Grameen Bank after a dispute with the government about his role. However, the Grameen Bank continues to operate today as he established it. As demonstrated here, the research supporting microfinance is not all positive, but on the whole, it demonstrates beneficial outcomes, particularly if the program is designed to support the specific needs of the participants.

What You Can Do Now

- Raise awareness about the status of women worldwide and why this is important to social development.
- Volunteer with local agencies. Many of these issues, such as intimate partner violence, are not only experienced by those in the Global South.
- Raise funds to help a local organization continue its work. What is small money to those in the United States can make a major difference in other countries.
- Understand the strengths and weaknesses of arguments relating to women's issues and cultural relativity. Be able to respond articulately to those who state, "That's just their culture; we shouldn't interfere."
- Help to donate goods such as computers and digital cameras to organizations that need them.
- Work to fight stereotypes based on gender in your own life.

What You Can Do as a Professional Social Worker

- Work for an international NGO such as those listed in the Appendix.
- Work for a domestic agency that focuses on issues faced by women and girls. Change created in one country can spread to others and no country is immune to these issues.

World Wide Web Resources

Association for Women in Development (www.awid.org): An international organization committed to achieving gender equality, sustainable development, and human rights for women. The goal is to create policy, institutional, and individual change to improve the lives of women and girls.

The Campaign to End Fistula (www.endfistula.org): The website of the UNFPA campaign to raise money and awareness concerning fistulas.

Council of Europe Web site on violence against women (http://www.coe.int/t/dg2/equality/domesticviolencecampaign/default_en.asp): This Web site contains a variety of information on the campaign within Europe to combat intimate partner violence.

DAWN (Development Alternatives with Women for a New Era) (www.dawnnet.org): A network of women scholars and activists from the Global South who engage in feminist research and analysis and are committed to working for economic justice, gender justice, and democracy.

Eldis Interactions (interactions.eldis.org): A collection of research focusing on three central themes: activism against gender-based violence; health of women and girls in low-income urban settings; and the visibility of unpaid care work in public policy.

Grameen Bank (www.grameen-info.org): The home page of the Grameen Bank.

The International Center for Research on Women (www.icrw.org): Research on a variety of topics to advocate for women on an international basis.

One-by-One (www.fightfistula.org): A US-based campaign to raise awareness and money to reduce the incidence of fistulas.

Social Institutions and Gender Index (www.genderindex.org): Research developed by the OECD to assess countries in the Global South on "discriminatory social institutions, such as early marriage, discriminatory inheritance practices, violence against women, son preference, restricted access to public space, and restricted access to land and credit."

United Nations Population Fund (www.unfpa.org): A Web site containing information on a broad variety of issues related to reproductive health, including HIV/AIDS and female genital cutting. Up-to-date reports as well as intervention strategies are available.

United Nations Secretary-General Campaign to End Violence against Women (http://endviolence.un.org): The UN Web site on the campaign to end violence against women. It contains useful fact sheets and reports.

United Nations Womenwatch (www.un.org/womenwatch): This UN site provides information and resources on gender equality and empowerment of women.

UN Women (www.unwomen.org): This UN site also provides information and resources on gender equality and empowerment of women.

UN Women Virtual Knowledge Centre (http://www.endvawnow. org): A compendium of information on evidence-based strategies to end violence against women.

VAWnet compendium of research on IPV (snow.vawnet.org). A compendium of information on violence against women. It is US focused but has some global information.

World Health Organization—Gender-based violence (http://www. who.int/topics/gender_based_violence/en/): Information on a variety of forms of violence against women.

Women's Human Rights Resources (www.law-lib.utoronto. ca/Diana/index.htm): "Collects, organizes and disseminates information on women's human rights law to facilitate research, teaching, and cooperation." There is a database with links to hundreds of documents relating to women's human rights as well as bibliographies and research guides.

Women's Refugee Commission (http://womensrefugeecommission. org/): Part of the International Rescue Committee, this commission works to monitor the care and condition of refugee women and children. It gathers information and advocates on issues as needed.

8

Social Work and the Physical Environment

Grave changes are occurring within the Earth's physical environment. Attention has been growing within the profession that social workers need to increase their awareness of environmental issues and the impact they have on populations we serve. Despite social work's focus on the "Person-in-Environment," this has been defined primarily as person in the *social* environment, with little attention on the physical environment. Social workers have long been aware that disempowered communities bear the brunt of the downside of progress, such as locating toxic dumps in impoverished communities and receive little attention when disasters affect them, such as the Union Carbide gas leak in Bhopal, India. However, issues related to the physical environment have been given relatively little attention by the profession with the exception of a few scholars such as Mary Rogge and Fred Besthorn. With the increasing advent of climate change, and its disproportionate impact on the poor and disempowered, this can no longer be the case.

Recent publications seek to raise awareness in the profession regarding these issues, including *Environmental Social Work* (Gray, Coates, & Hetherington, 2013) and *Green Social Work: From Environmental Crises to Environmental Justice* (Dominelli, 2012). Gray et al. (2013) note the following environmental issues as important to social workers: destruction of natural resources; climate change; toxic materials production and disposal; pollution of air, soil, and water; the extinction of species;

natural disasters; and sustainable development. Therefore, the 2012 Global Agenda for social work developed jointly by the International Association of Schools of Social Work, the International Council on Social Welfare, and the International Federation of Social Workers places working toward environmental sustainability as one of the four priority areas.

While at first, it can be unclear how these issues relate to human rights and social work, a further examination of the impact these changes are having makes this clear. Due to the relatively recent awareness of these changes, this issue is not specifically named in the UDHR, but it can be regarded as being part of the collective rights, specifically Article 28, which states, "Everyone is entitled to a social and international order in which the rights and freedoms set forth in this Declaration can be fully realized" (as noted by Hawkins, 2010). The United Nations High Commissioner for Human Rights (2009) also notes that a healthy physical environment undergirds the achievement of a number of other rights, including the right to life, health, food, water, and housing. Recognizing these ties, the Nobel Peace Prize has been awarded to those working on environmental issues in recent years. It was given to Wangari Maathai in 2004 for her work in sustainable development and reforestation through the Green Belt Movement. In 2007, it was awarded to the Intergovernmental Panel on Climate Change (IPCC) and former US Vice President Al Gore for their work in advancing knowledge of climate change. At the national level, the countries of Ecuador and Bolivia have passed legislation recognizing the rights of the natural world to exist and reproduce (Besthorn, 2013).

A growing threat to the sustainability of life on this planet is the overuse of its resources, including its forests, animals, and energy sources. Currently the wealthiest billion people (14% of the population) use 72% of the resources. Clearly, as we seek to raise up the bottom billion, who use 1% of the resources, this level of consumption is not sustainable (United Nations, 2013). Despite the fact that it is the Global North who uses a disproportionate amount of resources and is therefore disproportionately responsible for the decline in sustainable ecosystems, it is those in the Global South who bear the heaviest burden as a result of them. For example, although the continent of Africa contributes little to the emission of greenhouse gases, it is experiencing increasing desertification and drought.

The decreasing availability of resources is especially concerning in light of the increasing population. The United Nations estimates that Earth's population will increase from the current 7 billion to 9 billion by 2040. By 2030, at least 50% more food, 45% more energy, and 30% more water will be required to sustain the population (United Nations High-Level Panel on Global Sustainability, 2012). Clearly the current levels of consumption in the Global North cannot continue. However, these consumers typically seek to "go green" as opposed to reducing their consumption and look to develop the most economically efficient way to reduce emissions. In contrast, those in the Global South are more likely to focus on more inclusionary practices in decision-making, proportionate rights to emissions, and compensating for past injustices (Mearns & Norton, 2010). For example, Bolivia states that because the developed countries are primarily responsible for the negative impacts being suffered by the developing countries, there is a "climate debt" (People's World Conference on Climate Change, 2010).

The expected impacts of resource over-use are widespread (Besthorn & Meyer, 2010). Forests are being lost as a result of climate change and human consumption. The deforestation of the planet for firewood as well as to clear land for agriculture and grazing, together with those forests lost to climate change, not only reduces these natural oxygenating environments but also creates a loss of habitat for the species that inhabit them and can lead to extinction. Further loss of the Amazon rain forest is anticipated as the climate changes it to savannah (resulting in the loss of associated plant and animal life) (Verner, 2010). Deforestation can also lead to further mudslides and floods due to a reduced ability to retain water in the land.

Access to potable water is a growing issue. Many people do not have ready access to potable water, necessitating long trips each day to gather water for cooking and drinking. Climate change will further reduce the availability. In Latin America and the Caribbean, drinking water will be affected by rising sea levels in nations such as the Bahamas and loss of glaciers in nations such as Bolivia (Verner, 2010). On the island of Bequia in the Grenadines, the rural poor rely on rainwater to drink; however, summer rainfall is expected to decline, forcing these people to purchase water (Rossing, 2010). Conversely, in the United States, marketing has convinced consumers not to drink tap water, even when the water is safe. Tap water companies must meet a high level of health standards, while federal law exempts many bottled water companies from these standards (Santa Clara Valley Water District, 2013).

This water must be bottled in a factory, transported to the store and then transported home. There is a large energy footprint involved with bottled water, adding to detrimental environmental impacts. Energy is required to make the plastic, shape it into a bottle, process the water, fill and seal the bottle, transport the product, and chill it (Gleick & Cooley, 2009). The amount of energy involved can vary markedly. For example, in transportation costs, some companies bottle near major US cities for US consumption, but Fiji Spring Water ships its product from the island of Fiji in the South Pacific and Evian ships from France (Gleick & Cooley, 2009).

Not only does the energy footprint to produce and transport the bottle to the consumer affect the planet, but this negative impact continues after the water is consumed as well. The plastic bottle in which it comes is then all too rarely recycled, helping to increase the plastic garbage dump in the Pacific. Thus, the simple act of choosing to consume bottled water can have large implications for the planet. This has helped to lead Concord, Massachusetts to ban the sale of small disposable water bottles (Locker, 2013).

Climate Change

Climate change has been defined as "a change of climate which is attributed directly or indirectly to human activity that alters the composition of the global atmosphere and which is in addition to natural climate variability observed over comparable time periods" (United Nations, 1992, p. 7). Climate change is expected to have a major impact on populations served by social workers due to increases in temperature extremes, natural disasters, drought, hunger, poverty, armed conflict, and migration. These impacts are also clearly interlinking and do not stand apart from one another. Systems that have lower amounts of resources, be they nations, communities, or individuals, suffer disproportionately from these effects.

While some continue to debate whether or not these changes are occurring, the science clearly supports that they are and the debate is moving to center around what must be done. The Earth is warmer than it ever has been in recorded history, and this trend is only accelerating ("Earth warms," 2013). The Intergovernmental Panel on Climate Change (2013) states that the global average temperature has risen, as have global average sea levels, while the Northern Hemisphere snow cover is decreasing, together with the Arctic ice. Some areas of the world have experienced a marked increase in precipitation, while others have a marked decrease. Droughts have become more intense and more frequent, as have heat waves. The Panel states that "it is *extremely likely* that human influence has been the dominant cause of the observed warming since the mid-20th century" (p. SPM-12; Italics original). If nothing is done, these changes will not only continue, but worsen. These changes lead to increasing poverty, thus increasing the risk of the human rights violations discussed in the other chapters.

The United Nations Development Program states that unless environmental issues are tended to, the gains made in eradicating poverty and improving health could be erased (Provost, 2013). Climate change is expected to negatively affect health in a variety of ways. Starvation is anticipated to increase as a result of the rising population and diminishing crop yields (Vidal, 2013). Extreme temperatures can cause heat stroke or hypothermia, while the range of mosquito-borne diseases such as malaria and dengue fever will shift to areas with less resistance. Water-borne illnesses such as cholera are expected to increase, as is malnutrition (Andersen, Geary, Pörtner, & Verner, 2010). These health impacts, of course, then impact other factors such as the ability to attend school or to work, reducing income, as well as potentially increasing medical expenses (Andersen, Geary, et al., 2010).

Climate change is expected to continue to play havoc with water, creating increased flooding, rising sea levels, evaporation of fresh water, and increased drought. This will also create the loss of arable land due to loss of fertile topsoil and desertification (Besthorn & Meyer, 2010). Water security will decrease as a result of glacier melt, decreased rainfall, rising sea levels, and natural disasters such as hurricanes and typhoons (Rossing, 2010). For example, in Nepal, the availability of potable water has decreased, while water-borne illness has increased. The crop output has decreased concurrent with reduced rainfall, while at the same time, floods and landslides have increased (Charmaker & Mijar, 2009).

As noted, the continent of Africa is expected to continue to experience negative impacts as a result of the changes. Changes in water, including both drought and flooding, are expected to cause increases of water-borne illnesses (such as cholera), malaria, and wildfires. The melting of the ice caps on the tropical mountains of Uganda is expected to cause increases in both flooding as well as long-term water scarcity (Kumssa & Jones, 2010). Due to the increases in drought and decreases in arable land, hunger and poverty are expected to increase in affected areas as farmers will be unable to grow sufficient food to feed others and earn money for themselves. While there are seeds that are more resistant to these changes, impoverished countries have a harder time accessing them, as do their farmers. For example, in Swaziland, the curator of the national food bank has been unable to get these seeds to the farmers due to a lack of funds and the farmers are often unable to get to him ("No seeds," 2013). Fishing yields are also expected to decrease as a result of the rising water temperatures, and those living near the coast will be at an increased risk of flooding (Kumssa & Jones, 2010).

Physical health is not the only type of health that will be affected. Psychologists are examining the mental health impacts of the effects of climate change and have noted the development of "psychoterratic" syndromes (Albrecht, 2011). Humans relate innately to the "rhythms and patterns" of their home environment and are affected when these are disrupted (Albrecht, 2011). People can also suffer mental trauma from natural disasters, even if they are unharmed. Anxiety, Post-Traumatic Stress Disorder, depression, and other difficulties may result, and again, vulnerable populations suffer disproportionately from these effects (Simpson, Weissbecker, & Sephton, 2011).

In the Caribbean, tourism and the ability to earn a living from it are likely to be affected due to the impact of increasing natural disasters, such as hurricanes and floods, as well as decreasing water supplies. Natural disasters can damage or destroy infrastructure, including roads, airports, and hotels. Tourism requires a great deal of water for activities such as bathing, drinking, swimming in a pool, and watering landscapes; in Barbados the average tourist uses 178 gallons of water every day (Drosdoff, as cited in Nielsen, 2010). As noted, islands such as the Bahamas have been experiencing decreasing amounts of fresh water, and this is expected to further decrease due to rising sea levels.

The impacts of climate change are disproportionately felt by the most vulnerable in society, including women, children, the elderly, the impoverished, and indigenous peoples. Due to their disproportionate lack of assets and access to information, they also suffer disproportionately. As women are typically responsible for fetching the water needed for the household, the growing scarcity of potable water will be felt by them.

Girls may be pulled out of school in order to complete this chore. Women are also often responsible for food production, so declining agricultural output will affect them (Wenden, 2011). Women are more likely to die during a natural disaster than men, due to such reasons as being less likely to be able to swim or wearing clothing that inhibits movement, as well as looking after children (UN High Commissioner for Human Rights, 2009). However, women tend to be excluded from decision-making as they are often seen as unqualified or ill-suited for this public role and most countries do not have gender-sensitive disaster policies (Demetriades & Esplen, 2010; "Putting women," 2013). When gender is considered, it tends to focus on women as a vulnerable population (victim role) as opposed to including their voices in determining solutions (Bee, Bierman, & Tschakert, 2013; Okali & Naess, 2013).

Nigeria has experienced increased temperature, a decreased rainy season, increasing desertification, and a drying of surface water. This has resulted in decreased yields from farms. Nigerian gender roles position men as heads of households and policymakers, giving them access to decision-making, career opportunities, credit and information. Women are responsible for the household —household members and livestock—and engage in food production with men. Women are typically excluded from power and decisions. Due to the decreasing agricultural yields, men have been migrating to the cities to seek other sources of income, options from which women are excluded. Women remain on the farms, trying to eke out a living, but lack access to credit and knowledge to successfully adapt. However, women have begun organizing against the multinational oil companies in Nigeria that have been causing environmental damage, in some cases marching and in others occupying their facilities. (summarized from Odigie-Emmanuel, 2010)

Children are expected to experience increased malnutrition, morbidity, and mortality as a result of changes wrought by climate change. Childhood malnourishment leads to stunting, lower educational achievement, and lower earnings as an adult (Heltberg, Siegel, & Jorgensen, 2010). Temperature extremes, heat waves and freezes, have increased, including in the Global North. Those who live in poverty are less able to modify their home environment to a moderate temperature. They are also more likely to live in areas that are susceptible to damage from natural disasters and less likely to have insurance or savings to repair them, as exemplified in the United States by the impacts of Hurricane Katrina. The impoverished are also more likely to depend on subsistence agriculture and thus be affected quickly by the altering climate (Kumssa & Jones, 2010). The elderly are more susceptible to the deleterious effects of these extremes and are more likely to have them be fatal. The impoverished, the elderly, and those with disabilities are also less able to migrate to avoid the impacts of these climate events.

The World Bank (2008) states that although indigenous peoples account for only 5% of the world's population, they care for 22% of the Earth's surface, including 80% of its biodiversity. Indigenous peoples are likely to live in lands quickly affected by climate change due to their environmental sensitivity (e.g., arctic regions, tropical forests), and their lives are closely tied to their ecosystems. For example, Inuit communities living in polar regions have already had to relocate due to these changes (UN High Commissioner for Human Rights, 2009). In the Andes, herders are facing loss of water for their livestock and those in the Amazon region are coping with the impacts of deforestation (Oleson, 2010).

The United Nations agency that assists refugees, UNHCR, has been preparing to assist those who are displaced due to these issues. While they dislike the term "environmental refugee" that has been used by some because, as noted in Chapter 5, the term "refugee" has a very specific legal meaning, they do believe that assisting many of these persons will fall within their mandate (UNHCR, 2009). The term "environmentally displaced persons" has been suggested by others (Besthord & Meyer, 2010). UNHCR states climate-related displacement may occur due to the following reasons: hydro-meteorological disasters (such as flooding, hurricanes, mudslides, etc.); slower onset disasters, including recurrent flooding, reduced availability of potable water, and desertification); the sinking of island states; areas being banned from habitation due to increased risks such as the aforementioned; and increased armed conflict due to increased competition for natural resources that have decreased due to climate change (potable water, arable land, food, etc.). Persons may also migrate for labor reasons as their previous methods of earning income are no longer an option (Andersen, Lund, & Verner, 2010).

When they migrate, they leave their support networks and become more vulnerable.

The number of natural disasters has more than doubled over the past 20 years from approximately 200 a year to more than 400 a year, and 9 out of 10 of them are climate-related (Holmes, 2008 as cited in UNHCR, 2009). Between 2008 and 2012, approximately 144 million people were displaced as a result of natural disasters. In this time period, 83% of these disasters were related to weather and climate change, but in 2012, 98% of them were (Internal Displacement Monitoring Centre, 2013). As the United States saw with Hurricane Katrina, these disasters can cause mass displacement of people, and it is the poor who are disproportionately affected. While social workers have been increasingly involved with the provision of services to those affected, comparatively little attention has been given by the profession as to why these disasters are increasing in number and what the profession can do about it.

Island states such as Tuvalu and the Maldives are preparing for the possibility of the loss of their nations due to rising sea levels. The mass displacement that would result may cause citizens of these nations to become stateless if they are not taken in by other countries. Indeed, the government of the Maldives has begun saving to buy a new homeland if their current country becomes uninhabitable (Tutu, 2009).

It is expected that climate change will increase the likelihood of armed conflict and statistical models have supported this theory (Devitt & Tol, 2012). Some have argued that the conflict occurring in the Darfur region of Sudan was provoked by a competition for increasingly scarce resources, such as arable land and potable water (UNHCR, 2009). The risk of conflict also increases if there are large numbers of young men who do not feel that there is an alternative way to meet their needs. If it is felt that there is support, such as from an established welfare system, this decreases this propensity, but many nations in the Global South lack this due to their relative poverty (Barnett & Adger, 2007).

Facing the Challenge

As progress toward reducing the changes wrought by climate change is proceeding very slowly, adaption to this new reality has become necessary. Those affected will face a new set of risks to which they must determine how they will react. For example, will subsistence farmers whose crop yields continue to decrease remain on their land and attempt to change their crop or migrate to the city to attempt to earn a living in new ways? Will those who face threats from slow- or rapid-onset changes due to their living arrangements (e.g., near a coast that faces an increased risk of flooding) make changes to their living arrangements to protect their property? Clearly, the ability to make adjustments is constrained by the person's capital: income, education, and social status. These individual-level decisions then have effects on the macro level. If farmers are abandoning their fields, that can lead to food shortages, increased food prices, and malnutrition. If certain foods can no longer be grown in their traditional regions, dietary changes may be needed (Dow et al., 2013).

On the macro level, a country's ability to adapt is contingent on several factors: "economic wealth, technology, information and skills, infrastructure, institutions and equity" (Furlow, Smith, Anderson, Breed, & Padgham, 2011, p. 413). Unfortunately, the countries currently most affected by climate change (due to their physical location or reliance on agriculture) also have the least ability to adapt. Furlow et al. (2011) note that they particularly lack wealth and technology. Helping these systems gain access to these needed adaptation supports is vital, for example, through development projects. Under President Obama, USAID has been shaping its aid to assist nations in this process (Furlow et al., 2011).

Resiliency is also a necessary characteristic for adaptation. Communities that are resilient to these changes tend to have four types of supports: economic development; social capital; information and communications; and community competence, including a tradition of solving one's own problems and collaboration (Edwards & Wiseman, 2011). Social workers can assist communities in developing and honing these protective factors. For example, social capital varies between communities and can be a strong force for revitalization when present. In 2007/2008, Bolivia was struck by widespread devastating floods. The community of Mecapaca exhibited strong social networks and reached out to help those affected, enabling them to remain in the town. In contrast, the community of Palca did not have these bonds. When they found out a new irrigation system would be required at a cost of USD$10,000, they became despondent and sent the young people to La Paz to find work, weakening the community further (Rossing & Rubin,

2010). Social workers can help communities organize to obtain the resources they need to survive and strengthen social bonds.

As changes are made, it is vital to assure that they are sustainable. Sustainable development has been defined by the World Commission on Environment and Development (1987, p. 41) in its report Our Common Future, also known as the Brundtland report, as:

Sustainable development is development that meets the needs of the present without compromising the ability of future generations to meet their own needs. It contains within it two key concepts:

- *the concept of "needs," in particular the essential needs of the world's poor, to which overriding priority should be given; and*
- *the idea of limitations imposed by the state of technology and social organization on the environment's ability to meet present and future needs.*

Social workers' historical role in community organizing and development will stand us in good stead here. Proactive interventions to address this issue are required at all system levels, from the individual to the global. As has been seen with numerous disasters, international assistance tends to be delayed until the crisis is extreme and then is only temporary and is not integrated into long-term development. Knowing that the oppressed and vulnerable are disproportionately affected and have the least ability to adapt, many are calling for "pro-poor" policies that focus on assisting and developing the assets of this group, in line with the values of sustainable development.

Besthorn and Meyer (2010) note that cultural competence is a core value of the profession and encourage social workers to look past the micro and mezzo systems to apply it to a global system in which the interconnections between countries become clear. They state that anti-oppressive practice requires social workers to examine these global changes and the role that social workers can play. It is essential that changes and plans be developed jointly with those in the affected communities, and sustainable development requires that the needs of the poor are given priority. If plans to protect the natural environment are made without sufficient consideration of their impact on people's ability to earn a living, they will not be accepted (Nielsen, 2010). Including the voices of those affected is essential, including women's voices.

As noted earlier, women tend to be excluded from these policy discussions as it is seen outside their role or that they do not have knowledge to contribute. However, women make up half of the world's agricultural laborers and are the main producer of staple crops (Dankelman & Jansen, 2010). Women are also the vast majority of those responsible for supplying household water, knowledge passed from mother to daughter, and therefore have specific knowledge in local water management (Dankelman & Jansen, 2010). Women should be accorded access to education and training, land ownership, markets, and supportive services in order to help them successfully face the challenges posed by climate change (Ajani, Onwubuya, & Mgbenka, 2013). In 2004, the Nobel Peace Prize was given to Wangari Maathai for her work in sustainable development and reforestation through the Green Belt Movement. Beginning in 1977, this movement to replant trees developed into one that empowers women through training and income generation (Ajani et al., 2013).

In Brazil, the award-winning Pintadas Solar project was developed to assist farmers in developing efficient irrigation methods for their crops. This project has paid particular attention to gender roles and the inclusion of women. First, a woman was selected to lead the project. The family was treated as the system level of intervention and as such, men and women were treated on an equal basis for participation, including training and access to micro-credit. For travel to training and meetings, women were selected when possible. Additionally, the focus of the project included not only the technical aspects, but was also inclusive of other outcomes including communication, responsibility and respect, more "feminine" qualities. (summarized from Corral, 2010)

The inclusion of indigenous knowledge can be invaluable in adapting to the hanging weather patterns. Using techniques such as terraces and dams (from the Otomí people in Mexico) or *waru-waru* (from those in the Andes), in which elevated soil beds connected by earthen channels regulate water flow, maintains soil humidity during dry spells and reducing flooding in wet ones (ELLA, 2012).

Social workers can be involved in all nations in helping people develop the knowledge and skills to help mitigate this crisis: understanding what is occurring and why; reducing consumption; changing to more renewable energy sources; gardening; and so on. We should also be working on the macro level to develop networks and advocate for change on a broad level to help steer the planet away from the brink for which we are heading (Peeters, 2012). Peeters (2012, p. 290) states that "[w]e have to search for an alternative to the dominant idea that well-being follows primarily from material prosperity and economic growth." Current levels of consumption are not only unsustainable, but potentially deadly. Societies of the Global North must scale back massively if the tide is to be turned. To turn away from the idea that consumption is how a country's progress is measured, UNDP has developed a different method for determining a country's progress. Traditionally, progress was assessed by the nation's Gross Domestic Product (GDP), based on the assumption that any monetary exchange was beneficial to the nation. In contrast UNDP developed the Human Development Index, which draws together the nation's progress in life expectancy, education, and income to include both social and economic development across a population (Gamble, 2013). By judging a nation on these measures as well draws attention to the fact that simply spending money does not assure progress.

The United Nations Development Programme calls climate change "one of the defining changes of our time" (2013, ¶1). As noted, it undergirds access to other vital rights necessary for survival. If we do not act quickly, the impacts will only accelerate. We must act, both on the individual and collective level, to make changes to avert outcomes even more disastrous than the ones currently occurring. This issue, more than any other in this book, is truly "international," as we will all bear the consequences if sufficient access is not taken.

Culture Box
CLIMATE CHANGE IN BOLIVIA

Bolivia, a land-locked nation in South America, has already been experiencing the effects of climate change, and these impacts are expected only to continue to increase. Since achieving its independence from Spain in 1825, Bolivia has experienced a great deal of political turmoil. Democracy was achieved in 1982 after almost 200 coups and countercoups, However, the country has been beset by widespread difficulties. It is near or at the bottom of Latin American countries in a number of areas of social development, including poverty, education, malnutrition, and mortality (CIA, 2013). Poverty is high—half of the population lives on under USD$2 a day and 25% of children aged 5–13 years are engaged in child labor. One-third of the population is engaged in agriculture (CIA, 2013) and thus more vulnerable to climate change. As noted in the main chapter, indigenous peoples are disproportionately affected by climate change. In Bolivia, almost two-thirds of the population is considered to be indigenous, the highest percentage in Latin America (Kronik & Verner, 2010). As in other nations, the rural population struggles more in access to education, potable water, and improved sanitation. However, in Bolivia, even the urban population has limited access to improved sanitation with only one-third of the urban population having such access (CIA, 2013). However, recent economic demand for its commodities, such as natural gas, has been high and trade surpluses have been recorded (CIA, 2013).

The geography of Bolivia varies greatly; the country contains almost every type of climate from desert to rain forest to glaciers. This diversity makes Bolivia vulnerable to a variety of climate change impacts. Deforestation has been continuing as land is cleared for agriculture or to meet the global demand for timber. Additionally, soil erosion has been a problem as a result of overgrazing and slash-and-burn agriculture (CIA, 2013). The effects of climate change have cost Bolivia hundreds of millions of dollars due to losses in crops, housing, and livestock (Chávez, 2012). These impacts are expected to only increase. Crop yields are expected to be reduced by 20%–30% by the year 2080 (Olesen, 2010). Less rain is predicted in the Amazon basin during the dry months, which threatens its viability (Seiler, Hutjes, & Kabat, 2013a). However, the warming of Bolivia, much of which is cold, may help to decrease income inequality (Andersen & Verner, 2010).

Bolivia is at risk of both increased floods and drought as a result of climate change (Rossing & Rubin, 2010; Seiler, Hutjes, & Kabat, 2013b). Bolivia contains approximately 20% of the world's tropical glaciers (Oxfam, 2009), which play an important role in water supply; they absorb excess water in the form of snow and ice and release fresh water (Verner, 2010). The Chacaltaya glacier in Bolivia was once the world's highest ski resort. However, by 2009 it had completely melted away, 6 years earlier than anticipated. The biggest impact of this was not the loss of the tourism dollars, but the lack of fresh water that it used to supply to the cities of La Paz and El Alto (Painter, 2009). The Tuni and Condoriri glaciers that also supply these cities are similarly melting and are projected to disappear by 2035 (Rossing, 2010).

Desertification has already caused large-scale migration from rural areas to El Alto, so the population, and thus need for water, has increased at the same time (Andersen, Lund, & Verner, 2010). The melting of the Andes glaciers has provided a temporary increase in the amount of fresh water, but this will fade away as they disappear. It is estimated that 70% of the Andean population will be at risk of losing their water supply by 2020 (Tikjøb & Verner, 2010). The decreased amount of water will also concentrate waste (El Alto has no sewage treatment system), resulting in increased disease (Verner, 2010). Other glaciers are expected to disappear, jeopardizing the water supply as well as the generation of hydroelectric power in the region—which generates half of all electricity to Bolivia, Peru, and Ecuador (Painter, 2009).

(continued)

Health factors are also being affected. While public health has overall been improving in Bolivia, the incidence of malaria has been rapidly increasing. In 1982, approximately 7,000 cases were recorded. By 1997, that had increased to over 50,000 (Andersen, Geary et al., 2010). By 2006, this had risen to 74,000 (World Health Organization, 2008). Measures such as the distribution of bed nets have now been implemented and they are helping to bring the number of cases back down (World Health Organization, 2012).

Bolivia has been working on the world stage to press for radical action to halt and reverse climate change. In 2010, president Evo Morales hosted the World's People's Congress on Climate Change. He stated that the talks in Copenhagen the previous year had been a total failure and developed this conference to highlight the voices of those most affected by climate change, the impoverished (Schipani & Vidal, 2010). The People's Accord produced by this event calls for a 50% reduction in emissions by the Global South before 2017, that a new human rights convention be developed on the Rights of Mother Earth, and that the Global North develop a fund equivalent to 6% of the GDP to help the Global South deal with the impacts of climate change. Under this accord as well, an international Tribunal on Environmental and Climate Justice would be developed with its base in Bolivia (Weinberg, 2010). Later that year, Bolivia took this Accord to the UN conference on climate change in Cancun, Mexico, but to no avail. A consensus must be achieved for action, and few countries were interested in the radical steps proposed by Bolivia. Nations worked to a compromise acceptable to almost all nations, but Bolivia held out, stating that this compromise still would result in continued increases in global warming to 4 degrees Celsius (Gray, 2010).

Bolivia is to be praised for the high importance it gives to climate issues. However, Bolivia also needs to examine its internal policies, which have been described as "piecemeal" (Chávez, 2012). Bolivia's Law of Mother Earth was based on the concept of the indigenous earth deity *Pachamama* and contains a variety of environmental protections, including that developers must remedy any environmental harm they cause, and gives preferences to indigenous people for redistributed farmland. However, it only requires that indigenous people be *notified* of development projects that may affect them or their land; it does not give them the right to approve or disapprove such projects (DeAngelis, 2013).

Strategies, tools, and financial plans need to be developed, and coordination between sectors must be increased (UNDP, 2009). More research needs to be conducted in order to gather more information on the potential impacts of climate change and there needs to be greater dialogue between these scientists and indigenous peoples, or this traditional knowledge, such as how to construct terraced farmland and artificial ponds to help protect against flooding, is at risk of being lost (DeAngelis, 2013; UNDP, 2011). For example, a pre-Incan farming technique called "camellones" is being reintroduced. This method utilizes raised seedbeds surround by water channels, rendering the plants less vulnerable to flooding as well as providing water during drought (Oxfam, 2009). Considering Bolivia's high risk for continuing severe impacts from climate change, there is a long road ahead.

What Can I Do Now?

- Calculate your own global footprint at http://myfootprint.org. How much is needed to sustain your lifestyle? How can you reduce your consumption?
- Don't purchase bottled water.
- Don't leave your electronic devices on "standby."
- Examine whether you can increase your use of renewable energy.
- Use public transportation when possible, and consider biking or walking instead of driving.
- Educate those around you about climate change and its impacts.
- Switch to locally grown foods, including growing your own if possible.
- Think about what temperature you set the interior climate to and the energy impacts of that choice.

What Can I Do as a Professional Social Worker?

- Help to develop community gardens.
- Join/build coalitions to advocate for smarter polices at all levels of government.
- Work with educational campaigns to inform people about what needs to occur.
- Work with those who have been displaced due to environmental changes.
- Help the development community assess how climate change will impact their projects and determine any needed adjustments.
- Ensure that voices of all those affected are included in projects and policy.
- Ensure that development projects are sustainable.
- Work to increase public transportation options.

World Wide Web Resources

Intergovernmental Panel on Climate Change (http://www.ipcc.ch): The international scientific body charged by the United Nations with assessing the impacts of climate change.

Social Resilience & Climate Change (http://www.worldbank.org): Contains a number of reports examining the impact of climate change on the most vulnerable and mechanisms to alleviate it.

United Nations Development Programme (http://www.undp.org/climatechange): UNDP's Web site on the effects of climate change on human development.

9

Millennium Development Goals and Beyond

Thinking about how to solve the issues discussed in this text can be overwhelming. The scope of the issues and their interlinking nature can create a hydra's head: When one problem appears to be solved, two more grow to takes its place. But it is precisely the interlinking nature of these issues that can lead to solutions. By examining the root causes of these issues and addressing them, the problem can be addressed before it grows.

The Millennium Development Goals (see Box 9.1) were developed in 2000 by the United Nations in an attempt to address the primary issues and provide a roadmap to solutions. The goals were derived from the UN's Millennium Declaration, which affirmed a collective responsibility for global equality and equity and was signed by 189 nations (UNDP, n.d.). The Millennium Development Goals set clear and precise targets for achieving the commitments made in the Millennium Declaration by 2015. While previously, development goals tended to focus on economic growth, these goals focus on social development (UNDP, 2003). They also are aligned with the human rights guaranteed by the UDHR (UNDP, 2003). The goals are connected in that the achievement of one makes it easier to achieve the others. As noted throughout this text, poverty, lack of education, and discrimination are risk factors for many social problems, and therefore reducing them can reduce other issues as well. The targets to meet these goals were altered slightly in 2007 to add four new targets (United Nations Statistical Division, n.d.). Overall, there is much

BOX 9.1 The UN Millennium Development Goals

Goal 1: Eradicate extreme poverty and hunger
- Reduce by half the proportion of people living in extreme poverty.
- Reduce by half the proportion of people who suffer from hunger.
- Achieve full and productive employment and decent work for all, including women and young people.

Goal 2: Achieve universal primary education
- Ensure that all boys and girls complete a full course of primary education.

Goal 3: Promote gender equality and empower women
- Eliminate gender disparity in primary and secondary education, preferably by 2005, and at all levels by 2015.

Goal 4: Reduce child mortality
- Reduce by two-thirds the mortality rate among children under five.

Goal 5: Improve maternal health
- Reduce by three-quarters the maternal mortality ratio.
- Achieve universal access to reproductive health.

Goal 6: Combat HIV/AIDS, malaria, and other diseases
- Halt and begin to reverse the spread of HIV/AIDS.
- Achieve, by 2010, universal access to treatment for HIV/AIDS for all those who need it.
- Halt and begin to reverse the incidence of malaria and other major diseases.

Goal 7: Ensure environmental sustainability
- Integrate the principles of sustainable development into country policies and programmes; reverse loss of environmental resources.
- Reduce biodiversity loss, achieving, by 2010, a significant reduction in the rate of loss.
- Reduce by half the proportion of people without sustainable access to safe drinking water and basic sanitation.
- Achieve significant improvement in lives of at least 100 million slum dwellers by 2020.

Goal 8: Develop a global partnership for development
- Develop further an open, rule-based, predictable, nondiscriminatory trading and financial system.
- Address the least developed countries' special needs.
- Address the special needs of landlocked and small island developing states.
- Deal comprehensively with developing countries' debt problems through national and international measures to make debt sustainable in the long term.
- In cooperation with pharmaceutical companies, provide access to affordable essential drugs in developing countries.
- In cooperation with the private sector, make available the benefits of new technologies—especially information and communication technologies.

to celebrate regarding achievement of these goals, although there is also much more work to be done.

The primary responsibility for the achievement of Goals 1–7 lies within these nations themselves, although wealthier nations play a part in helping to achieve these goals, as demonstrated in Goal 8. In addition to sharing knowledge and technology such as water purification and advanced medicines, the wealthier nations must also examine the structures that make it difficult for other nations to develop, such as trade policies and debt.

Modernization theory states that more industrialized nations can give aid to other countries to help them develop. However, although the nations of the Organisation for Economic Co-operation and Development (OECD, primarily nations in the Global North) have pledged to donate 0.7% of their gross national income to the countries in the Global South to help them develop, the vast majority do not. Five countries (Denmark, Luxembourg, the Netherlands, Norway, and Sweden) currently meet the 0.7% target. The United States, although its aid increased markedly under President George W. Bush, still donates only 0.2% of gross domestic product and has set no plans to meet the target (United Nations, 2012; United Nations Statistics Division, 2012).

Progress on the Millennium Development Goals

Progress on the goals has been mixed. Some goals are closer to being achieved than others, and some regions are closer to achieving the goals than others. Progress toward each goal is discussed next. One limitation to this data is that reporting is subject to the limits of the data provided by the countries themselves. An additional limitation is that examining a country's or a region's progress can mask inequalities within that country or region, for example, between urban and rural dwellers. All information that follows concerning progress toward the goals was gathered from the United Nations Development Goals Report (2013), except as noted.

Goal 1: Eradicate Extreme Poverty and Hunger

The first target under this goal is to halve the number of people living in extreme poverty. This target originally was defined as living on less than USD$1 a day, but it was redefined to USD$1.25 a day. The excellent news is that this overall target was achieved in 2010, and extreme poverty is declining in every region. The proportion of those living under this poverty line declined from 47% to 22%, representing a decrease of 700 million people. However, the achievement was heavily influenced by the growth in China (where the rate dropped from 60% in 1990 to 12% in 2010) and without that, the goal would not have been reached. It is estimated that approximately 970 million people will still be living in extreme poverty as of 2015.

The second target under this goal, added in 2007, is to have full and productive employment for all, including women and young people. While there was solid progress on this target between 2000 and 2008, this was driven heavily by the aforementioned growth in China. Progress worldwide has slowed since 2008 and many remain in vulnerable employment, especially women. Young people were especially hard-hit by global economic crisis. The third target is to halve the number of people who suffer from hunger. As of 2013, this goal was considered to be "within reach," as it had declined from 23.2% in 1990 to 14.9%. While the percentage has decreased, one in eight people, or 870 million, remain food insecure.

Goal 2: Achieve Universal Primary Education

The one target under this goal is that by 2015 all children, both boys and girls, will complete primary school. All regions have made large gains on this target, with 90% of children in the Global South now enrolled in school. All regions except sub-Saharan Africa have enrollment rates over 90%; sub-Saharan African is at 77%, an increase from 53% in 1990. Globally, 90% of children completed primary school, ranging from 70% in sub-Saharan Africa to near 100% in Latin America and the Caribbean, as well as in Caucasus and Central Asia (United Nations, 2012). Literacy is increasing and gender gaps are narrowing. However, progress has slowed and it is doubted that the goal of universal primary education will be met by 2015. The United Nations states that the largest barrier is familial poverty.

Goal 3: Promote Gender Equality and Empower Women

While there is only one target under this goal, to eliminate gender disparity in all levels of education, it has three disparate indicators: the ratios of girls to boys in primary, secondary, and tertiary education; the share of women in wage employment in the nonagricultural sector; and the proportion of seats held by women in national parliament. The gender ratio in all levels of education is considered to be at parity; however, there is wide variation between regions. Southern Asia has increased parity greatly, increasing its ratio from .74 in 1990 to .98 currently. Girls struggle with access to primary school, particularly in sub-Saharan Africa and Western Asia, while in Eastern Asia they have greater access than boys.

Only a small amount of progress was made on the second target regarding women's employment. Globally, women were 35% of the non-agricultural workers in 1990; in 2010, this figure had risen only 5%. It also varies greatly by region, with the Global North, as well as the Caucasus/ Central Asia being close to parity, while Western and Southern Asia as well as Northern Africa are only at 20% of parity. Even when women are employed, they tend to be segregated in lower paying fields. Progress has been made on the third target, the proportion of women in national legislatures, but it remains at a disappointingly low 21%. There is not a great deal of difference on this measure between the Global North (23.8%) and the Global South (20%). Oceania is the lowest at 3%, while Latin America and the Caribbean represent the high end, with 24.5% of seats being held by women.

Goal 4: Reduce Child Mortality

The target under this goal is to reduce the mortality rate of children under 5 years old by two-thirds. The rate has decreased by 47%, a tremendous achievement, but insufficient to reach the goal of a two-thirds reduction ("Global child mortality rates," 2013). All regions showed reductions, half of them more than 50% reductions, but only Northern Africa and East Asia have reached the target. However, while the overall mortality rate for those under 5 years has been decreasing, it has been increasing for children in the first month of life. Additionally, children living in rural areas, as well as those born into poor families, are disproportionately more likely to die. The education level of mothers has an impact on child mortality: The higher the education of mothers, the higher the child survival rate.

Goal 5: Improve Maternal Health

The first target for this goal is to reduce the maternal mortality ratio by three-quarters. While substantial progress has been made, and the rate has been reduced by half, this will not be sufficient to reach the 75% reduction goal. No region has met the target. One of the things that can help to achieve this target is to have a skilled attendant present during the birth. Some regions have shown remarkable increases in assisted deliveries, such as Southeastern Asia and Northern Africa. However, in sub-Saharan Africa and Southern Asia, only about half of births are attended by a skilled professional. There is a marked urban/rural gap in this; in sub-Saharan Africa, for example, 76% of urban births are attended as compared to only 40% of rural births.

Another factor that has limited the progress toward this goal is the limited availability of contraceptives to those women who desire to limit or space their children. Access to contraceptives helps reduce mortality through reducing the number of pregnancies as well as unsafe abortions. Thus, the United Nations added targets to this goal of assuring universal access to reproductive health care by 2015 (which includes access to contraceptives), as well as measuring the adolescent birth rate and access to prenatal care. Of those women who are married or in a union, 72% of those in the Global North and 62% of those in the Global South were using contraceptives. There was marked progress between 1990 and 2000, but this has slowed since that time. Rates between regions also vary greatly, with Eastern Asia at 84% and sub-Saharan Africa at 25%. The adolescent birth rate has shown a similar pattern, with marked progress between 1990 and 2000 that has now slowed or even reversed in some regions (such as Southeastern Asia). Prenatal care for pregnant women has improved with 81% of women in the Global South visiting a health professional at least once during her pregnancy, although only 51% visit at least four times.

Goal 6: Combat HIV/AIDS, Malaria, and Other Diseases

The first target under this goal is to halt and begin to reverse the spread of HIV/AIDS by 2015. As noted in Chapter 6, good progress is being made on this goal. The number of new infections continues to decline (a 21% decrease between 2001 and 2011), including in some of the hardest hit countries. A second target was added of providing universal access to treatment for HIV/AIDS for those who need it. The number of those receiving medication has increased markedly, and it is possible to reach the goal of universal access by 2015, but it is uncertain.

The third target under this goal is to halt and begin to reverse the incidence of malaria and other major diseases by 2015. The fight against malaria has rapidly increased in recent years, with funds coming from the Global Fund, the Gates Foundation, and the U.S. Malaria Initiative to purchase and distribute malaria nets. While the hoped-for 50% reduction will not be achieved, significant progress has been made. Since 2000, the incidence of malaria has decreased 17% and malaria deaths have decreased more than 25%, saving 1.1 million lives. Substantial progress is also being made in the fight against tuberculosis with a reduction in the number of new cases, as well as improvements in treatment of those infected. Tuberculosis deaths have been halved globally, which has resulted in averting 20 million deaths.

Goal 7: Ensure Environmental Sustainability

The first target under this goal is to integrate the policies of sustainable development into the policies and programs of countries and to reverse the loss of environmental resources. As part of the measurement of this goal, the proportion of land area covered by forests is measured. Forests continue to shrink, especially in Africa and South America. A major reason for this is to clear land for agricultural production to feed the world's increasing population. The emission of greenhouse gases is also tracked. Despite slowing slightly during the global financial crisis, they are now increasing again and have increased 46% since 1990. The second target under this goal, added in 2007, is to reduce biodiversity loss, achieving by 2010 a significant reduction in the rate of loss. While the percentage of protected areas is increasing, the loss of biodiversity continues. Overfishing continues and fishing yields have suffered. More species are headed for extinction.

Third is to halve the proportion of people without sustainable access to safe drinking water and basic sanitation. Globally, the target for access to water was met in 2010, 5 years ahead of schedule. However, neither sub-Saharan Africa nor Oceania is expected to meet the goal. It is possible for the goal for access to sanitation to be met, but it requires a major push, especially in the reduction of open defecation (people who have no access to any type of facility). As with the previous goals, those living in rural areas and/or in poverty are less likely to have access to clean water or basic sanitation.

The last target under this goal is to achieve a "significant improvement" in the lives of at least 100 million slum dwellers by 2020. While the achievement of this goal was in doubt in the first edition of this text, it has been achieved ahead of schedule. As of 2013, 200 million slum dwellers improved their lives through access to clean water, basic sanitation, and/or durable housing. The largest gains were made in Southern, Southeastern, and Eastern Asia. However, the numbers of slum dwellers continues to grow due in large part to rapid urbanization.

Goal 8: Develop a Global Partnership for Development

There are six targets under this goal, two of which include addressing the special needs of the least developed nations, landlocked countries, and small island developing countries. Official development aid dropped in 2012 to 0.29% of the Gross National Income of OECD countries, less than half of the goal of 0.7%. Additionally, aid to the Least Developed Countries is being reduced in favor of aid to middle-income nations (OECD, 2013).

The third target is to further develop a nondiscriminatory trading and financial system. This has improved for countries in the Global South, including those designated as Least Developed Countries. Duty-free access to global markets has improved, and tariffs are currently at a record low. The next target is to deal comprehensively with the debt of nations in the Global South. Debt payments have fallen substantially for 29 heavily indebted countries. Debt payments have fallen from 12% of external payments in 2000 to 3.1% in 2011. This is due both to debt forgiveness as well as increasing exports.

The fifth goal is to provide access to affordable essential medications for the Global South. The Millennium Development Goals report does not provide any data for this. However, as noted in Chapter 6, access has substantially increased, particularly for medications that treat HIV, but many more people continue to require essential medications.

The last goal is to help broaden access to advances in technology, especially information and communication. Access to communication technology has risen rapidly: The number of cell telephone subscribers has increased markedly. Access to the Internet continues to grow rapidly, with almost two-thirds of Internet users now located in the Global South.

Beyond 2015

As 2015 approaches, the United Nations is preparing to sunset the Millennium Development Goals and to prepare a new set of goals to build on them. The United Nations member states have agreed that these goals, rather than focusing on poorer nations and being funded by wealthier ones, are aimed at *all* nations. Human rights, gender equality, and the rule of law will be the undergirding principles (Ford, 2013).

A panel, led by David Cameron of the United Kingdom, Ellen Johnson Sirleaf of Liberia, and Dr. Susilo Banbang Yudhoyono of Indonesia, developed the new proposed set of goals, submitted to the Secretary-General in 2013. These goals were based on what they termed "five big transformational shifts" that they deem necessary to remove the barriers to full social inclusion and achievement for all (United Nations, 2013b):

1. *Leave no one behind*: To focus on excluded groups and move to *ending* issues such as poverty, not merely reducing them.
2. *Put sustainable development at the core*: To integrate the "social, economic and environmental dimensions of sustainability" (p. 8); here countries of the Global North have a unique role through sharing technology to achieve this as well as reducing their disproportionate consumption.
3. *Transform economies for jobs and inclusive growth*: Again focusing on sustainable development and growth, they call for economies that provide all citizens with the opportunity to earn a decent living. This requires not only education skills but also health care, clean water, electricity, transportation, and telecommunications.
4. *Build peace and effective, open and accountable institutions for all*: In order to build a prosperous society, peace and transparent governance are needed.
5. *Forge new global partnerships*: "Perhaps the most important transformative shift is towards a new spirit of solidarity, cooperation and mutual accountability."

The panel stated that tracking of the goals must be as disaggregated as possible to be able to track subgroups and monitor divides such as rural/urban, male/female, rich/poor, and so forth. They also state that countries of the Global North have a more important role to play than in the Millennium Development Goals by truly joining in partnership with the rest of the world. They note that the 1.2 billion poorest people are responsible for only 1% of the world's goods and services consumed each year, while the billion richest are responsible for 72% of consumption. In other words, approximately 14% of the population consumes nearly three-quarters of its resources. The panel noted, therefore, that the growth models of countries in the Global North must be "reimagined."

They suggested a set of 12 new goals:

1. End poverty (as defined by living on less than $1.25/day).
2. Empower girls and women to achieve gender equality.
3. Provide quality education and lifelong learning.
4. Ensure healthy lives.
5. Ensure food security and good nutrition.
6. Achieve universal access to water and sanitation.
7. Secure sustainable energy.
8. Create jobs, sustainable livelihoods, and equitable growth.
9. Manage natural resource assets sustainably.
10. Ensure good governance and effective institutions.
11. Ensure stable and peaceful societies.
12. Create a global enabling environment and catalyze long-term finance.

The reaction to these propositions came quickly. Applauded were the zero-based goals, such as the elimination, and not just the reduction, of poverty (Tran, 2013). Also lauded were the focus on environmental sustainability and the focus on a truly global development agenda that is inclusive of all countries (Beyond 2015, 2013). Of course, all goals have their limitations, and these are no exception. One criticism was the idea of leaving USD$1.25 a day as the definition of extreme poverty because it was felt this is still too low to alleviate the risks associated with poverty (Woodward, 2013). Another criticism was that the goals only focused on poverty as opposed to income inequality (Tran, 2013). Beyond 2015 (2013), a coalition of 700 organizations, notes that the report positions "rapid and sustained" growth as a primary solution, rather than a primary problem.

What Can I Do Now?

- Go to one.org, an organization dedicated to fighting global poverty and work with them on their action items.
- Reduce your own levels of consumption, including both goods and services, as well as intangibles such as electricity.
- Contact your representatives in Washington to tell them you support an increase of development aid to 0.7%.
- Go to the UN Web site to determine the final set of goals for post-2015 (not yet available as this book goes to press).

What Can I Do as a Professional Social Worker?

- Any of the suggestions from previous chapters will help achieve the goals.

World Wide Web Resources

Center for Social Development (gwbweb.wustl.edu/csd): This center at the George Warren Brown School of Social Work takes a global approach to working from an asset-building approach as opposed to a deficit model.

Millennium Campaign (http://www.endpoverty2015. org/): Coordinated by the UNDP. This site "informs, inspires and encourages people's involvement and action for the realization of the Millennium Development Goals. An initiative of the United Nations, the Campaign supports citizens' efforts to hold their government to account for the Millennium promise."

One.org (www.one.org): The American branch of the project to make global poverty and AIDS history.

Social Watch Indicator Map (www.socialwatch.org/): Provides information by country on progress toward the Millennium Development Goals.

United Nations Development Programme (www.undp.org/ mdg): Provides background information as well as current information on the Millennium Goals.

United Nations Millennium Development Indicators (unstats.un.org/ unsd/mi/mi_worldmillennium_new.asp): Provides information by region and by country on progress toward each of the goals.

United Nations Millennium Project (www.unmillenniumproject. org): The Millennium Project's goal is to develop a concrete plan to realize the Millennium Goals. This site offers information about the goals and plans to achieve them.

10

A Call to Action

Never doubt that a small group of thoughtful, committed people can change the world. Indeed, it is the only thing that ever has.
                                                            —Margaret Mead

This text has focused on issues as they occur in the Global South to help those living in the Global North to understand how these issues can be both similar to and different from what occurs in their own nations. The enormity of these issues and the distance between the nations often provoke the response that an individual cannot help solve these problems. However, at the end of each chapter is a list of actions that people can take right now to help create change, as well as what they can do professionally.

Homan (2004) discusses factors that can prevent someone from taking action to create macro-level change. Examples include the following: "It's so large and I'm only one person," "I really don't know enough about the situation," and "I really don't know what to do." In Will Schwalbe's nonfiction book *The End of Your Life Book Club* (2012, p. 255), his mother tells him, "Too many people use the excuse that they don't think they can do enough, so they decide they don't have to do anything. There's never a good excuse for not doing anything" and goes on to discuss small actions a person can take. While it is true that a single person cannot solve all the problems of the world, people gathered together to create change can be extraordinarily effective. As systems theory teaches us, a system is greater than the sum of its subsystems. As the introductory quote by Margaret Mead illustrates, this is precisely the power of change that is needed to make a difference in the issues discussed in this text.

We currently see a dramatic rise in awareness of issues related to international social work and social development within the United States.

The Council on Social Work Education (CSWE), the accrediting body for social work programs in the United States, has established the Katherine A. Kendall Institute to increase international content in social work education (CSWE, 2007). Katherine Kendall is one of the social workers in the United States who have helped to bring these issues to the forefront of academia and raise our awareness. Dr. Kendall was one of the founders of CSWE and was the first salaried Secretary-General for the International Association of Schools of Social Work.

Other social work academics, such as Lynne Healy, M. C. Hokenstad, Karen Lyons, and James Midgely, have written books and articles to help broaden knowledge and awareness of social work and social work issues around the world. A growing number of Masters in Social Work programs are offering international social work concentrations and international placements. On both the bachelor's and master's level, there is an increasing amount of integration of international material in classes across the curriculum, as well as classes focusing specifically on international social work and social development. For those who are interested in global issues, there has never been a better time to be able to step forward and make a contribution. The 2008 Educational Policy and Accreditation Standards issued by CSWE state that social workers must have "a global perspective" (p. 1) and "recognize the global interconnections of oppression" (p. 5).

As discussed in the Preface, international issues affect not only social workers practicing outside of the Global North but also those within the Global North countries. The increasing global migration, both voluntary and forced, brings these issues to those working with the countries of the Global North. Whether it is helping refugees adjust to their new country, assisting someone who has been trafficked, or working with an undocumented worker who is being abused, international issues touch all social workers. Therefore, to uphold the core value of social work of practicing with competence, social workers must be educated about these issues that touch all of our lives on a growing basis.

As reflected by the new chapter added to this edition, issues related to the physical environment are growing in prominence as well as impact. The responsibility for a healthy planet is something that touches us all, student or professional, personal life or private. This is an issue that is easy to engage with on a simple level, but it also requires macro-level intervention in order for true change to occur.

Just as we saw social work develop as a profession at the end of the 19th century largely in response to immigration, so today we see a new era of social work developing due to this new wave of migration. The effects of technology make our interconnections with those around the world clearer than ever. The importance of understanding social work issues from a global context is important even for those who will never leave our hometown. The international has now come to us, whether we are prepared or not. To practice ethical social work, therefore, we must be prepared to help effect change.

In working to create solutions to these problems, the suggestions at the end of each chapter offer ideas that are "do-able" for people, as well as potential career paths. However, the ideas should not be viewed as the only ways to make a difference; they are simply ways to get started. The role that social workers can play in creating a more equitable world is an important one. Social workers offer vital, unique skills that can be used toward this goal. Diaz, Mama, and Lopez (2006) and Van Soest and Crosby (1997) note the following skills that social workers can offer in the international arena. Due to the generalist nature of entry-level social work, these tips still hold true 25 years later:

- Social workers' skills are portable to any area or level of practice. Social workers are trained to consider a problem at the micro, mezzo, and macro levels.
- Social workers are task-oriented and know how to develop and implement solutions in full partnership with the client.
- Social workers understand the role of culture.
- Social workers can analyze a situation and use all variables to effect change (problem-solving skills).
- Social workers have the ability to bring the human element to planning, policy, and service development. They understand the connection between a client's well-being and the political, economic, and social context in which he or she lives.
- Social workers have the training to bring all the actors and elements together to develop strategies and plans and implement programs (coordination).
- The principles of social work mirror those of social development, including empowerment of the client (having the client define his or her own needs and develop his or her own solutions).

Social work clearly has much to offer as social issues around the globe grow in importance. Social workers of all levels, whether experienced practitioners or first-year BSW students, can help to create positive change. Operating from a human rights standpoint and advancing social justice, we can "promote social change and problem-solving in human relationships and the empowerment and liberation of people to enhance well-being," as specified in the International Federation of Social Workers definition of social work (International Federation of Social Workers, 2000, ¶1).

Appendix A: Universal Declaration of Human Rights

PREAMBLE

Whereas recognition of the inherent dignity and of the equal and inalienable rights of all members of the human family is the foundation of freedom, justice and peace in the world,

Whereas disregard and contempt for human rights have resulted in barbarous acts which have outraged the conscience of mankind, and the advent of a world in which human beings shall enjoy freedom of speech and belief and freedom from fear and want has been proclaimed as the highest aspiration of the common people,

Whereas it is essential, if man is not to be compelled to have recourse, as a last resort, to rebellion against tyranny and oppression, that human rights should be protected by the rule of law,

Whereas it is essential to promote the development of friendly relations between nations,

Whereas the peoples of the United Nations have in the Charter reaffirmed their faith in fundamental human rights, in the dignity and worth of the human person and in the equal rights of men and women and have determined to promote social progress and better standards of life in larger freedom,

Whereas Member States have pledged themselves to achieve, in cooperation with the United Nations, the promotion of universal respect for and observance of human rights and fundamental freedoms,

Whereas a common understanding of these rights and freedoms is of the greatest importance for the full realization of this pledge,

Now, therefore,

The General Assembly,

Proclaims this Universal Declaration of Human Rights as a common standard of achievement for all peoples and all nations, to the end that every individual and every organ of society, keeping this Declaration constantly in mind, shall strive by teaching and education to promote respect for these rights and freedoms and by progressive measures, national and international, to secure their universal and effective recognition and observance, both among the peoples of Member States themselves and among the peoples of territories under their jurisdiction.

ARTICLE 1

All human beings are born free and equal in dignity and rights. They are endowed with reason and conscience and should act towards one another in a spirit of brotherhood.

ARTICLE 2

Everyone is entitled to all the rights and freedoms set forth in this Declaration, without distinction of any kind, such as race, colour, sex, language, religion, political or other opinion, national or social origin, property, birth or other status.

Furthermore, no distinction shall be made on the basis of the political, jurisdictional or international status of the country or territory to which a person belongs, whether it be independent, trust, non-self-governing or under any other limitation of sovereignty.

ARTICLE 3

Everyone has the right to life, liberty and security of person.

ARTICLE 4

No one shall be held in slavery or servitude; slavery and the slave trade shall be prohibited in all their forms.

ARTICLE 5

No one shall be subjected to torture or to cruel, inhuman or degrading treatment or punishment.

ARTICLE 6

Everyone has the right to recognition everywhere as a person before the law.

ARTICLE 7

All are equal before the law and are entitled without any discrimination to equal protection of the law. All are entitled to equal protection against any discrimination in violation of this Declaration and against any incitement to such discrimination.

ARTICLE 8

Everyone has the right to an effective remedy by the competent national tribunals for acts violating the fundamental rights granted him by the constitution or by law.

ARTICLE 9

No one shall be subjected to arbitrary arrest, detention or exile.

ARTICLE 10

Everyone is entitled in full equality to a fair and public hearing by an independent and impartial tribunal, in the determination of his rights and obligations and of any criminal charge against him.

ARTICLE 11

1. Everyone charged with a penal offence has the right to be presumed innocent until proved guilty according to law in a public trial at which he has had all the guarantees necessary for his defence.
2. No one shall be held guilty of any penal offence on account of any act or omission which did not constitute a penal offence, under national or international law, at the time when it was committed. Nor shall a heavier penalty be imposed than the one that was applicable at the time the penal offence was committed.

ARTICLE 12

No one shall be subjected to arbitrary interference with his privacy, family, home or correspondence, nor to attacks upon his honour and reputation. Everyone has the right to the protection of the law against such interference or attacks.

ARTICLE 13

1. Everyone has the right to freedom of movement and residence within the borders of each State.
2. Everyone has the right to leave any country, including his own, and to return to his country.

ARTICLE 14

1. Everyone has the right to seek and to enjoy in other countries asylum from persecution.
2. This right may not be invoked in the case of prosecutions genuinely arising from non-political crimes or from acts contrary to the purposes and principles of the United Nations.

ARTICLE 15

1. Everyone has the right to a nationality.
2. No one shall be arbitrarily deprived of his nationality nor denied the right to change his nationality.

ARTICLE 16

1. Men and women of full age, without any limitation due to race, nationality or religion, have the right to marry and to found a family. They are entitled to equal rights as to marriage, during marriage and at its dissolution.
2. Marriage shall be entered into only with the free and full consent of the intending spouses.
3. The family is the natural and fundamental group unit of society and is entitled to protection by society and the State.

ARTICLE 17

1. Everyone has the right to own property alone as well as in association with others.
2. No one shall be arbitrarily deprived of his property.

ARTICLE 18

Everyone has the right to freedom of thought, conscience and religion; this right includes freedom to change his religion or belief, and freedom, either alone or in community with others and in public or private, to manifest his religion or belief in teaching, practice, worship and observance.

ARTICLE 19

Everyone has the right to freedom of opinion and expression; this right includes freedom to hold opinions without interference and to seek, receive and impart information and ideas through any media and regardless of frontiers.

ARTICLE 20

1. Everyone has the right to freedom of peaceful assembly and association.
2. No one may be compelled to belong to an association.

ARTICLE 21

1. Everyone has the right to take part in the government of his country, directly or through freely chosen representatives.
2. Everyone has the right to equal access to public service in his country.
3. The will of the people shall be the basis of the authority of government; this will be expressed in periodic and genuine elections which shall be by universal and equal suffrage and shall be held by secret vote or by equivalent free voting procedures.

ARTICLE 22

Everyone, as a member of society, has the right to social security and is entitled to realization, through national effort and

international cooperation and in accordance with the organization
and resources of each State, of the economic, social and cultural
rights indispensable for his dignity and the free development of
his personality.

ARTICLE 23

1. Everyone has the right to work, to free choice of employment,
   to just and favourable conditions of work and to protection
   against unemployment.
2. Everyone, without any discrimination, has the right to equal
   pay for equal work.
3. Everyone who works has the right to just and favourable
   remuneration ensuring for himself and his family an existence
   worthy of human dignity, and supplemented, if necessary, by
   other means of social protection.
4. Everyone has the right to form and to join trade unions for the
   protection of his interests.

ARTICLE 24

Everyone has the right to rest and leisure, including reasonable
limitation of working hours and periodic holidays with pay.

ARTICLE 25

1. Everyone has the right to a standard of living adequate
   for the health and well-being of himself and of his family,
   including food, clothing, housing and medical care and
   necessary social services, and the right to security in the event
   of unemployment, sickness, disability, widowhood, old age or
   other lack of livelihood in circumstances beyond his control.
2. Motherhood and childhood are entitled to special care and
   assistance. All children, whether born in or out of wedlock,
   shall enjoy the same social protection.

ARTICLE 26

1. Everyone has the right to education. Education shall be free, at least in the elementary and fundamental stages. Elementary education shall be compulsory. Technical and professional education shall be made generally available and higher education shall be equally accessible to all on the basis of merit.
2. Education shall be directed to the full development of the human personality and to the strengthening of respect for human rights and fundamental freedoms. It shall promote understanding, tolerance and friendship among all nations, racial or religious groups, and shall further the activities of the United Nations for the maintenance of peace.
3. Parents have a prior right to choose the kind of education that shall be given to their children.

ARTICLE 27

1. Everyone has the right freely to participate in the cultural life of the community, to enjoy the arts and to share in scientific advancement and its benefits.
2. Everyone has the right to the protection of the moral and material interests resulting from any scientific, literary or artistic production of which he is the author.

ARTICLE 28

Everyone is entitled to a social and international order in which the rights and freedoms set forth in this Declaration can be fully realized.

ARTICLE 29

1. Everyone has duties to the community in which alone the free and full development of his personality is possible.

2. In the exercise of his rights and freedoms, everyone shall be subject only to such limitations as are determined by law solely for the purpose of securing due recognition and respect for the rights and freedoms of others and of meeting the just requirements of morality, public order and the general welfare in a democratic society.

3. These rights and freedoms may in no case be exercised contrary to the purposes and principles of the United Nations.

ARTICLE 30

Nothing in this Declaration may be interpreted as implying for any State, group or person any right to engage in any activity or to perform any act aimed at the destruction of any of the rights and freedoms set forth herein.

© *The Office of the High Commissioner for Human Rights*

Appendix B: Opportunities in International Social Work

JOBS

ADVENTIST DEVELOPMENT & RELIEF AGENCY (ADRA)
http://www.adra.org/site/PageServer
An affiliate agency to the Seventh-day Adventist Church that works to improve communities and quality of life through disaster relief services and prevention developments. The ADRA works against discrimination of all kinds—age, gender, ethnicity, and political or religious association.

AFRICAN MEDICAL & RESEARCH FOUNDATION, INC. (AMREF)
http://www.amrefusa.org/
Work to train health professionals from all African countries to improve the health of vulnerable populations in Africa in an effort to alleviate poverty and increase quality of life. Headquarters are located in Nairobi, Kenya.

AFRICARE
http://www.africare.org/
Africare is a leading nongovernmental organization that works to improve the quality of life in Africa through development programs focused on food, water, environment, health, and emergency aid as well as business development and governmental affairs. Africare supports over 150 self-help development programs in 26 African nations.

AMERICAN ENTERPRISE INSTITUTE FOR PUBLIC POLICY RESEARCH
http://www.aei.org
The American Enterprise Institute for Public Policy Research (AEI) is a
nonprofit institute focused on research and education on issues of government, politics, economics, and social welfare. AEI works to defend the
principles and improve the institutions of American freedom and democratic capitalism. AEI offers research and staff assistant positions in economic policy studies, foreign and defense policy studies, and social and
political studies. Openings are posted as they become available.

AMERICAN FRIENDS SERVICE COMMITTEE
http://www.afcs.org
The American Friends Service Committee (AFSC) is an organization
based on the expression of the faith of the Religious Society of Friends
(Quakers). The AFSC stands committed to the principles of nonviolence
and justice and works to draw on the transforming power of human and
divine love. AFSC regularly posts available positions on its Web site.

AMERICAN REFUGEE COMMITTEE
http://www.arcrelief.org
The American Refugee Committee (ARC) works with refugees, displaced
persons, and those at risk of being displaced to help them survive crises and
rebuild lives of dignity, health, security, and self-sufficiency. Employment
opportunities may be searched according to geographic location, as ARC
works throughout the world. Positions are posted as they become available.

AMERICARES FOUNDATION INC.
http://www.americares.org/
AmeriCares provides emergency response and disaster relief humanitarian as well as long-term humanitarian assistance programs around the
world. They operate without regard to race, creed, or political association.

AMERICA'S DEVELOPMENT FOUNDATION (ADF)
http://www.interaction.org/organization/americas-development-foundation
The ADF focuses on the expansion of democratic principles through the
foundation of a strong civil society, and autonomous economic, social,
cultural, and political systems.

AMIGOS DE LAS AMERICAS (AMIGOS)

http://www.amigoslink.org/

AMIGOS works to develop community programs which focus on empowering young leaders in order to develop communities and strengthen multicultural understanding in the Americas.

ANANDA MARGA UNIVERSAL RELIEF TEAM (AMURT)

http://www.amurt.net/

Originally based in the areas of the Indian subcontinent, AMURT aims to meet the needs of disaster victims and has established a network of humanitarian aid programs in 80 countries. AMURT goals include providing long-term assistance to those in poverty in order to break the cycle and improve quality of life.

BERESFORD BLAKE THOMAS

http://www.bbtworldwide.com

Beresford Blake Thomas serves as a recruiting consultancy, providing both temporary and permanent staff members to organizations across the globe. Candidates in health and social care may search for jobs based on country, location, and specialization. Beresford Blake Thomas also provides job placement assistance, including consultations regarding placement options, career direction, and procurement of necessary documentation.

BIENESTAR HUMAN SERVICES, INC.

http://www.bienestar.org

Bienestar is a grassroots nonprofit organization dedicated to enhancing the health and well-being of the Latino community and other underserved communities.

CARE

http://www.care.org

CARE is an international organization dedicated to eradicating global poverty. Specializing in working with impoverished women, CARE strives to improve basic education, prevent the spread of HIV, increase access to clean water and sanitation, protect natural resources, and expand economic opportunity. Information about short-term, part-time, and full-term positions can be accessed through the Web site. Regions include Africa, Asia, Europe, and the United States.

Catholic Medical Mission Board (CMMB)
http://www.cmmb.org/
The CMMB operates in collaboration with other programs to provide quality health care and services without discrimination to all peoples. They are work according to their motto as being "rooted in the healing ministry of Jesus."

Catholic Relief Services
http://www.catholicrelief.org/
Provide essential and direct assistance for immediate needs and further encourage communities around the world to contribute to their own development. Catholic Relief Services works to empower vulnerable populations to create productive, just, and secure communities.

Christian Children's Fund (CCF)
http://www.childfund.org/
The CCF works to create a positive and nurturing environment for children, families, and communities through the use and development of practical tools and skills for lasting change. Their mission is to ensure children in need have the opportunity to fulfill their potential.

Church World Service (CWS)
http://www.cwsglobal.org/
CWS is a relief, development, and refugee assistance organization comprised of 36 Protestant, Orthodox, and Anglican denominations in the United States. They partner with indigenous organizations in more than 80 countries and work to meet needs and foster autonomy.

Citizens Development Corps (CDC)
http://www.cdcdevelopmentsolutions.org/
The CDC provides practical strategies and solutions, program developments, and professional expertise to emerging and transitioning economies

around the world. This mission will aid in the development of the private sector as well as whole economies.

Citizens Network for Foreign Affairs, The (CNFA)
http://www.cnfa.org/
The CNFA partners with US companies, entrepreneurs, farm groups, and various organizations to stimulate continuous growth of international markets and opportunities.

Concern Worldwide US Inc.
http://www.concernusa.org/
Concern Worldwide US Inc. is made up of bipartisan organizations which work to lead, speak, and act on behalf of the vulnerable populations of the hungry, poor, and victims of crisis. They are involved both domestically and internationally.

Cooperative Housing Foundation
http://www.chfinternational.org
The Cooperative Housing Foundation (CHF) is an organization dedicated to being a catalyst for sustainable positive change in low- and moderate-income communities around the world. CHF strives to help these communities improve their economic, social, and environmental conditions. CHF offers consultancy positions, as well as employment both at headquarters and in the field. Openings are posted along with descriptions as they become available.

Council on Foreign Relations
http://www.cfr.org
The Council on Foreign Relations is a national membership organization and scholarly center that is dedicated to the production and dissemination of ideas that allow for a better understanding of the world and foreign policy choices facing both the United States and other governments. The Council on Foreign Relations offers positions in both the New York and Washington, DC offices. Available positions and descriptions are posted as openings arise.

COUNTERPART INTERNATIONAL, INC.

http://www.counterpart.org/about

Counterpart International is a global development organization working in collaboration with communities to ensure economic security, food and nutritional stability, and the development of effective governments and similar institutions.

DOCTORS WITHOUT BORDERS/MÉDECINS SANS FRONTIÉRES

http://www.dwb.org

http://www.msf.org

Doctors Without Borders/Médecins Sans Frontières (MSF) is an independent and international medically based humanitarian organization that delivers emergency aid to global citizens adversely affected by armed conflict, epidemics, natural or human-made disasters, or poor health care in more than 70 countries throughout the world. Available positions are updated regularly.

ELDIS, UK

http://www.eldis.org/

Provides financial services to the world's poorest families so they can become more self-sufficient through employment, raising income, and improving standards of living. Eldis, UK operates within a global network of locally managed and self-supporting institutions.

FOREIGN POLICY ASSOCIATION

http://www.fpa.org

The Foreign Policy Association (FPA) is a nonprofit organization that is committed to inspiring the American public to educate themselves about the world. FPA offers independent publications as well as programs and forums that increase public awareness of and encourage participation in matters relating to policy issues. FPA offers a job board database; available positions may be located by category. Open positions may be with a variety of FPA's affiliate organizations.

GLOBAL HEALTH COUNCIL

http://www.globalhealth.org/

The Global Health Council is an international humanitarian agency working to alleviate the prevalence and suffering of poverty. The GHC focuses particularly on the more than 2 billion people living on less than $2 per day. They are instrumental in ensuring access to health care and influencing international health policies.

GOAL USA
http://www.goalusa.org
GOAL USA is a nondenominational Christian humanitarian agency that builds simple, affordable housing in partnership with those who need of adequate shelter. They offer emergency assistance to those in need including health care, food assistance, and transitional shelter for displaced persons.

Grassroots International
http://www.grassrootsonline.org
Grassroots International is an organization that works to promote global justice through its partnerships with social change organizations. Through these partnerships, Grassroots International strives to advance political, economic, and social rights and support development alternatives in developing nations. Programs include grant-making, education, and advocacy. Positions are available at the Boston headquarters and are posted as they become available.

Habitat for Humanity International (HFHI)
http://www.habitat.org/
HFHI works to achieve sustainable advances in health care by implementing health education programs, conducting health policy research, and providing humanitarian aid. Thereby, HFHI contributes to the improvement of human dignity, the promotion of international understanding, and social and economic development.

Health Opportunities for People Everywhere (HOPE)
http://www.projecthope.org/
HOPE is a global humanitarian organization working to inspire, empower, and mobilize individuals to serve the needs of the poor in communities around the world. They function collaboratively to promote quality health care, alleviate hunger, establish resources, and educate.

HOLT INTERNATIONAL CHILDREN'S SERVICES
http://www.holtinternational.org/
Holt International Children's Services supports the institution of demo-cratic systems in developing societies through the use of research and analysis as well as "country-specific expertise." This approach ensures sensitivity and success within countries of operation in partnering with governments and nongovernmental organizations.

IFES (CURRENTLY IS—DERIVED FROM INTERNATIONAL FEDERATION FOR ELECTORAL SYSTEMS)
http://www.ifes.org/
IFES supports and implements systems for citizens' rights to exercise their right to participate in the political process. They provide communi-ties the training, technical assistance, and grants they need to solve their own problems and further shape their government system.

IMA WORLD HEALTH
IMA World Health provides health care services and medical supplies around the world, primarily in the Global South. It is a nonprofit, faith-based organization and they aim to "restore health, hope and dignity to those most in need."

INTERACTION: AMERICAN COUNCIL FOR VOLUNTARY INTERNATIONAL ACTION (IA)
http://www.interaction.org/
The IA is global humanitarian agency dedicated to providing interna-tional aid and development training to indigenous churches so as to cre-ate a network of resources for communities in need.

INTERNATIONAL AID (IA)
http://www.internationalaid.org/
International Aid is an organization committed to improving the lives of women in poverty, advancing equality and human rights, and contributing to broader economic and social well-being.

INTERNATIONAL CRISIS GROUP (ICG)
http://www.crisisgroup.org
The ICG works to prevent conflict worldwide and provides policy analyses and resolution proposals. They partner with international governmental organizations such as the United Nations, European Union, and World Bank to work on prevention and resolution strategies for international conflicts.

INSTITUTE FOR SUSTAINABLE COMMUNITIES (ISC)
http://www.iscvt.org/
The ISC is the largest alliance of US-based international development and humanitarian nongovernmental organizations. They work with more than 160 partner organizations based in over 100 countries to alleviate the cycle of poverty, advance social justice, and ensure basic dignity for all people.

INTERNATIONAL FEDERATION FOR SOCIAL WORKERS (IFSW)
http://ifsw.org/
The IFSW acknowledges that social work is made up of various humanitarian, religious, and democratic ideals. Additionally, the IFSW recognizes the need for international interventions so as to fully develop human potential. The IFSW facilitates a network of social workers from all countries and provides a space for discussion of prevalent needs and research findings. These methods are then criticized and applied to international conflicts.

INTERNATIONAL INSTITUTE OF RURAL RECONSTRUCTION (IIRR)
http://www.iirr.org/
The IIRR is a small international development and research organization working at the grassroots level. They are people centered and aim to establish sustainable resources in Africa, Asia, and Latin America. The IIRR is dedicated to saving lives and to relieving suffering through health care training and medical relief programs. They operate as a private, voluntary, nonpolitical, nonsectarian organization.

INTERNATIONAL JUSTICE MISSION

http://www.ijm.org

International Justice Mission is a human rights agency that rescues victims of violence, sexual exploitation, slavery, and oppression. It is based in the United States and has agencies around the world.

INTERNATIONAL MEDICAL CORPS

http://www.imcworldwide.org

The International Medical Corps (IMC) is a nonprofit organization that works to save lives and relieve suffering through health care training and relief and development programs. IMC offers training and health care to high-risk populations and rehabilitates health care systems. A variety of positions are available; positions are posted regularly.

INTERNATIONAL ORTHODOX CHRISTIAN CHARITIES (IOCC)

http://www.iocc.org/

The IOCC provides cost-effective emergency relief and implements development programs through its network of churches worldwide.

INTERNATIONAL RESCUE COMMITTEE

http://www.theirc.org

The IRC works around the globe to deliver lifesaving aid in emergencies, rebuild shattered communities, and provide other social services. For refugees afforded sanctuary in the United States, IRC offices across the country provide a range of assistance to help new arrivals get settled and acquire the skills to become self-sufficient.

INTERNATIONAL SOCIAL SERVICE—UNITED STATES OF AMERICA BRANCH, INC. (ISS-USA)

http://www.iss-usa.org/

The ISS-USA operates as a nonsectarian international social work agency that provides resources for children, families, and adults who experience a socio-legal need. They work with over 150 international correspondents to communicate in an effort to resolve these socio-legal problems.

INTERNATIONAL WOMEN'S HEALTH COALITION (IWHC)

http://www.iwhc.org/

The IWHC aims to support and protect the rights and health of women and girls through the development of health and population policies, programs, and funding. They work primarily with countries in Africa, Asia, and Latin America and those transitioning in post-socialist transition.

INTERNATIONAL YOUTH FOUNDATION (IYF)

http://www.iyfnet.org/

The IYF is present in approximately 70 countries and is working to improve the conditions and potential for youth and their environments. They work collaboratively with organizations around the world to bolster humanitarian resources available for young people. This is to ensure they have adequate access to educational programs and other opportunities which will contribute to their quality of life.

INTERVIDA FOUNDATION USA

http://www.intervida.org/en/

The US branch of the Intervida Foundation works to support developing countries with a focus on the well-being of the nation's children.

JESUIT REFUGEE SERVICE/USA (JRS-USA)

http://jrsusa.org/

The JRS-USA agency works to accompany, serve, and advocate for the rights of refugees and people who have been forcibly displaced as a result of national, international, and political conflicts. They facilitate services at the national and regional levels.

MEDICAL CARE DEVELOPMENT (MCDI)

http://mcd.org/

Medical Care Development (International) assists vulnerable populations and communities in developing countries with health planning, management research, and training. They work in partnership with US agencies, states, foreign governments, global organizations and private sector agencies.

MENNONITE CENTRAL COMMITTEE, SERVICE TREE
http://www.mcc.org
The Mennonite Central Committee endeavors to demonstrate God's love through working with those suffering from poverty, conflict, oppression, and natural disaster. MCC maintains a goal of establishing peace, justice, and dignity for all people by sharing experiences, resources, and faith in Jesus Christ. The Service Tree portion of MCC's Web site provides an area for international service workers. Available positions are sorted into sectors and updated as they become available.

MERCY CORPS
http://www.mercycorps.org/
The Mercy Corps mission is to "alleviate suffering, poverty and oppression by helping people build secure, productive and just communities." They operate with headquarters in Portland, Seattle, Cambridge, Washington, DC, and Edinburgh, Scotland.

MINNESOTA INTERNATIONAL HEALTH VOLUNTEERS (MIHV)
http://www.wellshareinternational.org/
MIHV works to improve the health of women, children, and communities on international and local levels through programs addressing health and child survival.

NATIONAL PEACE CORPS ASSOCIATION (NPCA)
http://www.peacecorpsconnect.org/
The NPCA is a membership-based program of people who have served in the Peace Corps: volunteers and staff, families, friends, and other individuals interested in issues of world peace. They provide a central network of 30,000 people and over 150 connection groups to advance community, national, and international services. The NPCA offers global education programs and advocacy campaigns.

NEAR EAST FOUNDATION (NEF)
http://www.neareast.org/
The Near East Foundation is committed to helping those experiencing rural and urban poverty in the areas of the Middle East and Africa. They

assist in community and interpersonal development and work closely with other indigenous services. The NEF aims to create productive communities through training and customized agriculture, self-sustaining projects, and health, literacy, and income-generation programs.

Northwest Medical Teams
http://www.medicalteams.org/
Northwest Medical Teams is a humanitarian aid organization working to reduce suffering around the world and in the Pacific Northwest.

Opportunity International-U.S. (OI-U.S.)
http://www.opportunity.org/
The approach of OI-U.S. is to create jobs and stimulate business in order to strengthen communities suffering from extreme poverty. They work with indigenous organizations to sponsor business loans, training, and guidance.

Oxfam America
http://www.oxfamamerica.org
http://www.oxfam.org
Oxfam aims to end global poverty through saving lives, strengthening communities, and campaigning for change. Positions are available both in the United States and in regional offices throughout the world. Additionally, Oxfam allows partner organizations to post available positions on the Web site.

Pact
http://pactworld.org/
PACT is a global organization and network that works to increase the capacity of local leaders and organizations in order to improve their abilities to address issues of social need. They operate with the principle that local communities themselves possess the energy to end poverty and injustice.

Partners for Development (PFD)
http://www.pfd.org/
PFD serves vulnerable and disadvantaged populations in developing countries to improve quality of life with programs in Cambodia, Nigeria,

and Bosnia and Herzegovina. They assist with issues of health, agriculture, water and sanitation, veterinary health, and credit.

PATHFINDER INTERNATIONAL
http://www.pathfind.org/
Pathfinder International is committed to the mission of developing programs that provide high-quality services for family planning.

PEACE CORP
http://www.peacecorps.gov/
Volunteers and employees associated with the Peace Corps work in areas of education, youth outreach, and community development, health and HIV/AIDS, agriculture, business development, and information technology. Responsibilities vary between community and volunteers/employees.

PHYSICIANS FOR HUMAN RIGHTS (PHR)
http://physiciansforhumanrights.org/
PHR uses science and medical services to advocate for victims of mass atrocities and violations of human rights. They impact indigenous organizations, national governments, and international policies.

POPULATION ACTION INTERNATIONAL (PAI)
http://populationaction.org/
PAI is an independent group that works to influence policy through advocacy work on behalf of public awareness, political issues, and financial issues. They work globally to support population programs and individual rights. PAI focuses on the rights of women and children and their access to food and a safe environment. They look to strengthen communities and aim to improve the availability of reproductive health care around the world.

REFUGEE INTERNATIONAL (RI)
http://refugeesinternational.org/
RI is an independent organization operating without government or UN funding. They work to advocated for refugees seeking lifesaving assistance and protection as displaced persons. RI aims to increase

community stability and individual quality of life through advocacy and direct relief work.

Relief International (RI)
http://www.ri.org/

Relief International (RI) is a nonprofit humanitarian agency working to provide emergency relief, development support, and rehabilitation services to communities affected by natural and human--made disasters. RI operates with the mission of reducing human suffering and advocating for individual rights.

Relief Web
http://reliefweb.int/

Relief Web is considered a gateway to information on humanitarian emergencies as it provides assistance and research for current events and underlying emergencies. Relief Web serves as a resource for the international humanitarian community of service delivery.

RESULTS
http://www.results.org/

RESULTS is an organization dedicated to creating political will to end hunger and poverty through empowering individuals to exercise their rights. They seek to influence policies and introduce strategies to affect the issues of hunger and poverty.

Save the Children (SC/US)
http://www.savethechildren.org/

SC/US is an independent organization working for positive and sustainable change for children in need in the United States and around the world. This organization operates as a member of the International Save the Children Alliance made up of 27 national organizations working in more than 100 countries.

SHARE Foundation (SHARE)
http://www.share-elsalvador.org/

SHARE serves to empower and support the poor and historically marginalized communities of El Salvador in an effort to meet immediate needs.

They aim to build sustainable solutions to problems of poverty, housing, underdevelopment, and social injustice.

STRATEGIC ACTIONS FOR A JUST ECONOMY
http://www.saje.org
Strategic Actions for a Just Economy is an economic justice and education center that works to build economic power for working-class people in Los Angeles. SAJE posts available employment opportunities on a regular basis.

SYNERGOS INSTITUTE, THE
http://www.synergos.org/
The Synergos Institute is an organization based out of New York that works in partnership with organizations around the world to fight poverty. With this network, The Synergos Institute is dedicated to building local human, financial, and social capital needed to create sustainable solutions to the problem of poverty.

TRICKLE UP PROGRAM, THE
http://www.trickleup.org/
The Trickle Up Program assists people living in poverty around the world to take the first steps to surpass their destitution. They provide business training, support services, and conditional capital.

UNITED JEWISH COMMUNITIES (UJC)
http://unitedjewishcommunities.orghub.net/
The UJC is made up of 155 Jewish federations and 400 independent Jewish communities across North America. It reflects the values of social justice and human rights that define Jewish people. They hold the value of caring highly as it is seen to transform lives and perform miracles.

WORLD CONFERENCES OF RELIGIONS FOR PEACE (WCRP)
http://www.religionsforpeace.org/
The WCRP works to orchestrate and mobilize religious communities to achieve common ground. It is made up of representatives of the various

religious communities and works to implement collaborative programs to address major societal challenges.

WORLD HOPE INTERNATIONAL
http://www.worldhope.org/
World Hope International is a Christian relief and development agency working to alleviate the poverty, social injustices, and suffering experienced by oppressed and vulnerable populations.

WORLD LEARNING
http://www.worldlearning.org/
World Learning is the only international organization with both academic and project capabilities dedicated to promoting international education, social justice, and world peace. Programs within this organization are focused on empowering leaders in education and management, contributing to global development, and effecting global change.

WORLD RELIEF (WR)
http://worldrelief.org/
WR works with evangelical churches around the world to bring relief to people suffering. Their mission states that they operate in the name of Christ by working in ministry to the impoverished, sick, and the hungry. They attend to those suffering from the effects of war and natural disasters and aim to meet the physical, emotional, and spiritual needs of the people they serve.

WORLD RESOURCES INSTITUTE (WRI)
http://www.wri.org/
The mission of WRI is to move human society to live in ways that protect Earth's environment and its capacity to provide for the needs and potential of current and future generations.

WORLD VISION INTERNATIONAL
http://www.wvi.org/
World Vision International is a Christian organization for the well-being of all people, especially children by way of emergency relief, education,

and health care programs. They work on economic development and the promotion of justice while helping communities help themselves. World Vision International is currently working on six continents.

WORLD VISION
http://www.worldvision.org
World Vision is a Christian relief and development organization dedicated to eliminating the causes of poverty and helping children and their communities worldwide. Both domestic and international positions are available.

INTERNSHIPS

ACADEMY FOR EDUCATIONAL DEVELOPMENT
http://www.aed.org
The Academy for Educational Development (AED) is a nonprofit organization dedicated to finding solutions to critical programs and building the capacity of individuals, communities, and institutions to become more self-sufficient. While AED works in all major areas of human development, it maintains a focus on improving education, health, and economic opportunities for the least advantaged individuals around the world. AED offers both paid and unpaid internships. Interns participate in research and writing, coordination of itineraries and meeting schedules, and proposal preparation and production.

AFRICA ACTION
http://www.africaaction.org
Africa Action is the oldest organization working on African affairs in the United States. Africa Action works alongside activists and civil society organizations in the United States and Africa to change US foreign policy and the policies of international institutions. Africa Action offers internships throughout the academic year and during the summer. Interns focus on campaigns to end HIV/AIDS in Africa, cancel Africa's debt, and stop genocide in Darfur, Sudan.

AMERICA-MIDEAST EDUCATIONAL AND TRAINING SERVICES, INC.

http://www.amideast.org

America-Mideast Educational and Training Services, Inc. (AMIDEAST) is a nonprofit organization dedicated to strengthening mutual understanding and cooperation between citizens of the United States, Middle East, and North Africa. AMIDEAST offers English language and professional skills training, educational advising, and testing services to individuals throughout the Middle East and North Africa. AMIDEAST offers internships based on the needs of the organization, generally a total of four to six positions yearly.

AMERICAN ENTERPRISE INSTITUTE FOR PUBLIC POLICY RESEARCH

http://www.aei.org

The American Enterprise Institute for Public Policy Research (AEI) is a nonprofit institute focused on research and education on issues of government, politics, economics, and social welfare. AEI works to defend the principles and improve the institutions of American freedom and democratic capitalism. AEI offers approximately 50 internship positions throughout the fall, spring, and summer in the Washington, DC office.

AMERICAN FRIENDS SERVICE COMMITTEE

http://www.afcs.org

The American Friends Service Committee (AFSC) is an organization based on the expression of the faith of the Religious Society of Friends (Quakers). The AFSC stands committed to the principles of nonviolence and justice and works to draw on the transforming power of human and divine love. AFSC offers internships to high school and college students at offices across the nation. Positions are posted as they become available.

ATLANTIC COUNCIL OF THE UNITED STATES

http://www.acus.org

The Atlantic Council of the United States works to promote constructive leadership and engagement in international affairs in the United States based on the central role of the Atlantic community in meeting global challenges in a modern world. The Council comprises a network of leaders who strive to bring ideas to power and give power to ideas.

The Council offers the John A. Baker internship program, providing 10 to 15 volunteer positions during the fall, spring, and summer. John A. Baker interns assist with Council projects, attend briefings and seminars, and complete independent research projects.

BREAD FOR THE WORLD
http://www.bread.org
Bread for the World is a national Christian movement that lobbies the nation's decision makers, seeking justice for hungry people around the world. Bread for the World offers internships in the fall, spring, and summer in the Washington, DC office. Interns are matched to specific jobs based on background, skills, interests, and the needs of the organization.

CARE
http://www.care.org
CARE is an international organization dedicated to eradicating global poverty. Specializing in working with impoverished women, CARE strives to improve basic education, prevent the spread of HIV, increase access to clean water and sanitation, protect natural resources, and expand economic opportunity. Available internships can be accessed through the Web site. Regions include Africa, Asia, Europe, and the United States.

THE CARTER CENTER
http://www.cartercenter.org
The Carter Center is an organization working in partnership with Emory University that, guided by its commitment to human rights and the alleviation of human suffering, seeks to prevent and resolve conflicts, enhance freedom and democracy, and improve heath. The Carter Center offers internship positions to college juniors, seniors, recent graduates, or graduate students. Interns are involved in a wide range of duties focusing on issues addressed by their particular program but may also be involved in office administration or other issues that span across programs.

CENTER FOR GLOBAL EDUCATION
The Center for Global Education offers various study abroad opportunities for George Mason University students and the general public.

Programs can be short or long term and offer international experience, internships, and intensive language programs.

CENTER FOR STRATEGIC AND INTERNATIONAL STUDIES
http://www.csis.org
The Center for Strategic and International Studies (CSIS) is a nonprofit organization that seeks to advance global security and prosperity by offering insights and policy solutions to decision makers. CSIS conducts research and analysis and develops policy initiatives for the US government. CSIS offers both full- and part-time internships in the fall, spring, and summer. Interns participate in a variety of activities that support individual programs.

CHRISTIAN REFORMED WORLD RELIEF COMMITTEE
http://www.crwrc.org
The Christian Reformed World Relief Committee (CRWRC) is a relief, development, and educational ministry of the Christian Reformed Church in North America. As a ministry, CRWRC partners with local agencies throughout the world that understand the local needs, then works with these partners to provide lasting change. CRWRC offers Program Hope!, a 30-month internship program in which individuals work in community-level projects in a variety of areas, including agriculture, income generation, health, and education. Interns may also have the opportunity to train leaders of local churches in need. Interns receive a small stipend each month, training, insurance, transportation, and field supervision.

COMMISSION ON SECURITY AND COOPERATION IN EUROPE
http://www.csce.gov
The Commission on Security and Cooperation in Europe (CSCE), also known as the Helsinki Commission, is an independent government agency that monitors and encourages compliance with the Helsinki Final Act, as well as other commitments. CSCE offers the Helsinki Commission Internship, a program that allows students to research Helsinki Final Act-relation issues regarding human rights, religious liberties, corruption and rule of law, and free media. Additionally, interns assist staff advisors and the communications director, compile press clippings, communicate with

the House and Senate regarding pending foreign policy initiatives, and conduct office duties. Internships last for one academic semester.

COUNCIL OF THE AMERICAS
http://www.americas-society.org
The Council of the Americas is a business organization composed of members who share a common commitment to free trade and open markets throughout the Americas. The Council of the Americas' programs and advocacy aim to educate, encourage, and promote free trade and integrated markets for the benefit of the member companies, as well as companies throughout the Americas. The Council of the Americas offers internships at its New York and Washington, DC locations. Positions are posted as they become available.

COUNCIL ON FOREIGN RELATIONS
http://www.cfr.org
The Council on Foreign Relations is an organization and nonpartisan center for scholars that is committed to producing and disseminating ideas that will better allow members, policymakers, journalists, students, and US and world citizens to understand the foreign policy choices facing the United States and other governments. The Council on Foreign Relations offers fall, spring, and summer internships at both the New York and Washington, DC offices. Internships available at each location are posted as openings arise.

DEVELOPMENT ASSOCIATES
http://www.devassoc.com
Development Associates is a firm specializing in economic and social development programs both in the United States and overseas. Development Associates provides nations around the world with counsel, technical assistance, training, and management services that help them to achieve results. Development Associates offers internships year round. Potential topics are posted on the firm's Web site.

DOCTORS WITHOUT BORDERS/MÉDECINS SANS FRONTIÈRES
http://www.dwb.org
http://www.msf.org

Doctors Without Borders/Médecins Sans Frontières (MSF) is an independent and international medically based humanitarian organization that delivers emergency aid to global citizens adversely affected by armed conflict, epidemics, natural or human-made disasters, or poor health care in more than 70 countries throughout the world. Interns with DWB/MSF obtain experience in development, human resources, communication, executive, or program departments, in addition to a valuable basic introduction to the field of international medical humanitarian aid and advocacy. Terms are available in the fall, spring, and summer and take place in the New York office. All internships are unpaid, but work-study funds and course credit may be provided to qualifying students.

ETHIOPIAN COMMUNITY DEVELOPMENT COUNCIL, INC.
http://www.ecdcinternational.org

Ethiopian Community Development Council, Inc. (ECDC) is an organization that works to resettle refugees; promote educational, cultural, and socioeconomic development in the refugee and immigrant populations in the United States; and carry out humanitarian and development programs in the Horn of Africa.

FELLOWSHIP OF RECONCILIATION
http://www.forusa.org

The Fellowship of Reconciliation (FOR) is an international, interfaith movement with branches and groups in over 40 nations. FOR works to replace violence, war, racism, and economic injustice with nonviolence, peace, and economic justice. To achieve these goals, FOR educates, trains, builds coalitions, and engages in nonviolent and compassionate actions on a local, national, and global front. FOR offers the Freeman Peace Internships. Freeman interns commit to an 11-month position during which they will receive a monthly stipend, medical insurance, housing, 4 weeks of vacation, experienced mentors, and expanding opportunities.

FOOD FOR THE HUNGRY

http://www.fh.org

Food for the Hungry is an international relief and development organization striving to meet the physical and spiritual needs of those in need in more than 45 nations. Food for the Hungry works alongside churches, leaders, and families to bring forth the resources needed to help communities become self-sufficient and self-sustaining. Food for the Hungry offers internships in the fall, spring, summer, and entire academic year in Washington, DC, Phoenix, and abroad. Interns receive training and coaching, mentorship, community interaction, and a placement based on personal interest and talents.

FOUNDATION FOR SUSTAINABLE DEVELOPMENT

http://www.fsdinternational.org

The Foundation for Sustainable Development (FSD) supports grassroots development organizations that are working to better their communities, environments, and the economic opportunities around them. FSD upholds the philosophy that economic development begins with community development and is sustainable only if it comes from and is continually supported by the members of those communities. FSD also works to raise awareness about international issues. FSD offers both summer and long-term international internships. Interns may work in health, human rights, education, women's issues, environmental issues, microfinance, community development, or other areas.

FREEDOM HOUSE

http://www.freedomhouse.org

Freedom House is a nongovernmental organization that works to support the expansion of freedom throughout the world. By supporting nonviolent civic initiatives around the world, Freedom House acts as a catalyst for freedom, democracy, and the rule of law. Freedom House accepts volunteers through its American Volunteers for International Development (AVID) program. This program identifies, mobilizes, and sponsors American professionals who will then work in conjunction with counterparts in emerging democracies. Volunteers receive basic living expenses, roundtrip air transportation, and medical evacuation insurance.

GLOBAL EXCHANGE
http://www.globalexchange.org
Global Exchange is a membership-based human rights organization working to promote social, economic, and environmental justice around the
world. Global Exchange is dedicated to increasing public awareness of the
root causes of injustice while establishing international partnerships and
mobilizing for change. Global Exchange offers structured internships in
the summer, with more informal positions in the fall, winter, and spring.
Interns work in the San Francisco office on campaigns and programs and
are expected to bring some knowledge and experience to the position.

GLOBAL SERVICE CORPS
http://www.globalservicecorps.org
The Global Service Corps is an international nonprofit volunteer organization that provides service-learning opportunities to live and work in
Thailand and Tanzania. Programs include HIV/AIDS prevention, sustainable agriculture, health care, English instruction, Buddhist immersion,
and the Seeds of Sustenance Fellowship. Global Service Corps offers
internships for a period of 9 weeks throughout the year.

GRASSROOTS INTERNATIONAL
http://www.grassrootsonline.org
Grassroots International is an organization that works to promote global
justice through its partnerships with social change organizations. Through
these partnerships, Grassroots International strives to advance political, economic, and social rights and support development alternatives
in developing nations. Programs include grant-making, education, and
advocacy. Grassroots International offers internships at its Boston office.
Interns must commit to at least 10 hours of service per week, and a two-
semester commitment is preferred.

HUDSON INSTITUTE
http://www.hudson.org
The Hudson Institute is a nonpartisan policy research organization that is
dedicated to innovative research and analysis that promotes global security, prosperity, and freedom. The Hudson Institute works to challenge

conventional thinking and manage strategic transitions to the future through interdisciplinary and collaborative studies. The Hudson Institute offers internships in its Washington, DC office, working in areas such as campaign reform, economic and employment policy, Middle East studies, philanthropy and civic renewal, national security studies, and science in public policy.

IMA WORLD HEALTH

IMA World Health provides health care services and medical supplies around the world, primarily in the Global South. It is a nonprofit, faith-based organization and they aim to "restore health, hope and dignity to those most in need."

INSTITUTE FOR POLICY STUDIES
http://www.ips-dc.org

The Institute for Policy Studies uses independent research, visionary thinking, and links to the grassroots, scholars, and elected officials to strengthen social movements. IPS's projects are divided into three clusters: democracy and fairness, global justice, and peace and security. IPS accepts interns into a variety of their ongoing projects. Details regarding the positions and contact information are posted regularly.

INTERNATIONAL CENTER FOR RESEARCH ON WOMEN
http://www.icrw.org

The International Center for Research on Women is a private, nonprofit organization that is dedicated to improving the lives of women living in poverty, as well as advancing equality and human rights and contributing to broader economic and social well-being. To achieve these goals, ICRW works in partnership with other agencies to research and to build capacity and advocacy on issues affecting women's economic, health, and social status in low- and middle-income nations. ICRW accepts interns into the Sally Yudelman Internship program each summer in the Washington, DC office.

INTERNATIONAL CENTER—UNIVERSITY OF MICHIGAN
http://internationalcenter.umich.edu/

The International Center at the University of Michigan is an independent, nonprofit, multinational organization, with over 100 staff members on five continents, working to analyze and advocate to prevent and resolve violent and deadly conflicts.

INTERNATIONAL INSTITUTE

http://www.intlinst.org

The International Institute is a nonprofit agency and United Way member that works to assist refugees and immigrants into independence by providing English lessons, finding employment, and providing adjustment services. The International Institute offers internships in a variety of different sections/departments, including education, employment, health/mental health, individual development accounts, micro-enterprise, senior VP for individuals and families, and social services.

INTERNATIONAL JUSTICE MISSION

http://www.ijm.org

International Justice Mission is a human rights agency that rescues victims of violence, sexual exploitation, slavery, and oppression. It is based in the United States and has agencies around the world.

INTERNATIONAL RESCUE COMMITTEE

http://www.theirc.org

The IRC works around the globe to deliver lifesaving aid in emergencies, rebuild shattered communities, and provide other social services. For refugees afforded sanctuary in the United States, IRC offices across the country provide a range of assistance aimed to help new arrivals get settled and acquire the skills to become self-sufficient.

INTERNATIONAL RESEARCH & EXCHANGES BOARD (IREX)

http://www.irex.org/

The IREX is an international organization that works to build education programs, independent media, Internet development, and civil society programs in the countries of the United States, Europe, Eurasia, the Middle East, North Africa, and Asia.

LANDMINE SURVIVORS NETWORK
http://landminesurvivors.org
Landmine Survivors Network is an organization which works to empower individuals and communities affected by landmines to recover from trauma, reclaim their lives, and fulfill their rights. Senior Social Workers with international experience are preferred for this position in an effort to provide best service to those affected by landmines.

LIFELONG EDUCATION ALTERNATIVES AND PROGRAMS NOW
http://www.leapnow.org
Lifelong Education Alternatives and Programs Now (LEAP Now) specializes in alternative education programs in the United States and abroad. LEAP Now offers 3-month and longer internships around the world. Internships are available in arts and crafts, schools and teaching, social service, environment and ecology, animals, outdoor work, and more. Positions, along with details, are posted as they become available.

MADRE
http://www.madre.org
MADRE is an international women's human rights organization that works in conjunction with community-based women's organizations across the globe to confront the issues of health and reproductive rights, economic development, education, and other human rights. MADRE provides these organizations with resources, training, and support to ensure that they will be able to meet the concrete needs of their communities while striving to shift the balance of power to encourage long-term development and social justice. Internships are available at the New York City office in the fall, spring, and summer. Interns receive a small daily stipend and must be available for at least 2 to 3 months.

OXFAM
http://www.oxfamamerica.org
http://www.oxfam.org
Oxfam America is an affiliate of Oxfam International. As a nonprofit organization, Oxfam America aims to end global poverty through saving lives, strengthening communities, and campaigning for change. Internships are

available at both the Boston and Washington, DC offices. Positions are posted, along with descriptions, as they become available.

PAN-AMERICAN DEVELOPMENT FOUNDATION
http://www.padf.org
The Pan-American Development Foundation stems from an agreement between the Organization of American States and the private sector. As an organization, the PADF facilitates the creation of public–private partnerships that will assist the least advantaged individuals in Latin America and the Caribbean. PADF selects interns for the fall, spring, and summer to assist in different departments throughout the organization. Descriptions of internships are posted as positions become available within certain programs.

PARTNERS OF THE AMERICAS
http://www.partners.net
Partners of the Americas upholds the philosophy that working together across borders builds understanding and improves the lives of all people in the Western Hemisphere. As an organization, Partners of the Americas creates opportunities that inspire hope and celebrate diversity. Internships are available at the Washington, DC office in a variety of programs. Positions are posted as they become available.

PEARL S. BUCK INTERNATIONAL
http://www.psbi.org
Pearl S. Buck International works to continue the vision of Pearl S. Buck, including her deep commitment to improving quality of life of and expanding opportunities for children, promoting understanding of the values and attributes of other cultures, and the need for humanitarianism throughout the world. Internships are available through the Welcome House Adoption Program.

REDR
http://www.redr.org.uk
RedR works to provide disaster relief as international charity with organization branches in Australia, India, Malaysia, Lanka, New Zealand,

and the United Kingdom. The goal of RedR is to provide professional guidance to individuals and communities in order to recover and rebuild from the destruction of natural and human-made disasters. The UK branch of RedR has an opening in the position of Head of Humanitarian Services.

SISTER CITIES INTERNATIONAL

http://www.sister-cities.org

Sister Cities International is a nonprofit diplomacy network that generates and strengthens partnerships between communities in the United States and abroad to increase global cooperation at the local level.

The mission of Sister Cities International is to promote peace through mutual respect, understanding, and cooperation: one individual, one community at a time. Internships are available in communications and sustainable development.

UN UNIVERSITY, OFFICE AT THE UNITED NATIONS, NEW YORK (UNU-ONY)

http://www.ony.unu.edu/

The New York office location of the United Nations University works to distribute information about the United Nations University to various offices of the United Nations and other nongovernmental organizations in an effort to build a network of humanitarian aid. They also work to build resources of research and information to bolster the legitimacy of its authority.

UNITARIAN UNIVERSALIST SERVICE COMMITTEE

http://www.uusc.org/index.shtml

The Unitarian Universalist Service Committee aims to advance human rights and social justice around the world through partnership with those who experience unjust power structures and mobilizing these individuals to challenge oppressive policies. Internships with the UUSC are available at the Cambridge, Massachusetts, location. Potential interns work in conjunction with UUSC staff and their advisors to design their own internship. Interns are considered for all departments.

UNITED STATES AGENCY FOR INTERNATIONAL DEVELOPMENT (USAID)
http://www.usaid.gov/
USAID is an independent federal government organization that receives guidance from the Secretary of State. It supports the development and sustainability of economic growth initiatives as well as advances the implementation of proposed US foreign policy. The mission of USAID is to build foundations for increased economic growth, agriculture and trade, global health, democracy, conflict prevention and resolution, and humanitarian assistance.

U.S. ASSOCIATION FOR THE UNITED NATIONS HIGH COMMISSIONER FOR REFUGEES (USA FOR UNHCR)
http://www.unrefugees.org/site/c.lfIQKSOwFqG/b.4778881/k.BE35/ Home.htm
USA for UNHCR works with people who have fled their countries because of well-founded fear of persecution for reasons of their race, religion, nationality, political affiliation, or social group. In particular, USA for UNHCR works with those who cannot or do not want to return to their country of origin.

U.S. COMMITTEE FOR REFUGEES AND IMMIGRANTS
http://www.refugees.org
The U.S. Committee for Refugees and Immigrants works to address the needs and rights of migrants worldwide by advancing fair and humane public policy, facilitating and providing direct professional services, and promoting the full participation of migrants in community life. Internships are available in the Washington, DC office in a variety of sectors. A small stipend is provided and academic credit can be arranged.

U.S. FUND FOR UNICEF
http://www.unicefusa.org/
The U.S. Fund for UNICEF supports the work of the UN Children's Fund by raising support for its programs and increasing public awareness of challenges facing the world's youth. They work as part of a worldwide effort to advance humanity with health, education, equality, and protection of every child.

VOICES ON THE BORDER
http://www.votb.org
Voices on the Border is an organization that builds solidarity between communities throughout the United States and El Salvador to promote sustainable and equitable development in the latter. Special emphasis is placed on promoting Salvadoran activism on all levels and educating US citizens about the impact of US policy abroad. Internships are available at the Washington, DC office; interns work closely with the executive director. Hours and start dates for the internship are arranged between the executive director and the intern.

WINROCK INTERNATIONAL (WI)
http://www.winrock.org/
Winrock International works with people around the world to increase economic opportunity, sustain natural resources, and protect the environment. Volunteers work with farmers and businesses and local governments on short-term projects related to environmental sustainability and effective use of resources.

WITNESS FOR PEACE
http://www.witnessforpeace.org
Witness for Peace is a nonprofit grassroots organization dedicated to protecting human rights and establishing economic justice through nonviolent means. The organization's mission is to change US foreign and economic policies in Latin America and the Caribbean while providing just alternatives. Internships are available in three areas: legislative/grassroots organizing, delegation planning and support, and development.

WOMEN'S INTERNATIONAL LEAGUE FOR PEACE AND FREEDOM
http://www.wilpf.org
The Women's International League for Peace and Freedom strives to achieve world disarmament, full rights for women, racial and economic justice, an end to all forms of violence, and the establishment of political, psychological, and social conditions that ensure peace, freedom, and justice for all world citizens. A variety of internships are available throughout the year at the Philadelphia, New York, and Geneva, Swit-zerland, offices.

WORLD VISION

http://www.worldvision.org

World Vision is a Christian relief and development organization dedicated to eliminating the causes of poverty and helping children and their communities worldwide. Internships are available at World Vision headquarters in Federal Way, Washington. Interns work in a variety of departments and participate in weekly intern gatherings.

VOLUNTEER WORK

AGRICULTURAL COOPERATIVE DEVELOPMENT INTERNATIONAL

http://www.acdivoca.org

Agricultural Cooperative Development International (ACDI/VOCA) is a nonprofit organization working to promote broad-based economic growth and the development of civil society in developing nations. ACDI/VOCA offers a range of technical assistance services. ACDI/VOCA offers 2- to 4-week volunteer placements around the world. Volunteers are typically mid-career and senior professionals who work side by side with farmers and entrepreneurs in developing countries.

AMERICAN FRIENDS SERVICE COMMITTEE

http://www.afcs.org

The American Friends Service Committee (AFSC) is an organization based on the expression of the faith of the Religious Society of Friends (Quakers). The AFSC stands committed to the principles of nonviolence and justice and works to draw on the transforming power of human and divine love. AFSC offers volunteer positions across the globe. Openings are posted as they become available.

AMERICAN JEWISH WORLD SERVICE

http://www.ajws.org

The American Jewish World Service (AJWS) is an international development organization dedicated to the alleviation of poverty, hunger, and disease among the citizens of the developing world. AJWS, with the assistance of grants to grassroots organizations, volunteer service, advocacy, and education, fosters civil society, sustainable development, and human rights for all people. AJWS Volunteer Corps places Jewish professionals with grassroots organizations throughout the world to provide skills training to nongovernmental organizations. The volunteers also train staff members in their area of expertise. Placements last from 3 to 12 months.

AMERICAN REFUGEE COMMITTEE
http://www.arcrelief.org
The American Refugee Committee (ARC) works with refugees, displaced persons, and those at risk of being displaced to help them survive crises and rebuild lives of dignity, health, security, and self-sufficiency. ARC offers volunteer positions in locations throughout the world. Opportunities are posted as they become available.

BRETHREN VOLUNTEER SERVICE
http://www.brethren.org/genbd/bvs
The Brethren Volunteer Service (BVS) is a ministry of the Church of the Brethren, General Board. BVS works to provide hope to shattered lives and to establish understanding between individuals, groups, nations, and humanity. BVS offers placements in the United States and abroad. Volunteers receive room, board, medical insurance, transportation to the project site, and a small stipend.

CHRISTIAN FOUNDATION FOR CHILDREN AND AGING
http://www.cfcausa.org
The Christian Foundation for Children and Aging (CFCA) is a lay Catholic organization dedicated to creating relationships between sponsors in the United States and children and aging individuals in 26 developing countries across the globe. CFCA offers volunteer positions both at its headquarters in Kansas City and at its international mission sites. International volunteers must be able to serve for at least a 6-month period.

CHURCH WORLD SERVICE, IMMIGRATION AND REFUGEE PROGRAM
http://www.churchworldservice.org
The Church World Service (CWS) Immigration and Refugee Service Immigration and Refugee Program is a network of denominations and local affiliate offices that serves the needs of refugees and immigrants. Co-sponsor congregations across the United States welcome the uprooted and displaced and create a hospitable community. Volunteer opportunities are available at the local affiliate offices throughout the

United States. Volunteers may work directly with refugees as well as assist with office duties.

CONCERN AMERICA
http://www.concernamerica.org/
A nondenominational, humanitarian organization dedicated to the relief assistance and advancement of people in need, particularly in developing countries. Concern America concentrates on the "poorest people" in its 27 countries of operation in Africa, Asia, Central America, and Eastern Europe.

CONGRESSIONAL HUNGER CENTER (CHC)
http://www.hungercenter.org/
Collaborates with communities located in transitioning societies in order to help them develop autonomous institutions and resources for social, environmental, economic, health, and educational advancement.

CROSS-CULTURAL SOLUTIONS
http://www.crossculturalsolutions.org
Cross-Cultural Solutions is a nonprofit organization and leader in the field of international volunteering. Volunteers with Cross-Cultural Solutions assist with Partner Programs, each of which is a dynamic, community-led initiative. These community programs include caring for children/infants, teaching children, teaching English, assisting teachers, providing medical and HIV/AIDS work, caring for the elderly and disabled, providing special education, and empowering women. Volunteer sites include Brazil, China, Costa Rica, Ghana, Guatemala, India, Peru, Russia, Tanzania, and Thailand. A fee and specific dates apply to each volunteer program. College credit may be provided for extended stays.

DIRECT RELIEF INTERNATIONAL
http://www.directrelief.org
Direct Relief International is an international organization that provides material medical aid, including medicines, medical supplies, and equipment, to impoverished people around the world. The mission of Direct Relief International is to improve the health of people living in developing nations, as well as those who are victims of natural disasters, war, and

civil unrest. Direct Relief International offers volunteer positions at its office and warehouse in Santa Barbara, California. Volunteers assist with a wide variety of tasks, including administrative, clerical, research, and writing, as well as providing staffing at special events.

DOCTORS WITHOUT BORDERS
http://www.dwb.org http://www.doctorswithoutborders.org/volunteer/field/index.cfm
Doctors Without Borders/Médecins Sans Frontières (MSF) is an independent and international medically based humanitarian organization that delivers emergency aid to global citizens adversely affected by armed conflict, epidemics, natural or human-made disasters, or poor health care in more than 70 countries throughout the world. MSF seeks volunteers with mental health training. Volunteer opportunities include working with individuals suffering from Post-Traumatic Stress Disorder stemming from conflict situations, increasing mental health programs, providing mental health care for people living with HIV/AIDS, and training local mental health workers. The recruitment process is competitive, and specific criteria must be met.

ETHIOPIAN COMMUNITY DEVELOPMENT COUNCIL, INC.
http://www.ecdcinternational.org
Ethiopian Community Development Council, Inc. (ECDC) is an organization that works to resettle refugees; promote educational, cultural, and socioeconomic development in the refugee and immigrant populations in the United States; and carry out humanitarian and development programs in the Horn of Africa. Volunteer positions are available.

FELLOWSHIP OF RECONCILIATION
http://www.forusa.org
The Fellowship of Reconciliation (FOR) is an international, interfaith movement with branches and groups in over 40 nations. FOR works to replace violence, war, racism, and economic injustice with nonviolence, peace, and economic justice. To achieve these goals, FOR educates, trains, builds coalitions, and engages in nonviolent and compassionate actions on a local, national, and global front. FOR offers volunteer positions at its

office in Nyack, New York. Volunteers assist with a variety of tasks and programs.

FOOD AND AGRICULTURE PROGRAM OF THE UNITED NATIONS
http://www.fao.org

The Food and Agriculture Organization of the United Nations (FAO) endeavors to defeat hunger by serving as a forum where both developed and developing nations gather to reach agreements and debate policies. FAO also stands as a source of knowledge and information and helps developing nations to improve agriculture, forestry, and fishery practices; modernize; and ensure good nutrition for citizens. FAO offers volunteer opportunities in several locations throughout the world. Volunteers must be a citizen of an FAO member nation and fluent in at least one of FAO's working languages. Applications must submit an assignment proposal outlining objectives and expected results of a volunteer position with FAO.

FOSTER PARENTS PLAN
http://www.fosterparentsplan.ca

Foster Parents Plan is an international development organization centered on children. It currently works in 45 developing nations to bring about effective, lasting change in all aspects of the well-being of children, including health, education, shelter, and livelihood. Volunteer positions are available at its Toronto office. Openings are posted, along with details, as they become available.

FOUNDATION FOR INTERNATIONAL COMMUNITY ASSISTANCE
http://www.villagebanking.org

The Foundation for International Community Assistance (FICA) is a nonprofit agency known for the innovation of the "village banking method," which provides microcredit to developing nations. FICA's other programs include education loans, home improvement loans, revolving lines of credit, and services such as insurance, savings, and basic business training. FICA accepts volunteers at its headquarters in Washington, DC, as well as in affiliate offices in developing countries. Volunteers help with a variety of projects and assignments in the areas of human resources, administration, finance, legal, marketing, or information technology.

FOUNDATION FOR SUSTAINABLE DEVELOPMENT

http://www.fsdinternational.org

The Foundation for Sustainable Development (FSD) supports grass-roots development organizations that are working to better their communities, environments, and the economic opportunities around them. FSD upholds the philosophy that economic development begins with community development and is sustainable only if it comes from and is continually supported by the members of those communities. FSD also works to raise awareness about international issues. FSD offers short-term international volunteer positions that last from 1 to 6 weeks. Participants volunteer with local organizations and stay with local families.

GLOBAL SERVICE CORPS

http://www.globalservicecorps.org

The Global Service Corps is an international nonprofit volunteer organization that provides service-learning opportunities to live and work in Thailand and Tanzania. Programs include HIV/AIDS prevention, sustainable agriculture, health care, English instruction, Buddhist immersion, and the Seeds of Sustenance Fellowship. Volunteer positions are available for 2, 4, or 6 or more weeks.

HEART TO HEART INTERNATIONAL (H2H)

http://www.hearttoheart.org/

H2H is a global health initiative that works to connect people and resources around the world. H2H provides and supports programs of medical education, medical assistance, and crisis response, as well as community development and health resources.

HEIFER INTERNATIONAL

http://www.heifer.org

Heifer International works with communities to end hunger and poverty and to care for the Earth in order to bring about a world of communities that live together in peace and equitable sharing of resources. Heifer International brings resources into needy communities that will provide a source of nourishment and income. Heifer International offers two types of volunteer positions: community volunteers and learning center volunteers. Community volunteers work closely with regional offices to assist with educational programs, training programs, and community outreach. Learning center volunteers immerse themselves at one of Heifer International's three locations: Ceres Center in California, Heifer Ranch in Arkansas, and Overlook Farm in Massachusetts. Learning center volunteers view Heifer International's theory in practice by tending gardens, helping with livestock, and assisting in educational programs.

INTERNATIONAL CULTURAL YOUTH EXCHANGE
http://www.icye.org
The International Cultural Youth Exchange (ICYE) is an international nonprofit exchange organization for youth that works to promote mobility, intercultural learning, and international voluntary service. ICYE organizes both short- and long-term volunteer exchanges in more than 34 nations around the world.

INTERNATIONAL JUSTICE MISSION
http://www.ijm.org
International Justice Mission is a human rights agency that rescues victims of violence, sexual exploitation, slavery, and oppression. It is based in the United States and has agencies around the world.

INTERNATIONAL MEDICAL CORPS
http://www.imcworldwide.org
The International Medical Corps is an international nonprofit organization that is dedicated to saving lives and relieving suffering through providing health care training and relief and development programs. The mission of the International Medical Corps is to improve quality of life through planned health interventions and related activities that serve to build the local capacity in areas throughout the world. It accepts both domestic and general international volunteers. International volunteers must serve for at least 2 months, and they receive a per diem during their time of service. Domestic volunteers serve at IMC's offices in Los Angeles, London, or Washington, DC.

INTERPLAST

http://www.interplast.org.au/

Interplast is the first international humanitarian organization to provide reconstructive procedures and surgeries free of charge to people in developing countries. They make a direct and profound impact on the lives of thousands of children every year who suffer from congenital physical deformities or injuries. Interplast partners with volunteers and international medical personnel to provide these services and other medical programs around the world.

INTERNATIONAL RELIEF TEAMS (IRT)

http://irteams.org/

The IRT is dedicated to forming volunteer teams that work to provide medical and nonmedical assistance to victims of disasters and abject poverty around the world.

JESUIT VOLUNTEER CORPS

http://www.jesuitvolunteers.org

The Jesuit Volunteer Corps offers individuals an opportunity to work for justice and peace in a full-time volunteer placement. Those who choose to serve with the Jesuit Volunteer Corps are called to the mission of directly serving the impoverished, working for structural change in the United States, and accompanying citizens of developing nations. Applicants for volunteer positions should be at least 21 years old and have a college degree or applicable work experience. Positions are available in the United States and internationally.

LIFE FOR RELIEF & DEVELOPMENT (LIFE)

http://www.lifeusa.org/site/PageServer

LIFE is a nonprofit humanitarian charity that works to alleviate suffering around the world without regard to race, color, religion, or culture. They offer various services for health, education, and community development programs. LIFE attends to the needs of refugees and victims of natural or human-made disasters.

Lutheran Volunteer Corps

http://www.lutheranvolunteercorps.org

The Lutheran Volunteer Corps works to uphold its mission of being a community of faith that unites people to work together for peace and justice. LVC offers a 1-year domestic volunteer program. Volunteers must be at least 21 years of age. Placements are posted as they become available.

Mennonite Voluntary Service

http://www.mennonitemission.net

The Mennonite Voluntary Service is the mission agency of the Mennonite Church in the United States. MVS works with the disadvantaged and those suffering from injustice, participates in the issues and activities crucial to local neighborhoods and faith communities, and encourages volunteers to live simply in shared households in order to affirm and nurture relationships and serve as an extension of the local congregation. Volunteer positions require a 1- or 2-year commitment. Most positions are in the United States, with some openings in the United Kingdom. Available volunteer sites are posted regularly.

Operation USA (OpUSA)

http://www.opusa.org

Operation USA is a nonprofit disaster relief agency based in Los Angeles. For 27 years, Operation USA has assisted developing communities both in the United States and abroad in confronting problems related to natural and human-made disasters and chronic poverty. By providing essential materials, training, advocacy, and financial support, Operation USA promotes sustainable health and nutrition and aids in disaster response. Volunteer opportunities are available at Operation USA's Port of Los Angeles Warehouse in Wilmington, California. Volunteers assist in processing, loading, and unloading shipments.

Oxfam America

http://www.oxfamamerica.org

Oxfam America is an affiliate of Oxfam International. As a nonprofit organization, Oxfam America aims to end global poverty through saving lives, strengthening communities, and campaigning for change. Volunteer positions are available at both the Boston and Washington, DC offices. Openings are posted, along with descriptions, as they become available.

PHYSICIANS FOR PEACE (PFP)
http://www.physiciansforpeace.org/
PFP is an independent organization that provides training and support to areas underserved in medical services. PFP sends medical volunteers around the world to introduce skills and to help close service gaps by mobilizing and sponsoring programs for new equipment and trainings.

PROJECT CONCERN
http://www.projectconcern.org
Project Concern is an international organization that strives to prevent disease, improve community health, and promote sustainable development. Lifesaving programs are provided to individuals in Africa, Asia, and the Americas. Project Concern offers both domestic and international volunteer opportunities. Positions in the United States are available at the international office in San Diego, as well as the Mexican border region. Responsibilities vary and openings are posted as they become available. For international volunteer opportunities, duties typically include research development and writing, public health education, and community-level interventions.

RURAL UPGRADE SUPPORT ORGANISATION
http://www.interconnection.org/ruso
The Rural Upgrade Support Organisation (RUSO) is a nongovernmental organization dedicated to empowering local communities and contributing sustainable grassroots solutions to rural challenges in Ghana. RUSO also uses volunteers to provide health care, education, and social development. Placements with VOLU vary in length according to volunteer preference and nature of the project. All volunteers must be at least 18 years of age, in good health, and willing to work hard and live in the rural community.

SERVICE CIVIL INTERNATIONAL

http://www.sci-ivs.org

Service Civil International promotes short-term and long-term volunteer placements to work on political, social, and humanitarian issues across the globe. Both summer work camps and long-term placements are available in many nations. Availability can be searched according to country and program type.

SEVA FOUNDATION

http://www.seva.org

Seva is an international organization driven by "compassionate capitalism": the perception that Western technology and skills must be applied abroad in ways that are sustainable and that can be shared with those individuals and communities that lack access to capital and resources. Seva aims to serve an ever-changing vision that incorporates the ancient and modern in ways that promote health and human harmony. Seva offers both domestic and international volunteer opportunities. Volunteers within the United States staff information tables at festivals and concerts and assist with data entry, mailings, filing, and packaging merchandise. International volunteers are needed to work with the Sight Program and other development programs in Africa and Asia.

STUDENTS PARTNERSHIP WORLDWIDE

http://www.spw.org

Students Partnership Worldwide (SPW) is an international development charity that recruits and trains young people (aged 18–28 years) to be volunteer peer educators. Peer educators lead programs that address pressing health and environmental issues in Africa and Asia. SPW offers volunteer programs in India, Nepal, South Africa, Tanzania, Uganda, and Zambia. Openings, along with position details, are posted as they become available.

UNITARIAN UNIVERSALIST SERVICE COMMITTEE (UUSC)

http://www.uusc.org/

The UUSC is a nonsectarian organization working to promote human rights and social justice on a global level while maintaining partnerships in the United States, South and Southeast Asia, Central Africa, Latin

America, and the Caribbean. Programs under the UUSC are founded on Unitarian Universalist principles which affirm the dignity and worth of every person.

UNITED METHODIST COMMITTEE ON RELIEF
http://gbgm-umc.org/umcor
The United Methodist Committee on Relief (UMCOR) is a nonprofit humanitarian aid organization. With open hearts and minds, UMCOR works to alleviate all forms of human suffering, regardless of the source. Volunteers with UMCOR may participate in disaster relief, ranging from immediately following the disaster to several years later. Further opportunities are available processing disaster relief supplies at the Sager Brown Depot. International volunteer placements are available through the United Methodist Volunteers in Mission.

UNITED NATIONS VOLUNTEERS FOR PEACE AND DEVELOPMENT
http://www.unv.org
The United Nations Volunteers is the UN organization that encourages global sustainable human development by promoting volunteerism. Volunteer positions are available both in the United States and abroad and vary according to sector and responsibilities. Positions are posted as they become available.

UNITED STATES CONFERENCE OF CATHOLIC BISHOPS MIGRATION AND REFUGEE SERVICES
http://www.nccbuscc.org
Migration and Refugee Services serves and advocates for immigrants, refugees, and people on the move. The Conference of Catholic Bishops works with the federal government and local churches in the resettlement process, providing caring and supportive communities. Volunteers with Migration and Refugee Services may assist with social services, such as finding appropriate housing, English translation/tutoring, job search assistance, and so forth. Volunteers may also provide pastoral care, helping the newcomer into the community, settling the newcomer into a worship community, and aiding in cultural orientation and transition.

UN UNIVERSITY, OFFICE AT THE UNITED NATIONS, NEW YORK (UNU-ONY)

U.S. ASSOCIATION FOR THE UNITED NATIONS HIGH COMMISSIONER FOR REFUGEES (USA FOR UNHCR)

VISIONS IN ACTION

http://www.visionsinaction.org

Visions in Action is a nonprofit international organization with a commitment to achieving social and economic justice throughout the developing world by placing communities of volunteers. Volunteer types are divided according to sector (agriculture, education, small business, human rights and law, etc.). Placements are available in Africa and Mexico.

VOLUNTARY WORKCAMPS ASSOCIATION OF GHANA

http://www.volu.org

Membership in the Voluntary Workcamps Association of Ghana (VOLU) is open to all persons age 16 years and over. VOLU has numerous partner organizations throughout Europe, North America, and Asia. VOLU offers two cycles of work camps, winter and summer. Volunteers with VOLU work on a variety of projects, including constructing schools, hospitals, and roads, in addition to cocoa plantation, literacy projects, community development, oil palm production, reforestation, and AIDS awareness campaigns. Camps vary in length from 3 to 4 weeks.

VOLUNTEER AFRICA

http://www.volunteerafrica.org

Volunteer Africa is an international nonprofit organization run by a team of volunteers who are stationed around the world. Volunteer Africa links people from around the world with community-initiated projects in developing nations. Volunteer Africa offers 4-, 7-, and 10-week programs in three locations in Africa. Program dates and costs are updated regularly.

Volunteer in Asia

http://www.viaprograms.org

Volunteer in Asia (VIA) is a nonprofit organization that is dedicated to increasing understanding between the United States and Asia. VIA strives to offer young Americans the opportunity to work and live within an Asian culture while meeting the needs of an Asian host organization. VIA offers both summer and long-term (1- and 2-year) programs. Most participants work in Asian nations teaching English.

Volunteer Match

http://www.volunteermatch.org

Volunteer Match is an organization offering online services that support a community of nonprofit, volunteer, and business leaders committed to civic engagement. Volunteer Match offers a search function for volunteer positions: those seeking placements enter their ZIP code, distance willing to travel, and area of interest.

World Concern

http://www.worldconcern.org

World Concern is a Christian humanitarian organization whose goal is to provide emergency relief and community development throughout the world. Volunteer opportunities include volunteer prayer advocacy and assisting in the seed shipping process.

World Education (WEI)

http://worlded.org/WEIInternet/

WEI is dedicated to improving the lives of the poor through economic and social development programs. They provide training and technical assistance in nonformal education for children and adults. WEI particularly focuses on programs of income generation, private sector development, literacy, environmental education, reproductive and maternal health, and HIV/AIDS education.

World Neighbors

http://wn.org

World Neighbors is an international organization dedicated to the development of remote and marginalized communities in poverty-stricken areas of Africa, Asia, and Latin America. Local people are assisted in developing, managing, and sustaining their own programs. These programs incorporate food security, farming, literacy, community health, environmental conservation, water and sanitation, nonformal education, savings and credit, and income-generation activities. Volunteers assist in planning and execution of annual events as well as providing support in the Oklahoma City Village Volunteer Program.

WorldTeach
http://www.worldteach.org
WorldTeach is a nonprofit organization that offers opportunities for individuals to volunteer as teachers in developing nations. Most volunteers teach English, although other opportunities are available. Both summer and full-year placements are available at a variety of locations throughout the world.

World Vision
http://www.worldvision.org
World Vision is a Christian relief and development organization dedicated to eliminating the causes of poverty and helping children and their communities worldwide. Volunteer opportunities are available at World Vision headquarters in Federal Way, Washington, as well as in offices across the nation. World Vision does not currently send volunteers abroad.

YMCA Go Global
http://www.internationalymca.org/GoGlobal/Go_Global_Service_Corps. shtml
YMCA Go Global is a voluntary service and capacity-building program that places young Americans at YMCAs and community organizations around the world. The Go Global Service Corps is a long-term opportunity to share individual skills with YMCAs and community organizations in developing countries, ranging from 6 months to 1 year.

SEARCH ENGINES

DevNetJobs
http://www.devnetjobs.org
DevNetJobs serves as a database of positions available in the international development, nongovernmental organization, and environmental sector. Potential employees may access availability information free of charge or post their résumé for a small fee.

Foreign Policy Association
http://www.fpa.org/jobs_contact2423/jobs_contact.htm
Jobs are listed on this Web site and are available in a weekly e-mail in areas such as development assistance, environment, health, and youth.

Human Rights Internet
http://www.hri.ca/jobboard
This Web site is designed to facilitate the transfer of information in the human rights community, including the posting of jobs.

Idealist.Org
http://www.idealist.org
Idealist.org is part of Action Without Borders, an organization that connects people, organizations, and resources to help to build a world where people live free and dignified lives. Idealist.org lists available employment, internship, and volunteer opportunities. Openings may be searched by country, state or province, town, area of focus, and project description.

Interaction
http://www.interaction.org
Interaction is an alliance of international development and humanitarian nongovernmental organizations. They have an e-mail newsletter with job opportunities available by subscription.

INTERNATIONAL JOBS

http://www.internationaljobs.org/

Offers information on international jobs to its members; information on "hot jobs" is available to all.

RELIEFWEB

http://www/reliefweb.int/w/rwb.nsf

ReliefWeb is run by the UN Office for the Coordination of Humanitarian Affairs and provides a job listing for international jobs from a host of different types of employers.

VOLUNTEERS FOR PEACE

http://www.vfp.org

Volunteers for Peace is a nonprofit organization that provides consultation and placement services for international work camps. Work camp availability may be searched according to dates of availability, country, or type of camp.

VOLUNTEER MATCH

http://www.volunteermatch.org

Volunteer Match is an organization offering online services that support a community of nonprofit, volunteer, and business leaders committed to civic engagement. Volunteer Match offers a search function for volunteer positions: those seeking placements enter their ZIP code, distance willing to travel, and area of interest.

WORLD VOLUNTEER WEB

http://www.worldvolunteerweb.org/

The World Volunteer Web stems from the United Nations' volunteer program. With an overall goal of serving as a global clearinghouse for information and resources linked to volunteerism, the World Volunteer Web may be effectively used for campaigning, advocacy, networking, and mobilizing volunteer action. Information may be accessed according to nation of interest, sector of work, or the particular volunteer issue at hand.

References

Chapter One

Center for Applied Linguistics. (2010). *Foreign language teaching in U.S. schools: Results of a national survey.* Retrieved from http://www.cal.org/resources/pubs/fl_teaching.html

Diaz, L., Mama, R., & Lopez, L. (2006, August). *Making the social work profession an essential partner in international development.* Paper presented at the biennial conference of the International Federation of Social Workers, Munich, Germany.

Herscovitch, L. (2001). International relief and development practice. In L. Healy (Ed.), *International social work: Professional action in an interdependent world* (pp. 170–192). New York, NY: Oxford University Press.

Institute of International Education. (2012). *Open doors 2012.* Retrieved from http://www.iie.org/en/Who-We-Are/News-and-Events/Press-Center/Press-Releases/2012/11-13-2012-Open-Doors-International-Students

Isbister, J. (2003). *Promises not kept: Poverty and the betrayal of Third World development* (6th ed.). Bloomfield, CT: Kumarian Press.

Kaiser, W. L., & Wood, D. (2001). *Seeing through maps.* Amherst, MA: ODT Incorporated.

Macionis, J. J. (2006). *Society: The basics* (8th ed.). Upper Saddle River, NJ: Pearson/Prentice Hall.

Midgley, J. (1997). Social work and international social development: Promoting a developmental perspective in the profession. In M. C. Hokenstad & J. Midgley

(Eds.), *Issues in international social work: Global challenges for a new century* (pp. 11–26). Washington, DC: NASW Press.

Modern Language Association. (2009). *Enrollments in languages other than English in United States institutions of higher education, Fall 2009.* Retrieved from http://www.mla.org/2009_enrollmentsurvey

National Geographic. (2002). *2002 global geographic literacy survey.* Retrieved from http://geosurvey.nationalgeographic.com/geosurvey/download/Roper Survey.pdf/

National Geographic. (2006). *2006 global geographic literacy survey.* Retrieved from http://www.nationalgeographic.com/roper2006/pdf/FINALReport 2006GeogLitSurvey.pdf

Rodney, W. (2005). How Europe underdeveloped Africa. In P. S. Rothenberg (Ed.). *Beyond borders: Thinking critically about global issues* (pp. 107–125). New York, NY: Worth Publishers.

Schultz, E. A., & Lavenda, R. H. (2005). *Cultural anthropology: A perspective on the human condition* (6th ed.). New York, NY: Oxford University Press.

Thomas-Slayter, B. P. (2003). *Southern exposure: International development and the global south in the twenty-first century.* Bloomfield, CT: Kumarian Press.

United Nations. (1999). *About the World Summit for Social Development.* Retrieved from http://www.visionoffice.com/socdev/wssd.htm.

United Nations Development Programme. (2003). *Human development report 2003.* New York, NY: Oxford University Press.

United Nations–Division for the Advancement of Women. (2005). *Creating an enabling environment for girls' and women's participation in education.* Retrieved from http://www.un.org/womenwatch/daw/egm/enabling-environment2005/docs/EGM-WPD-EE-2005-EP.8%20%20A.pdf

University of London, Department of Geography. (n.d.). *The power of maps: Bias and distortion on a world map.* Retrieved from http://www.geog.qmul.ac.uk/map

US Department of Education. (2010). *The nation's report card: Geography 2010.* Retrieved from http://nationsreportcard.gov/geography_2010/geography_2010_report/

Chapter Two

Amnesty International. (2005). *Human rights for human dignity: A primer on economic, social and cultural rights.* Retrieved from http://web.amnesty.org/library/pdf/POL340092005ENGLISH/$File/POL3400905.pdf

Ayton-Shenker, D. (1995). *The challenge of human rights and cultural relativism.* Retrieved from http://www.un.org/rights/dpi1627e.htm

George, J. (1999). Conceptual muddle, practical dilemma: Human rights, social development and social work education. *International Social Work, 42*(1), 15–26.

Ghai, Y. (2001). *Human rights and social development: Toward democratization and social justice.* Geneva, Switzerland: United Nations Research Institute for Social Development. Retrieved from http://www.unrisd.org/unrisd/website/document.nsf/(httpPublications)/ECD0417EB1177C52 80256B5E004BCAFA?OpenDocument

Healy, L. (2001). *International social work: Professional action in an interdependent world.* New York, NY: Oxford University Press.

Human Rights Watch. (1996). *Death by default: A policy of fatal neglect in China's state orphanages.* Retrieved from http://www.hrw.org/summaries/s.china961.html

Ife, J., & Fiske, L. (2006). Human rights and community work. *International Social Work, 49*(3), 297–308.

International Committee of the Red Cross. (2006). *International conference paves the way for Red Crystal.* Retrieved from http://www.icrc.org/web/eng/siteeng0.nsf/html/geneva-news-220606?opendocument

Jahan, S. (2005). *Human rights-based approach to poverty reduction: Analytical linkages, practical work and UNDP.* Retrieved from http://www.undp.org/poverty/HRPR.doc

MacFarquhar, N. (2009, May 12). U.S. joins rights panel after a vote at the U.N. *New York Times.* Retrieved from http://www.nytimes.com

Muntarbhorn, V. (2005, September 14). Human rights and globalisation. *The Bangkok Post.* Retrieved from http://www.bangkokpost.com

Red Cross of Latvia. (n.d.). *International humanitarian law.* Retrieved from http://www.redcross.lv/en/conventions.htm

Reichert, E. (2003). *Social work and human rights.* New York, NY: Columbia University Press.

Skegg, A. (2005). Human rights and social work: A Western imposition or empowerment to the people? *International Social Work, 48*(5), 667–672.

UNICEF. (1999). *Human rights for children and women: How UNICEF helps make them a reality.* Retrieved from http://www.unicef.org/publications/index_5587.html

United Nations High Commissioner for Human Rights (2006a). *International Covenant on Civil and Political Rights*. Retrieved from http://www.ohchr.org/english/countries/ratification/4.htm

United Nations High Commissioner for Human Rights (2006b). *International Covenant on Economic, Social and Cultural Rights*. Retrieved from http://www.ohchr.org/english/countries/ratification/3.htm

United Nations. (n.d.): *Membership of the Human Rights Council*. Retrieved from http://www.ohchr.org/EN/HRBodies/HRC/Pages/Membership.aspx

Chapter Three

Anti-Slavery International. (n.d.). *About Timidria*. Retrieved from http://www.antislavery.org

Anti-Slavery International. (2001). *The enslavement of Dalit and indigenous communities in India, Nepal and Pakistan through debt bondage*. Retrieved from http://www.antislavery.org/homepage/resources/goonesekere.pdf

Anti-Slavery International. (2009). *Information on Nepal*. Retrieved from http://www.antislavery.org

Ask, B. (2011, March 31). Sweden: Why we criminalized purchase of sexual services. *CNN*. Retrieved from http://www.cnn.com

Balch, O. (2013, April 3). Corporate initiative can play a major role in anti-trafficking movement. *The Guardian*. Retrieved from http://www.guardian.co.uk

Bales, K. (2004). *Disposable people: New slavery in the global economy*. Los Angeles, CA: University of California Press.

Bales, K. (2007). What predicts human trafficking? *International Journal of Comparative and Applied Criminal Justice, 31*(2), 269–279.

Bales, K. (2012). Preface to the 2012 edition. In. K. Bales *Disposable people: New slavery in the global economy* (pp. xv–xxxvi). Los Angeles, CA: University of California Press.

Bales, K., & Trodd, Z. (2008). *To plead our own cause: Personal stories by today's slaves*. Ithaca, NY: Cornell University.

Bennetts, L. (2011, July 25). The john next door. *Newsweek*, 60–63.

Blackburn, A. G., Taylor, R. W., & Davis, J. B. (2010). Understanding the complexities of human trafficking and child sexual exploitation: The case of Southeast Asia. *Women & Criminal Justice, 20*(1/2), 105–126.

Blumhofer, R. D., Shah, N., Grodin, M. A., & Crosby, S. S. (2011). Clinical issues in caring for former chattel slaves. *Journal of Immigrant Minority Health, 13,* 323–332.

Bodeen, C. (2013, January 7). Will China really end "forced labor"? *Christian Science Monitor*. Retrieved from http://www.csmonitor.com/World/Latest-News-Wires/2013/0107/Will-China-really-end-forced-labor

Cabinet approves anti-trafficking plan. (2013, March 19). *Library of Congress*. Retrieved from http://www.loc.gov/lawweb/servlet/lloc_news?disp3_1205403524_text

Children trafficked to sell flowers and beg. (2012, June 4). *IRIN News*. Retrieved from http://www.irinnews.org/PrintReport.aspx?ReportID=95566

Cho, S., Dreher, A., & Neumayer, E. (2013). Does legalized prostitution increase human trafficking? *World Development, 41*, 67–82.

Cho, S., & Vadlamannati, K. C. (2012). Compliance with the anti-trafficking protocol. *European Journal of Political Economy, 28*, 249–265.

Danailova-Trainor, G., & Laczko, F. (2010). Trafficking in persons and development: Towards greater policy coherence. *International Migration, 48*(4), 38–83.

Deane, T. (2010). Cross-border trafficking in Nepal and India: Violating women's rights. *Human Rights Review, 11*, 491–513.

Decker, M. R., McCauley, H. L., Phuengsamran, D., Janyam, S., & Silverman, J. G. (2011). Sex trafficking, sexual risk, sexually transmitted infection and reproductive health among female sex workers in Thailand. *Journal of Epidemiology and Community Health, 65*, 334–339.

Demir, O. O., & Finckenauer, J. O. (2010). Victims of sex trafficking in Turkey: Characteristics, motivations, and dynamics. *Women & Criminal Justice, 20*(1/2), 57–88.

Disabled—and at risk of being trafficked. (2011, March 14). *IRIN News*. Retrieved from http://www.irinnews.org/PrintReport.aspx?ReportID=92183

Dottridge, M. (2006). *Action to prevent child trafficking in South Eastern Europe: A preliminary assessment*. Retrieved from http://www.unicef.org/ceecis/Assessment_report_June_06.pdf

Family pressures exacerbate trafficking. (2011, May 26). *IRIN News*. Retrieved from http://www.irinnews.org/PrintReport.aspx?ReportID=92813

Fitzpatrick, S. (2009, September 20). Diplomatic immunity leaves abused workers in shadows. *Washington Post*. Retrieved from http://articles.washingtonpost.com/2009-09-20/news/36810213_1_diplomatic-immunity-foreign-diplomats-claim-immunity

French, H. W. (2005). A village grows rich off its main export: Its daughters. *New York Times*, p. A4.

Gooch, L. (2012, December 3). Malaysia urged to protect domestic workers. *New York Times*. Retrieved from http://www.nytimes.com

Harlan, C. (2013, September 12). Population of North Korea's gulag has shrunk, experts say. *The Washington Post*. Retrieved from http://www.washingtonpost.com

Hodge, D. R., & Lietz, C. A. (2007). The international sexual trafficking of women and children: A review of the literature. *Affilia, 22*(2), 163–174.

Huijsmans, R. (2008). Children working beyond their localities: Lao children working in Thailand. *Childhood, 15*, 331–353.

Human Rights Watch. (2001). *Burma violates own ban in use of forced labor.* Retrieved from http://hrw.org/english/docs/2001/03/07/burma347_txt.htm

Human Rights Watch. (2005). *Malaysia: Migrant workers fall prey to abuse.* Retrieved from http://hrw.org/english/docs/2005/05/17/malays10959_txt.htm

Human Rights Watch. (2011a). *"They deceived us at every step": Abuse of Cambodian domestic workers migrating to Malaysia.* Retrieved from http://www.hrw.org/reports/2011/10/31/they-deceived-us-every-step

Human Rights Watch. (2011b). *ILO: New landmark treaty to protect domestic workers*. Retrieved from http://www.hrw.org/news/2011/06/16/ilo-new-landmark-treaty-protect-domestic-workers

Indonesia revokes ban on sending migrant workers to Malaysia. (2011, December 1). *Jakarta Globe*. Retrieved from http://www.thejakartaglobe.com

International Labour Office. (2005). *In Asia: Debt bondage, trafficking and state-imposed forced labour.* Retrieved from http://www.ilo.org/public/english/bureau/inf/features/05/debt_asia.htm

International Labour Office. (2009). *Operational indicators of trafficking in human beings.* Retrieved from http://www.ilo.org/sapfl/Informationresources/Factsheetsandbrochures/WCMS_105023/lang--en/index.htm

International Labour Organization. (2009). West-African court slavery judgement. *International Union Rights, 16*(2), 18–19.

International Labour Organization. (2012a). *ILO global estimate of forced labour 2012: Results and methodology.* Retrieved from http://www.ilo.org/sapfl/Informationresources/ILOPublications/WCMS_182004/lang--en/index.htm

International Labour Organization. (2012b). *Questions and answers on forced labour.* Retrieved from http://www.ilo.org

International Labour Organization. (2013). *Tricked and trapped: Human trafficking in the Middle East*. Retrieved from http://www.ilo.org/addisababa/information-resources/publications/WCMS_210110/lang--en/index.htm

International Organization for Migration. (2003). *Seduction, sale & slavery: Trafficking in women and children for sexual exploitation in Southern Africa*. Retrieved from http://www.iom.org.za/site/media/docs/Trafficking Report3rdEd.pdf

Jacobs, A. (2013, July 15). Court ruling deals public blow to China's labor-camp system. *New York Times*. Retrieved from http://www.nytimes.com

Jayagupta, R. (2009). The Thai government's repatriation and reintegration programmes: Responding to trafficked female commercial sex workers from the Greater Mekong Subregion. *International Migration, 47*(2), 227–253.

Keeping watch for traffickers. (2010, December 13). *IRIN News*. Retrieved from http://www.irinnews.org/PrintReport.aspx?ReportID=91357

Kim, E., Yun, M., Park, M., & Williams, H. (2009). Cross border North Korean women trafficking and victimization between North Korea and China: An ethnographic case study. *International Journal of Law, Crime and Justice, 37*, 154–169.

Lee, J. J. H. (2005). Human trafficking in East Asia: Current trends, data collection, and knowledge gaps. In F. Laczko and E. Gozdziak (Eds.), *Data and research on human trafficking: A global survey* (pp. 165–201). Geneva, Switzerland: International Organization for Migration.

Mauritania pledges help for freed slaves. (2013, March 22). Retrieved from http://reliefweb.int/report/mauritania/mauritania-pledges-help-freed-slaves

Men trafficked into "slavery" at sea. (2011, August 29). *IRIN News*. Retrieved from http://www.irinnews.org/PrintReport.aspx?ReportID=93606

Muico, N. K. (2005). *An absence of choice: The sexual exploitation of North Korean women in China*. Retrieved from http://www.antislavery.org/homepage/resources/PDF/Full%20Korea %20report% 202005.pdf

Muico, N. K. (2007). *Forced labour in North Korean prison camps*. Retrieved from http://www.antislavery.org/english/resources/reports/download_antislavery_publications/forced_labour_reports.aspx

Nadi, N. M. (2013, May 16). Thai raid on fishing operations frees dozens of enslaved migrants. *Democratic Voice of Burma*. Retrieved from http://www.dvb.no

Neubauer, C. (2012, December 13). Diplomats immune to charges of human trafficking. *Washington Times*. Retrieved from http://www.washingtontimes.

com/news/2012/dec/13/workers-abused-by-immune-diplomats/?
page=all

New California law combats human slavery. (2012, January 26). *Christian Science Monitor*. Retrieved from http://www.csmonitor.com

Nikolic-Ristanovic, V. (2010). Supporting victims of trafficking. Towards reconciling the security of victims and states. *Security and Human Rights, 21*(3), 189–202.

Onishi, N. (2005, February 16). Japan, easygoing till now, plans sex traffic crackdown. *New York Times*, p. A3.

Oram, S., Stöckl, H., Busza, J., Howard, L. M., & Zimmerman, C. (2012). Prevalence and risk of violence and the physical, mental, and sexual health problems associated with human trafficking: Systematic review. *PLoS Medicine, 9*(5). Retrieved from http://www.plosmedicine.org

Patel, R. (2013). The trafficking of women in India: A four-dimensional analysis. *The Georgetown Journal of Gender and the Law, 14*(1), 159–188.

Pattisson, P. (2013, September 25). Revealed: Qatar's World Cup "slaves." *The Guardian*. Retrieved from http://www.theguardian.com

Pearson, E. (2001). *Human rights and trafficking in person: A handbook*. Bangkok, Thailand: Global Alliance Against Traffic in Women. Retrieved from http://gaatw.net/books_pdf/Human%20Rights%20and%20Trafficking%20in%20Person.pdf

Raghavan, S. (2013, June 1). Timbuktu's slaves liberated as Islamists flee. *Washington Post*. Retrieved form http://www.washingtonpost.com

Seelke, C. R. (2012). Trafficking in persons in Latin America and the Caribbean. *Congressional Research Service*. Retrieved from http://www.fas.org/sgp/crs/row/RL33200.pdf

Shahinian, G. (2010a). *Report of the Special Rapporteur on contemporary forms of slavery, including its causes and consequences: Mission to Brazil*. Retrieved from http://www2.ohchr.org/english/bodies/hrcouncil/docs/15session/A.HRC.15.20..Add.4_en.pdf

Shahinian, G. (2010b). *Report of the Special Rapporteur on contemporary forms of slavery, including its causes and consequences [focus on domestic servitude]*. Retrieved from http://www.ohchr.org/EN/Issues/Slavery/SRSlavery/Pages/SRSlaveryIndex.aspx

Shen, A., Antonopoulos, G. A., & Papanicolaou, G. (2013). China's stolen children: Internal child trafficking in the People's Republic of China. *Trends in Organized Crime, 16*, 31–48.

Shubert, A. (2011, March 30). *The battle against sex trafficking: Sweden vs. Denmark*. Retrieved from http://thecnnfreedomproject.blogs.cnn.com

Smit, M. (2011). Trafficking in human beings for labour exploitation: The case of the Netherlands. *Trends in Organized Crime, 14*, 184–197.

Smith, C. S. (2005, June 26). Turkey's growing sex trade snares many Slavic women. *New York Times*, p. A4.

Special Rapporteur on Contemporary Forms of Slavery. (2010). *Report of the Special Rapporteur on contemporary forms of slavery, including its causes and consequences, Gulnara Shahinian. Addendum: Mission to Mauritania*. Retrieved from http://www2.ohchr.org/english/issues/slavery/rapporteur/docs/A.HRC.15.20.Add.2_en.pdf

Srivastava, R. S. (2005). Bonded labour in India: Its incidence and pattern. *International Labour Office*. Retrieved from http://www.ilo.org/sapfl/Informationresources/ILOPublications/WCMS_081967/lang--en/index.htm

Supplementary Convention on the Abolition of Slavery, the Slave Trade, and Institutions and Practices Similar to Slavery. (1957). Retrieved from http://www.ohchr.org/english/law/slavetrade.htm

Swedish Institute. (2010). *The ban against the purchase of sexual services. An evaluation 1999-2008*. Retrieved from http://www.government.se/sb/d/13420/a/151488

Tavcer, D. S. (2006). The trafficking of women for sexual exploitation: The situation from the Republic of Moldova to Western Europe. *Police Practice and Research, 7*(2), 135–147.

Transparency International. (2012). *2012 corruptions perceptions index*. Retrieved from http://cpi.transparency.org/cpi2012/

Tverdova, Y. V. (2011). Human trafficking in Russia and other post-Soviet states. *Human Rights Review, 12*, 329–344.

U.N. High Commissioner for Human Rights (2002). *Recommended principles and guidelines on human rights and human trafficking*. Retrieved from http://www.ohchr.org/Documents/Publications/Traffickingen.pdf

U.N. member states appraise global action plan to combat human trafficking. (2013, May 13). Retrieved from http://www.un.org/apps/news/printnews.asp?nid=44885

UNICEF. (2012). *UNICEF aids Restavek victims of abuse and exploitation in Haiti*. Retrieved from http://www.unicef.org/infobycountry/hati_61518.html

United Nations. (2011). *Nepal must improve conditions of former indentured labourers, UN says.* Retrieved from http://www.un.org/apps/news/story.asp?NewsID=39460#.UaSXUkbD85s

United Nations. (2013). *Protocol to Prevent, Suppress and Punish Trafficking in Persons, Especially Women and Children, supplementing the United Nations Convention against Transnational Organized Crime.* Retrieved from http://treaties.un.org

United Nations Office on Drugs and Crime. (2013). *United Nations Convention against Transnational Organized Crime and the Protocols thereto.* Retrieved from http://www.unodc.org/unodc/treaties/CTOC

United Nations- Nepal Information Platform. (2012). *Bonded labour.* Retrieved from http://un.org.np/oneun/bondedlabour

US concerned by slow Thai response to human-trafficking cases: Surapong. (2013, May 10). *Pattaya Mail.* Retrieved from http://www.pattayamail.com

US Department of State. (2011). *Trafficking in persons report 2011.* Retrieved from http://www.state.gov/j/tip/rls/tiprpt/2011/164220.htm

US Department of State. (2012a). *United States-Myanmar Joint Plan on Trafficking in Persons.* Retrieved from http://www.state.gov/r/pa/prs/ps/2012/11/200675.htm

US Department of State. (2012b). *Trafficking in persons report 2012.* Retrieved from http://www.state.gov/j/tip/rls/tiprpt/2012/index.htm

US Department of State. (2013a). *Country reports on human rights practices for 2012.* Retrieved from http://www.state.gov/j/drl/rls/hrrpt/humanrightsreport

US Department of State. (2013b). *Trafficking in persons report 2013.* Retrieved from http://www.state.gov/j/tip/rls/tiprpt/2013/index.htm

Vijeyarasa, R. (2012). The Cinderella syndrome: Economic expectations, false hopes and the exploitation of trafficked Ukrainian women. *Women's Studies International Forum, 35,* 53–62.

Vlieger, A. (2012). Domestic workers in Saudi Arabia and the Emirates: Trafficking victims? *International Migration, 50*(6), 180–194.

Waldman, A. (2005, May 8). Sri Lankan maids pay dearly for perilous jobs overseas. *New York Times,* p. A1, p. A6.

Walk Free Foundation. (2013). *The global slavery index 2013.* Retrieved from http://www.globalslaveryindex.org

Chapter Four

Adinkrah. M. (2011). Child witch hunts in contemporary Ghana. *Child Abuse & Neglect, 35*, 741–752. doi: 10.1016/j.chiabu.2011.05.011

Buckley, C. (2013, November 15). China to ease longtime policy of 1-child limit. *New York Times.* Retrieved from http://www.nytimes.com

Casey, N. (2012, May 18). Identity on a divided island. *Wall Street Journal.* Retrieved from http://online.wsj.com/article/SB10001424052702303505 504577406210848911828.html

Cash grants for food incentivize birth registrations. (2011, October 4). *IRIN News.* Retrieved from http://www.irinnews.org/printreport.aspx? reportid=93878

Central Intelligence Agency (CIA). (2012). *China.* Retrieved from https:// www.cia.gov/library/publications/the-world-factbook/geos/ch.html

Chen, J., Dunne, M. P., & Han, P. (2007). Prevention of child sexual abuse in China: Knowledge, attitudes, and communication practices of children of elementary school children. *Child Abuse & Neglect, 31*, 747–755.

China's one child policy may be coming to an end. (2013, January 22). *South China Morning Post.* Retrieved from http://www.scmp.com/news/china/ article/1133667/signs-chinas-one-child-policy-may-be-coming-end?page=all

Cimpric, A. (2010). *Children accused of witchcraft: An anthropological study of contemporary practices in Africa.* Retrieved from http://www.unicef.org/ wcaro/wcaro_children-accused-of-witchcraft-in-Africa.pdf

Clawson, H. J., Salomon, A., & Grace, L. G. (2008). *Treating the hidden wounds: Trauma treatment and mental health recovery for victims of human trafficking.* Retrieved from http://aspe.hhs.gov/hsp/07/HumanTrafficking/ Treating/ib.htm

Crary, D. (2010, March 28). Adopting China's special needs kids. *MSNBC.* Retrieved from http://www.msnbc.msn.com/id/36037857/ns/health- childrens_health/t/adopting-chinas-special-needs-kids/

Custer, C. (2013, July 24). Carried off: Abduction, adoption and two families' search for answers. *China File.* Retrieved from http://www.chinafile.com

Fiszbein, A. & Schady, N. (2009). *Conditional cash transfers: Reducing present and future poverty.* Retrieved from http://siteresources.worldbank.org/ INTCCT/Resources/5757608-1234228266004/PRR-CCT_web_ noembargo.pdf

Global child mortality rates "halved." (2013, September 13). *IRIN News*. Retrieved from http://www.irinnews.org/printreport.aspx?reportid=98750

Hamid, J. (2006, July 26). Sabah's "undocumented" children in stateless limbo. *The Bangkok Post*. Retrieved from http://www.bangkokpost.com

Helderman, R. S. (2012, December 4). Senate rejects treaty to protect disabled around the world. *Washington Post*. Retrieved from http://articles.washingtonpost.com/2012-12-04/politics/35624605_1_treaty-disabled-children-americans-with-disabilities-act

Human Rights Watch. (1996). *Death by default: A policy of fatal neglect in China's state orphanages*. Retrieved from http://www.hrw.org

Human Rights Watch. (1997). *Voices of child soldiers*. Retrieved from http://hrw.org

Human Rights Watch. (2003). *Small change: Bonded child labor in India's silk industry*. Retrieved from http://www.hrw.org/reports/2003/india

International Food Policy Research Institute. (2010). *Study finds Bolsa Familia children healthier, doing better in in school*. Retrieved from http://www.ifpri.org/pressrelease/study-finds-bolsa-familia-children-healthier-doing-better-school

International Labour Organization. (n.d.). *Facts on child labour in agriculture*. Retrieved from http://www.ilo.org

International Labour Organization. (2010). *Facts on child labour 2010*. Retrieved from http://www.ilo.org/wcmsp5/groups/public/@dgreports/@dcomm/documents/publication/wcms_126685.pdf

International Labour Organization. (2012). *ILO 2012 global estimate of forced labour*. Retrieved from http://www.ilo.org/washington/WCMS_182004/lang--en/index.htm

International Labour Organization. (2013). *Making progress against child labour: Global estimates and trends 2000-2012*. Retrieved from http://www.ilo.org

Jacobs, A. (2009, April 5). Chinese hunger for sons fuels boys' abductions. *New York Times*. Retrieved from http://www.nytimes.com

Johnson, K., Banghan, H., & Liyao, W. (1998). Infant abandonment and adoption in China. *Population and Development Review*, 24(3), 469–510.

Johnson, K. (2002). Politics of international and domestic adoption in China. *Law and Society Review*, 36(2), 379–396.

Johnson, K. A. (2004). *Wanting a daughter, needing a son: Abandonment, adoption and orphanage care in China*. St. Paul, MN: Yeong & Yeong Book Company.

Johnson, K. (2012). Challenging the discourse of intercountry adoption: Perspectives from rural China. In J. L. Gibbins & K. S. Rotabi (Eds.), *Intercountry adoption: Policies, practices and outcomes* (pp. 103–118). Burlington, VT: Ashgate.

Kazmin, A. (2012, August 29). India proposes ban on child labor. *The Washington Post.* Retrieved from http://www.washingtonpost.com/world/india-proposes-ban-on-child-labor/2012/08/29/ef9d802a-f1f2-11e1-a612-3cfc842a6d89_story.html

Kombarakaran, F. A. (2004). Street children of Bombay: Their stresses and strategies of coping. *Children and Youth Services Review, 26,* 853–871.

Kudrati, M. Plummer, M. L., & Yousif, N. D. E. H. (2008). Children of the sug: A study of the daily lives of street children in Khartoum, Sudan, with intervention recommendations. *Child Abuse & Neglect, 32,* 439–448. doi: 10.1016/j.chiabu.2007.07.009

LaFraniere, S. (2009, April 21). Name not on our list? Change it, China says. *New York Times.* Retrieved from http://www.nytimes.com

LaFraniere, S. (2011, April 7). As China ages, birthrate policy may prove difficult to reverse. *New York Times,* pp. A4, A9.

LaFraniere, S. (2011, August 4). Chinese officials seized and sold babies, parents say. *New York Times.* Retrieved from http://www.nytimes.com

Lakshmi, R. (2013, July 26). In India, a rise in surrogate births for West. *Washington Post.* Retrieved from http://www.washingtonpost.com

Mantra may help kids escape abuse. (2005, October 18). *Bangkok Post.* Retrieved from http://www.bangkokpost.com

Martorano, B., & Sanfilippo, M. (2012). *Innovative features in conditional cash transfers: An impact evaluation of Chile Solidario on households and children.* Retrieved from http://www.unicef-irc.org/publications/656

Mathur, M., Rathore P., & Mathur, M. (2009). Incidence, type and intensity of abuse in street children in India. *Child Abuse & Neglect, 33,* 907–913. doi: 10.1016/j.chiabu.2009.01.003

Moore, M. (2012, June 1). Chinese couple pay £130,000 to have a second child to avoid one-child policy. *The Telegraph.* Retrieved from http://www.telegraph.co.uk

Mouravieff-Apostol, E. (2006). The significance of birth registration in today's world. In N. Hall (Ed.) *Social work: Making a world of difference* (pp. 103–113). Berne, Switzerland: International Federation of Social Workers.

Niles, C. (2012, September 26). *United Nations Secretary-General launches global education initiative.* Retrieved from http://www.unicef.org/education/bege_65956.html

No ID, no government services. (2012). *IRIN News.* Retrieved from http://www.irinnews.org/Report/95890/EGYPT-No-ID-no-government-services

No more child soldiers. (2012). *IRIN News.* Retrieved from http://www.irinnews.org/printreport.aspx?reportid=95947

Norman, J., & Bathori-Tartsi, Z. (2010). Improvisational international research: Seeking to help children in Ukrainian orphanages sooner than later. *Families in Society, 91*(4), 421–425. doi: 10.1606/1044-3894.4037

Pinheiro, P. S. (2006). *World report on violence against children.* Geneva, Switzerland: United Nations.

Pinzón-Rondón, A. M., Hofferth, S., & Briceño, L. (2008). Children working in the streets of Colombian cities: Different pathways to the street lead to different populations. *Children and Youth Services, 30,* 1417–1424.

Plan India. (2010). *Count every child: Ensuring universal birth registration in India.* Retrieved from http://plan-international.org/birthregistration/count-every-child-in-india

Plan International. (2012a). *Mother to child: How discrimination prevents women from registering the birth of their child.* Retrieved from http://plan-international.org/birthregistration/files/mother-to-child-1

Plan International. (2012b). *Because I am a girl: The state of the world's girls 2012.* Retrieved from http://plan-international.org/girls/pdfs/2012-report/The-State-of-the-World-s-Girls-Learning-for-Life-Plan-International-2012.pdf

Plan International. (n.d.). *Bolivia.* Retrieved from http://plan-international.org/birthregistration/resources/country-case-studies/bolivia

Plummer, M. L., Kudrati, M., & Yousif, N. D. E. H. (2007). Beginning street life: Factors contributing to children working and living on the streets of Khartoum, Sudan. *Child Abuse & Neglect, 29,* 1520–1536. doi: 10.1016/j.chiabu.2007.06.008

Provost, C. (2013, June 11). Drop in aid for primary schools puts education MDG at risk. *The Guardian.* Retrieved from http://www.guardian.co.uk

Refugees International. (2009). *Nationality rights for all: A progress report and global survey on statelessness.* Retrieved from http://www.refugeesinternational.org/sites/default/files/RI%20Stateless%20Report_FINAL_031109.pdf

Refugees International. (2007). *Malaysia: Undocumented children in Sabah vulnerable to statelessness.* Retrieved from http://www.unhcr.org/refworld/pdfid/47a6ee98d.pdf

Refugees International & Open Society Justice Initiative. (2011). *Without citizenship: Statelessness, discrimination and repression in Kuwait.* Retrieved from http://www.refugeesinternational.org/sites/default/files/120511_Kuwait_With_Citizenship_0.pdf

Rotabi, K. S., & Bromfield, N. F. (2012). The decline in intercountry adoptions and new practices of global surrogacy: Global exploitation and human rights concerns. *Affilia, 27,* 129–141. doi: 10.1177/0886100912444102

Rotabi, K. S., Pennell, J., Roby, J. L., & Bunkers, K. M. (2012). Family group conferencing as a culturally adaptable intervention: Reforming intercountry adoption in Guatemala. *International Social Work, 55,* 402–416. doi:10.1177/0020872812437229

Shakya, A. (2011). Experiences of children in armed conflict in Nepal. *Children and Youth Services Review, 33,* 557–563. doi: 10.1016/j.childyouth.2010.08.018

Sinha, K. (2012, March 2). 25% of Indian births not registered. *Times of India.* Retrieved from http://articles.timesofindia.indiatimes.com

Speizer, I. S., Goodwin, M., Whittle, L., Clyde, M., & Rogers, J. (2008). Dimensions of child sexual abuse before age 15 in three Central American countries: Honduras, El Salvador, and Guatemala. *Child Abuse & Neglect, 32,* 455–462.

Swarns, R. L. (2013, January 24). American adoptions from abroad at their lowest levels in years. *New York Times.* Retrieved from http://www.nytimes.com

Stateless: When is a Dominican not one? (2011, December 31). *The Economist.* Retrieved from http://www.economist.com/node/21542182

Texting for birth certificates. (2012). *IRIN News.* Retrieved from http://www.irinnews.org/printreport.aspx?reportid=96066

UNESCO. (2013). *Children still battling to go to school.* Retrieved from http://unesdoc.unesco.org/images/0022/002216/221668E.pdf

UNICEF. (2001). *Adult wars, child soldiers.* Retrieved from http://www.unicef.org

UNICEF. (2005). *Convention on the Rights of the Child.* Retrieved from http://www.unicef.org/crc/index_protecting.html

UNICEF. (2006). *State of the world's children 2006.* Retrieved from http://www.unicef.org/publications/index_30398.html

UNICEF. (2006b). *Birth registration*. Retrieved from http://www.unicef.org/protection/files/birthregistration_2006.pdf

UNICEF. (2007). *Birth registration and armed conflict*. Retrieved from http://www.unicef.org/protection/birth_registration_and_armed_conflict(1).pdf

UNICEF. (2009). *Progress for children*. Retrieved from http://www.unicef.org/protection/files/Progress_for_Children-No.8_EN_081309(1).pdf

UNICEF. (2011a). *Child protection from violence, exploitation, and abuse: A statistical snapshot.* Retrieved from http://www.childinfo.org/files/ChildProtection__from_violence_exploitation_abuse.pdf

UNICEF. (2011b). *State of the world's children 2011*. Retrieved from http://www.unicef.org/sowc2011/pdfs/SOWC-2011-Main-Report_EN_02092011.pdf (note child labour stats)

UNICEF. (2012a). *2012 progress report on committing to child survival: A promise renewed.* Retrieved from http://www.unicefusa.org/assets/pdf/zero/APR_Progress_Report_2012_final.pdf

UNICEF. (2012b). *State of the world's children 2012*. Retrieved from http://www.unicef.org/sowc2012/pdfs/SOWC%202012-Main%20Report_EN_13Mar2012.pdf

UNICEF. (2012c). *Statistics by area: Education*. Retrieved from http://www.childinfo.org/education.html

United Nations High Commissioner for Refugees. (2011). *Global trends 2011*. Retrieved from http://www.unhcr.org/4fd6f87f9.html

United Nations. (2012). *Report of the Special Representative of the Secretary-General for Children and Armed Conflict*. Retrieved from http://childrenandarmed-conflict.un.org/library/

United Nations. (n.d.). *Education First*. Retrieved from http://www.globaleducationfirst.org/

United Nations Human Rights Council. (2012). *Resolution 31*. Retrieved from http://www.crin.org/docs/Resolution_31.doc

United Nations Security Council. (2012). *Children and armed conflict: Report of the Secretary-General*. Retrieved from http://childrenandarmedconflict.un.org/library/

United Nations Security Council. (2012). *Report of the Secretary-General on the situation of children and armed conflict affected by the Lord's Resistance Army.* Retrieved from http://childrenandarmedconflict.un.org/library

US Department of Health and Human Services. (2009). *Understanding the effects of maltreatment on brain development*. Retrieved from http://www.childwelfare.gov/pubs/issue_briefs/brain_development/effects.cfm

US State Department. (2011). *FY 2011 annual report on intercountry adoption.* Retrieved from http://adoption.state.gov/content/pdf/fy2011_annual_report.pdf

US State Department. (2012). *China.* Retrieved from http://adoption.state.gov/country_information/country_specific_info.php?country-select=china

US State Department. (2012). *Romania.* Retrieved from http://adoption.state.gov/country_information/country_specific_alerts_notices.php?alert_notice_type=notices&alert_notice_file=romania_1

War, poverty and ignorance fuel sexual abuse of children. (2007, June 6). *IRIN News.* Retrieved from http://www.irinnews.org/PrintReport.aspx?ReportId=72578

Ward, C. L., & Seager, J. R. (2010). South African street children: A survey and recommendations for services. *Development Southern Africa, 27*(1), 85–100. doi: 10.1080/03768350903519374

Whetten, K., Ostermann, J., Whetten, R. A., Pence, B. W., O'Donnell, K., Messer, L. C.,...The Positive Outcomes for Orphans Research Team. (2009). A comparison of the wellbeing of orphans and abandoned children ages 6-12 in institutional and community-based care setting in 5 less wealthy nations. *PLoS One, 4*(12), 1–11.

Wilson, S. L., Weaver, T. L. Cradock, M. M., & Kuebli, J. E. (2008). A preliminary study of the cognitive and motor skills acquisition of young international adoptees. *Children & Youth Services Review, 30,* 585–596.

Wong, E. (2012, July 22). Reports of forced abortions fuel push to end Chinese law. *New York Times.* Retrieved from http://www.nytimes.com

World Bank. (2009). *Abolishing school fees in Africa: Lessons from Ethiopia, Ghana, Kenya, Malawi, and Mozambique.* Retrieved from http://www.unicef.org/publications/files/Aboloshing_School_Fees_in_Africa.pdf

Zhao, Q., Li, X., Kaljee, L. M., Fang, X., Stanton, B., & Zhang, L. (2009). AIDS orphanages in China: Reality and challenges. *AIDS Patient Care and STDs, 23*(4), 297–303. doi: 10.1089/apc.2008.0190

Zijuan, S., Shuzhuo, L., & Feldman, M. W. (2012). *Policy responses of gender imbalance in China: The "Care for Girls" campaign.* Retrieved from http://hsblogs.stanford.edu/morrison/files/2012/11/125-n0ilb4.pdf

Chapter Five

Activists rap Australia's offshore processing of migrants. (2013, January 14). *IRIN News.* Retrieved from http://www.irinnews.org/printreport.aspx?reportid=97243

African asylum-seekers must quit Tel Aviv. (2009, February 24). *IRIN News*. Retrieved from http://www.irinnews.org/printreport.aspx?reportid=83111

Aid workers welcome Burmese refugee census. (2011, June 9). *IRIN News*. Retrieved from http://www.irinnews.org/printreport.aspx?reportid=92941

Albuja, S., & Ceballos, M. (2010). Urban displacement and migration in Colombia. *Forced Migration Review, 34*, 10–11. Retrieved from http://repository.forcedmigration.org/show_metadata.jsp?pid=fmo:5585

Ali, L. (2013, January 6). Rape flourishes in Mogadishu's IDP camps. *Al-Jazeera*. Retrieved from www/aljazeera.com

American Red Cross. (2011). *Summary of the Geneva Conventions of 1949 and their additional protocols*. Retrieved from http://www.redcross.org/images/MEDIA_CustomProductCatalog/m3640104_IHL_SummaryGenevaConv.pdf

Amnesty International. (2011). *"This is what we demand, justice!": Impunity for sexual violence against women in Colombia's armed conflict*. Retrieved from http://www.amnesty.org/en/library/info/AMR23/018/2011/en

Amnesty International. (2012a). *Nauru camp: A catastrophe with no end in sight*. Retrieved from http://www.amnesty.org/en/library/info/ASA42/002/2012/en

Amnesty International. (2012b). *Hidden from justice. Impunity for conflict-related sexual violence*. Retrieved from http://www.amnesty.org/en/news/colombian-authorities-fail-stop-or-punish-sexual-violence-against-women-2012-10-04

Amnesty International. (2012c). *The Victims and Land Restitution Law: An Amnesty International analysis*. Retrieved from http://www.amnesty.org/en/library/info/AMR23/018/2012/en

Armstrong, P. (2011, December 5). What are "conflict diamonds"? *CNN*. Retrieved from http://articles.cnn.com/2011-12-05/africa/ world_africa_conflict-diamonds-explainer_1_world-diamond-council-marange-conflict-diamonds?_s=PM:AFRICA

Asylum-seekers detained, harassed. (2009, February 4). *IRIN News*. Retrieved from http://www.irinnews.org/printreport.aspx?reportid=82739

Attanayake, V., McKay, R., Joffres, M., Singh, S., Burkle, F., & Mills, E. (2009). Prevalence of mental disorders among children exposed to war: A systemic review of 7,290 children. *Medicine, Conflict and Survival, 25*(1), 4–19. doi:10.1080/13623690802568913

Australia asylum bill voted down. (2012, June 28). *BBC News*. Retrieved from http://bbc.co.uk

Australia's offshore asylum process. (2012, November 30). *IRIN News*. Retrieved from http://www.irinnews.org/report/96940/Analysis-Australia-s-offshore-asylum-process

Australia to send all boatpeople to poverty-hit Papua New Guinea. (2013, July 23). *South China Morning Post*. Retrieved from http://www.scmp.com

Barrie, L., & Mendes, P. (2011). The experiences of unaccompanied asylum-seeking children in and leaving the out-of-home care system in the UK and Australia: A critical review of the literature. *International Social Work, 54*(4), 485–503.

Bartels, S. A., Scott, J. A., Leaning, J., Kelly, J. T., Mukwege, D., Joyce, N. R., & VanRooyen, M. J. (2012). Sexual violence trends between 2004 and 2008 in South Kivu, Democratic Republic of Congo. *Prehospital and Disaster Medicine, 26*(6), 408–413. doi: 10.1017/S1049023X12000179

Bernstein, N. (2006, October 8). In New York immigration court, asylum roulette. *New York Times*. Retrieved from http://www.nytimes.com

Bernstein, N. (2009, August 5). U.S. to reform policy on detention for immigrants. *New York Times*. Retrieved from http://www.nytimes.com

Bernstein, N. (2011, September 28). Companies use immigration crackdown to turn a profit. *New York Times*. Retrieved from http://www.nytimes.com

Bleak prospects for country's estimated 1.5 million widows. (2008, January 30). *IRIN News*. Retrieved from http://www.irinnews.org/printreport.aspx?reportid=76492

Byrne, O., & Miller, E. (2012). The flow of unaccompanied children through the immigration system. *Vera Institute of Justice*. Retrieved from http://www.vera.org/pubs/flow-unaccompanied-children-through-immigration-system-resource-practitioners -policy-makers-and

Burnham, G., Lafta, R., Doocy, S., & Roberts, L. (2006). Mortality after the 2003 invasion of Iraq: A cross-sectional cluster sample survey. *Lancet, 368*(9545), 1421–1428.

Cambridge, P., & Williams, L. (2004). Approaches to advocacy for refugees and asylum seekers: A developmental case study for a local support and advice service. *Journal of Refugee Studies, 17*(1), 97–113.

Camps offer little refuge from rape. (2008, January 28). *IRIN News*. Retrieved from http://www.irinnews.org/printreport.aspx?reportid=76454

Cemlyn, S., & Briskman, L. (2003). Asylum, children's rights, and social work. *Child and Family Social Work, 8*, 163–178.

Children's Commissioner. (2012). *Landing in Dover*. Retrieved from http://www.childrenscommissioner.gov.uk/content/publications/content_556

Christian, M., Safari, O., Ramazani, P., Burnham, G. & Glass, N. (2011). Sexual and gender based violence against men in the Democratic Republic of Congo: Effects on survivors, their families and the community. *Medicine, Conflict and Survival, 27*(4), 227–246.

Cluster Munition Coalition. (2012). *Cluster munition monitor 2012*. Retrieved from   http://www.the-monitor.org/index.php/publications/display?url= cmm/2012/

Coalition to Stop the Use of Child Soldiers. (2007). *Frontiers: Childhood at the borderline*. Retrieved from http://www.child-soldiers.org/2007-23-02-Colombia_frontiers_report-FINAL.pdf

Coghlan, B., Brennan, R. J., Ngoy, P., Dofara, D., Otto, B., Clements, M., & Stewart, T. (2006). Mortality in the Democratic Republic of Congo: A nationwide survey. *The Lancet, 367*, 44–51.

Columbia peace talks: Farc says progress is "modest." (2013, October 4). *BBC News*. Retrieved from http://www.bbc.co.uk

Culture of disbelief works against asylum seekers. (2013, April 24). *IRIN News*. Retrieved from http://www.irinnews.org/printreport.aspx?reportid=97906

De Jong, K., & Kleber, R. J. (2007). Emergency conflict-related psychosocial interventions in Sierra Leone and Uganda: Lessons from Médecins Sans Frontières. *Journal of Health Psychology, 12*, 485–497.

Deacon, Z., & Sullivan, C. (2009). Responding to the complex and gendered needs of refugee women. *Affilia, 24*(3), 272–284.

Degomme, O., & Guha-Sapir, D. (2010). Patterns of mortality rates in Darfur conflict. *Lancet, 375*(9711), 294–300.

Doctors Without Borders. (2005a). *Mental health*. Retrieved from http://www. doctorswithoutborders.org/news/mentalhealth.htm

Doctors Without Borders. (2005b). *The crushing burden of rape: Sexual violence in Darfur*. Retrieved from http://www.doctorswith outborders.org/ publications/reports/2005/sudan03.pdf

Doctors Without Borders. (2013). *Working in the field: Mental health specialists*. Retrieved from http://www.doctorswithoutborders.org/work/field/ profiles.cfm?id=2537

Doucet, D., & Denov, M. (2012). The power of sweet words: Local forms of intervention with war-affected women in rural Sierra Leone. *International Social Work, 55*, 612–628.

Dozens of children die in Afghanistan cold. (2012, February 21). *The Guardian*. Retrieved from http://www.guardian.co.uk/world/2012/feb/21/dozens-children-die-afghanistan-cold

Engstrom, D. W., & Okamura, A. (2004). A plague of our time: Torture, human rights, and social work. *Families in Society, 85,* 291–300.

Gates, S., Hegre, H., Nygård, H. M., & Strand, H. (2012). Development consequences of armed conflict. *World Development, 40*(9), 1713–1722.

Gettleman, J. (2009, August 4). Symbol of unhealed Congo: Male rape victims. *New York Times.* Retrieved from http://www.nytimes.com

Giacaman, R., Rabaia, Y., & Nguyen-Gillham, V. (2010). Domestic and political violence: The Palestinian predicament. *The Lancet, 375*(9711), 259–260.

Global Witness. (2011). *Global Witness leaves Kimberley Process, calls for diamond trade to be held accountable.* Retrieved from http://www. globalwitness.org/library/global-witness-leaves-kimberley-process-calls-diamond-trade-be-held-accountable

Global Witness. (n.d.). *Conflict minerals.* Retrieved from http://www. global witness.org/campaigns/conflict/conflict-minerals

Governance and Social Development Resource Centre. (2009). *The impact of conflict on women's education, employment and health care.* Retrieved from http://www.gsdrc.org/docs/open/HD588.pdf

Gower, M. (2013). Ending child immigration detention. *House of Commons Library.* Retrieved from http://www.parliament.uk/briefing-papers/ SN05591

Green, E. C., & Honwana, A. (1999). Indigenous healing of children in Africa. *IK Notes, 10.* Retrieved from http://www.worldbank.org/afr/ik/iknt10.pdf

Green-Rauerhorst, M., Jacobsen, K., & Pyne, S. (2008). *Invisible in Thailand.* Retrieved from http://sites.tufts.edu/feinstein/2008/invisible-in-thailand

Greenberg, J. (2012, November 2). Israel's crackdown on illegal African migrants draws critics. *Washington Post.* Retrieved from http://www. washingtonpost.com

Hoge, W. (2005, June 22). U.N. relief official condemns use of rape in African wars. *New York Times,* p. A4.

Hoge, W. (2005, July 30). U.N. charges Sudan ignores rape in Darfur by military and police. *New York Times.* Retrieved September 29, 2006, from http:// www.nytimes.com

Honwana, A. (2006). *Child soldiers in Africa.* Philadelphia, PA: University of Pennsylvania Press.

Hopkins, P., & Hill, M. (2010). The needs and strengths of unaccompanied asylum-seeking children and young people in Scotland. *Child & Family Social Work, 15,* 399–408.

Human Rights Watch. (2003). *"You'll learn not to cry:" Child combatants in Colombia*. Retrieved from http://www.hrw.org/reports/2003/colombia0903

Human Rights Watch. (2004). *Refugee and internally-displaced women: Gender-based asylum claims*. Retrieved from http://www.hrw.org/women/refugees.html

Human Rights Watch. (2010). *Paramilitaries' heirs: The new face of violence in Colombia*. Retrieved from http://www.hrw.org/reports/2010/02/03/paramilitaries-heirs

Human Rights Watch. (2012a). *Israel: Asylum seekers blocked at border*. Retrieved from http://www.hrw.org

Human Rights Watch. (2012b). *Ad hoc and inadequate: Thailand's treatment of refugees and asylum seekers*. Retrieved from http://www.hrw.org/reports/2012/09/12/ad-hoc-and-inadequate

Husain, F., Anderson, M., Cardozo, B. L., Becknell, K., Blanton, C., Araki, D., & Vithana, E. K. (2011). Prevalence of war-related mental health conditions and association with displacement status in postwar Jaffna District, Sri Lanka. *JAMA, 306*(5), 522–531.

IBON Foundation. (2006). *Uncounted lives: Children, women and conflict in the Philippines: A needs assessment of children and women affected by armed conflict*. Retrieved from http://www.internal-displacement.org/8025708F004CE90B/(httpDocuments)/4195F736A00885CCC1257289005B3781/$file/Uncounted+Lives+-Oct+2006.pdf

Immigration and Customs Enforcement. (2012). *Detention reform accomplishments*. Retrieved from http://www.ice.gov/detention-reform/detention-reform.htm

Imprisoned Eritreans complain of being forced to leave Israel. (2013, March 11). *IRIN News*. Retrieved from http://www.irinnews.org/printreport.aspx?reportid=97623

Internal Displacement Monitoring Centre. (2006). *Colombia: Government "peace process" cements injustice for IDPs*. Retrieved from http://www.internal-displacement.org/8025708F004BE3B1/(httpInfoFiles)/2F1618E6C169F2EBC125719C002F6421/$file/Special%20Country%20Report%20Colombia.pdf

Internal Displacement Monitoring Centre. (2011). *Colombia: Property restitution in sight but integration still distant*. Retrieved from http://www.internal-displacement.org/8025708F004BE3B1/(httpInfoFiles)/D46F6EF1CC3666AEC1257975005F3FC6/$file/Colombia+-December+2011.pdf

International Association of National Public Health Institutes. (2013). *Colombia.* Retrieved from http://www.ianphi.org/member-countries/country.cfm/count_id/8058FD57-168B-4FAF-9BE2-24467C2E2A9F

International Campaign to Ban Landmines. (n.d.). *The treaty.* Retrieved from http://www.icbl.org/index.php/icbl/Treaty

International Campaign to Ban Landmines. (2012). *Landmine monitor 2012.* Retrieved from http://www.the-monitor.org/index.php/publications/display?url=lm/2012/

International Committee of the Red Cross. (2012). *Colombia: Displacement.* Retrieved from http://www.icrc.org/eng/resources/documents/feature/2012/colombia-report-2011-displacement.htm

IRIN. (2012). *From pillar to post: The plight of Afghans abroad.* Retrieved from http://www.irinnews.org/InDepthMain.aspx?indepthid=95&reportid=94960

Israel's migration policy bites hard. (2012, November 21). *IRIN News.* Retrieved from http://www.irinnews.org/Report/96800/In-Depth-Migration-policy-bites-hard

Johnson, K., Scott, J., Rughita, B., Kisielewski, M., Asher, J., Ong, R., & Lawry, L. (2010). Association of sexual violence and human rights violations with physical and mental health in territories of the eastern Democratic Republic of the Congo. *Journal of the American Medical Association, 304*(5), 553–562.

Kershner, I. (2012, June 18). Crackdown on migrants tugs at soul of Israelis. *New York Times.* Retrieved from http://www.nytimes.com

Kershner, I. (2012, June 4). Israeli leader pledges hard line on migrants. *New York Times.* Retrieved from http://www.nytimes.com

Kilpatrick, R., & Leitch, R. (2004). Teachers' and pupils' educational experiences and school-based responses to the conflict in Northern Ireland. *Journal of Social Issues, 60*(3), 563–586.

Kohli, R., & Mather, R. (2003). Promoting psychosocial well-being in unaccompanied asylum-seeking young people in the United Kingdom. *Child and Family Social Work, 8*, 201–212.

KPMG. (2012). *Conflict minerals—Does compliance really matter? Ask California, Australia, and the EU.* Retrieved from http://www.kpmg.com/US/en/IssuesAndInsights/ArticlesPublications/dodd-frank-series/Pages/conflict-minerals-does-compliance-really-matter.aspx

Levinson, A. (2011). Unaccompanied immigrant children: A growing phenomenon with few easy solutions. *Migration Information Source.* Retrieved from http://www.migrationinformation.org/Feature/print.cfm?ID=823

Lidchi, V., Tombs, N., Magalhaes, T., & Lopez, J. (2004). Hidden voices: The family biogram for working with families forcibly displaced in Colombia. *Australian and New Zealand Journal of Family Therapy, 25*(4), 212–221.

Liptak, A. (2005, December 26). Courts criticize judges' handling of asylum cases. *New York Times.* Retrieved from the LexisNexis database.

Loughna, S. (2002). *FMO country guide: Colombia.* Retrieved, from http://www.forcedmigration.org/guides/fmo003/fmo003.pdf

Machel, G. (2001). *The impact of war on children.* New York, NY: Palgrave.

Machel, G. (1996). *The impact of armed conflict on children.* Retrieved from http://www.un.org/rights/impact.htm

Mapp, S. (2013). Children and armed conflict. In C. Franklin (Ed.), *Encyclopedia of social work online.* New York, NY: Oxford University Press. doi: 10.1093/acrefore/9780199975839.013.870

Martin, S. (2005). *Must boys be boys? Ending sexual exploitation and abuse in UN peacekeeping missions.* Retrieved from http://www.refugeesinternational.org

Médecins Sans Frontières. (2006). *Living in fear: Colombia's cycle of violence.* Retrieved from http://www.msf.org/source/countries/americas/colombia/2006/report/living_in_fear.pdf

Médecins Sans Frontières. (2009). *Shattered lives: Immediate medical care vital for sexual violence victims.* Retrieved from http://www.doctorswithoutborders.org/publications/article.cfm?id=3422

Médecins Sans Frontières. (2011). *Psychosocial and mental health interventions in areas of mass violence.* Retrieved from http://www.msf.org/source/mentalhealth/guidelines/MSF_mentalhealthguidelines.pdf

Médecins Sans Frontières. (2012). *South Sudan's hidden crisis.* Retrieved from http://www.doctorswithoutborders.org/publications/article.cfm?id=6438

Meleigy, M. (2010). Yemen conflict takes its toll on civilians. *Lancet, 375*(9711), 269–270.

Mitchell, F. (2003). The social services response to unaccompanied children in England. *Child and Family Social Work, 8,* 179–189.

Murthy, R. S., & Lakshminarayana, R. (2006). Mental health consequences of war: A brief review of research findings. *World Psychiatry, 5*(1), 25–30.

Nelson, B. D., Collins, L., Van Rooyen, M. J., Joyce, N., Mukwege, D., & Bartels, S. (2011). Impact of sexual violence on children in the Eastern Democratic Republic of Congo. *Medicine, Conflict and Survival, 27*(4), 211–225. doi:10.1080/13623699.2011.645148

New Australian refugee quota welcomed. (2012, August 24). *IRIN News*. Retrieved from http://www.irinnews.org/printreport.aspx?reportid=96164

No school today—Why Syrian refugee children miss out on education. (2012, August 8). *IRIN News*. Retrieved from http://www.irinnews.org/printreport.aspx?reportid=96053

Onyango, M. A., & Hampanda, K. (2011). Social constructions of masculinity and male survivors of wartime sexual violence: An analytical review. *International Journal of Sexual Health, 23*, 237–247.

Oxfam International. (2009). *In her own words: Iraqi women talk about their greatest challenges*. Retrieved from http://www.oxfam.org

Paz, Y. (2011). Ordered disorder: African asylum seekers in Israel and discursive challenges to an emerging refugee regime. *UNHCR*. Retrieved from www.unhcr.org/4d7a26ba9.pdf

Pazzano, C. (2012, November 16). Asylum seekers: Where Australia stands. *SBS*. Retrieved from http://www.sbs.com.au/news/article/1295782/Asylum-seekers-Where-Australia-stands

The plight of LGBTI asylum seekers, refugees. (2013, May 7). *IRIN News*. Retrieved from http://www.irinnews.org/printreport.aspx?reportid=97989

Povoledo, E. (2012, December 28). In Italy, shantytowns of refugees reflect paradox on asylum. *New York Times*, p. A12.

Private prisons profit from illegal immigrants. (2012, August 2). *CBS News*. Retrieved from http://www.cbsnews.com/8301-201_162-57485392/ap-private-prisons-profit-from-illegal-immigrants/

Rape on the rise amid "climate of fear" in Mogadishu IDP camps. (2011, December 22). *IRIN News*. Retrieved from http://www.irinnews.org/printreport.aspx?reportid=94520

Refugee Council of Australia. (2012a). *Mandatory detention*. Retrieved from http://www.refugeecouncil.org.au/f/as-det.php

Refugee Council of Australia. (2012b). *Boat arrivals*. Retrieved from http://www.refugeecouncil.org.au/f/as-boat.php

Refugees International. (2005a). *Colombia*. Retrieved from http://www.refugeesinternational.org/content/country/detail/2934

Refugees International. (2005b). *Saiza voices: Massacre and return*. Retrieved from http://www.refugeesinternational.org/content/article/detail/5044

Refugees International. (2006). *Colombia: Thousands of displaced people face destitution in urban areas*. Retrieved from http://www.refugeesinternational.org/content/article/detail/8978

Refugees International. (2009). *Displaced women demand their rights*. Retrieved from http://refugeesinternational.org/policy/field-report/colombia-displaced-women-demand-their-rights

Refugees International. (2012). *Transformational change must include urban IDPs*. Retrieved from http://refugeesinternational.org/policy/field-report/colombia-transformational-change-must-include-urban-idps

Risser, G. (2007). *Children caught in conflicts: The impact of armed conflict on children in Southeast Asia*. Retrieved from the Child Rights Information Network Web site: http://www.crin.org/docs/CIDA_Caught_Conflict.pdf

Savage, C. (2008, August 24). Vetted judges more likely to reject asylum bids. *New York Times*. Retrieved from http://www.nytimes.com

Schmidt, S. (2005). *Liberian refugees: Cultural considerations for social service providers*. Retrieved from http://www.brycs.org/documents/Liberian_Cultural_Considerations.pdf

Schwartz, E. P., & Hetfield, M. (2013, August 2). Israel turns its back on African refugees. *Washington Post*. Retrieved from http://www.washingtonpost.com

Sexual abuse survivors in north denied justice—Amnesty. (2007, November 30). *IRIN News*. Retrieved from http://www.irinnews.org/printreport.aspx?reportid=75620

Sexual violence continues in IDP camps. (2008, March 4). *IRIN News*. Retrieved from http://www.irinnews.org/Report.aspx?ReportId=77102

Shakya, A. (2011). Experiences of children in armed conflict in Nepal. *Children and Youth Services Review, 33*, 557–563.

Sieff, K. (2013, February 2). Alleged terrorism ties foil some Afghan interpreters' U.S. visa hopes. *Washington Post*. Retrieved from http://www.washingtonpost.com

Siegel, M. (2011, November 26). Australia eases detentions of refugees coming by sea. *New York Times*, p. A7.

Sivakumaran, S. (2007). Sexual violence against men in armed conflict. *The European Journal of International Law, 18*(2), 253–276.

Sonke Gender Justice Network. (2012). *Gender relations, sexual violence and the effects of conflict on women and men in North Kivu, eastern Democratic Republic of Congo*. Retrieved from http://www.genderjustice.org.za/resources/reports.html?view=docman

South Africa's flawed asylum system. (2013, April 30). *IRIN News*. Retrieved from http://www.irinnews.org/printreport.aspx?reportid=97944

Spindler, W. (2003). Indigenous Colombians: "We are here today and tomorrow we disappear." *Refugees Magazine, 132*. Retrieved from http://www.unhcr.org/publ/PUBL/4135ca574.html

Suárez-Orozco, C. (2001). Psychocultural factors in the adaptation of immigrant youth: Gendered responses. In M. Agosín (Ed.), *Women, gender and human rights: A global perspective* (pp. 170–188). New Brunswick, NJ: Rutgers University Press.

Tavernise, S. (2006, October 8). Sectarian havoc freezes the lives of young Iraqis. *New York Times*. Retrieved from http://www.nytimes.com

Thomas, M. (2012, December 7). Conflict diamond definition won't change. *The Times of India*. Retrieved from http://articles.timesofindia.indiatimes.com/2012-12-07/surat/35669944_1_conflict-diamonds-kpcs-kp-chair

UNESCO. (2013). *Children still battling to go to school*. Retrieved from http://unesdoc.unesco.org/images/0022/002216/221668E.pdf

UNICEF. (2005). *The impact of conflict on women and girls in west and central Africa and the UNICEF response*. Retrieved from http://www.unicef.org/publications/index_25262.html

United Nations. (2013, July 2). UN agency welcomes extension of stay for Afghan refugees in Pakistan. Retrieved from http://www.un.org/apps/news/story.asp?NewsID=45324&#.UgUSWkbD85s

United Nations. (n.d.). *The six grave violations*. Retrieved from http://childrenandarmedconflict.un.org/effects-of-conflict/six-grave-violations/

United Nations High Commissioner for Refugees. (2004). *Helping refugees: An introduction to UNHCR*. Retrieved from http://www.unhcr.org/cgi-bin/texis/vtx/basics/opendoc.htm? tbl=BASICS&id=420 cc0432

United Nations High Commissioner for Refugees. (2006a). *Afghans in Pakistan get registered for first ever identification*. Retrieved from http://www.unhcr.org/news/NEWS/453391fd4.html

United Nations High Commissioner for Refugees. (2006b). *The state of the world's refugees 2006: Human displacement in the new millennium*. Retrieved from http://www.unhcr.org/cgi-bin/texis/vtx/publ/opendoc.htm?tbl=PUBL&id=4444d3cc2

United Nations High Commissioner for Refugees. (2011). The 1951 Convention relating to the status of refugees and its 1967 Protocol. Retrieved from http://www.unhcr.org/pages/49da0e466.html

United Nations High Commissioner for Refugees. (2012). *UNHCR Global Report 2011*. Retrieved from http://www.unhcr.org/4fd6f87f9.html

United Nations High Commissioner for Refugees. (2013a). *2013 UNHCR country operations profile—Thailand.* Retrieved from http://www.unhcr. org/cgi-bin/texis/vtx/page?page=49e489646&submit=GO

United Nations High Commissioner for Refugees. (2013b). *2013 UNHCR country operations profile—Pakistan.* Retrieved from http://www.unhcr. org/cgi-bin/texis/vtx/page?page=49e487016&submit=GO

United Nations High Commissioner for Refugees. (2013c). *2013 UNHCR regional operations profile—North America and the Caribbean.* Retrieved from http:// www.unhcr.org/cgi-bin/texis/vtx/page?page=49e492086&submit=GO

United Nations High Commissioner for Refugees. (2013d). *UNHCR Mission to Manus Island, Papua New Guinea.* Retrieved from http://unhcr.org.au/ unhcr/images/2013-02-04%20Manus%20Island%20Report%20Final.pdf

United Nations High Commissioner for Refugees. (2013e). *2013 UNHCR country operations profile—Colombia.* Retrieved from http://www.unhcr. org/pages/49e492ad6.html

United Nations High Commissioner for Refugees. (n.d.). *Asylum seekers.* Retrieved from http://www.unhcr.org/pages/49c3646c137.html

United Nations High Commissioner for Refugees—Thailand. (n.d.). *UNHCR Thailand.* Retrieved from http://unhcr.or.th/about/thailand

United Nations Security Council. (2012a). *Conflict-related sexual violence: Report of the Secretary-General.* Retrieved from http://www.unhcr. org/refworld/docid/4f27a19c2.html

United Nations Security Council. (2012b). *Children and armed conflict: Report of the Secretary-General.* Retrieved from http://childrenandarmedconflict. un.org/library/

United Nations Special Representative of the Secretary-General for Children and Armed Conflict. (2012). *Colombia.* Retrieved from http:// childrenandarmedconflict.un.org/countries/colombia/

United Nations Special Representative on Sexual Violence in Conflict. (2012a). *Press conference by Secretary-General's Special Representative on Sexual Violence in Conflict.* Retrieved from http://www.un.org/News/briefings/ docs/2012/121220_Bangura.doc.htm

United Nations Special Representative of the Secretary-General on Sexual Violence in Conflict (2012b). *Visit to Colombia.* Retrieved from http:// www.internal-displacement.org/8025708F004CE90B/(httpDocuments)/ 496B11B58A67B6D6C1257A530054E006/$file/FinalColombiaReport. pdf

United States Commission on International Religious Freedom. (2005). *Report on asylum seekers in expedited removal*. Retrieved from http://www.uscirf. gov/index.php?option=com_content&task=view&id=1892

Urrego, Z., Abaakouk, Z., Roman, C., & Contreras, R. (2009). Evaluation of results from a single session psychotherapeutic intervention in population affected by the Colombian internal armed conflict. *Médecins Sans Frontières*. Retrieved from http://hdl.handle.net/10144/223391

Vélez, O. R., & Bello, A. H. (2010). Family breakdown in Bogotá. *Forced Migration Review*, *34*, 69–70. Retrieved from http://repository.forcedmigration. org/show_metadata.jsp?pid=fmo:5618

Ward, J., & Marsh, M. (2006). *Sexual violence against women and girls in war and its aftermath: Realities, responses, and required resources*. Retrieved from http://www.unfpa.org/emergencies/symposium06/docs/finalbrussels briefingpaper.pdf

Wasem, R. E. (2011). Asylum and "credible fear" issues in U.S. immigration policy. *Congressional Research Service*. Retrieved from www.fas.org/sgp/ crs/homesec/R41753.pdf

World Bank. (2011). *GINI Index*. Retrieved from http://data.worldbank.org/ indicator/SI.POV.GINI

Zongwe, D. P. (2012). The new sexual violence legislation in the Congo: Dressing indelible scars on human dignity. *African Studies Review*, *24*(2), 37–57.

Zwi, A. B., Grove, N. J., Kelly, P., Gayer, M., Ramos-Jimenez, P., & Sommerfield, J. (2006). Child health in armed conflict: Time to rethink. *The Lancet*, *367*, 1886–1888.

Chapter Six

Adamczyk, A., & Grief, M. (2011). Education and risky sex in Africa: Unraveling the link between women's education and reproductive health behaviors in Kenya. *Social Science Research*, *40*, 654–666.

Agot, K. E., Stoep, A. V., Tracy, M., Obare, B. A., Bukusi, E. A., Ndinya-Achola, J. O.,…Weiss, N. S. (2010). Widow inheritance and HIV prevalence in Bondo district, Kenya: Baseline results from a prospective cohort study. *PLoS ONE*, *5*(11). Retrieved from http://www.plosone.org/article/ info:doi/10.1371/journal.pone.0014028

Aluisio, A., Richardson, B. A., Bosire, R., John-Stewart, G., Mbori-Ngacha, D., & Farquhar, C. (2011). Male antenatal attendance and HIV testing are associated with decreased infant HIV infection and increased HIV-free survival. *Journal of Acquired Immune Deficiency Syndrome, 56*(1), 76–82.

Asiedu, C., Asiedu, E., & Owusu, F. (2010). Young women's marital status and HIV risk in sub-Saharan Africa: Evidence from Lesotho, Swaziland and Zimbabwe. *Journal of African Development, 12*(2), 33–46.

Avert. (2013a). *Children, HIV, and AIDS*. Retrieved from http://www.avert.org/children.htm

Avert. (2013b). *AIDS, drug prices and generic drugs*. Retrieved from http://www.avert.org/generic.htm

Bajaj, M. (2009). Sugar daddies and the danger of sugar: Cross-generational relationships, HIV/AIDS, and secondary schooling in Zambia. *International Perspectives on Education and Society, 10*, 123–143.

Basic healthcare crucial to beating HIV, study. (2009, May 27). *IRIN News*. Retrieved from http://www.plusnews.org/PrintReport.aspx?ReportID=84567

Better paediatric HIV formulations. (2012, July 23). *IRIN News*. Retrieved from http://www.irinnews.org/PrintReport.aspx?ReportID=95933

Bharat, S. (2011). A systematic review of HIV/AIDS-related stigma and discrimination in India: Current understanding and future needs. *Journal of Social Aspects of HIV/AIDS, 8*(3), 138–149. Retrieved from http://www.ajol.info

Bhattacharya, G. (2004). Sociocultural and behavioral contexts of condom use in heterosexual married couples in India: Challenges to the HIV prevention program. *Health Education and Behavior, 31*(1), 101–117.

Birdthistle, I., Floyd, S., Nyagadza, A., Mudziwapasi, N., Gregson, S., & Glynn, J. R. (2009). Is education the link between orphanhood and HIV/HSV-2 risk among female adolescents in urban Zimbabwe? *Social Science & Medicine, 68*, 1810–1818.

Botswana women allowed to inherit. (2012, October 12). *BBC News*. Retrieved from http://www.bbc.co.uk

Bryceson, D. F., & Fonseca, J. (2005). *Risking death for survival: Peasant response to hunger and HIV/AIDS in Malawi*. Retrieved from http://www.ifpri.org/events/conferences/2005/durban/papers/brycesonWP.pdf

Busza, J. R., Balakireva, O. M., Teltschik, A., Bondar, T. V., Sereda, Y. V., Meynell, C., & Sakovych, O. (2011). Street-based children at high risk of HIV in Ukraine. *Journal of Epidemiology and Community Health, 65*(12), 1166–1170.

Cairns, G. (2013, March 4). *VOICE trial's disappointing result poses big questions for PrEP*. Retrieved from http://www.aidsmap.com/page/2586636/?utm_source=dlvr.it&utm_medium=twitter

Cash payments reduce risky behaviour. (2012, September 7). *IRIN News*. Retrieved from http://www.irinnews.org/PrintReport.aspx?ReportID=96264

Centers for Disease Control. (2012). *Malawi*. Retrieved from http://www.cdc.gov/globalaids/Global-HIV-AIDS-at-CDC/countries/Malawi

Central Intelligence Agency (CIA). (2013). *Malawi*. Retrieved from https://www.cia.gov/library/publications/the-world-factbook/geos/mi.html

Cockcroft, A., Kunda, J. L., Kgakole, L., Masisi, M., Laetsang, D., Ho-Foster, A.,...Andersson, N. (2010). Community views of inter-generational sex: Findings from focus groups in Botswana, Namibia and Swaziland. *Psychology, Health & Medicine, 15*(5), 507–514.

Commission on HIV/AIDS and governance in Africa. (n.d.). *The impacts of HIV/AIDS on families and communities in Africa*. Retrieved from http://repository.uneca.org/handle/10855/5541

Condoms continue to confound Uganda. (2013, March 1). *IRIN News*. Retrieved from http://www.irinnews.org/Report/97573/Analysis-Condoms-continue-to-confound-Uganda

Criminalization of sex work hinders HIV prevention efforts. (2011, November 17). *IRIN News*. Retrieved from http://www.plusnews.org/PrintReport.aspx?ReportID=94231

Crissman, H. P., Adanu, R. M., & Harlow, S. D. (2012). Women's sexual empowerment and contraceptive use in Ghana. *Studies in Family Planning, 43*(3), 201–212.

Curnow, R., & Watts, J. (2013, March 21). Lawyer fights "widow sex" tradition in Malawi. *CNN*. Retrieved from http://www.cnn.com/2013/03/21/world/africa/seodi-white-women-malawi

D'Adesky, A. (2004). *Moving mountains: The race to treat global AIDS*. New York, NY: Verso.

D'Agnes, T. (2001). *From condoms to cabbages: An authorized biography of Mechai Viravaidya*. Bangkok, Thailand: Post Books.

Department of Social Development, South African Social Security Agency, & UNICEF. (2012). *The South African child support grant impact assessment*. Retrieved from http://www.unicef.org/southafrica/SAF_resources_csg2012s.pdf

Doctors Without Borders. (2005). *MSF's projects for people with HIV/AIDS.* Retrieved from http://www.doctorswithoutborders.org/news/hiv-aids/hiv-aids.htm

Doctors Without Borders. (2011). *International Activity Report 2011—Malwai.* Retrieved from http://www.doctorswithoutborders.org/publications/ar/report.cfm?id=6210

El-Bassel, N., Gilbert, L., Terlikbayeva, A., West, B., Bearman, P., Wu, E.,...Brisson, A. (2011). Implications of mobility patterns and HIV risks for HIV prevention among migrant market workers in Kazakhstan. *American Journal of Public Health, 101*(6), 1075–1081.

Eliminate bottlenecks to end mother-to-child HIV transmission. (2010, May 28). *IRIN News.* Retrieved from http://www.plusnews.org/PrintReport.aspx?ReportID=89281

Farmer, P. (2005). *Pathologies of power: Health, human rights, and the new war on the poor.* Los Angeles, CA: University of California Press.

Farmer, P. E., Nutt, C. T., Wagner, C. M., Sekabaraga, C., Nuthulaganti, T., Weigel, J. L.,...Drobac, P. C. (2013). Reduced premature mortality in Rwanda: Lessons from success. *BMJ, 346.* Retrieved from http://www.bmj.com/content/346/bmj.f65

Fattah, H. M. (2006, August 8). Saudi Arabia begins to face its hidden AIDS problem. *New York Times,* p. A3.

Ford, E. (2010, March 27). Chinese demand for Durex condoms boosts SSL sales. *The Times.* Retrieved from http://www.thetimes.co.uk

Furin, J. J., Behforouz, H. L., Shin, S. S., Mukherjee, J. S., Bayona, J., Farmer, P. E.,...Keshavjee, S. (2008). Expanding global HIV treatment: Case studies from the field. *Annals of the New York Academy of Sciences, 1136,* 12–20.

Gausset, Q. (2001). AIDS and cultural practices in Africa: The case of the Tonga (Zambia). *Social Science and Medicine, 52,* 509–518.

Hageman, K. M., Dube, H. M. B., Mugurungi, O., Gavin, L. E., Hader, S. L., & St. Louis, M. E. (2010). Beyond monogamy: Opportunities to further reduce risk for HIV infection among married Zimbabwean women with only one lifetime partner. *AIDS and Behavior, 14*(1), 113–124.

Hallfors, D. D., Cho, H., Mbai, I., Milimo, B., & Itindi, J. (2012). Process and outcome evaluation of a community intervention for orphan adolescents in western Kenya. *Journal of Community Health, 37*(5), 1101–1109.

Hallfors, D. D., Cho, H., Rusakaniko, S., Iritani, B., Mapfumo, J., &Halpern, C. (2011). Supporting adolescent orphan girls to stay in school as HIV risk prevention: Evidence from a randomized controlled trial in Zimbabwe. *American Journal of Public Health, 101*(6), 1082–1088.

Heffron, R., Donnell, D., Rees, H., Celum, C., Mugo, N., Were, E.,…Baeton, J. M. (2012). Use of hormonal contraceptives and risk of HIV-1 transmission: A prospective cohort study. *The Lancet Infectious Diseases, 12*(1), 19–26.

Hindin, M. J., & Fatusi, A. O. (2009). Adolescent sexual and reproductive health in developing countries: An overview of trends and interventions. *International Perspectives on Sexual and Reproductive Health, 35*(2), 58–62.

HIV-positive people battle health care discrimination. (2011, August 31). *IRIN News.* Retrieved from http://www.plusnews.org/PrintReport. aspx?ReportID=93624

HIV stigma still a barrier. (2012, November 12). *IRIN News.* Retrieved from http://www.plusnews.org/PrintReport.aspx?ReportID=96761

Human Rights Watch. (2005). *The less they know, the better: Abstinence-only HIV/ AIDS programs in Uganda.* Retrieved from http://hrw.org/reports/2005/ uganda0305/uganda0305.pdf

Indonesia to override patents for live-saving medicines. (2013, March 25). *IRIN News.* Retrieved from http://www.plusnews.org/PrintReport. aspx?ReportID=97728

Insensitive health workers drive pregnant HIV-positive women away. (2009, June 15). *IRIN News.* Retrieved from http://www.plusnews.org/Print Report.aspx?ReportID=84838

Jacobs, A. (2010, November 13). Law banning discrimination over H.I.V. fails in China. *New York Times,* p. A5.

Kanabus, A. (2005). *HIV and AIDS in China.* Retrieved from http://www. avert.org/aidschina.htm

Kanabus, A., & Fredriksson, J. (2005). *HIV and AIDS in Thailand.* Retrieved from http://www.avert.org/aidsthai.htm

Kang, M., Dunbar, M., Laver, S., & Padian, N. (2008). Maternal versus paternal orphans and HIV/STI risk among adolescent girls in Zimbabwe. *AIDS Care, 20*(2), 221–224.

Karmacharya, D., Yu, D., Dixit, S., Rajbhandari, R., Subedi, B., Shrestha, S.,…Santangelo, S. L. (2012). A study of the prevalence and risk factors leading to HIV infection among a sample of street children and youth of Kathmandu. *AIDS Research and Therapy, 9.* Retrieved from http://www. aidsrestherapy.com/content/9/1/25

Kenya condom advert pulled after religious complaints. (2013, March 20). *BBC News*. Retrieved from http://www.bbc.co.uk/news/world-africa-21859665

Kidder, T. (2003). *Mountains beyond mountains: The quest of Dr. Paul Farmer, a man who would cure the world.* New York, NY: Random House.

Kim, J., Ferrari, G., Abramsky, T., Watts, C., Hargreaves, J., Morison, L., ... Pronyk, P. (2009). Assessing the incremental effects of combining economic and health interventions: The IMAGE study in South Africa. *Bulletin of the World Health Organization, 87*, 824–832.

Lacey, M. (2008, August 7). Vulnerable to HIV, resistant to labels. *New York Times*. Retrieved from http://www.nytimes.com

LaFraniere, S. (2004, June 14). Mandatory tests bolster Botswana's war on AIDS. *New York Times*. Retrieved from http://www.nytimes.com

LaFraniere, S. (2005, December 30). Women's rights laws and African custom clash. *New York Times*. Retrieved from http://www.nytimes.com

Levin, D. (2013, January 2). In China, grass-roots groups take on H.I.V./AIDS outreach work. *New York Times*. Retrieved from http://www.nytimes.com

Lim, S., & Cameron, M. (2004). *Reducing HIV/AIDS prevalence: A dynamic model of labour migration in Northeast Thailand*. Paper presented at the annual conference of the New Zealand Association of Economists, Wellington, New Zealand. Retrieved from http://www.nzae.org.nz/conferences/2004/95-Lim-Cameron.pdf

Lwanda, J. (2003). The (in)visibility of HIV/AIDS in the Malawi public sphere. *African Journal of AIDS Research, 2*(2), 113–126.

Lwanda, J. (2005). *Politics, culture and medicine in Malawi: Historical continuities and ruptures with special references to HIV/AIDS*. Zomba, Malawi: Kachere Series.

Lwanda, J. L. (2004). Politics, culture, and medicine: An unholy trinity? Historical continuities and ruptures in the HIV/AIDS story in Malawi. In E. Kalipeni, S. Craddock, J. R. Oppong, & J. Ghosh (Eds.), *HIV and AIDS in Africa: Beyond epidemiology* (pp. 29–42). Malden, MA: Blackwell Publishers.

Makofane, K., Gueboguo, C., Lyons, D., & Sandfort, T. (2013). Men who have sex with men inadequately addressed in African AIDS National Strategic Plans. *Global Public Health, 8*(2), 129–143.

Malawi Government. (2012). *2012 Global AIDS response progress report: Malawi country report for 2012 and 2011*. Retrieved from http://www.unaids.org/en/dataanalysis/knowyourresponse/countryprogressreports/2012countries/ce_MW_Narrative_Report[1].pdf

Malawi's never-ending drug shortage problem. (2013, February 19). *IRIN* News. Retrieved from http://www.irinnews.org/printreport.aspx?reportid=97503

Mass male circumcision—what will it mean for women? (2007, July 24). *IRIN News*. Retrieved from http://www.irinnews.org/printreport.aspx?reportid=73285

McClanahan, P. (2013, June 10). Poorest countries eye additional grace period on intellectual property rules. *The Guardian*. Retrieved from http://www.guardian.co.uk

McCoy, D., Chopra, M., Loewenson, R., Aitken, J., Ngulube, T., Muula, A....Rowson, M. (2005). Expanding access to antiretroviral therapy in sub-Saharan Africa: Avoiding the pitfalls and dangers, capitalizing on the opportunities. *American Journal of Public Health, 95*(1), 18–22.

Médecins Sans Frontières. (2011). *Newer drugs are priced out of reach*. Retrieved from http://www.msfaccess.org/our-work/hiv-aids/article/1342

Mhaka-Mutepfa, M. (2010). Types of services for children infected and affected by HIV and AIDS: Results and implications of a Zimbabwean study. *International Journal of Psychology and Counselling, 2*(6), 100–106.

Migrant sex workers off the HIV prevention radar. (2012, May 31). *IRIN News*. Retrieved from http://www.irinnews.org/PrintReport.aspx?ReportID=95561

Miller, T., Hallfors, D., Cho, H., Luseno, W., & Waehrer, G. (2013). Cost-effectiveness of school support for orphan girls to prevent HIV infection in Zimbabwe. *Prevention Science, 14*, 503–512. doi: 10.1007/s11121-012-0315-0

Ministry of Health-Botswana. (2012). *HIV counseling and testing programme*. Retrieved from http://www.hiv.gov.bw/content/hiv-counseling-and-testing-programme

Ministry of Health, Kingdom of Saudi Arabia. (2012). *UNGASS country progress report 2012*. Retrieved from http://www.unaids.org/en/dataanalysis/knowyourresponse/countryprogressreports/2012countries/Final%20Version%20Narrative%20Report_Saudi%20Arabia.pdf

Mkandawire, P., Tenkorang, E., & Luginaah, I. N. (2013). Orphan status and time to first sex among adolescents in northern Malawi. *AIDS and Behavior, 17*(3), 939–950.

Mkandawire-Valhmu, L. Wendland, C., Stevens, P. E., Kako, P. M., Dressel, A., & Kibicho, J. (2013). Marriage as a risk factor for HIV: Learning from the experiences of HIV-infected women in Malawi. *Global Public Health, 8*(2), 187–201.

Mmari, K., Michaelis, A., & Kiro, K. (2009). Risk and protective factors for HIV among orphans and non-orphans in Tanzania. *Culture, Health, & Sexuality*, *11*(8), 799–809.

Mother-to-child HIV transmission still falling. (2012, July 23). *IRIN News*. Retrieved from http://www.irinnews.org/PrintReport.aspx?ReportID=95929

Muslim clerics declare war on condoms. (2008, May 12). *IRIN News*. Retrieved from http://www.irinnews.org/Report/78160/KENYA-Muslim-clerics-declare-war-on-condoms

Mutume, G. (2001). Malawi battles AIDS orphan nightmare. *Africa Recovery*. Retrieved from http://www.un.org/ecosocdeve/geninfo/afrec/vol15no3/153chil5.htm

Nada, K. H., & Suliman, E. D. A. (2010). Violence, abuse, alcohol and drug use and sexual behaviors in street children of Greater Cairo and Alexandria, Egypt. *AIDS, 24*(Supplement 2), S39–S44.

Naicker, S., Plange-Rhule, J., Tutt, R. C., & Eastwood, J. B. (2009). Shortage of health care workers in developing countries—Africa. *Ethnicity & Disease, 19*, S1-60–S1-64.

National AIDS Commission. (2003). *HIV/AIDS in Malawi*. Retrieved from http://www.synergyaids.com/documents/MAL_AIDS.pdf

New ARV tender drops prices, changes treatment. (2012, November 30). *IRIN News*. Retrieved from http://www.plusnews.org/PrintReport.aspx?ReportID=96930

New light shed on male sex work. (2011, June 20). *IRIN News*. Retrieved from http://www.plusnews.org/PrintReport.aspx?ReportID=93018

New WHO guidelines urge decriminalization of sex work. (2012, December 18). *IRIN News*. Retrieved from http://www.plusnews.org/PrintReport.aspx?ReportID=97077

Nullis, C. (2005, May 6). South African official touts nutrition over anti-AIDS drugs. *The Patriot News*, p. A12.

Oyefara, J. L. (2007). Food insecurity, HIV/AIDS pandemic and sexual behavior of female commercial sex workers in Lagos metropolis, Nigeria. *Journal of Social Aspects of HIV/AIDS, 4*(2), 626–635.

Partners in Health. (2005). *Rwanda: Project overview*. Retrieved from http://www.pih.org/wherewework/rwanda/index.html

Partners in Health. (2013a). *Our work*. Retrieved from http://www.pih.org/our-work

Partners in Health. (2013b). *HIV/AIDS*. Retrieved from http://www.pih.org/priority-programs/hiv-aids/about

Partners in Health. (2013c). *Health on wheels: How dirt bikes help hard-to-reach patients in Malawi*. Retrieved from http://www.pih.org/blog/health-on-wheels-how-dirt-bikes-help-hard-to-reach-patients-in-malawi

Partners in Health. (n.d.). *Haiti*. Retrieved from http://www.pih.org/country/haiti/about

Pettifor, A., MacPhail, C., Nguyen, N., & Rosenberg, M. (2012). Can money prevent the spread of HIV? A review of cash payments for HIV prevention. *AIDS and Behavior, 16*, 1729–1738.

Phiri, Z. (2002). *Inculturating African widowhood rites*. Retrieved from http://www.jctr.org.zm/bulletins/incult-widows.htm

Plusnews. (2003, March 28). *Traditional culture spreading HIV/AIDS*. Retrieved from http://new.hst.org.za/news/index.php/20030401

Protecting widows from dangerous customs. (2007, June 19). *IRIN News*. Retrieved from http://www.irinnews.org/PrintReport.aspx?ReportID=72821

Push to meet 2013 male circumcision targets. (2012, November 6). *IRIN News*. Retrieved from http://www.plusnews.org/PrintReport.aspx?ReportID=96717

Queer Malawi lifts the gay curtain. (2011, May 11). *IRIN News*. Retrieved from http://www.plusnews.org/PrintReport.aspx?ReportID=92681

Rajaraman, D., Russell, S., & Heymann, J. (2006). HIV/AIDS, income loss and economic survival in Botswana. *AIDS Care, 18*(7), 656–662.

Rankin, S. H., Lindgren, T., Rankin, W. W., & Ng'oma, J. (2005). Donkey work: Women, religion and HIV/AIDS in Malawi. *Health Care for Women International, 26*, 4–16.

Reducing the HIV risk of girls living on the street. (2012, May 8). *IRIN News*. Retrieved from http://www.irinnews.org/PrintReport.aspx?ReportID=95427

Rimal, R. N., Böse, K., Brown, J., Mkandawire, G., & Folda, L. (2009). Extending the purview of the risk perception attitude framework: Findings from HIV/AIDS prevention research in Malwai. *Health Communication, 24*, 210–218.

Rosenberg, T. (2006, August 6). When a pill is not enough. *New York Times*. Retrieved from http://www.nytimes.com

Rowan, D., & Kabwira, D. B. (2009). Empowering HIV/AIDS orphans through teaching vocational trades: A SWOT analysis of a community-based orphan training program in Malawi. *Journal of Global Social Work Practice, 2*(1). Retrieved from http://www.globalsocialwork.org/vol2no1_Rowan.html

Sáez-Cirión, A., Bacchus, C., Hocqueloux, L., Avettand-Fenoel, V., Girault I., Lecuroux, C.,...the ANRS VISCONTI Study Group. (2013).

Post-treatment HIV-1 controllers with a long-term virological remission after the interruption of early initiated antiretroviral therapy ANRS VISCONTI Study. *PLoS Pathogens, 9*(3), e1003211.

Shaban, N. (2012, May). *The role of cash transfers in Kenya in empowering women and girls and reducing their vulnerability and impact to HIV and AIDS.* Presented at the 2012 GlobalPOWER Women Network African conference, Harare, Zimbabwe. Retrieved from http://www.globalpower-womennetworkafrica.org/wp-content/uploads/2012/05/The-role-of-cash-transfers-in-empowering-women-and-girls-and-their-vulnerability-to-HIV-in-Kenya.pdf

Solving health worker shortages. (2008, October 1). *IRIN News.* Retrieved from http://www.irinews.org/PrintReport.aspx?ReportID=80698

Stigma hinders participation in clinical HIV trials. (2011, December 21). *IRIN News.* Retrieved from http://www.plusnews.org/PrintReport.aspx?ReportID=94513

Stockman, J. K., Lucea, M. B., & Campbell, J. C. (2013). Forced sexual initiation, sexual intimate partner violence and HIV risk in women: A global review of the literature. *AIDS and Behavior, 17*(3), 832–847.

Study shows HIV stigma a barrier to health facility births. (2012, September 10). *IRIN News.* Retrieved from http://www.plusnews.org/PrintReport.aspx?ReportID=96279

Sunmola, A. M. (2005). Sexual practices, barriers to condom use and its consistent use among long distance truck drivers in Nigeria. *AIDS Care, 17*(2), 208–221.

Supply the main challenge in male circumcision. (2012, May 30). *IRIN News.* Retrieved from http://www.plusnews.org/PrintReport.aspx?ReportID=95551

Survey reveals gaps in HIV programming for MSM. (2011, July 14). *IRIN News.* Retrieved from http://www.plusnews.org/PrintReport.aspx?ReportID=93230

Tamboli, B. L. (2010). Role of unmanned condoms depots in promotion of condoms in the community during HIV/AIDS epidemic in India. *National Journal of Community Medicine, 1*(2), 118–121.

Taylor-Smith, K., Tweya, H., Harries, A., Schoutene, E., & Jahn, A. (2010). Gender differences in retention and survival on antiretroviral therapy of HIV-1 infected adults in Malawi. *Malawi Medical Journal, 22*(2), 49–56.

Tenkorang, E. (2012). Negotiating safer sex among married women in Ghana. *Archives of Sexual Behavior, 41*(6), 1353–1362.

The downside of male involvement in PMTCT. (2012, January 16). *IRIN News*. Retrieved from http://www.irinnews.org/PrintReport. aspx?ReportID=94652

Tlilane, N. K. (2004). Healthcare funding problems in Algeria. *International Social Security Review, 57*, 91–110.

Ugandan HIV campaign targets "cheaters." (2013, January 23). *IRIN News*. Retrieved from http://www.plusnews.org/PrintReport.aspx?ReportID= 97317

UNAIDS. (2004). *UNAIDS at country level*. Retrieved from http://www.unaids. org/en/Regions_Countries/Countries/malawi.asp

UNAIDS. (2005a). *Women and girls bear brunt of AIDS worldwide, UN rights experts recall*. Retrieved from http://www.unhchr.ch/huricane/huricane. nsf/view01/74F1E47D756C89E5C12570CA003 357F7?opendocument

UNAIDS. (2005b). *AIDS in Africa: Three scenarios to 2025*. Retrieved from http://www.unaids.org/unaids_resources/images/AIDSScenarios/ AIDS-scenarios-2025_report_en.pdf

UNAIDS. (2005c). *The female AIDS epidemic: 2005*. Retrieved from http:// womenandaids.unaids.org/womenandaidsnovfin.doc

UNAIDS. (2006). *2006 report on the global AIDS epidemic*. Retrieved from http://www.unaids.org/en/HIV_data/2006GlobalReport/default.asp

UNAIDS. (2011). *Synthesis of strategic information on HIV and young people*. Retrieved from http://www.unaids.org/en/media/unaids/contentassets/ documents/unaidspublication/2011/20110727_JC2112_Synthesis_ report_en.pdf

UNAIDS. (2011b). *Malawi*. Retrieved from http://www.unaids.org/en/ regionscountries/countries/malawi/

UNAIDS. (2012a). *UNAIDS report on the global AIDS epidemic 2012*. Retrieved from http://www.unaids.org/en/media/unaids/contentassets/ documents/epidemiology/2012/gr2012/20121120_UNAIDS_Global_ Report_2012_with_annexes_en.pdf

UNAIDS. (2012b). *Women out loud: How women living with HIV will help the world end AIDS*. Retrieved from http://www.unaids.org/en/media/unaids/ contentassets/documents/unaidspublication/2012/20121211_Women_ Out_Loud_en.pdf

UNAIDS. (2012c). *Thailand*. Retrieved from http://www.unaids.org/en/ regionscountries/countries/thailand/

UNAIDS. (n.d.a). *Preventing HIV infection in girls and young women*. Retrieved from http://data.unaids.org/gcwa/gcwa_bg_prevention_en.pdf

UNAIDS. (n.d.b). *Economic security for women fights AIDS*. Retrieved from http://data.unaids.org/pub/BriefingNote/2006/20060308_bn_gcwa_en.pdf

UNAIDS & the Athena Network. (2011). *Community innovation: Achieving sexual and reproductive health and rights for women and girls through the HIV response*. Retrieved from http://www.unaids.org/en/media/unaids/contentassets/documents/document/2011/07/20110719_Community%20innovation.pdf

UNICEF. (2012a). *Global and regional trends*. Retrieved from http://www.childinfo.org/hiv_aids.html

UNICEF. (2012b). *Prevention of infection among adolescents and young people*. Retrieved from http://www.childinfo.org/hiv_aids_young_people.html

UNICEF. (2012c). *Provide paeditric treatment*. Retrieved from http://www.childinfo.org/hiv_aids_treatment_care.html

UNICEF. (n.d.a). *China: "Four frees and one care."* Retrieved from http://www.unicef.org

UNICEF. (n.d.b). *Malawi: Monica's struggle for education*. Retrieved from http://www.unicef.org

United Nations Development Programme (UNDP). (2013). *2013 human development report*. Retrieved from http://www.undp.org/content/undp/en/home/librarypage/hdr/human-development-report-2013

United Nations Development Programme (UNDP). (n.d.). *HIV/AIDS in Africa*. Retrieved from http://web.undp.org

Van, K., & Dung, T. (2006, February 8). Street children miss HIV/AIDS fight. *VietNam News*. Retrieved from http://www.asianews net.net/print_template.php?news_id=52190&13sec=12

Vasavya Mahila Mandali. (2009). *Second innings: A report on pioneering responses to grannies affected by HIV/AIDS in Andhra Pradesh, India*. Retrieved from http://www.ovcsupport.net/s/library.php?ld=1057

Waldman, A. (2005, December 6). On India's roads, cargo and a deadly passenger. *New York Times*. Retrieved from LexisNexis database.

Where is HIV/AIDS on Banda's to-do list? (2012, June 6). *IRIN News*. Retrieved from http://www.plusnews.org/PrintReport.aspx?ReportID=95594

Wood, E. B. (2010). HIV-related sexual risk behaviours among late-adolescent Jamaican girls with older male partners. *West Indian Medical Journal*, *59*(4), 403–408.

World Bank. (2013). *Malawi*. Retrieved from http://data.worldbank.org/country/malawi#cp_wdi

World Food Programme. (n.d.). *Malawi*. Retrieved from http://www.wfp.org/countries/malawi/overview

World Health Organization. (2010). Thailand's new condom crusade. *Bulletin of the World Health Organization, 88*(6). Retrieved from http://www.who.int/bulletin/volumes/88/6/10-010610/en/

World Health Organization. (2011). *Prevention and treatment of HIV and other sexually transmitted infections among men who have sex with men and transgender people: Recommendations for a public health approach*. Retrieved from http://whqlibdoc.who.int/publications/2011/9789241501750_eng.pdf

Wyrod, R., Fritz, K., Woelk, G., Jain, S., Kellogg, T., Chirowodza, A., ... McFarland, W. (2011). Beyond sugar daddies: Intergenerational sex and AIDS in urban Zimbabwe. *AIDS and Behavior, 15*, 1275–1282.

Young, M. R., Odoyo-June, E., Nordstrom, S. K., Irwin, T. E., Ongong'a, D. O., Ochomo, B., ... Bailey, R. C. (2012). Factors associated with uptake of infant male circumcision for HIV prevention in western Kenya. *Pediatrics, 130*(1), e175–e182.

Zhao, Q., Li, X., Kaljee, L. M., Fang, X., Stanton, B., & Zhang, L. (2009). AIDS orphanages in China: Reality and challenges. *AIDS Patient Care and STDs, 23*(4), 297–303. doi: 10.1089/apc.2008.0190

Zuilkowski, S. S., & Jukes, M. C. H. (2011). The impact of education on sexual behavior in sub-Saharan Africa: A review of the evidence. *AIDS Care, 24*(5), 562–576.

Chapter Seven

Abdelmoneium, A. O. (2005). Challenges facing children in education and labour: Case study of displaced children in Khartoum-Sudan. *Ahfad Journal, 22*(2), 64–76.

Afghan women navigate a challenging judicial landscape. (2013, March 12). *IRIN News*. Retrieved from http://www.irinnews.org/printreport.aspx?reportid=97631

Afkhami, M. (2001). Gender apartheid, cultural relativism, and women's human rights in Muslim societies. In M. Agosín (Ed.), *Women, gender and human rights: A global perspective* (pp. 234–245). New Brunswick, NJ: Rutgers University Press.

Agosín, M. (2001). Introduction. In M. Agosín (Ed.), *Women, gender and human rights: A global perspective* (pp. 1–11). New Brunswick, NJ: Rutgers University Press.

Ahmed, S. M. (2009). Capability development among the ultra-poor in Bangladesh: A case study. *Journal of Health, Population and Nutrition, 27*(4), 528–535.

Almond, D., & Edlund, L. (2008). Son-biased sex ratios in the 2000 United States Census. *PNAS: Proceedings of the National Academy of Sciences, 105*(15), 5681–5682.

Ashraf, N., Karlan, D., & Yin, W. (2010). Female empowerment: Impact of a commitment savings product in the Philippines. *World Development, 38*(3), 333–344.

Ayton-Shenker, D. (1995). *The challenge of human rights and cultural relativism.* Retrieved from http://www.un.org/rights/dpi1627e.htm

Azhar, N. (2012). *Violence against women in Pakistan.* Retrieved from http://www.af.org.pk/PDF/VAW%20Reports%20AND%20PR/Violence%20Against%20Women%20Annual%20Report%202011.pdf

Balatchandirane, G. (2003). Gender discrimination in education and economic development: A study of South Korea, China and India. *International Studies, 40*(4), 349–378.

Ban term "bride price." (2013, February 4). *New Vision.* Retrieved from LexisNexis database.

Ban welcomes UN General Assembly resolutions eliminating female genital mutilation. *UN News Centre.* Retrieved from http://www.un.org/apps/news/printnews.asp?nid=43839

Banda, F. (2008). *Project on a mechanism to address laws that discriminate against women.* Retrieved from http://www.ohchr.org/Documents/Publications/laws_that_discriminate_against_women.pdf

Basargekar, P. (2010). Measuring effectiveness of social capital in microfinance: A case study of urban microfinance in India. *International Journal of Social Inquiry, 3*(2), 25–43.

Basher, A. (2007). Empowerment of microcredit participants and its spillover effects: Evidence from the Grameen Bank of Bangladesh. *The Journal of Developing Areas, 40*(2), 173–183.

Bedi, R. (2012, February 27). Indian dowry deaths on the rise. *The Telegraph.* Retrieved from http://www.telegraph.co.uk

Benard, C. (2002). *Veiled courage: Inside the Afghan women's resistance.* New York, NY: Broadway Books.

Bernasek, A. (2003). Banking on social change: Grameen Bank lending to women. *International Journal of Politics, Culture and Society, 16*(3), 369–385.

Bhatt, E. (2006). *We are poor but so many: The story of self-employed women in India*. New York, NY: Oxford University Press.

Bilefsky, D. (2006, July 16). How to avoid honor killing in Turkey? Honor suicide. *New York Times*. Retrieved from http://www.nytimes.com

Botswana women allowed to inherit. (2012, October 12). *BBC News*. Retrieved from http://www.bbc.co.uk

Branigan, T. (2011, November 2). China's great gender crisis. *The Guardian*. Retrieved from http://www.guardian.co.uk

Breakthrough in Saudi Arabia: Women allowed in Parliament. (2013, January 11). *Al Arabiya*. Retrieved from http://english.alarabiya.net/articles/2013/01/11/259881.html

Bridging the north-south maternal death divide. (2012, July 6). *IRIN News*. Retrieved from http://www.irinnews.org/printreport.aspx?reportid=95812

Brodsky, A. (2003). *With all our strength*. New York, NY: Routledge.

Bronner, E., & Kershner, I. (2012, January 14). Israelis facing a seismic rift over role of women. *New York Times*. Retrieved from http://www.nytimes.com

Broom, A., Sibbritt, D., Nayar, K. R., Doron, A., & Nilan, P. (2012). Men's experiences of family, domestic and honour-related violence in Gujarat and Uttar Pradesh, India. *Asian Social Science, 8*(6), 3–10.

Cash incentives for raising girls. (2008, March 4). *New York Times*, p. A10.

Central Intelligence Agency (CIA). (2013). *The world factbook: Bangladesh*. Retrieved from https://www.cia.gov/library/publications/the-world-factbook/geos/bg.html

Chemin, M. (2008). The benefits and costs of microfinance: Evidence from Bangladesh. *Journal of Development Studies, 44*(4), 463–484.

Chesler, P. (2010). Worldwide trends in honor killings. *Middle East Quarterly, 17*(2), 3–11.

Chun, H., & Gupta, M. D. (2009). Gender discrimination in sex selective abortions and its transition in South Korea. *Women's Studies International, 32*, 89–97.

Chung, W., & Gupta, M. D. (2007). The decline of son preference in South Korea: The roles of development and public policy. *Population and Development Review, 33*(4), 757–783.

Coleman, I. (2005). Development: The payoff from women's rights. In R. J. Griffiths (Ed.), *Developing World 05/06: Annual editions* (pp. 191–196). Dubuque, IA: McGraw/Hill.

Csillag, R. (2012). Canadian imans declare fatwa against "honor killings." *Christian Century, 129*(5), 19.

Demand-side financing bolsters maternal health. (2012, July 19). *IRIN News*. Retrieved from http://www.irinnews.org/printreport.aspx?reportid=95898

Dennis, S., & Anderson, S (2009). *US government renews commitment to Cairo; Increases funding for ICPD*. Retrieved from http://populationaction.org/2009/04/08/us_government_renews_commitmen/

Develtere, P., & Huybrechts, A. (2005). The impact of microcredit on the poor of Bangladesh. *Alternatives, 30,* 165–189.

Devraj, R. (2003). *A murderous arithmetic*. Retrieved from http://www.indiatogether.org/2003/jul/wom-girls.htm

Diop, N. J., & Askew, I. (2009). The effectiveness of a community-based education program on abandoning female genital mutilation/cutting in Senegal. *Studies in Family Planning, 40*(4), 307–318.

Easton, P., Monkman, K., & Miles, R. (2003). Social policy from the bottom up: Abandoning FGC in sub-Saharan Africa. *Development in Practice, 13*(5), 445–458.

FGM/C regulations mistaken for endorsement, experts fear. (2011, September 1). *IRIN News*. Retrieved from http://www.irinnews.org/printreport.aspx?reportid=93628

Fighting for women's right to land. (2012, June 22). *IRIN News*. Retrieved from http://www.irinnews.org/printreport.aspx?reportid=95705

Freeman, M. A. (2009). *Reservations to CEDAW: An analysis for UNICEF*. Retrieved from http://www.unicef.org/gender/files/Reservations_to_CEDAW-an_Analysis_for_UNICEF.pdf

Gakidou, E., Cowling, K., Lozano, R., & Murray, C. (2010). Increased educational attainment and its effect on child mortality in 175 countries between 1970 and 2009: A systematic analysis. *Lancet, 376,* 959–974.

Girl's death prompts search for new strategies to fight FGM. (2007, September 27). *IRIN News*. Retrieved from http://www.irinnews.org/printreport.aspx?reportid=74529

Grameen Bank. (2002). *A short history of Grameen Bank*. Retrieved from http://www.grameen-info.org/bank/hist.html

Grameen Bank. (2011). *Grameen Bank*. Retrieved from http://www.grameen-info.org/index.php?option=com_content&task=view&id=26&Itemid=175

Grameen Bank. (n.d.). *The 16 decisions of Grameen Bank*. Retrieved from http://www.grameen-info.org/index.php?option=com_content&task=view&id=22&Itemid=109

Grameen Bank. (2013). *10 indicators*. Retrieved from http://www.grameen-info. org/index.php?option=com_content&task=view&id=23&Itemid=126

Hackett, M. (2011). Domestic violence against women: Statistical analysis of crimes across India. *Journal of Comparative Family Studies, 42*(2), 267–288.

Haile, H. B., Bock, B., & Folmer, H. (2012). Microfinance and female empowerment: Do institutions matter? *Women's Studies International Forum, 35,* 256–265.

Harding, L. (2012). Saudi Arabia criticized over text alerts tracking women's movements. *The Guardian.* Retrieved from http://www.guardian.co.uk/ world/2012/nov/23/saudi-arabia-text-alerts-women/print

Hayford, S. R. (2005). Conformity and change: Community effects on female genital cutting in Kenya. *Journal of Health and Social Behavior, 46*(2), 121–140.

Hesketh, T., Lu, L., & Xing, Z. W. (2011). The consequences of son preference and sex-selective abortion in China and other Asian countries. *Canadian Medical Association Journal, 183*(12), 1374–1377.

The hidden costs of early marriage. (2012, June 15). *IRIN News.* Retrieved from http://www.irinnews.org/printreport.aspx?reportid=95654

Hogan, M., C., Foreman, K. J., Naghavi, M., Ahn, S. Y., Wang, M. Maleka, S. M.,…Murray, C. J. L. (2010). Maternal mortality for 181 countries, 1980–2008: A systematic analysis of progress towards Millennium Development Goal 5. *The Lancet, 375,* 1609–1623. doi: 10.1016/ S0140-6736(10)60518-1

Homolo, V. (2006, April 14). Turkish man sentenced in "honor killing" of sister. *New York Times.* Retrieved from http://www.nytimes.com

Hoque, M., & Itohara, Y. (2009). Women empowerment through participation in micro-credit programme: A case study from Bangladesh. *Journal of Social Sciences, 5*(3), 244–250.

Human Rights Watch. (2006). *Forms of violence against women in Pakistan.* Retrieved from http://www.hrw.org/campaigns/pakistan/.forms.htm

Human Rights Watch. (2011). "He loves you, he beats you": Family violence in Turkey and access to protection. Retrieved from http://www.hrw.org/ sites/default/files/reports/turkey0511webwcover.pdf

Human Rights Watch. (2012). *"I had to run away": Women and girls imprisoned for "moral crimes" in Afghanistan.* Retrieved from http://www.hrw.org/ sites/default/files/reports/afghanistan0312webwcover_0.pdf

Hvistendahl, M. (2011). *Unnatural selection: Choosing boys over girls, and the consequences of a world full of men.* Jackson, TN: Public Affairs.

International Center for Research on Women. (2007). *How to end child marriage: Action strategies for prevention and protection*. Retrieved from http://www.icrw.org/files/publications/How-to-End-Child-Marriage-Action-Strategies-for-Prevention-and-Protection-Brief.pdf

Islam, A., & Choe, C. (2013). Child labor and schooling responses to access to microcredit in rural Bangladesh. *Economic Inquiry, 51*(1), 46–61.

Jackson, S. (2013, July 14). Gender equality funds must go to women's groups in poor countries. *The Guardian*. Retrieved from http://www.guardian.co.uk

Jahiruddin, A. T. M., Short, P., Dressler, W., & Khan, M. A. (2011). Can microfinance worsen poverty? Cases of exacerbated poverty in Bangladesh. *Development in Practice, 21*(8), 1109–1121.

Jha, P., Kumar, R., Vasa, P., Dhingra, N., Thiruchelvam, D., & Moineddin, R. (2006). Low male-to-female sex ratio of children born in India: National survey of 1.1 million households. *Lancet, 367*, 211–218.

Karim, L. (2008). Demystifying micro-credit: The Grameen Bank, NGOs, and neoliberlaism in Bangladesh. *Cultural Dynamics, 20*(5), 5–29.

Karmaker, B., Kandala, N., Chung, D., & Clarker, A. (2011). Factors associated with female genital mutilation in Burkina Faso and its policy implications. *International Journal for Equity in Health, 10*. Retrieved from http://www.equityhealthj.com/content/10/1/20

Kassindja, F. (1998). *Do they hear you when you cry?* New York, NY: Dell.

Kaur, G. (2006). *Foeticide journeys*. Retrieved from http://www.indiatogether.org/2006/aug/wom-usfoet.htm

Khan, S. (2012, November 3). Pakistani Taliban target female students with acid attack. *CNN*. Retrieved from http://www.cnn.com/2012/11/03/world/asia/pakistan-acid-attack/index.html

Kishwar, M. P. (2005). Destined to fail. *Manushi, 148*. Retrieved from http://www.indiatogether.org/manushi/issue148.dowry.htm

Kizilhan, J. I. (2011). Impact of psychological disorders after female genital mutilation among Kurdish girls in Northern Iraq. *European Journal of Psychiatry, 25*(2), 92–100.

Kotla, H. (2011, April 7). India's skewed sex ratio: An aversion to having daughters is leading to millions of missing girls. *The Economist*. Retrieved from http://www.economist.com

Kristof, N., & WuDunn, S. (2009). *Half the sky*. New York, NY: Alfred A. Knopf.

Kulczycki, A., & Windle, S. (2011). Honor killings in the Middle East and North Africa: A systematic review of the literature. *Violence Against Women*, *17*(11), 1442–1464.

Lederer, E.M. (2004). Eighty-five nations endorse U.N. population agenda, but Bush administration refuses to sign. *Associated Press*. Retrieved from LexisNexis database.

Mai, M. (2006). *In the name of honor*. New York, NY: Atria Books.

MacFarquhar, N. (2010, April 13). Big banks draw profits from microloans to poor. *New York Times*. Retrieved from http://www.nytimes.com

MacFarquhar, N. (2011, September 25). Saudi monarch grants women right to vote. *New York Times*. Retrieved from http://www.nytimes.com

Mahjabeen, R. (2008). Microfinancing in Bangladesh: Impact on households, consumption and welfare. *Journal of Policy Modeling, 30*, 1083–1092.

Malkin, E. (2008, April 5). Problems for microfinancing in Mexico. *New York Times*. Retrieved from http://www.nytimes.com

McCloskey, L. A., Williams, C., & Larsen, U. (2005). Gender inequality and intimate partner violence among women in Moshi, Tanzania. *International Family Planning Perspectives, 31*(3), 124–130.

Medical house visits cut maternal mortality. (2009, April 15). *IRIN News*. Retrieved from http://www.irinnews.org/printreport.aspx?reportid=83939

Meleigy, M. (2007). Egypt tightens ban on female genital mutilation after 12 year old girl dies. *BMJ, 335*(7609), 15.

Microfinance institutions pushed loans, admits major GO. (2011, April 20). *IRIN News*. Retrieved from http://www.irinnews.org/printreport.aspx?reportid=92528

Moloney, A. (2009) Bolivia tackles maternal and child deaths. *The Lancet, 374*, 442.

Nasrullah, M., Haqqi, S., & Cummings, K. J. (2009). The epidemiological patterns of honour killings of women in Pakistan. *European Journal of Public Health, 19*(2), 193–197.

Nawaz, S. (2010). Microfinance and poverty reduction: Evidence from a village study in Bangladesh. *Journal of Asian and African Studies, 45*, 670–683.

Nepal's maternal mortality decline paradox. (2013, March 18). *IRIN News*. Retrieved from http://www.irinnews.org/printreport.aspx?reportid=97667

Oldenburg, V. T. (2002). *Dowry murder: The imperial origins of a cultural crime*. New York, NY: Oxford University Press.

Online birth data to prevent child marriage. (2012, July 3). *IRIN News*. Retrieved from http://www.irinnews.org/printreport.aspx?reportid=95782

Onolemhemhen, D. N. (2005). *A social worker's investigation of childbirth-injured women in northern Nigeria*. New York, NY: University Press of America.

Plan International. (2008). *Learn without fear: The global campaign to end violence in schools*. Retrieved from http://plan-international.org/learnwithoutfear/files/learn-without-fear-global-campaign-report-english

Polgreen, L., & Bajaj, V. (2010, November 17). India microcredit faces collapse from defaults. *New York Times*. Retrieved from http://www.nytimes.com

Population Reference Bureau. (2010). *Female genital mutilation/cutting: Data and trends—Update 2010*. Retrieved from http://www.prb.org/pdf10/fgm-wallchart2010.pdf

Rani, M., Bonu, S., & Diop-Sidibé, N. (2004). An empirical investigation of attitudes towards wife beating among men and women in seven sub-Saharan African countries. *African Journal of Reproductive Health, 8*(3), 116–136.

Rubin, A. J. (2010, November 7). For Afghan wives, a desperate, fiery way out. *New York Times*. Retrieved from http://www.nytimes.com

Rubin, A. J. (2013, May 18). Efforts to strengthen an Afghan law on women may backfire. *New York Times*. Retrieved from http://www.nytimes.com

Salhi, Z. S. (2003). Algerian women, citizenship, and the "family code." *Gender and Development, 11*(3), 27–35.

Sang-Hun, C. (2007, December 23). Where boys were kings, a shift towards baby girls. *New York Times*. Retrieved from http://www.nytimes.com

Save the Children Denmark, Ministry of Education, & Ministry of Women's Affairs. (2008). *A study on violence against girls in primary schools and its impacts on girls' education in Ethiopia*. Retrieved from http://www.ungei.org/resources/files/Study_on_Violence_Against_schoolgfils_final.pdf

Self-Employed Women's Association [SEWA]. (n.d.). *SEWA: Self-Employed Women's Association*. Retrieved from http://www.sewa.org

Sev'er, A., & Yurdakul, G. (2005). Culture of honor, culture of change: A feminist analysis of honor killings in rural Turkey. In P. S. Rothenberg (Ed.), *Beyond borders: Thinking critically about global issues* (pp. 288–306). New York, NY: Worth Publishers.

Sheth, S. S. (2006). Missing female births in India. *Lancet, 367*, 185–186.

Shortage of midvives "deadly." (2009, May 5). *IRIN News*. Retrieved from http://www.irinnews.org/printreport.aspx?reportid=84241

Singh, A. (2011, March 3). Ending child marriage in India. *The Guardian.* http://www.guardian.co.uk/global-development/poverty-matters/2011/mar/03/ending-child-marriage-india-health

Sipsma, H. L., Chen, P. G., Ofori-Atta, A., Ilozumba, U. O., Karfo, K., & Bradley, E. H. (2012). Female genital cutting: Current practices and beliefs in western Africa. *Bulletin of the World Health Organization, 90,* 120–127F.

Slashing the maternal mortality rate in Bo. (2012, November 22). *IRIN News.* Retrieved from http://www.irinnews.org/printreport.aspx?reportid=96847

Social Institutions and Gender Index. (2012a). *2012 SIGI.* Retrieved from http://www.genderindex.org/sites/default/files/2012SIGIsummaryresults.pdf

Social Institutions and Gender Index. (2012b). *Thailand.* Retrieved from http://genderindex.org/country/thailand

Surtees, R. (2003). Negotiating violence and non-violence in Cambodian marriages. *Gender and Development, 11*(2), 30–41.

Tanveer, K. (2005, December 29). Pakistani father admits slaying 4 over "honor." *The Patriot-News,* p. A9.

UNESCO. (2011). *Adult and youth literacy.* Retrieved from http://www.uis.unesco.org/FactSheets/Documents/FS16-2011-Literacy-EN.pdf

UNICEF. (2005). *Changing a harmful social convention: Female genital mutilation/cutting.* Retrieved from http://www.unicef-icdc.org/publications/pdf/fgm-gb-2005.pdf

UNICEF. (2011a). *Child protection from violence, exploitation, and abuse: A statistical snapshot.* Retrieved from http://www.childinfo.org/files/ChildProtection__from_violence_exploitation_abuse.pdf

UNICEF. (2011b). *Adolescent clubs empower young girls to resist early marriage in India.* Retrieved from http://www.unicef.org/infobycountry/india_58294.html

UNICEF. (2012). *Statistics by area: Education.* Retrieved from http://www.childinfo.org/education.html

UNICEF. (2013). *Female genital mutilation/cutting: A statistical overview and exploration of the dynamics of change.* Retrieved from http://www.unicef.org/media/files/FGCM_Lo_res.pdf

UNICEF. (n.d.). *Factsheet: Female genital mutilation/cutting.* Retrieved from http://www.unicef.org

United Nations. (2005). *Creating an enabling environment for girls' and women's participation in education.* Retrieved from http://www.

un.org/womenwatch/daw/egm/enabling-environment2005/docs/
EGM-WPD-EE-2005-EP.8%20%20A.pdf

United Nations. (2009). *Reservations to CEDAW*. Retrieved from http://www.
un.org/womenwatch/daw/cedaw/reservations.htm

United Nations. (2013). *Convention on the Elimination of All Forms of
Discrimination against Women*. Retrieved from http://treaties.un.org/Pages/
ViewDetails.aspx?src=TREATY&mtdsg_no=IV-8&chapter=4&lang=en

United Nations. (n.d.). *Gender mainstreaming*. Retrieved from http://www.
un.org/womenwatch/osagi/gendermainstreaming.htm

United Nations Assistance Mission in Afghanistan. (2012). *Still a long way to
go: Implementation of the law on elimination of violence against women in
Afghanistan*. Retrieved from http://unama.unmissions.org/LinkClick.aspx
?fileticket=Qy9mDiEa5Rw%3d&tabid=12254&language=en-US

United Nations Population Fund (UNFPA). (2004). *State of the world population 2004*. Retrieved from http://www.unfpa.org/swp/2004/english/ch1/
index.htm

United Nations Population Fund (UNFPA). (2005). *State of the world population
2005*. Retrieved from http://www.unfpa.org/upload/lib_pub_file/493_
filename_en_swp05.pdf

United Nations Population Fund (UNFPA). (2009). *Campaign to End Fistula: The
year in review*. Retrieved from http://www.unfpa.org/webdav/site/global/
shared/documents/publications/2009/fistula_annual_report_2008.pdf

United Nations Population Fund (UNFPA). (2012). *Sex imbalances at
birth: Current trends, consequences and policy implications*. Retrieved from
http://www.unfpa.org/public/home/publications/pid/12405

United Nations Population Fund (UNFPA), UNICEF, WHO, World Bank
(2012). *Trends in maternal mortality: 1990–2010*. Retrieved from http://
www.unfpa.org/public/home/publications/pid/10728

United Nations Population Fund (UNFPA). (n.d.). *Technical resources*. Retrieved
from http://www.endfistula.org/public/pid/7433

United Nations Secretary-General. (2006). *In-depth study on all forms of violence
against women*. Retrieved from www.un.org/womenwatch/daw/vaw/v-sg-
study.htm.

Valerio, A., Bardasi, E., Chambal, A., & Lobo, M. F. (2006). Mozambique:
School fees and primary school enrollment and retention. In A. Coudouel,
A. A. Dani, & S. Paternostro (Eds.), *Poverty & social impact analysis of reforms:
Lessons and examples from implementation* (pp. 93–148). Washington, DC:
World Bank.

Van Rooyen, C., Stewart, R., & De Wet, T. (2012). The impact of microfinance in sub-Saharan Africa: A systematic review of the literature. *World Development, 40*(11), 2249–2262.

Van Soest, D., & Crosby, J. (1997). *Challenges of violence worldwide.* Washington, DC: NASW Press.

Vonderlack-Navarro, R. (2010). Targeting women versus addressing gender in microcredit: Lessons from Honduras. *Affilia, 25*(2). 123–134.

Vojvoda, R. (2012, October 11). Celebrating International Day of the Girl Child. *UNGEI.* Retrieved from www.ungei.org/infobycountry/247_3112.html

Watson, K. (2012, December 12). Winning the case for women in work: Saudi Arabia's steps to reform. *BBC News.* Retrieved from http://www.bbc.co.uk/news/business-20697030

Williams, R. (2013, March 11). Why girls in India are still missing out on the education they need. *The Guardian.* Retrieved from http://www.guardian.co.uk

Wipatayotin, A. (2005, November 29). Abuse of women, children soars. *Bangkok Post.* Retrieved from http://www.bangkokpost.com

Women yet to regain their place. (2013, May 6). *IRIN News.* Retrieved from http://www.irinnews.org/printreport.aspx?reportid=97976

Women's equality in theory, but not in practice. (2009, February 9). *IRIN News.* Retrieved from http://www.irinnews.org/printreport.aspx?reportid=82824

World Health Organization. (2005). *WHO multi-country study on women's health and domestic violence against women.* Retrieved from http://www.who.int/gender/violence/who_multicountry_study/summary_report/summary_report_English2.pdf

World Health Organization. (2006). Female genital mutilation and obstetric outcome: WHO collaborative prospective study in six African countries. *Lancet, 367,* 1835–1841.

World Health Organization. (2012a). *Safe and unsafe induced abortion.* Retrieved from http://apps.who.int/iris/bitstream/10665/75174/1/WHO_RHR_12.02_eng.pdf

World Health Organization. (2012b). *Unsafe abortion incidence and mortality.* Retrieved from http://apps.who.int/iris/bitstream/10665/75173/1/WHO_RHR_12.01_eng.pdf

Wu, Z., Viisainen, K., Wang, Y., & Hemminki, E. (2003). Perinatal mortality in rural China: Retrospective cohort study. *British Medical Journal, 327.* Retrieved from http://www.bmj.com

Xu, X., Zhu, F., O'Campo, P., Koenig, M. A., Mock, V., & Campbell, J. (2005). Prevalence of and risk factors for intimate partner violence in China. *American Journal of Public Health, 95*(1), 78–85.

Zaman, A. (2005, May 24). Where girls marry rapists for honour. *Los Angeles Times*. Retrieved from http://www.kwahk.org/index.asp? id=71

Zhu, W. X., Lu., L., & Hesketh, T. (2009). China's excess males, sex selective abortion, and one child policy: Analysis of data from 2005 national inter-census survey. *BMJ, 338*. Retrieved from www.bmj.com/cgi/reprint/338/apr09_2/b1211.pd

Zijuan, S., Shuzhuo, L., & Feldman, M. W. (2012). *Policy responses of gender imbalance in China: The "Care for Girls" campaign*. Retrieved from http://hsblogs.stanford.edu/morrison/files/2012/11/125-n0ilb4.pdf

Chapter Eight

Ajani, E. N., Onwubuya, E. A., & Mgenka, R. N. (2013). Approaches to eco-nomic empowerment of rural women for climate change mitigation and adaptation: Implications for policy. *Journal of Agricultural Extension, 17*(1). Retrieved from http://www.eldis.org/go/display&type=Document&id=65317#.Ufz8S0bD85s

Albrecht, G. (2011). Chronic environmental change: Emerging "psychoter-ratic" syndromes. In I. Weissbecker (Ed.). *Climate change and human well-being: Global challenges and opportunities* (pp. 43–56). New York, NY: Springer.

Andersen, L., Geary, J., Pörtner, C., & Verner, D. (2010). Human health and climate change. In D. Verner (Ed.), *Reducing poverty, protecting livelihoods, and building assets in a changing climate: Social implications of climate change in Latin America and the Caribbean* (pp. 167–194.). Washington, DC: World Bank.

Andersen, L., Lund., L., & Verner, D. (2010). Migration and climate change. In D. Verner (Ed.), *Reducing poverty, protecting livelihoods, and building assets in a changing climate: Social implications of climate change in Latin America and the Caribbean* (pp. 195–220). Washington, DC: World Bank.

Andersen, L., & Verner, D. (2010). Simulating the effects of climate change on poverty and inequality. In D. Verner (Ed.), *Reducing poverty, protecting liveli-hoods, and building assets in a changing climate: Social implications of climate change in Latin America and the Caribbean* (pp. 249–265). Washington, DC: World Bank.

Barnett, J., & Adger, W. N. (2007). Climate change, human security and violent conflict. *Political Geography, 26,* 639–655.

Bee, B., Biermann, M., & Tschakert, P. (2013). Gender, development, and rights-based approaches: Lessons for climate change adaptation and adaptive social protection. In M. Alston & K. Whittenbury (Eds.), *Research, action and policy: Addressing the gendered impacts of climate change* (pp. 95–108). New York, NY: Springer.

Besthorn, F. H. (2013). Radical equalitarian ecological justice: A social work call to action. In M. Gray, J. Coates, & T. Hetherington, (Eds)., *Environmental social work* (pp. 31–45). New York, NY: Routledge.

Besthorn, F. H., & Meyer, E. E. (2010). Environmentally displaced persons: Broadening social work's helping imperative. *Critical Social Work, 11*(3). Retrieved from http://www1.uwindsor.ca/criticalsocialwork

Charmaker, S., & Mijar, D. (2009). Impact of climate change on poor and marginalized people in high mountain region, Nepal. *IOP Conference Series: Earth and Environmental Science, 6.* Retrieved from http://m.iopscience.iop.org/1755-1315/6/14/142017

Chávez, F. (2012, June 29). Bolivia in need of coordinated climate change policies. *Inter Press Service News agency.* Retrieved from www.ipsnews.net

CIA World Factbook. (2013). *Bolivia.* Retrieved from https://www.cia.gov/library/publications/the-world-factbook/geos/bl.html

Corral, T. (2010). Gender perspectives in adaptation strategies: The case of Pintadas Solar in the semi-arid region of Brazil. In I. Dankelman (Ed.), *Gender and climate change: An introduction* (pp. 138–144). Sterling, VA: Earthscan.

Dankelman, I., & Jansen, W. (2010). Gender, environment and climate change: Understanding the linkages. In I. Dankelman (Ed.) *Gender and climate change: An introduction* (pp. 21–54). Sterling, VA: Earthscan.

DeAngelis, K. (2013). Building resilience to climate change through indigenous knowledge: The case of Bolivia. *Climate Change and Development Network.* Retrieved from http://cdkn.org/resource/building-resilience-to-climate-change-through-indigenous-knowledge-the-case-of-bolivia

Demetriades, J., & Esplen, E. (2010). The gender dimension of poverty and climate change adaptation. In R. Mearns & A. Norton (Eds.), *Social dimensions of climate change: Equity and vulnerability in a warming world* (pp. 133–143). Washington, DC: World Bank.

Devitt, C., & Tol, R. S. J. (2012). Civil war, climate change, and development: A scenario study for sub-Saharan Africa. *Journal of Peace Research, 49*(1), 129–145.

Dominelli, L. (2012). *Green social work: From environmental crises to environmental justice.* Cambridge, UK: Polity.

Dow, K., Berkhout, F., Preston, B. L., Klein, R. J. T., Midgley, G., & Shaw, M. R. (2013). Limits to adaptation. *Nature Climate Change, 3,* 305–307.

Earth warms at record-breaking pace. (2013, July 3). *IRIN News.* Retrieved from http://www.irinnews.org/printreport.aspx?reportid=98352

Edwards, T., & Wiseman, J. (2011). Climate change, resilience and transformation: Challenges and opportunities for local communities. In I. Weissbecker (Ed.), *Climate change and human well-being: Global challenges and opportunities* (pp. 185–200). New York, NY: Springer.

ELLA. (2012): *How traditional knowledge and technologies are contributing to climate change adaptation in Latin America's mountains.* Retrieved from http://ella.practicalaction.org/node/1028

Furlow, J., Smith, J. B., Anderson, G., Breed, W., & Padgham, J. (2011). Building resilience to climate change through development assistance: USAID's climate adaptation program. *Climatic Change, 108,* 411–421.

Gamble, D. N. (2013). Sustainable development. *Encyclopedia of social work online.* Retrieved from http://socialwork.oxfordre.com

Gleick, P. H., & Cooley, H. S. (2009). Energy implications of bottled water. *Environmental Resource Letters, 4.* Retrieved from http://iopscience.iop.org/1748-9326/4/1

Gray, L. (2010). Cancun climate change summit: Bolivians dance to a different beat, but fail to derail the talks. *The Telegraph.* Retrieved from http://www.telegraph.co.uk

Gray, M., Coates, J., & Hetherington, T. (2013). *Environmental social work.* New York, NY: Routledge.

Hawkins, C. A. (2010). Sustainability, human rights, and environmental justice: Critical connections for social work. *Critical Social Work, 11*(3). Retrieved from http://www1.uwindsor.ca/criticalsocialwork

Heltberg, R., Siegel, P. B., & Jorgensen, S. L. (2010). Social policies for adaptation to climate change. In R. Mearns & A. Norton (Eds.), *Social dimensions of climate change: Equity and vulnerability in a warming world* (pp. 259–275). Washington, DC: World Bank.

Intergovernmental Panel on Climate Change. (2013). *Working group I contribution to the IPCC fifth assessment report. Climate change 2013:The physical science basis.* Retrieved from http://www.ipcc.ch

Internal Displacement Monitoring Centre. (2013). *Global estimates 2012: People displaced by disasters.* Retrieved from http://www.internal-displacement.org

International Association of Schools of Social Work, the International Council on Social Welfare, & the International Federation of Social Workers. (2012). *The global agenda*. Retrieved from http://www.globalsocialagenda.org

Kronik, J., & Verner, D. (2010). The role of indigenous knowledge in crafting adaptation and mitigation strategies for climate change in Latin America. In R. Mearns & A. Norton (Eds.), *Social dimensions of climate change: Equity and vulnerability in a warming world* (pp. 145–169). Washington, DC: World Bank.

Kumssa, A., & Jones, J. F. (2010). Climate change and human security in Africa. *International Journal of Sustainable Development & World Ecology, 17*(6), 453–461.

Locker, M. (2013, January 4). Massachusetts town bans plastic water bottles. *Time.* Retrieved from http://newsfeed.time.com/2013/01/04/massachusett-town-bans-plastic-water-bottles

Mearns, R., & Norton, A. (2010). Equity and vulnerability in a warming world: Introduction and overview. In R. Mearns & A. Norton (Eds.), *Social dimensions of climate change: Equity and vulnerability in a warming world* (pp. 1–44). Washington, DC: World Bank.

Nielsen, S. T. (2010). Coastal livelihoods and climate change. In D. Verner (Ed.), *Reducing poverty, protecting livelihoods, and building assets in a changing climate: Social implications of climate change in Latin America and the Caribbean* (pp. 123–165). Washington, DC: World Bank.

No seeds to weather climate change. (2013, January 31). *IRIN News.* Retrieved from http://www.irinnews.org/printreport.aspx?reportid=97378

Odigie-Emmanuel, O. (2010). The gender impact of climate change in Nigeria. In I. Dankelman (Ed.), *Gender and climate change: An introduction* (pp. 123–129). Sterling, VA: Earthscan.

Okali, C., & Naess, L. O. (2013). *Making sense of gender, climate change and agriculture in sub-Saharan Africa: Creating gender-responsive climate adaptation policy*. Retrieved from http://www.eldis.org/go/display&type=Document&id=65144#.Ufz9nUbD85s

Olesen, J. E. (2010). Agrarian livelihoods and climate change. In D. Verner (Ed.), *Reducing poverty, protecting livelihoods, and building assets in a changing climate: Social implications of climate change in Latin America and the Caribbean* (pp. 93–122). Washington, DC: World Bank.

Oxfam. (2009). *People-centered resilience: Working with vulnerable farmers towards climate change adaptation and food security*. Retrieved from http://www.oxfam.org/en/policy/people-centered-resilience

Painter. J. (2009, May 12). Huge Bolivian glacier disappears. *BBC News*. Retrieved from http://news.bbc.co.uk/2/hi/8046540.stm

Peeters, J. (2012). The place of social work in sustainable development: Towards ecosocial practice. *International Journal of Social Welfare, 21*, 287–298.

People's World Conference on Climate Change. (2010, April 30). *Bolivia submits Cochabamba Conference outcome to UNFCCC*. Retrieved from http://pwccc.wordpress.com

Provost, C. (2013, March 14). Environmental threats could push billions into extreme poverty, warns UN. *The Guardian*. Retrieved from http://www.guardian.co.uk

Putting women on the disaster risk reduction agenda. (2013, June 6). *IRIN News*. Retrieved from http://www.irinnews.org/printreport.aspx?reportid=98177

Rossing, T. (2010). Water scarcity, climate change, and the poor. In D. Verner (Ed.), *Reducing poverty, protecting livelihoods, and building assets in a changing climate: Social implications of climate change in Latin America and the Caribbean* (pp. 21–62). Washington, DC: World Bank.

Rossing, T., & Rubin, O. (2010). Climate change, disaster hot spots, and asset erosion. In D. Verner (Ed.), *Reducing poverty, protecting livelihoods, and building assets in a changing climate: Social implications of climate change in Latin America and the Caribbean* (pp. 63–91). Washington, DC: World Bank.

Santa Clara Valley Water District. (2013). *Regulation and monitoring*. Retrieved from http://www.valleywater.org/EkContent.aspx?id=327

Schipani, A., & Vidal, J. (2010, April 18). Bolivia climate change talks to give poor a voice. *The Guardian*. Retrieved from http://www.guardian.co.uk

Seiler, C., Hutjes, R. W. A., & Kabat, P. (2013a). Likely ranges of climate change in Bolivia. *Journal of Applied Meteorology and Climatology, 52*, 1303–1317.

Seiler, C., Hutjes, R. W. A., & Kabat, P. (2013b). Climate variability and trends in Bolivia. *Journal of Applied Meteorology and Climatology, 52*, 130–146.

Simpson, D. M., Weissbecker, I., & Sephton, S. E. (2011). Extreme weather-related events: Implications for mental health and well-being. In I. Weissbecker (Ed.), *Climate change and human well-being: Global challenges and opportunities* (pp. 57–78). New York, NY: Springer.

Tikjøb, S., & Verner, D. (2010). Conclusion. In D. Verner (Ed.), *Reducing poverty, protecting livelihoods, and building assets in a changing climate: Social implications of climate change in Latin America and the Caribbean* (pp. 305–338). Washington, DC: World Bank.

Tutu, D. (2009, October 23). Spirit that freed South Africa must now rescue the planet. *The Age*. Retrieved from http://www.theage.com.au/

federal-politics/political-opinion/spirit-that-freed-south-africa-must-now-rescue-the-planet-20091022-hbch.html

United Nations. (1992). *United Nations Framework Convention on Climate Change*. Retrieved from http://unfccc.int/files/essential_background/background_publications_htmlpdf/application/pdf/conveng.pdf

United Nations. (2013). *A new global partnership: Eradicate poverty and transform economies through sustainable development*. Retrieved from http://www.un.org/sg/management/pdf/HLP_P2015_Report.pdf

UNHCR. (2009). *Climate change, natural disasters and human displacement: A UNHCR perspective*. Retrieved from http://www.unhcr.org/4901e81a4.html

United Nations Development Programme [UNDP]. (2011). *Tras las huellas del cambio climático en Bolivia: Estado del arte del conocimiento sobre adaptación al cambio climático. Agua y seguridad alimentaria*. Retrieved from http://cambioclimatico-pnud.org.bo/paginas/admin/uploaded/traslashuellas.pdf

United Nations Development Programme. (2013). *Climate change*. Retrieved from http://www.undp.org/content/undp/en/home/ourwork/environmentandenergy/strategic_themes/climate_change.html

United Nations High Commissioner for Human Rights. (2009). *Report of the office of the United Nations High Commissioner for Human Rights on the relationship between climate change and human rights*. Retrieved from http://www.ohchr.org/EN/Issues/HRAndClimateChange/Pages/Study.aspx

United Nations High-Level Panel on Global Sustainability. (2012). *Resilient people, resilient planet: A future worth choosing*. Retrieved from http://www.un.org/gsp/gsp/report

Verner, D. (2010). Introduction. In D. Verner (Ed.), *Reducing poverty, protecting livelihoods, and building assets in a changing climate: Social implications of climate change in Latin America and the Caribbean* (pp. 1–19). Washington, DC: World Bank.

Vidal, J. (2013, April 13). Millions face starvation as world warms, say scientists. *The Guardian*. Retrieved from http://www.guardian.co.uk

Weinberg, B. (2010). Bolivia's new water wars: Climate change and indigenous struggle. *NACLA Report on the Americas*. Retrieved from http://nacla.org

Wenden, A. L. (2011). Women and climate change: Vulnerabilities and challenges. In I. Weissbecker (Ed.), *Climate change and human well-being: Global challenges and opportunities* (pp. 119–133). New York, NY: Springer.

World Bank. (2008). *Social dimensions of climate change: Workshop report 2008*. Retrieved from http://web.worldbank.org

World Commission on Environment and Development. (1987). *Our common future*. Retrieved from http://www.un-documents.net/our-common-future.pdf

World Health Organization. (2008). *World malaria report 2008*. Retrieved from http://www.who.int/malaria/publications/country-profiles/2008/mal2008-bolivia-en.pdf

World Health Organization. (2012). *World malaria report 2012*. Retrieved from http://www.who.int/malaria/publications/world_malaria_report_2012/wmr2012_country_profiles.pdf

Chapter Nine

Beyond 2015. (2013). *Beyond 2015*. Retrieved from http://www.beyond2015.org/hlp-report

Ford, L. (2013, September 25). New UN development goals must focus on rights and apply to all countries. *The Guardian*. Retrieved from http://www.theguardian.com

Global child mortality rates "halved." (2013, September 13). *IRIN News*. Retrieved from http://www.irinnews.org/printreport.aspx?reportid=98750

Organisation for Economic Co-operation and Development (OECD). (2013, March 4). *Aid to poor countries slips further as governments tighten budgets*. Retrieved from http://www.oecd.org/dac/stats/aidtopoorcountries slipsfurtherasgovernmentstightenbudgets.htm

Tran, M. (2013, May 30). New UN goals call for end to extreme poverty by 2030. *The Guardian*. Retrieved from http://www.guardian.co.uk

United Nations. (2012). *The Millennium Development Goals report 2012*. Retrieved from http://www.un.org/millenniumgoals/reports.shtml

United Nations. (2013a). *The Millennium Development Goals report 2013*. Retrieved from http://www.un.org/millenniumgoals/reports.shtml

United Nations. (2013b). *A new global partnership: Eradicate poverty and transform economies through sustainable development*. Retrieved from http://www.un.org/sg/management/pdf/HLP_P2015_Report.pdf

United Nations Development Programme. (2003). *Human development report 2003*. New York, NY: Oxford University Press.

United Nations Development Programme. (n.d.). *About the MDGs: Basics*. Retrieved from http://www.undp.org

United Nations Statistics Division. (2012). *Net ODA as percentage of OECD/DAC donors GNI*. Retrieved from http://data.un.org

United Nations Statistics Division. (n.d.). *About the Millennium Development Goals indicators.* Retrieved from http://mdgs.un.org/unsd/mdg/Host.aspx?Content=Indicators/About.htm

Woodward, D. (2013, June 7). How progressive is the push to eradicate extreme poverty? *The Guardian.* Retrieved from http://http://www.guardian.co.uk

Chapter Ten

Council on Social Work Education [CSWE]. (2007). *Katherine A. Kendall Institute for International Social Work Education.* Retrieved from http://www.cswe.org/CentersInitiatives/KAKI.aspx

Council on Social Work Education [CSWE]. (2007). *Educational and policy accreditation standards.* Retrieved from http://www.cswe.org/Accreditation/2008EPASDescription.aspx

Diaz, L., Mama, R., & Lopez, L. (2006, August). *Making the social work profession an essential partner in international development.* Paper presented at the biennial conference of the International Federation of Social Workers, Munich, Germany.

Homan, M. S. (2004). *Promoting community change: Making it happen in the real world* (3rd ed.). Belmont, CA: Wadsworth/Thomson.

International Federation of Social Workers. (2000). *Definition of social work.* Retrieved from http://www.ifsw.org/en/p38000208.html

Schwalbe, W. (2012). *The end of your life book club.* New York, NY: Vintage.

Van Soest, D., & Crosby, J. (1997). *Challenges of violence worldwide: A curriculum module.* Washington, DC: NASW Press.

Index

AIDS
    and anti-retroviral treatment: 141–144
    and behavior change: 128
    and children: 124–125, 131–132,
        141–142
    and condoms: 139–140
    and females: 123, 129–131, 132–136
    and male circumcision: 140–141
    and men: 122–123, 128–129
    and men who have sex with
        men: 124–125, 131–132, 141–142
    and poverty: 122–128
    and sex workers: 138
    and stigma: 136–137
Afghanistan: 58, 96, 101–102, 164,
    169–171
Australia: 106–108

Bangladesh: 60, 181–183
Bolivia: 77, 189, 196, 200–201
Bolsa Familia: 59, 60
Botswana: 146
Brazil: 35–36, 198
Burkina Faso: 161–162

Cambodia: 72
Child labor: 57–61
Child maltreatment: 68–70
Child soldiers: 65–68
China: 32, 33, 71, 72, 76, 83–84,
    145–146, 156, 157, 158
Climate change: 190–201
Cluster munitions: 96–97
Colombia: 67–68, 115–118
Conditional Cash Transfers: 59–60,
    172–173
Conflict diamonds: 112–113

Conflict minerals: 112–113
Convention on the Elimination of All
    Forms of Discrimination Against
    Women: 153–154
Convention on the Rights of the
    Child: 28, 56, 65
Cultural relativism: 18

Democratic Republic of the Congo: 91,
    92, 93, 94, 95, 113
Dependency theory: 10–12
Dowry deaths: 165–166

Early marriage: 162–163
Education: 78–80
    and girls: 78–79, 175–176
    Universal Primary Education: 79–80
Ethiopia: 71

FARC: 67–68, 115–116
Female genital cutting: 158–162
Fistulas: 173–175

Geneva Conventions: 19, 87–88
Grameen Bank: 181–183
Guatemala: 72–73

Haiti: 38–39, 76, 126–128
Hague Convention on Intercountry
    Adoption: 71
Honor killings: 166–168
Human trafficking
    and human rights: 27–29
    Debt bondage: 33–36
    Definition: 29–30

Human trafficking (*Cont.*)
  Descent-based: 39–40
  Domestic workers: 36–39
  Estimates: 27
  Exploitation by the state: 31
  Forced marriage: 44–45
  Sex trafficking: 41

India: 33–34, 42, 58, 60–61, 73, 77,
    136–137, 140, 156, 158, 165–166,
    177–178
International adoption: 70–74
  Trafficking: 72–73
Intercountry surrogacy: 73
Intimate partner violence: 163–164
Iraq: 95, 96
Israel: 105–106, 168, 169

Kenya: 139–140
Kuwait: 76

Landmines: 96–97
Laos: 50–51
Lord's Resistance Army: 66–67

Malawi: 148
Malaysia: 75–76
Maps: 2–5
  Mercator: 3–4
  Peters: 4
Maternal mortality: 172–173
Mauritania: 39
Mechai Viravaidhya: 145
Microfinance: 133, 178–180,
    181–183
Millennium Development Goals: 8,
    204–212
Modernization theory: 9–10
Mohammed Yunus: 181–183
Mukhtar Mai: 168
Myanmar: 31–32, 56, 65–66,
    100–101

Nepal: 34, 42, 77
Niger: 39–40
Nigeria: 193
North Korea: 32, 33

Pakistan: 101–102, 163–164, 168
Paul Farmer: 127, 143

Qatar: 34–35

Romania: 74
Russia: 71

Saudi Arabia: 168, 169
Self–Employed Women's Association: 49,
    177–178
Sex–selective abortion: 155–158
Social development: 7–9
South Africa: 141
South Korea: 71, 157
Sri Lanka: 68
Stateless children: 74–78
Street children: 61–62
  and witchcraft: 61–62
  and AIDS: 131–132
Structural Adjustment Policies: 8, 125, 177
Sudan: 63, 64, 92–93
Sweden: 46–47

Tamil Tigers: 68
Thailand: 42, 43, 50–51, 76, 100–101,
    144–145
Turkey: 42–43

Uganda: 66–67, 79–80, 139–140, 165
United Kingdom: 108
United Nations
  Role in human rights: 20–21
United States; 102–105, 109, 110
Universal Declaration of Human
    Rights: 15–17
Uzbekistan: 32

War and conflict
  Impacts of: 88–90, 95
  Sexual violence during: 90–94
  Refugees and asylum seekers: 98–112
Water: 189–190, 191–192
Women's health: 171
Women and the Law: 168–171
World Bank: 8, 125, 177